Anglo-German Dramatic and Poetic Encounters

STUDIES IN TEXT AND PRINT CULTURE

General Editor: Sandro Jung
Shanghai University of Finance and Economics

This series focuses on up-to-date, text-specific, and text-theoretical approaches to the literature and culture of Britain, Europe, and America from the fifteenth to the mid-nineteenth centuries. It publishes innovative scholarship that promotes an understanding of literature as closely related to, and informed by, other discursive forms, especially the multifarious visual cultures of a given time.

Advisory Board:
Barbara Benedict, Trinity College, Hartford, Connecticut
Margaret Ezell, Texas A&M University
Hilary Fraser, Birkbeck College, University of London
Stana Nenadic, University of Edinburgh
Andrew Prescott, University of Glasgow
James Raven, Essex University and Cambridge University

Michael Wood and Sandro Jung, *Anglo-German Dramatic and Poetic Encounters: Perspectives on Exchange in the Sattelzeit*

Sandro Jung, *James Thomson's* The Seasons, *Print Culture, and Visual Interpretation, 1730–1842*

Betsy Bowden, *The Wife of Bath in Afterlife: Ballads to Blake*

Michael Edson, *Annotation in Eighteenth-Century Poetry*

Sandro Jung, *The Publishing and Marketing of Illustrated Literature in Scotland, 1760–1825*

Herbet Gottfried, *Erie Railway Tourist, 1854–1886: Transporting Visual Culture*

Sandro Jung and Kwinten Van De Walle, *The Genres of Thomson's The Seasons*

Anglo-German Dramatic and Poetic Encounters

Perspectives on Exchange in the Sattelzeit

Edited by Michael Wood and Sandro Jung

LEHIGH UNIVERSITY PRESS
Bethlehem

Published by Lehigh University Press
Copublished by The Rowman & Littlefield Publishing Group, Inc.
4501 Forbes Boulevard, Suite 200, Lanham, Maryland 20706
www.rowman.com

Unit A, Whitacre Mews, 26-34 Stannary Street, London SE11 4AB

Copyright © 2019 by The Rowman & Littlefield Publishing Group

All rights reserved. No part of this book may be reproduced in any form or by any electronic or mechanical means, including information storage and retrieval systems, without written permission from the publisher, except by a reviewer who may quote passages in a review.

British Library Cataloguing in Publication Information Available

Library of Congress Cataloging-in-Publication Data

Names: Wood, Michael, 1986- editor. | Jung, Sandro, editor.
Title: Anglo-German dramatic and poetic encounters : perspectives on exchange in the Sattelzeit / edited by Michael Wood and Sandro Jung.
Description: Bethlehem : Lehigh University Press, [2019] | Series: Studies in text and print culture | Includes bibliographical references and index.
Identifiers: LCCN 2019011411 (print) | LCCN 2019016996 (ebook) | ISBN 9781611462937 (Electronic) | ISBN 9781611462920 (cloth) ISBN 9781611462944 (pbk)
Subjects: LCSH: Comparative literature—English and German. | Comparative literature—German and English. | English literature—18th century—History and criticism. | English literature—19th century—History and criticism. | German literature—18th century—History and criticism. | German literature—19th century—History and criticism.
Classification: LCC PR129.G3 (ebook) | LCC PR129.G3 A63 2019 (print) | DDC 820.9/006—dc23
LC record available at https://lccn.loc.gov/2019011411

Contents

Acknowledgments	vii
Illustrations and Tables	ix
Note on the Text	xi
Introduction: Traditions and Genres in Dialogue *Michael Wood*	1
1 British Ghosts of the Gothic Novel: Dramatic Adaptation as a Medium of Anglo-German Cultural Transfer in the 1790s *Barry Murnane*	23
2 "From Scotland New Come Home": Scottish Ghosts and Afterlives of Bürger's "Lenore" *Lucy Wood*	47
3 Of German Genres and Scottish Sentiments: Henry Mackenzie, Walter Scott, and the *Schauspiel* *Michael Wood*	69
4 Kotzebue's Adaptations of English Comedies: Colman, Cumberland, and Conservatism after 1815 *Johannes Birgfeld*	95
5 Surveying Shakespeare's Impact on German Drama: Taking a Computational Approach to an Epoch *Nils Reiter and Marcus Willand*	117
6 Milton in Germany: Translation and Creative Response *John Guthrie*	145

7   The Female Body in Text and Image: Amelia, Lavinia, and
    Musidora in the German Translations of Thomson's *The
    Seasons* and Beyond   169
    Sandro Jung

8   Student Experiences: John Stuart Blackie and William
    Edmonstoune Aytoun in Germany (1829–1830 and 1833–1834)   201
    Bernhard Maier

Select Bibliography   223

Index   231

About the Authors   243

Acknowledgments

This collection has come about as a result of a Royal Society of Edinburgh Susan Manning Symposium on the topic of "Anglo-German Encounters with Drama and Poetry, 1760–1835" that was held at the Institute for Advanced Studies in the Humanities (IASH) at the University of Edinburgh. The pieces here constitute a selection of contributions to that symposium that have, since then, been expanded and further developed. Needless to say, without that symposium, this book would never have come about. To that end, the editors would first and foremost like to thank IASH for hosting the original event. Its then director, Professor Jo Shaw, generously supported the event, as did the Royal Society of Edinburgh, for which we are grateful. We are also grateful to the various further speakers and chairs at that conference for their contributions to discussion. Sandro Jung wishes to acknowledge additional funding received as part of a European Institutes of Advanced Studies Fellowship (co-funded by the European Commission's Marie-Skodowska-Curie Action—COFUND Programme—FP7) and through the Fonds Wetenschappelijk Onderzoek–funded "Transnational Textual Cultures" network. Michael Wood wishes to thank the Department of European Languages and Cultures in the School of Literatures, Languages and Cultures at the University of Edinburgh for its additional financial support of this event as part of the "Cultural Encounters/Dialogues" research strand. He also thanks the British Academy for the Postdoctoral Fellowship that has made editing this collection possible in the first place.

Of course, no edited volume would be possible without its contributors, and we would like to express our enormous debt of gratitude to the authors of the chapters in this collection for their rigor, patience, their understanding, and their willingness to engage with feedback. We would also like to thank the two anonymous reviewers of the manuscript of this collection for their commentaries on the individual essays and on the collection as a whole. Their assistance has been invaluable. Last but by no means least, we owe our thanks to Kate Crassons and Trish Moore of Lehigh University Press, who have been supportive of this project from the very start.

Illustrations and Tables

Figure 5.1	Average number of acts and scenes. All values have been scaled, so that the maximum value in each category is 1. Unscaled values are shown inside the bars.	126
Figure 5.2	Standard deviations of scenes per act, restricted to plays with five acts.	127
Figure 5.3	Average number of utterances, sentences, and tokens. All values have been scaled so that the maximum value in each category is 1. Unscaled values are shown inside the bars.	129
Figure 5.4	Distribution of number of tokens per subcorpus.	130
Figure 5.5	Distribution of the number of figures in the *dramatis personae* per subcorpus. Plays without a printed list of *dramatis personae* are excluded.	131
Figure 5.6	First appearances of the five most speaking figures per play.	132
Figure 5.7	Figure ranks according to first appearance (x axis) and *dramatis personae* (y axis). Dots are scaled according to the number of figures at this rank.	133
Figure 5.8	Relative frequency of interjections per play.	135
Table 5.1	List of texts with assignments to subcorpus.	137
Figure 7.1	William Kent, "Sommer," *B.H. Brockes aus dem Englischen übersetzte Jahreszeiten des Herrn Thomson* (Hamburg: Herold, 1745).	186

Figure 7.2a	G.L. Crusius, "Sommer," in *Jacob Thomsons Jahrszeiten aus dem Englischen nach der neuesten Ausgabe übersetzt von Johann Franz von Palthen. Mit Kupfern* (Rostock: Koppe, 1757).	187
Figure 7.2b	Detail from Figure 7.2a.	188
Figure 7.3	Salomon Gessner, title vignette, in *Sommer* (Zurich: Gessner und Orell, 1761).	189
Figure 7.4	Johann Sebastian Bach, "Damon und Musidora" (1777).	190

Note on the Text

Unless otherwise indicated, translations into English are provided by the authors of individual contributions. Inevitably, with any collected volume like this, individual authors make repeated references to particular works and particular collected editions throughout their chapters and therefore abbreviate these for ease. Details of such abbreviations can be found in the individual chapters.

Last but not least, dates given in parentheses next to titles of works denote the year of a work's first publication.

Introduction
Traditions and Genres in Dialogue
Michael Wood

In his poem *Die Tageszeiten* (The Times of the Day), first published in 1756, Justus Friedrich Wilhelm Zachariae makes a decisive statement in support of intercultural literary exchange. Toward the end of the second book, "Mittag" (Midday), Zachariae is explicit in stating that German writers have been well-advised in looking to their British counterparts for inspiration:

Und warum ists falscher Geschmack, dem Britten zu folgen?
Ist er nicht näher mit uns verwandt, als *Galliens* Sklaven,
Denen Gebrauch und Grammatik die stärksten Flügel beschneidet?
Deutsches sächsisches Blut schlägt in Britanniens Barden.
Schande genug, daß Enkel von uns, uns längst übertroffen.
Aber noch größere Schande, wenn wir nicht Enkel verstünden,
Und die gedankenreichsten Gesänge für schwülstig erklärten.

Aber noch brennt auch in unserm Deutschland das heilige Feuer,
Das von Germanischen Barden auf Brittische Barden gekommen.
Großer *Milton*, wer konnt' auch bey uns dich schöner verewgen,
Als ein *Bodmer* und *Klopstock* durch ihre göttlichen Lieder!
Die unsterbliche *Row* [sic] singt aus dem fühlenden *Wieland*;
Du, mein *Gärtner*, *Giseke*, *Gleim*, und *Gellert*, und *Schlegel*,
Rammler [sic], *Leßing*, und *Uz*; und du freymüthiger *Huber*,
Ihre seid alle Germaniens Zierde; und alle Verehrer
Der mit uns so nahe verschwisterten Brittischen Musen.
Und könnt' ich dich, *Ebert*, vergessen! Du, der du die Sprache
Dieses denkenden Volkes zu deinem Eigenthum machest?—
Du, der Herold von jedem Genie der dichtrischen Insel,
Wirst mit mir voll Mitleid die kriechenden *Dunse* verachten,
Die ihre Prosa voll hinkender Reime zur Göttinn erheben.

Oder vielleicht glüht schon ein glücklicher Schüler von *Popen*,
Welcher die stolzen Zwerge mit *Dunciaden* verewigt.¹

[And why is it in bad to taste to follow the Briton? Is he not more closely related to us than *Gaul*'s slaves to whose customs and grammar the strongest wings are clipped? German, Saxon blood beats in Britain's bards. It is disgrace enough that our grandsons have long surpassed us; but it is an even greater disgrace if we cannot understand our own grandsons and write-off verses rich with ideas as fustian.

But in our Germany that sacred fire still burns that had come from Germanic bards to British bards. Great *Milton*, who could immortalize you in our eyes more beautifully than *Bodmer* and *Klopstock* in their divine songs! The immortal *Rowe* sings through the feeling *Wieland*; you, my *Gärtner, Giseke, Gleim*, and *Gellert*, and *Schlegel, Ramler, Lessing*, and *Uz*; and you, forthright *Huber*, you are all the ornament of Germania, and all of you worshippers of the British muses that are so closely related to us. And how could I forget you, *Ebert*! You, who has made the language of this thinking people your very own? You, the herald of every genius of that island of poets, with me you will spurn the grovelling *Dunses* who elevate their prose full of limping rhymes to the status of a goddess. Or maybe there's already the first glow of some happy pupil of *Pope*, who immortalizes these haughty dwarves in *Dunciads*.]

Here, Zachariae, the translator of *Paradise Lost*, evokes a whole tradition of British poets that he regards as benefiting German life and letters. He clearly sees no need to make explicit reference to Scottish poet James Thomson, author of *The Seasons* (1730), a work that inspired Zachariae's own. Instead, he cites John Milton, Nicholas Rowe, and Alexander Pope as the foremost muses of German culture. And as Zachariae's choice of German writers makes clear, the German literary tradition responding to British literature is one that is relatively young, consisting of writers all born in the last forty years—with the notable exception of Zurich-based Johann Jakob Bodmer, whose inclusion we will briefly consider in the following.

Zachariae's appraisal of recent British literary influence in the German-speaking world does not, however, stop at providing a one-sided depiction whereby one culture takes from another. Not only does Zachariae emphasize the similarities between and common roots shared by British Anglo-Saxons and the current Germanic inhabitants of central Europe, but he also highlights the significant influence of the German muse on what has since become British literature; what once flowed from East to West is now making its way East again. Importantly, Zachariae's opening rhetorical question signals that recent literary history has disproved the centuries-old dominance of French cultural paradigms that had made slaves of poets and playwrights alike, and his choice of German-speaking literary figures to name (Bodmer in particular) makes clear that his rhetorical question is directed at the likes of the Francophile Leipzig-based dramatic and linguistic reformer Johann Christoph Gottsched as well as a long line of early Enlightenment writers who condemned the apparent "Schwulst," or ornamental grandiloquence, of German baroque poetry.

While this passage from *Die Tageszeiten* foregrounds the role of the reception of British poets in establishing and improving a German literary tradition, Zachariae's choice of names demonstrates that British poetry has impacted more than just German verse. Johann Elias Schlegel and Gotthold Ephraim Lessing, for example, are picked out as dramatists who have been inspired by Britain's bards. Zachariae's inclusion of Christian Fürchtegott Gellert in this passage is also telling: Gellert not only composed poetry and drama, but the publication of his novel *Das Leben der schwedischen Gräfin von G**** (Life of the Swedish Countess of G***) in two instalments in 1747 and 1748 was a watershed moment in the history of the German novel. For Zachariae, the British poetic muse in the form of Milton, Rowe, Pope, and Thomson has rejuvenated German poetry and drama and fueled the emergence of the novel; he makes no mention of novelists such as Daniel Defoe, Samuel Richardson, or Henry Fielding, whose works had been translated into German directly on their publication in London and were reprinted as staples of the market for fiction throughout the eighteenth century. The transnational migration of poetry and drama, that is, has been a transgeneric movement, too.

The passage from *Die Tageszeiten* is worth dwelling on both for its support of looking to British literature and for its iteration of the historical shape of Anglo-German[2] exchange by the mid-eighteenth century. It occurs in a work that appears in the early stages of the German-speaking world's cultural awakening. It therefore captures Anglo-German literary exchange as something that is occurring in the present and is ushering in the very tradition that Zachariae and his contemporaries are establishing for German-language literature. Moreover, it comes at a historical point at which the newly emerging British and German literary traditions are to topple French cultural hegemony. Notably, Zachariae is writing in the mid-1750s, thus at the beginning of the period known within the History of Ideas as the "Sattelzeit" (ca. 1750–1850). Reinhard Koselleck singles this period out as historically significant in a number of respects, writing

> daß sich seit der Mitte des achtzehnten Jahrhunderts ein teifgreifender Bedeutungswandel klassischer topoi vollzogen, daß alte Worte neue Sinngehalte gewonnen, die mit Annäherung an unsere Gegenwart keiner Übersetzung mehr bedürftig sind. Der heuristische Vorgriff führt sozusagen eine "Sattelzeit" ein, in der sich die Herkunft zu unserer Präsenz wandelt.[3]

[that since the middle of the eighteenth century, a profound and far-reaching change in the meaning of classical topoi took place through which old words gained new meanings that, for their approximation with the present, no longer require translation. The heuristic anticipation ushers in, so to say, a "Saddle Period," in which the origin turns into our present.]

Not only, therefore, was the "Sattelzeit" a period of sweeping intellectual, philosophical, and technological advances, but it was a period in which many of the conceptual frameworks informing Western culture came about. In the field of European cultural production, we find the emergence of genres such as the novel, an exponential increase in the readerships of both fiction and non-fiction, and the codification of particular literary systems; we also find the emergence of modern concepts of nation and nationhood that are part and parcel of these advances. As Benedict Anderson argues in his influential study of nationalism, that the novel and the nation go hand in hand is no coincidence: for Anderson, the novel and the newspaper came to fruition in the eighteenth century and thus "provided the technical means for 're-presenting' the *kind* of imagined community that is the nation."[4]

In recent decades, theorists of cultural transfer and translation have concerned themselves with the roles of translated literatures and intercultural exchange in the development of national literary traditions. Itamar Even-Zohar's approach to literary transfer long ago identified the importance of translated literature in plugging "vacuums" in "young" literary cultures through processes in which translators select texts for translation and which aspects of these texts end up leaving their trace in another culture.[5] In Lawrence Venuti's words, "[t]ranslation changes the receiving cultural situation by bringing into existence something new and different, a text that is neither the source text nor an original composition in the translating language, and in the process it changes the values, beliefs, and representations that are housed in institutions."[6] And beyond constructing cultures and nations through literary interference or cultural transfer, translation has a role to play in conferring cultural capital on the products of one culture so that they can be received by another altogether.[7] Yet, to return to the specific concerns of the Sattelzeit and the growth of national awareness and the rise of the novel during it, the very choice of texts to translate and the ways in which they can be approached mean, in Venuti's words again, that in some cases a subject "identifies with cultural materials that are defined as national and thereby engage in a national collective," and the new text that arises from this "asserts a homogeneous language, culture, or identity."[8] Needless to say, translation is not the only way in which texts, ideas, and cultures move between nations, and adaptation and commentary are also fundamental forces that alter the conditions under which this movement can take place in the first place.

When we think of the birth of national traditions and national literatures, therefore, foreign literatures—whether in their original language or in translation—were central in aiding in the development of these "imagined communities." Yet contrary to Gayatri Chakravorty Spivak's assertion that "borders are easily crossed from metropolitan countries,"[9] Anglo-German exchange in the Sattelzeit was accompanied by ideological suspicion, aesthetic difference, and war, often purging these cultures of cultural capital in each other's eyes. And while "Britain" signified a unified entity, "Germany" remained a patchwork of distinct republics, kingdoms, and duchies until it was conquered by Napoleon, and then returned to a similar state after 1815. Given the historical significance of the period and the sheer amount and extent of intercultural dialogue taking place within it, it is no wonder that processes of literary and philosophical exchange in Europe in the eighteenth and nineteenth centuries have attracted sustained scholarly attention, often demonstrating how individual disciplines and cultures were brought into being by this exchange.[10] Exchange between Anglophone and Germanophone cultural spheres has long been a focus of research, and continues to result in edited volumes, scholarly monographs, and research articles[11]; moving beyond studying literary interchange, recent scholarship has begun to pay attention to the processes involved in language-learning and teaching in the period as an active component of cultural dialogue.[12] As a result, our current understanding of these patterns of exchange is complex and varied.

It is the contention of this book that until now—and certainly in recent scholarship—the novel has received a privileged position in research on Anglo-German exchange in the period in question that, while understandable to some degree, risks obscuring the significance of poetic and dramatic literature (and performance) in exchange between Britain and the German-speaking world from ca. 1750 to ca. 1850. This emphasis on the novel also risks obscuring some of the ways in which exchange in the period can inform how we think of processes of cultural transfer more generally. The present volume seeks to contribute to the current status of scholarship on Anglo-German exchange in the latter half of the eighteenth century and the first half of the nineteenth century. But beyond adding to what we already know, we hope to reframe and challenge some of the prevailing ways of conceptualizing how exchange took place, under what conditions, and what it resulted in. The focus of this book lies not on Anglo-German exchange in general, but on the places and the roles of poetry and drama in it. As the example from Zachariae shows, not only were poetry and drama integral in the development of the novel across Europe for the form and subject matter they could offer emerging prose writers, but they were also central to laying the foundations of cultural understanding upon which exchange could happen in the first place:

they provided German-speaking readers and writers with cultural products that gave a glimpse of the mores of a foreign people and therefore made these same people more accessible. While the novel was in the ascendency in the eighteenth century and continued to develop into the nineteenth century, the "Sattelzeit" also witnessed sweeping changes in poetic and dramatic traditions in both Britain and Ireland and present-day Germany, Austria, and Switzerland that were underwritten by processes of dialogue and interchange across national, cultural, linguistic, and generic borders. The chapters in this volume are therefore dedicated to exploring the dynamics of these processes. Moreover, while influence or unidirectional exchange has been the focus of much research until now,[13] the majority of chapters in this book look to uncover what Alessa Johns describes in her discussion of the translation and transmission of Richardson's *Clarissa* (1748) as "a dynamic and mutual interchange moving beyond simple ideas of reception or influence and challenging essential notions of national identity."[14] Thus they are concerned with tracing the status of drama and poetry in complex patterns of exchange, occurring with repeated movements across genres, media, traditions, languages, nations, and cultures.

SHIFTING FOCUS, ESTABLISHING TRADITIONS

The novel and the work of novelists and translators of novels have been a recurring focus in research into Anglo-German cultural exchange in the period. As hinted at previously, this is, of course, not without good reason. In both Britain and the German-speaking world—albeit at different points—the eighteenth century was the time at which the novel began to develop from an experimental genre into something that could boast exemplars of international renown and would come to dominate the literary marketplace; it could also come to develop into a site for imagining and fashioning a nation. As Steffen Martus writes, it is not surprising that the eighteenth century was the century of the novel:

> Keine andere Gattung war in diesen Jahren erfolgreicher; in keiner Gattung konnte die Aufklärung besser einen Menschen darstellen, der Fehler macht, sich deswegen entwickelt und aufgrund seiner Defizite lernt.[15]
>
> [no other genre was more successful in these years; in no other genre could the Enlightenment better depict people who make mistakes, develop because of them, and learn from their shortcomings].

Philosophically at least, narrative was the tool whereby authors could engage with the latest developments of their day. Yet the growth of the novel was certainly international in scale and facilitated by processes of exchange and by the popularity of products from other cultures. The relatively late rise of the German novel (in contrast to that of both France in the seventeenth century and Britain in the early eighteenth century), for example, was made possible by economic and cultural conditions that enabled the works of Defoe, Richardson, Fielding, and Laurence Sterne, for example, to cross the English Channel and find their way to a public that welcomed these British imports with open arms.[16] Although the German-speaking world had produced works such as Gellert's *Leben der schwedischen Gräfin* and Christoph Martin Wieland's *Geschichte des Agathon* (Story of Agathon, 1766–1767), the number of English novels being translated into German rose exponentially throughout the century; it only experienced a marginal decrease following the publication of Johann Wolfgang Goethe's *Die Leiden des jungen Werthers* in 1774[17] and then stagnated finally as the number of homegrown novelists took a sharp upward turn in the 1790s.[18] Ultimately, the British impact on the rise of the novel in Germany could be seen to have come full circle in the first half of the nineteenth century, as the very works of those novelists influenced by British prose came to exercise their influence on British writers in turn.[19]

For what it is worth, discussions of the intercultural processes underlying the growth and development of the English and German novel, however, rarely take the role of drama and poetry (even loosely defined) in these processes into account. And while both poetry and drama have received due attention over the years, scholarship continues to dwell on the position of a small number of figures. Where research into drama is concerned, two names tend to dominate discussions of Anglo-German exchange: William Shakespeare and August von Kotzebue. When compiling a bibliography of works on the influence of English literature on German literature, Lawrence Marsden Price writes, that "in the case of most other topics the difficulty of the investigator is in finding, in the case of Shakespeare the difficulty is in choosing."[20] While the first half of Price's statement—published in 1919—no longer holds, the second is still very much the case a hundred years later. Research consistently studies Shakespeare's role in the awakening and development of German culture throughout the eighteenth century and beyond,[21] and Price's own work is no exception to this trend: eighty out of 385 pages of the text of his 1953 study of *English Literature in Germany* from the seventeenth century to the mid-twentieth century are devoted to the topic "Shakespeare in Germany."[22] It is beyond doubt that Shakespeare's role in German culture is still rich in new findings, but its continued pre-eminence in scholarship occasionally overshadows anything else. In Lore Knapp and Eike Kronshage's 2016 volume of essays on *Britisch-deutscher Literaturtransfer 1756–1832*, for example, two out of twelve contributions focus on the influence of Shakespeare and only one of these considers the relationship between Shakespeare and German drama[23]; this is, of course, by no means the fault of the editors or the contributors in question, but perhaps indicates that scholarship still has its predilection for Shakespeare when it comes to studying British playwrights in eighteenth- and nineteenth-century German literature and culture.[24] Where this relationship is reversed, research has historically focused on "Kotzebuemania" in Britain in the 1790s and early 1800s, and British responses to the assumed moral depravity of Friedrich Schiller's *Die Räuber* (The Robbers, 1781).[25] Appropriately enough, the names of Shakespeare and Kotzebue occasionally become confused in this period: according to John Mander, when a production of Richard Brinsley Sheridan's adaptation of Kotzebue's *Die Spanier in Peru* (The Spaniards in Peru, 1796) as *Pizarro* (1798) was performed in Athlone, Ireland, in 1837, posters advertised "Shakespeare's celebrated play of Pizarro."[26] The phenomena of "Shakespeare in Germany" and "Kotzebue in Britain" are clearly important in the interchange of dramaturgical and performance practices as well as in demonstrating cultural affinities that could set the conditions for cultural exchange in the first place, but there are yet more dramatists that featured in and resulted from Anglo-German exchange in this period and that are due greater attention.

Again, the story of poetry's role in Anglo-German relations in this period has tended to focus on a set of particular writers and particular works. Discussions of the impact of German-language poets on British literature in the period regularly refer to Friedrich Gottlieb Klopstock, Salomon Gessner, and Goethe. Accounts of German literature in the eighteenth and nineteenth centuries would not, perhaps, be complete without considering the influence of figures such as Milton, Thomson, and Byron, and only in the last couple of decades have we begun to take account of the incomparable status of James MacPherson's "Ossian" poems in both the *Sturm und Drang* (Storm and Stress) and German Romanticism.[27]

It is one thing to show that research has a clear preference for certain key individuals and works and another thing altogether to claim that there is much more to be learned about a period—or indeed a whole set of processes. But, even still, why might poetry and drama be particularly promising avenues for research into Anglo-German relations, or, for that matter, into translation or comparative cultural studies? After all, intercultural exchange provided the necessary impetus for the development of the novel in Britain and thereafter in Germany. The very beginning of national prose traditions in the eighteenth century *required* looking to other literary cultures with their own fledgling traditions. As genres go, the novel was in its infancy in the eighteenth century. Poetry and drama, however, each belong to traditions stretching back millennia, and by the same point in time both English- and German-language poetry and drama had centuries-old indigenous traditions from which they had emerged and were continuing to emerge. Whereas the novel *needed* a spark from a foreign culture to come into being, these older forms already existed. Yet historically their development was always part and parcel of a process of learning from the products of other cultures in order to create cultural goods of one's own. Throughout the latter half of the eighteenth century and the first half of the nineteenth century, both Britain and the German-speaking world constantly either turned to each other to find models upon which to reform their own poetic and dramatic traditions or stumbled across one another, translating, adopting, and adapting each other's works for their own literary marketplaces.[28] As far as change goes, the more established genres of poetry and drama were, therefore, up for grabs just as much as the emerging novel, and intercultural dialogue played a central role in the ongoing development of these traditions. Furthermore, just as the novel acquired different ideological and "national" codings throughout this period, so too did drama and poetry. Indeed, research has only recently begun to move on from studying the ways in which the translation, adaptation, and performance of foreign dramatic traditions helped one culture study and respond to others. Birgit Tautz's recent *Translating the World* (2017), for example, demonstrates that German theater itself was a site for situating German culture within the wider world throughout the eighteenth century—before Weimar Classicism attempted to situate a German provincial capital as the center of that world.[29]

Despite the potential within poetry and drama to benefit from transnational exchange and despite the role of foreign dramatic and poetic works in the development of the novel, both receive surprisingly little attention in recent theoretical attempts to grasp both national and international cultural change. Current leading scholars in the field of World Literature, such as Pascale Casanova and Franco Moretti, almost exclusively deal with the processes by which prose forms historically develop through international transfer and by which new traditions and subgenres establish themselves, mutate, and often disappear.[30] Where Casanova mentions drama, for example, it is only in a national context (i.e., not as part of a movement between languages, cultures, and traditions) as a means of establishing the dominance of a native, performance-based tradition: "drama is at once a popular genre and an instrument for standardizing the language used in an emerging space. Its performance is directly related to the rediscovery and affirmation of traditional popular narratives."[31] In his study *What Is World Literature?* (2003), plotting the processes involved in the movement of literary works between languages and cultures, David Damrosch's interest in poetry seemingly runs out once the circulation of prose texts becomes established, and dramatic literature does not get a look-in among his case studies.[32]

In terms of contemporary book sales, the novel has the greatest international reach, and, historically speaking, prose has been a major driving force in how different cultures come into contact with one another and then sustain that contact. But this has not always been the case. It is without a doubt that both poetry and drama offer their own genre-specific difficulties for translators and foreign audiences alike: the condensation of poetic language and the cultural specificity of certain forms of rhyme and meter, the importance of tone and cultural convention in drama, and the centrality of gesture in performance, for example, all serve as potential barriers to the transfer of poetry and drama from culture to culture.[33] But they also offer opportunities for formal innovation and for circulating cultural capital. Theories that want to account for the forces involved in international literary transfer, the transnational networks involved in shaping a literary marketplace, and the intercultural factors that lead to the creation of national traditions and cultures need to take more than just prose forms into consideration. Indeed, Casanova's focus on the novel is a wider symptom of her debt to Anderson's work on nationalism, but we would do well to give fuller consideration to the many different functions of drama and poetry in cultural transfer.

Furthermore, poetry and drama have much to offer in terms of learning about other cultures. As Stephen Heath writes, drama is "a mode of presentation that can be seen across cultures through history"[34]; for Damrosch, through studying performance conditions "we can learn a good deal about a culture by seeing which elements a given tradition highlights, and how its writers use them."[35] Far from merely helping a culture to affirm its national tradition, based on a common language (as Casanova would suggest), drama and poetry are means of encountering another culture with its own traditions that are often traceable to orality and recognizing the differences and similarities between that culture and one's own.[36] Yopie Prins goes so far as to add "the circulation of poetry in print" to the novel and the newspaper as a space for the representation of an "imagined community"[37]; following Prins's logic, there would be no reason not to add the printed playtext to this list. If—as the potential linguistic and cultural barriers found in drama and poetry might suggest—it is difficult for one culture to fully assimilate the differences that it might find in printed documents between itself and another culture into its own system(s) of literature and culture, then poetic and dramatic works serve as possible means of encountering a difference that can promise the renewal of one's own traditions.

OUTLINE AND SCOPE

The eight chapters in this book each investigate the status and specific roles of drama and poetry in Anglo-German cultural exchange in the latter half of the eighteenth century and the first half of the nineteenth century. And rather than looking purely to the role of translation in processes of cultural transfer, the chapters here study translation alongside adaptation, the dissemination of texts and ideas, and the movement of individual people. Instead of opting for a specific, fixed period, the editors have chosen to explore the "Sattelzeit." Alongside our interest in importance of this period as one in which forms, genres, concepts, and nations crystallized, this choice of a nominal period over a set of dates serves an added pragmatic purpose. First of all, locating a start to the period is difficult, as Anglo-German cultural relations emerge gradually from the late sixteenth century into the seventeenth century. Knapp's and Kronshage's choice of 1756 to begin the period for their collection of essays is eminently sensible: 1756, as they write, is the year in which the Seven Years War broke out—which, incidentally, helped to solidify relations between Britain and a number of German principalities— and the Leipzig-based publisher Philipp Erasmus Reich traveled to England to visit Richardson.[38] Yet this is also the year in which, among much else, Zachariae's words in support of the British muse (cited previously) were first published and only three years before Lessing proclaimed that German culture would do well to forsake French literary models and turn instead to Shakespeare.[39] Then again, if we are looking for a point at which the German-speaking world began to turn to British drama or poetry, we might be equally justified in choosing 1732, the year in which Gottsched wrote his *Sterbender Cato* (Dying Cato), largely borrowing from Joseph Addison's 1712 tragedy *Cato*. A date for the British fascination with German-language literature may well be placed in 1761, when Mary Collyer's translation of Gessner's *Der Tod Abels* (The Death of Abel, 1758) was first published and, in the words of Violet Stockley, soon took "its place beside the *Bible* and the *Pilgrim's Progress* among the 'sacred classics' of the people."[40]

Finding an endpoint for the period is also difficult. Knapp and Kronshage argue that, being the year in which both Goethe and Walter Scott died, 1832 is a natural place to end their period.[41] Yet the processes of exchange set in motion by both figures were still ongoing. Indeed, it is difficult to find a specific date in which to round off the period in question: the translator and propagandist of German works Robert Pearse (or Pierce) Gillies established the *Foreign Quarterly Review* in July 1827 to disseminate European (and largely German) literature; 1828 saw the foundation of the first German university department in Britain, then at the University of London (now University College London), but this is presumably an indication of sustained and continued interest; indeed the English Goethe Society was not founded until 1886. Choosing precise dates in which to explore Anglo-German poetic and dramatic exchange in all of its forms is largely an exercise in tying down a moving—and arbitrary—target. But the roughly hundred years of the "Sattelzeit" featured such an intensity of exchange that it is worth pursuing in greater detail and from different angles.

Perhaps unsurprisingly, three of the chapters in this volume consider the period around 1800, but overall they reach to the beginning of the "Sattelzeit" and stretch to experiences gained during its final years that leave traces beyond the period. Four out of eight of the chapters study examples of Scottish works, figures, and contexts in cultural transfer in the period. Research until now has given considerable attention to the role of English figures in translating and adapting German works or to English writers being received in Germany. With the exception of Thomas Carlyle, the leading British figures that steered Anglo-German exchange in the period tend to be coded as English, thus scholarship has given thorough treatments to figures such as Henry Crabb Robinson, Samuel Taylor Coleridge, and Thomas De Quincey.[42] Germaine de Staël's role in facilitating Anglo-German exchange and helping to formulate the seeds of "Romanticism" has recently received renewed—and not undue—attention.[43] For all this, however, as some of the chapters here will demonstrate, we would do well to pay particular attention to the Scottish contexts of reception, transfer, and exchange. The role of Scottish periodicals such as *The Edinburgh Review* and *Blackwood's Magazine* and of Scottish individuals such as Gillies and John Gibson Lockhart to the reception of German literature in the early nineteenth century has been noted to some degree,[44] but this itself is rarely seen as more than a constituent part of English Romanticism.

In the first chapter in this volume, Barry Murnane provides a reassessment of the status of the German Gothic novel in Britain around 1800. So far, research has studied the relationship between German Gothic fiction and the growth of the Gothic novel in Britain, as well as linking this suspect German form to accusations of German immorality and political Jacobinism. Murnane's chapter, however, explores the networks of translation, adaptation, and performance that led the German Gothic novel to find its way on to the British stage. At a time when playwrights, directors, audiences, and producers sought sensation and spectacle, both of these were to be found in abundance in the works of novelists such as Benedikte Naubert, Heinrich Zschokke, and Christian August Vulpius. Thus the Gothic creations that found their way onto the British stage at the time were the result of the intermedial transformation of one genre *through* international transfer; moreover, as Murnane points out, the Gothic novel more generally played a larger role in the development of the melodrama as a theatrical form from Britain and France to the United States. Murnane goes further in demonstrating that the relative youth of the novel in the German-speaking world worked in its favor in this regard. The German novel was still a site of formal experimentation, and thus many of the novels that surfaced in Britain possessed a multigeneric quality, mixing prose with dialogue, sometimes lacking narrative entirely. Thus, as Murnane shows, the structural characteristics of the German novel were ideally suited to providing both new material and new ideas in an emerging British theater tradition.

While Murnane's chapter highlights the spectral presence of the German Gothic novel in the British theater, Lucy Wood identifies another specter in attempts to reinvigorate both British and German poetic traditions at the same time. Lucy Wood's chapter reexamines Scott's interaction with the ballads of Gottfried August Bürger in the mid-1790s and situates it within a circular form of cultural transfer whereby the British renewal of the ballad tradition would occur based on British sources, albeit mediated by the German reception of this same ballad tradition. Wood provides the example of William Taylor of Norwich's translation of Bürger's Gothic ballad "Lenore" as an attempt to transpose this German, Gothic rewriting of "Sweet William's Ghost" to a context and into a poetic form that might make it sit well with British tastes. Yet, as she demonstrates, Scott's treatment of this same ballad treads a difficult line between signaling the Germanness of Bürger's original and wanting to draw attention to the Scottish ballad tradition from which Bürger's ballad draws. Scott does not, however, stop at translating Bürger's ballads, nor is his treatment of them purely a case of translation. Rather, Scott recognizes much of Thomas Percy's *Reliques of Ancient English Poetry* (1765) in Bürger and introduces more of the old British ballad into his translations before going on to attempt to rejuvenate the British ballad tradition through an intriguing mix of lessons learned from both the older British tradition and its more recent Germanic revival.

Michael Wood's chapter likewise focuses on Scott and Scotland. Yet, rather than focusing on Scott's relationship with the German Gothic, he studies the reception of German drama in Scotland, exemplified through the experiences of Henry Mackenzie and Scott. Through an analysis of Mackenzie's important "Account of the German Theatre" of 1788 and Scott's subsequent interest in German plays, Wood identifies the significance of genre and generic categories in the Scottish reception of German drama at the end of the eighteenth and the beginning of the nineteenth centuries. While research to date has tended to interpret Scott's interaction with German drama as being guided by a passion for history and medieval and Gothic motifs, Wood argues that the basis for Scott's and Mackenzie's curiosity with regard to German plays and playwrights arises from the particular philosophical context in which they were reading and receiving them. When Scott, Mackenzie, and others came upon German drama at the end of the eighteenth century, they were drawn to concerns of the role of the passions, the ethics of theater, and formal innovation that bore a striking resemblance to their own Scottish interests. Indeed, the formal innovation of Lessing and his successors followed a period in which Lessing's interaction with Scottish Enlightenment philosophy led him to question traditional genre distinctions. Wood isolates the Scottish reception of German drama, using it to examine Scott's own attempt to write a play in 1799–1800 and pointing to ways in which his reappraisal may lead us to reassess the place of German drama in Scott's mature output.

One figure that is seemingly cast aside in the Scottish reception of German drama is Kotzebue. As indicated previously, Kotzebue's dominance on the English stage has long been a focus of research. Johannes Birgfeld's chapter, however, counts as one of the first pieces of scholarship to consider Kotzebue as a translator and adaptor of English plays. His contribution provides an analysis of two plays by Kotzebue based on eighteenth-century English works by Richard Cumberland and George Colman (the Elder). Birgfeld explores the ways in which Kotzebue adapted the morally dubious original plays to meet the demands of his performance context and his relatively conservative theatrical standards. In looking to provide plays that responded to the new cultural and political conditions of post-1815 German culture, Kotzebue looked beyond Germany in finding sources and themes with which to engage his audiences; in attempting to establish a new tradition of plays to be acted in the bourgeois home, he turned to English domestic comedies. Not only does Birgfeld's chapter provide a perspective into an overlooked element of Kotzebue's vast dramatic output, he also goes some way to pinning down an older Kotzebue, whose political and social conservatism after the peace of 1815 directly led to his assassination at the hands of the student Karl Ludwig Sand in 1819. In so doing, Birgfeld arguably exposes the other side of the coin of Anglo-German dramatic exchange in the period: while the importation of Kotzebue's works into England was tainted with suspicion of his moral depravity, his borrowing from the bawdy comedy of that same English theatrical tradition was guided by political conservatism.

Nils Reiter and Marcus Willand lead on from Birgfeld's chapter by keeping theater in focus, but they provide the first of two contributions to this volume that examine the status of a singular literary figure in another culture. Reiter and Willand adopt a Digital Humanities approach in giving a partial overview of the reception of Shakespeare in the German-speaking world in the eighteenth century. More specifically, they seek to explore and to challenge well-established claims about Shakespeare's influence on German playwrights in the second half of the eighteenth century. Their chapter begins by setting out a tradition of German Shakespeare criticism in the eighteenth century that focuses on apparent cases of formal innovation and rule-breaking in Shakespeare's plays. They identify aspects from the writings of Gottsched,

Johann Elias Schlegel, Lessing, and Goethe, in illustrating that German poetological discourse singled out a number of structural traits in Shakespeare's plays. Reiter and Willand then deploy cutting-edge technological means to explore over a hundred plays; this enables them to test assumptions about the uptake of certain aspects of Shakespearean form among eighteenth-century playwrights. They compare eighteenth-century works with translations of Shakespeare and with the contemporary critical discourse surrounding the relative merits and demerits of their formal composition. Perhaps not surprisingly, they find that the plays of the *Sturm und Drang* best represent Shakespeare's influence. Yet Reiter's and Willand's results argue that the *Sturm und Drang* playwrights are far from being the iconoclasts that they tend to be viewed as. Instead, they appear to be less innovative than Shakespeare and indeed than many other playwrights of the eighteenth century.

John Guthrie's chapter follows on from the computational approach of Reiter and Willand and instead engages in a philological treatment of the reception of Milton in the German-speaking world. Guthrie takes a long view starting in the late seventeenth century that enables him to trace the undulations and various meanderings of Milton's status in German culture in the eighteenth century. He examines the establishment of traditions in Milton criticism and translation before moving on to the mid- to late eighteenth century. Starting with the controversy between Zurich and Leipzig in the 1740s—when Johann Jakob Breitinger and Bodmer took on their Saxon opponent Gottsched in a famous, protracted war of words—Guthrie leads us through a history of leading figures in German culture, including Lessing, Goethe, Schiller, and Karl Philipp Moritz. What is perhaps most revealing in Guthrie's chapter is the way in which *Paradise Lost* serves as a touchstone and starting point for numerous debates, not only about translation, but about poetic form, the origins of language, the role of the marvelous in literature, and the place of feeling in poetry. His contribution elucidates the various competing German-speaking traditions that both shaped and were shaped by the reception of Milton and examines the genres and disciplines in which the reception of this English poet was central—including the psychological novel of Moritz and the complex heroes of the *Sturm und Drang* playwrights. Indeed, as Guthrie shows, the German tradition seemingly lost its reverence for Milton in the early nineteenth century, but not before his poetry had inspired some of its most significant creative minds.

Sandro Jung's contribution turns to the realm of translation studies, focusing his discussion on German translations of three interpolated tales from Thomson's *The Seasons*. As Jung's dense textual study of these three tales demonstrates, German translators were at pains to subdue Thomson's treatment of the body in order to give his text a place in both a canon of pious literature and in discourses of physico-theology. As Jung shows, the sheer volume of responses to Thomson's text illustrate that a long tradition of German writers (including first-tier figures such as Barthold Heinrich Brockes, Bodmer, and Zachariae) found very different ways of dealing with the eroticism of Thomson's text—even before we account for the number of writers who rewrote these three tales as separate works themselves. Scholarship is yet to fully comprehend the impact and the functions of illustration in Anglo-German exchange in the period. Besides merely depicting scenes in literary works, both vignettes and full-page illustrations enabled such works and the very ideas underlying them to undergo movements between genres and media. Jung, however, considers not only the range of approaches that German-speaking translators of the late eighteenth century adopted when tailoring the potentially erotic scenes to the demands of their readership; he also looks to the ways in which illustration adopted certain visual cues to connect Thomson's *Seasons* to the emotional and intellectual context of mid-eighteenth-century Germany and to dampen the translation of erotic poetic content into a visual representation. His interpretation of full-page illustrations, vignettes, and prints of Thomson's interpolated tales in the German-speaking world enriches our understanding of how this one Scottish poem might be turned into a modern classic and could feed into emerging traditions of German narrative poetry, helped along its way by being converted into another (visual) medium altogether.

Rounding off this volume, Bernhard Maier's chapter explores the effect of student experiences in Germany on two young Scotsmen: John Stuart Blackie and William Edmondstoune Aytoun. As Roger Paulin writes with regard to Staël and August Wilhelm Schlegel, "intercultural transfers . . . do not come about in the abstract: they require key persons to experience the alien culture at first hand."[45] It is beyond doubt that actual exchanges of individuals lent impetus and provided direction to transfer between Britain and the German-speaking world in the period. While Carlyle's, Coleridge's, and Crabb Robinson's activities as agents in Anglo-German exchange in the first half of the nineteenth century have been duly considered, Maier turns his attention to two figures who were to produce a profound effect on Scottish culture. As Maier demonstrates, Blackie and Aytoun were ahead of the curve in studying at German universities in the 1830s. Their experiences did not feature as part of a Grand Tour nor as part of an individual quest to get to know German culture and philosophy; rather, they were part of a tradition of Scottish students studying on the continent, but led the way in visiting German universities. It was these experiences and the personal connections made during them that enabled both Blackie and Aytoun to play essential roles in the later dissemination of German literature and thought in Britain. Moreover, their earlier student experiences left very visible traces on their later academic and poetic careers, with Blackie's academic interests resembling the paths of German Celtic scholars and Aytoun's own poetic works borrowing from the German poets he was still able to read and study.

In all, this book is intended to offer new insights into Anglo-German literary and cultural exchange in the second half of the eighteenth and the first half of the nineteenth century. Of course, any volume like this cannot hope to be exhaustive in its scope, and many notable figures and moments in Anglo-German exchange, such as Percy Bysshe Shelley's translation of Goethe's *Faust* (1808), Coleridge's reception of German drama and dramatic theory, and August Wilhelm Schlegel's writings on Shakespeare are not visited here; they are, however, covered in detail elsewhere. But the chapters presented in this volume constitute attempts to reconsider cases of Anglo-German encounters with and through drama and poetry in the Sattelzeit in a dual effort to provide new insights into these processes of exchange and cultural awakening and to redraw how we might think of intercultural transfer and the building of national traditions. Its contributors aim to challenge current assumptions by turning to new sources, asking new questions, and often reframing old questions. As the following chapters demonstrate, through studying the networks and movements of people and texts and affording these two older genres a privileged position in our analysis, we can gain a more nuanced perspective on the migration, adoption, and adaptation of genres and traditions across nations, cultures, and languages.

NOTES

1. Friedrich Wilhelm Zachariae, *Die Tageszeiten. Ein Gedicht, in vier Büchern* (Rostock and Leipzig: Koppe, 1756), 62–63. Emphasis in the original. Indeed, this passage is so illustrative that I have followed the lead of Lawrence Marsden Price, who uses this very passage (albeit from a later edition) to open his chapter on the eighteenth century in his *English Literature in Germany* (Berkeley, CA: University of California Press, 1953), 35.

2. Of course, the term "Anglo-German" may appear ahistorical and culturally insensitive to some readers, but will be adopted in the following when discussing exchange between Britain and the German-speaking world. To that end, "Anglo" is to be understood in terms of referring to the British side of exchange, unless a particular case is defined as being specifically English, Scottish, Irish, or Welsh; "German" refers to the entire German-speaking world, including the German-speaking states that were part of the Holy Roman Empire, or, following that, the German Confederation, Austria, and German-speaking Switzerland.

3. See Reinhart Koselleck, "Einleitung," in *Geschichtliche Grundbegriffe: Historisches Lexikon zur politisch-sozialen Sprache in Deutschland*, ed. Otto Brunner,

Werner Conze, and Reinhart Koselleck, eight volumes (Stuttgart: Klett, 1972–97), vol. 1, xv. See also Daniel Fulda and Elisabeth Décultot, eds., *Sattelzeit: Historiographiegeschichtliche Revisionen* (Berlin and Boston, MA: de Gruyter, 2016). Notably, the period of Koselleck's "Sattelzeit" coincides with the period identified and critiqued in Michel Foucault's *The Order of Things* (first published 1966).

4. Benedict Anderson, *Imagined Communities: Reflections on the Origin and Spread of Nationalism*, revised edition (London and New York: Verso, 2016), 25. Emphasis in the original. For a more detailed exposition on the role of the novel and the newspaper in Anderson's theory, see 22–36.

5. See, for example, Itamar Even-Zohar, "Translation Theory Today. A Call for Transfer Theory," *Poetics Today* 2, no. 4 (1981): 1–7; and Itamar Even-Zohar, "The Position of Translated Literature within the Literary Polystystem," *Poetics Today* 11, no. 1 (1990): 45–51.

6. Lawrence Venuti, *Translation Changes Everything: Theory and Practice* (London and New York: Routledge, 2013), 10. See also Lawrence Venuti, *The Translator's Invisibility: A History of Translation*, second edition (London and New York: Routledge, 2008), 14.

7. See, for example, Susan Bassnett and André Lefevere, *Constructing Cultures: Essays on Literary Translation* (Clevedon: Multilingual Matters, 1998), 7, 41–56.

8. Lawrence Venuti, "Local Contingencies: Translation and National Identities," in *Nation, Language, and the Ethics of Translation*, ed. Sandra Bermann and Michael Wood (Princeton and Oxford: Princeton University Press, 2005), 180, 189.

9. Gayatri Chakravorty Spivak, *Death of a Discipline* (New York: Columbia University Press, 2003), 16.

10. Three recent works on this topic that deserve particular attention are Maike Oergel, ed., *(Re)-Writing the Radical: Enlightenment, Revolution and Cultural Transfer in 1790s Germany, Britain and France* (Berlin and Boston, MA: de Gruyter, 2012); Stefanie Stockhorst, ed., *Cultural Transfer through Translation: The Circulation of Enlightenment Thought in Europe by Means of Translation* (Amsterdam and New York: Rodopi, 2010); and Birgit Tautz, *Translating the World: Toward a New History of German Literature Around 1800* (University Park, PA: Pennsylvania State University Press, 2017).

11. In the past few years alone, we can turn a number of works on the subject of Anglo-German exchange. Alessa Johns's pioneering *Blue-Stocking Feminism and British-German Cultural Transfer, 1750–1837* (Ann Arbor, MI: University of Michigan Press, 2014), for example, studies the development of discourses of liberty in Britain and the German-speaking world in this period, as informed by the ways in which the Personal Union enhanced the possibilities for cultural transfer. We also have the benefit of recent edited volumes, including Lore Knapp and Eike Kronshage, eds., *Britisch-deutscher Literaturtransfer 1756–1832* (Berlin and Boston, MA: de Gruyter, 2016), which consists of twelve essays studying the reception of British texts and concepts in Germany, as well as outlining some of the routes of transfer; and Ritchie Robertson and Michael White, eds., *Fontane and Cultural Mediation: Translation and Reception in Nineteenth-Century German Literature* (Cambridge/Leeds: Modern Humanities Research Association/Maney,

2015), whose contributions range across a number of subjects and therefore inform our understanding of relationships between German, British, and French literature and thought in the nineteenth century and beyond. Research has also begun following the lead of earlier twentieth-century scholars in exploring the rich pickings of the British periodical press and its role in Anglo-German exchange in the long eighteenth century. Catherine Angerson's "'A friend to rational piety': The Early Reception of Herder by Protestant Dissenters in Britain," *German Life and Letters* 69, no. 1 (2016): 1–21, for example, devotes attention to how the writers of *The Monthly Review* laid the groundwork for the reception of Johann Gottfried Herder's ideas in Britain.

12. For recent research into the teaching and learning of German among native English-speakers in the period, see Karl S. Guthke, "Deutsche Literatur aus zweiter Hand. Englische Lehr- und Lesebücher in der Goethezeit," *Jahrbuch des freien deutschen Hochstifts* (2011): 163–237; Nicola McLelland, "German as a Foreign Language in Britain: The History of German as a 'Useful' Language since 1600," *AN-GERMION* 8 (2015): 1–33; and Nicola McLelland, *German Through English Eyes: A History of Language Teaching and Learning in Britain 1500–2000* (Wiesbaden: Harrassowitz, 2015).

13. This includes the volumes edited by Lore Knapp and Eike Kronshage and Ritchie Robertson and Michael White, listed previously.

14. Johns, *Bluestocking Feminism*, 40.

15. Steffen Martus, *Aufklärung: Das Deutsche 18. Jahrhundert. Ein Epochenbild* (Berlin: Rowohlt, 2015), 885.

16. For further reading on the international dynamics of the rise of the novel in Germany and the Anglo-German book trade, for example, see Patrick Bridgwater, *The German Gothic Novel in Anglo-German Perspective* (Amsterdam and New York: Rodopi, 2013); Sarah Vandegrift Eldridge, "Expanding the Eighteenth-Century Novel between England and Germany: Sentiment, Experience, and the Self," in *Repopulating the Eighteenth Century: Second-Tier Writing in the German Enlightenment*, ed. Michael Wood and Johannes Birgfeld (Rochester, NY: Camden House, 2018), 90–106; Bernhard Fabian, *The English Book in Eighteenth-Century Germany* (London: British Library, 1992); H.R. Klieneberger, *The Novel in England and Germany: A Comparative Study* (London: Wolff, 1981); Michael Maurer, *Aufklärung und Anglophilie in Deutschland* (Göttingen: Vandenhoeck & Ruprecht, 1987); Bethany Wiggin, *Novel Translations: The European Novel and the German Book, 1680-1700* (Ithaca, NY: Cornell University Press, 2011); and Jennifer Willenberg, *Distribution und Übersetzung englischen Schrifttums im Deutschland des 18. Jahrhunderts* (Munich: Saur, 2008).

17. See Lawrence Marsden Price, "Introduction," in Mary Bell Price and Lawrence Marsden Price, *The Publication of English Literature in Germany in the Eighteenth Century*, (Berkeley, CA: University of California Press, 1934), 13–14.

18. For statistics on the number of living writers and number of new novels being published in Germany in the latter half of the eighteenth century, see Johann Wilhelm Appell, *Die Ritter-, Räuber- und Schauerromantik: Zur Geschichte der deutschen Unterhaltungs-Literatur* (Leipzig: Englemann, 1859), 11; and Marion Beaujean, *Der*

Trivialroman in der zweiten Hälfte des 18. Jahrhunderts: Die Ursprünge des modernen Unterhaltungsromans (Bonn: Bouvier, 1964), 178.

19. With reference to the relationship between German literature and British novelists and poets of the early nineteenth century, see Hilary Brown, *Benedikte Naubert (1756–1819) and her Relations to English Culture* (Leeds: Maney, 2005); Karl S. Guthke, *Englische Vorromantik und deutscher Sturm und Drang: M.G. Lewis' Stellung in der Geschichte der deutsch-englischen Literaturbeziehungen* (Göttingen: Vandenhoeck & Ruprecht, 1958); Peter Mortensen, *British Romanticism and Continental Influences: Writing in an Age of Europhobia* (Basingstoke: Palgrave Macmillan, 2004); Frauke Reitemeier, *Deutsch-englische Literaturbeziehungen: Der historische Roman Sir Walter Scotts und seine deutschen Vorläufer* (Paderborn: Schöningh, 2001); and Frank W. Stokoe, *German Influence in the English Romantic Period 1788–1818, with Special Reference to Scott, Coleridge, Shelley and Byron* (Cambridge: Cambridge University Press, 1926).

20. Lawrence Marsden Price, *English>German Literary Influences. Bibliography and Survey. Part I. Bibliography* (Berkeley, CA: University of California Press, 1919), 4.

21. See, for example, Hans Wolffheim, *Die Entdeckung Shakespeares: Deutsche Zeugnisse des 18. Jahrhunderts* (Hamburg: Hoffmann & Campe, 1959); Günther Erken, "Deutschland," in *Shakespeare-Handbuch: Die Zeit—Der Mensch—Das Werk—Die Nachwelt*, ed. Ina Schabert, fourth edition (Stuttgart: Kröner, 2000), 635–60; Roy Pascal, *The German Sturm und Drang* (Manchester: Manchester University Press, 1953), 233–95; Roger Paulin, *The Critical Reception of Shakespeare in Germany 1682–1914: Native Literature and Foreign Genius* (Hildesheim: Olms, 2003); and Roger Paulin, ed., *Shakespeare im 18. Jahrhundert* (Göttingen: Wallenstein, 2007).

22. Price, *English Literature in Germany*, 215–96. In his earlier version of this work, the section on Shakespeare counts for ninety out of 443 pages: see Lawrence Marsden Price, *The Reception of English Literature in Germany* (Berkeley, CA: University of California Press, 1932).

23. See Kira Liebert, "Die kreative Aneignung Shakespeares im Werk von Karl Philipp Moritz," in Knapp and Kronshage, *Britisch-deutscher Literaturtransfer*, 171–91; and Charlotte Lee, "'Durch Wunderkraft erschienen'—Affinitäten zwischen Goethes *Faust II* und Shakespeares *The Tempest*," in Knapp and Kronshage, *Britisch-deutscher Literaturtransfer*, 193–200.

24. One notable recent exception to this trend is Norbert Bachleitner's essay, "English Plays on the Austrian Lists of Banned Books between 1750 and 1848," in *Anglo-German Theatrical Exchange: "A sea-change into something rich and strange?"* ed. Rudolf Weiss, Ludwig Schnauder, and Dieter Fuchs (Leiden and Boston, MA: Brill, 2015), 19–41.

25. For references to published research on these topics, see notes in Michael Wood's and Johannes Birgfeld's chapters in this volume.

26. John Mander, *Our German Cousins: Anglo-German Relations in the 19th and 20th Centuries* (London: John Murray, 1974), 30.

27. Thanks largely to the efforts and the scholarship of Howard Gaskill, among others. Recent publications on Ossian in Germany include Howard Gaskill, "Introduction: The Translator's Ossian," *Translation and Literature* 22 (2013): 293–301; Caitríona Ó Dochartaigh, "Goethe's Translation from the Gaelic Ossian," in *The Reception of Ossian in Europe*, ed. Howard Gaskill (London: Continuum, 2004), 156–75; Wolf Gerhard Schmidt *"Homer des Nordens" und "Mutter der Romantik": James Macpherson's "Ossian" und seine Rezeption in der deutschsprachigen Literatur*, four volumes (Berlin and New York: de Gruyter, 2003–2004); and Wolf Gerhard Schmidt, "'Menschlichschön' and 'kolossalisch': The Discursive Function of *Ossian* in Schiller's Poetry and Aesthetics," in *Reception of Ossian in Europe*, Gaskill, 176–97. As research on *Ossian* in Germany demonstrates, there is still much work to be conducted into the relationship between German-language literature and non-English-language literature from the British Isles.

28. A detailed and essential work on the role of translation in the creation of both British and German literary traditions in the period 1750–1830 is Gauti Kristmannsson, *Literary Diplomacy*, two volumes (Frankfurt a.M.: Lang, 2005), volume 1: *The Role of Translation in the Construction of National Literatures in Britain and Germany, 1750–1830*.

29. See Tautz, *Translating the World*.

30. See Pascale Casanova, *The World Republic of Letters*, trans. M.B. DeBevoise (Cambridge, MA, and London: University of Harvard Press, 2004); Franco Moretti, *Atlas of the European Novel 1800–1900* (London and New York: Verso, 1998); Franco Moretti, *Graphs Maps Trees: Abstract Models for Literary History* (London and New York: Verso, 2007); and the relevant essays in Franco Moretti, *Distant Reading* (London and New York: Verso, 2013).

31. Casanova, *World Republic*, 228.

32. See David Damrosch, *What Is World Literature?* (Princeton and Oxford: Princeton University Press, 2003). Here Damrosch devotes chapters to the intercultural dissemination of ancient, medieval, and renaissance poetry before jumping on to Franz Kafka, P.G. Wodehouse, and Rigoberta Menchú.

33. See, for example, Susan Bassnett, "Translating for the Theatre: The Case Against Performability," *TTR: traduction, terminologie, redaction* 4, no. 1 (1991): 99–111; André Lefevere, "Mother Courage's Cucumbers: Text, System and Refraction in a Theory of Literature," *Modern Language Studies* 12, no. 4 (1982): 3–20; and Hanna Scolnicov, "Introduction," in *The Play Out of Context: Transferring Plays from Culture to Culture*, ed. Hanna Scolnicov and Peter Holland (Cambridge: Cambridge University Press, 1989), 1.

34. Stephen Heath, "The Politics of Genre," in *Debating World Literature*, ed. Christopher Prendergast (London and New York: Verso, 2004), 166.

35. David Damrosch, *How to Read World Literature* (Chichester: Wiley-Blackwell, 2009), 47. See also Gershom Shaked, "The Play: Gateway to Cultural Dialogue," in Holland and Scolnicov, *The Play Out of Context*, 18.

36. For cases of this in the poetry and drama of the period in question of this volume, see, for example, Peter Boerner, "National Images and Their Place in Literary

Research: Germany as Seen by Eighteenth-Century French and English Reading Audiences," *Monatshefte* 67, no. 4 (1975): 358–70; Michael White, "Herder and Fontane as Translators of Percy's *Reliques of Ancient Poetry*: The Ballad 'Edward, Edward,'" in *Fontane and Cultural Mediation*, Robertson and White, 107–19; and Michael Wood, "'An Old Friend in a Foreign Land': Walter Scott, *Götz von Berlichingen*, and Drama Between Cultures," *Oxford German Studies* 47, no. 1 (2018): 5–16.

37. See Yopie Prins, "Metrical Translation: Nineteenth-Century Homers and the Hexameter Mania," in Bermann and Wood, *Nation, Language, and the Ethics of Translation*, 228–56.

38. Lore Knapp and Eike Kronshage, "Einleitung," in Knapp and Kronshage, *Britisch-deutscher Literaturtransfer*, 3. On Reich's invaluable contribution to Anglo-German exchange in the period, see Martin Munke, "Philipp Erasmus Reich und die Verbreitung britischer Literatur in Deutschland. Import und Übersetzung," in Knapp and Kronshage, *Britisch-deutscher Literaturtransfer*, 21–38.

39. See Gotthold Ephraim Lessing, "Siebzehnter Brief [Den 16. Februar 1759]," in *Gotthold Ephraim Lessings Sämtliche Schriften*, ed. Karl Lchmann, third edition by Franz Muncker, twenty-three volumes (Stuttgart: Göschen, 1886–1924), volume 8, 41–44.

40. Violet Stockley, *German Literature as Known in England, 1750-1830* (London: Routledge, 1929), 5–6. For further treatment of the reception of *Der Tod Abels* in Britain at the time, see Sandra Richter, *Eine Weltgeschichte der deutschsprachigen Literatur* (Munich: Bertelsmann, 2017), 94–98.

41. Knapp and Kronshage, "Einleitung," 3.

42. See, for example, Manfred Engel and Jürgen Lehmann, "The Aesthetics of German Idealism and Its Reception in European Romanticism," in *Nonfictional Romantic Prose: Expanding Borders*, ed. Steven P. Sandrup, Virgil Nemoianu, and Gerald Gillespie (Amsterdam and Philadelphia, PA: John Benjamins, 2004), 89, where these three figures and Coleridge are given credit for rescuing the reputation of German idealist philosophy and literature in Britain in the early nineteenth century.

43. For some recent work on Staël's role in Anglo-German exchange and in the recognition and development of a European Romanticism, see John Claiborne Isbell, *The Birth of European Romanticism: Truth and Propaganda in Staël's "De l'Allemange," 1810–1815* (Cambridge: Cambridge University Press, 1994); and Roger Paulin, *The Life of August Wilhelm Schlegel: Cosmopolitan of Art and Poetry* (Cambridge: Open Book Publishers, 2016), 221–393.

44. See, for example, Frederic Ewen, "John Gibson Lockhart, Propagandist of German Literature," *Modern Language Notes* 49, no. 4 (1934): 260–65; Alan Lang Strout, "Writers on German Literature in *Blackwood's Magazine* (With a Footnote on Thomas Carlyle)," *The Library* 9 (1954): 35–44; and Harriet Harvey Wood, *Lockhart of the "Quarterly": "Prince of Biographers"* (Edinburgh: Sciennes Press, 2018), 36–40.

45. Paulin, *Life of August Wilhelm Schlegel*, 226–27.

Chapter One

British Ghosts of the Gothic Novel

Dramatic Adaptation as a Medium of Anglo-German Cultural Transfer in the 1790s

Barry Murnane

In the literary discourse surrounding Anglo-German cultural relations from the late 1780s onwards, German Gothic occupied a demonized position within the transnational frameworks of the emerging literary market. For the likes of Jane Austen and the *Anti-Jacobin*, Gothic fiction was synonymous with an image of Germany as a depraved site of necromancy, the supernatural, secret societies, revolutionary politics, and wanton sex and violence. Although the novel was the primary focus of British literary criticism of the time, German Gothic literature around 1800 was associated first and foremost with drama rather than with *Ritter-, Räuber-, und Schauerromane* (novels of chivalry, banditry, and horror). Samuel Taylor Coleridge's critique of the German Gothic in his 1816 review of *Bertram* by Charles Maturin is in fact a critique of what he terms "modern jacobinical *drama*."[1] And it is to the "German stage" in particular that the *Anti-Jacobin* objects with its polemical campaign against the radical "SYSTEM comprehending not Politics only, and Religion, but Morals and Manners, and generally whatever goes to the composition or holding together of Human Society" in German literature.[2] The apparent popularity and infamy of drama reminds us that it is unhelpful to limit the role of German literature within the emergent field of Gothic literature around 1800 to prose fiction alone; in literary discourse around 1800, "German" literature is primarily associated with works for the stage.[3]

This association of Germany with the stage was no accident: in 1799 alone, for example, fifteen plays by August von Kotzebue were published in English translations and multiple versions of his *Pizarro* (originally entitled *Die Spanier in Peru* [1794]) were performed on various London stages. Although Kotzebue's works were not actually Gothic, contemporary critics tended to view their perceived sexual and political licentiousness as affiliated with the mode. Add to this the various translations of works by Johann Wolfgang

Goethe, Friedrich Schiller, August Wilhelm Iffland, and melodramatic adaptations of German novels like *Herrmann von Unna* (1788), *Rinaldo Rinaldini* (1797), multiple versions of Matthew Gregory Lewis's "The Bleeding Nun" (taken from *The Monk*, 1796), and other British works purporting to be translations from the German, there was a clear precedent for seeing "German," "Gothic," and drama as going hand in hand—even if only as a result of paranoid reactions among British critics. For the *Anti-Jacobin*, the state of the British stage was a good indicator of the state of the British nation in revolutionary times: this was full of "German errors, German inconsistencies, German politics, and German blasphemies."[4]

The following chapter seeks to reconstruct the networks of translation and cultural transfer responsible for this perceived German invasion of the British stage. Given that many of the central texts under discussion actually gained notoriety as dramatic adaptations, I will suggest that any account of German Gothic in Britain that wishes to be comprehensive must take account of these transgeneric and transmedial contexts. To a great extent the popularity of German Gothic texts in Britain relied on their stage versions, only gaining a widespread audience as a result of their adaptation. Indeed many German novels were only received in their dramatized versions, meaning that the presence of German Gothic novels in Britain around 1800 was in many ways a spectral presence: as the stage ghosts of German novels.

GOTHIC AFTERLIVES AND GENERIC HEMORRHAGING: THE CASE OF THE "THE BLEEDING NUN"

It is not exactly surprising to find vitriolic polemics in a journal like the *Anti-Jacobin*, but even respectable literary journals like the *British Critic* or the *Monthly Review* joined in the chorus of fearful criticism of German drama: "In the present state of the drama, when pasteboard pageantries and German spectres have almost driven Shakespeare and Congreve from the stage, we cannot but applaud any attempt to 'hold the mirror up to Nature.'"[5] One perceived deficiency that critics found most objectionable in German literature was its anti-naturalist tendencies, although the knowledge base from which such judgments were reached was often questionable. On the whole the discussions in British literary journals centered on works in English translation, but equally as many referred to sham translations that were simply homegrown novels and plays written "in the German manner." Among those genuine translations a further difficulty arose in the lack of sufficient knowledge either of the foreign language or of the literary idiom on the part of the translator and commissioning editors. Writers who did have adequate

German, like Lewis and Thomas De Quincey, on the other hand, tended to produce adaptations and abridgements rather than translations, or to simply reproduce the most horrific parts of the source texts in isolation in their own works, as Lewis frequently did. Another issue often criticized was the apparent formlessness of German literature: alongside prose translations (and English novels purporting to be German), German novels were also available as stage adaptations, in redacted versions as prologues and epilogues (short, independent plays flanking the headline event), harlequinades (the forerunner to the pantomime), or epilogues, adapted into popular illustrated prose formats based on these stage versions in widely available chapbooks and bluebooks, and ultimately also into popular visual culture in the form of pantomimes, tableaux, and phantasmagoria shows. The British afterlife of Johann Karl August Musäus's "Die Entführung" (The Abduction) illustrates this generic multiplicity paradigmatically.

"Die Entführung," one of Musäus's *Volksmärchen der Deutschen* (Fairytales of the Germans, 1782–1786), gained notoriety in an abridged form as a central episode in Lewis's *The Monk* and has since been better known as "The Bleeding Nun."[6] This appears in an inset tale that Don Raymond tells Don Lorenzo about his attempted elopement with the latter's sister, Agnes. The action is removed temporarily from Madrid to Strasbourg and Germany, where Don Raymond has escaped from a band of murdering robbers with the Baroness Lindenberg, visits her castle, and falls in love with her niece, Agnes. Having been denied permission to marry him and knowing that she will be sent to a convent, Agnes plans to dress up as the castle's own specter, the fabled Bleeding Nun, in order to escape from the castle. In the first supernatural event of the novel, the escape plan goes wrong when Raymond greets the real Bleeding Nun at the gates of the castle instead of the disguised Agnes, promises himself to her in marriage, and hence locks himself into a cycle of nightly visitation that is only halted by the equally spectral exorcist figure of The Wandering Jew, himself modeled on the figures of the Armenian and the Sicilian in Schiller's *Geisterseher* (The Ghost-Seer, 1787–1789). This realistic framework is the first major piece of recontextualization from the German original: it locates a narrative that was marked as a fairy tale, a *Volksmärchen*, in Musäus's original text, firmly into the actual reality of the novel.

Musäus's tale is a convoluted "anecdote" (to use the subtitle he himself provides) about Lauenstein Castle that stretches over several hundred years, starting with the prehistory of the castle as a convent, how the dispossessed and disinterred nuns are said to have haunted the castle until an exorcist banished all but one of them, and finally finishing with a tale of love and intrigue between Emilie and a soldier named Fritz in the Thirty Years' War who plan to use the nun's appearance to elope. This tale prefigures Lewis's love story between Raymond and Agnes, with Fritz mistaking the ghost of the last remaining nun for Emilia and pledging his love for her so that her ghostly skeleton haunts him nightly. Musäus only mentions the visitation of the ghost in passing, however, and here the differences to Lewis's more horrific version become clear:

> Wie die Glocke zwölfe schlug, öffnete sich die Türe, die verlorne Reisegefährtin trat herein; doch nicht in Gestalt der reizenden Emilie, sondern der gespenstischen Nonne, als ein scheußliches Geripp. Der schöne Fritz wurde mit Entsetzen gewahr, daß er sich schlimm vergriffen hatte, schwitzte Todesschweiß, hob an sich zu kreuzen und zu segnen, und alle Stoßgebetlein zu intonieren, die ihm in der Angst einfielen.[7]

> [As the clock struck midnight, the door began to open and his missing female companion entered the room; but instead of Emilie's beautiful body the ghostly nun appeared in the shape of a horrible skeleton. Handsome Fritz realized in horror that he had made an awful mistake and, in fear for his life, began blessing himself and saying any prayer that came into his unhinged mind.]

The ghost of the Bleeding Nun in *The Monk* is elaborately developed and highly visual. Lewis focuses on the affect produced by what is clearly a violent ghostly presence rather than a light-hearted spectral apparition:

> By an involuntary movement I started up in my bed, and drew back the curtain. A single rush-light which glimmered upon the hearth shed a faint gleam through the apartment, which was hung with tapestry. The door was thrown open with violence. A figure entered, and drew near my Bed with solemn measured steps. With trembling apprehension I examined this midnight Visitor. God Almighty! It was the Bleeding Nun! It was my lost Companion! Her face was still veiled, but She no longer held her Lamp and dagger. She lifted up her veil slowly. What a sight presented itself to my startled eyes! I beheld before me an animated Corse. Her countenance was long and haggard; Her cheeks and lips were bloodless; The paleness of death was spread over her features, and her eyeballs fixed steadfastly upon me were lustreless and hollow.[8]

In keeping with this horrific spectacle, Lewis's Bleeding Nun mutates from a restless spirit whose grave had been disturbed into a sexual monster who has fled from a convent to become the concubine of a previous Baron Lindenberg. "Die Entführung" becomes a typically British Gothic story of the sins of the forefathers being revisited on younger generations.

This pattern in Lewis's adaptation is discernable at various junctures, not least in a comparison of the respective exorcisms. Musäus's text is not devoid of the supernatural and also features an exorcist who banishes the ghost: "Es wurden viele geheimnisvolle Zubereitungen gemacht . . . und auf des Meisters Ruf, erschien in einem dunklen Gemach . . . der mitternächtliche Geist diesmal in der Mittagsstunde" (He made various secretive preparations . . . and at the Master's command the midnight visitor appeared at midday . . . in the darkened room).[9] This is again narrated almost in passing, however, and by calling it "getriebner Unfug" (utter nonsense) the horror is rendered ludicrous. Lewis, on the other hand, develops an episode of radical, visual horror that relies on a powerful moment of performance in the exorcist's actions:

> He described a circle in the middle of the room. Round about this He placed various reliques, sculls, thigh-bones &c; I observed, that He disposed them all in the forms of Crosses. Lastly He took out a large Bible, and beckoned me to follow him into the Circle. I obeyed. . . . He spoke in a commanding tone, and drew the sable band from his forehead. In spite of his injunctions to the contrary, Curiosity would not suffer me to keep my eyes off his face: I raised them, and beheld a burning Cross impressed upon his brow. For the horror with which this object inspired me I cannot account, but I never felt its equal![10]

Lewis couples the plot and personnel of Musäus's text with a homegrown tale of blasphemy, sexual depravity, and violence that he clothes in an extravagantly dramatic, visual form of Gothic horror.[11]

This first stage of intertextual appropriation by Lewis was followed by multiple less "legitimate" instances, including plays, ballets, pantomimes, and chapbooks like *The Bleeding Nun of the Castle of Lindendorff; or, The History of Raymond and Agnes* (1799). Such popular adaptations draw on Lewis's reworking of "Die Entführung" rather than on Musäus's story itself, and it was presumably the visuality of Lewis's writing seen here that made the transition of the Gothic tale onto the stage relatively simple. This started with his production of Lewis's play *The Castle Spectre* (1797).[12] In *The Castle Spectre* the ghost of Evelina that appears in Conway Castle was modeled on the above description of the Bleeding Nun:

> The folding-doors unclose, and the Oratory is seen illuminated. In its centre stands a tall female figure, her white and flowing garments spotted with blood; her veil is thrown back, and discovers a pale and melancholy countenance; her eyes are lifted upwards, her arms extended towards heaven, and a large wound appears upon her bosom. Angela sinks upon her knees. . . . At length the Spectre advances slowly, to a soft and plaintive strain. . . . The music ceases. Angela rises with a wild look, and follows the Vision, extending her arms towards it.[13]

Even if *The Monk* is clearly the more familiar source text to readers today, "Die Entführung" becomes very much a British product here, and with it, a British *stage* product: an intermedial ghost of a German Gothic novel.

Following the spectacular success of this ghostly play, "The Bleeding Nun" enjoyed a stage afterlife of different proportions in less mainstream or legitimate theatrical contexts. The story also featured as a "ballet pantomime" called *Airs, Glees, and Chorusses in a New Grand Ballet Pantomime of Action, Called Raymond and Agnes; or the Castle of Lindenbergh*, performed in the Covent Garden theater in 1797 and organized by English actor Charles Farley. A melodramatic version of "The Bleeding Nun" in two acts entitled *Raymond and Agnes, the Travellers benighted* (published in 1804, performed in 1809) was attributed to Lewis himself; it also appeared with the alternative subtitle *The Bleeding Nun of Lindenberg*.[14] This success seems to have encouraged renowned director James Boaden to produce a dramatic adaptation of *Aurelio and Miranda* (1798),[15] but oddly enough, he opted to remove the nun from his dramatic adaptation, as the advertisement to the play outlines: "THIS play is avowedly founded on the Romance of the MONK. The Author enters not into the discussion which that work has produced. His attempt has been to dramatize the leading incident of the Romance, without recourse to supernatural agency."[16] Boaden mainly reproduces the structure, sequence, and content of Lewis's plot, but rather than privileging the supernatural episodes in Germany, the play focuses on the brutal events in Madrid, albeit without the gratuitous sex and violence of the novel.[17] These redactions are obviously a response to the scandal surrounding Lewis following publication of the novel, but it may also be a reaction to the criticism of the supernatural episode in *The Castle Spectre*: although this play was highly popular with audiences, the critical response viewed it as a rupture with the Aristotelian principles central to "proper" dramatic form.[18] Despite the star actors of the day, John Philip Kemble and Sarah Siddons, performing in the lead roles, the play was a disaster and was abandoned after only six nights. In his future Gothic productions, Boaden then returned to featuring ghostly apparitions.

As the fate of the "Bleeding Nun" shows, German and Gothic drama offered a dramatic mode that was both multigeneric (including music, masque, tableaux, and speaking roles), heavily intertextual (either as adaptations or redactions), and spectacular (including spectral apparitions and atmospheric effects). The diarist Hester Piozzi captures this formal diversity well: "taste, no longer classical, cried out for German plays and novels of a new sort, filled with what the Parisians call . . . *phantasmagoria*."[19] Although she lumps together both translations and adaptations under the same term here, Piozzi highlights a poetological illegitimacy of "German" drama: the deviation from classical taste stretches generic conventions to breaking point, confusing and discomforting critics in equal measure. Unlike text-based drama, phantasmagoria relies on an affect-driven performative poetics driven by suspense and fear, and it was familiar from popular, vernacular traditions such as the burlesque and vaudeville, available at non-patent theaters. Other critics like Coleridge and William Wordsworth were no less scathing in their response to these generically diverse works. Wordsworth can barely conceal his jealousy of Lewis's success (not least because his own *Borderers* of 1797 was rejected for performance),[20] and bemoaning how *The Castle Spectre* "fitted the taste of the audience like a glove" in a letter to William Hazlitt, he highlights the preoccupation with spectacle, performance, and affective spectatorship as an illegitimate, anti-Aristotelian model of drama.[21]

The practitioners of German and Gothic theater were well aware of this loosening of generic rules. Looking back on his fascination with German plays in the 1829 "Advertisement" to his *House of Aspen* (written in 1799–1800), Walter Scott terms his play more "a rifacimento of the original than a translation . . . since the whole is compressed, and the incidents and dialogue occasionally much varied."[22] This foregrounds streamlined plotting and tight, tension-inducing structuring as key characteristics of the Gothic drama that would provide a fast-paced and tension-filled play reliant on an affect-centered performance. In the prologue to *The Secret Tribunal* Boaden makes a similar argument, starting by lamenting the lack of formal coherence in other plays of the period, knowing full well that his play suffered from the same problems: "LONG hath the tragic muse, in secret mourn'd / Her pow'r abused, her empire overturn'd, / Her sacred laws in mixt confusion tost; / Her rights insulted, and her virtues lost."[23] Not that Boaden was necessarily intent on really curing this confusion, as he goes on to claim that his inclination is now "To waken Feeling, and to touch—The heart." With their privatized model of dramatic reception Wordsworth, Coleridge, Piozzi, and others argued that a properly dramatic effect could only be expected to be produced in the mind of a sensible reader rather than in the unpredictable situation of the theatrical spectacle endorsed by Boaden's dramatic inclination toward an affective mode of reception. In short, what Boaden's critics were responding to was the introduction of the melodrama onto the British stage in the late eighteenth century—a genre that, in a popular cartoon by Samuel de Wilde from 1807, was demonized as the "Monstrous Melo-Drama."[24]

MONSTROUS MELODRAMAS AND POLITICS: TRANSLATION AND TRANSFORMATION BETWEEN GERMANY, FRANCE, AND BRITAIN

The melodrama at the heart of these critical accounts was actually an innovative and relatively young format started in France's boulevard theaters by writers and directors like René Charles Pixérécourt. The melodrama's development in France and its arrival in Britain are intricately linked with German drama and the French Revolution, raising suspicions among paranoid conservative commentators in Britain of a conspiratorial, radical political context to what were generally quite harmless, entertaining romance narratives.[25] The reception of German writers like Iffland, Kotzebue, and Heinrich Zschokke had a formative influence on the melodrama in post-Revolutionary Paris, with Pixérécourt, for example, translating and staging various plays by Kotzebue, including *Pizarro* and *Die Hussiten vor Naumburg* (The Hussites at Naumburg, 1802),[26] and a version of Zschokke's *Aböllino, der große Bandit* (Abaellino, The Great Bandit, 1794) with the title *L'homme à trois visages* (The Man with Three Faces) in 1801.[27] The latter play is notable in that he simply calls it a "drame"—unlike Zschokke's own 1795 adaptation announced as a "tragedy"—showing the slippage of generic coordinates surrounding the melodrama. This slippage was at the heart of British critical responses.

Much has been written about the role of French mediation in the reception of English literature in Germany and of German literature in Britain.[28] French publishers based in Amsterdam and the Netherlands provided an initial and important point of transition to the continental book trade, with English works typically being translated into German from intermediary French versions and vice versa before homegrown translation industries emerged. While this may have been relatively unproblematic in the first half of the century, the outbreak of revolutionary and radical politics in the 1790s meant that any form of cultural transmission involving France became highly suspect to the British public—as the previously quoted passages from the *Anti-Jacobin* illustrate quite clearly. Thus for a British readership introduced to German literature primarily through French adaptations—which, as melodramas, were already held to be aesthetically dubious—German literature became recontextualized as conspiratorial, politically dangerous, and morally questionable. The reception of Benedikte Naubert's *Herrmann von Unna* offers a paradigmatic example of these recontextualizations.[29]

Celebrated in her day, Naubert was largely forgotten other than as a writer of fairy tales, and indeed the traditional accounts of the German Gothic novel that focused on Goethe, Schiller, and Carl Friedrich August Grosse often neglected her role as a formative figure in developing the Gothic in Germany and beyond.[30] *Herrmann von Unna*, a sentimental *Ritterroman*, was by far her most successful work in Britain and tells the story of Ida, the illegitimate daughter of a nobleman raised in a middle-class family in Nuremberg, who appears at the court of Emperor Wenceslas and instantly becomes the Empress's favorite. She falls in love with Herrmann, before becoming tied up in a series of conspiracies, which employ secret tribunals to separate the lovers and falsely imprisons her in various dungeons and convents. Ida is accused of witchcraft, murder, and high treason but in order to assist her, her adoptive father becomes a member of the so-called *Vehmgericht*, or Secret Tribunal. The *Vehmgericht* emerges as a traditional and respectable institution that has become tarnished by the corruption encouraged by Wenceslas. As a result, it has been infiltrated by debauched and corrupt judges more interested in their own personal enrichment, and hence become an invisible vehicle for a contingent and unjust use of power. When the young couple, Herrmann and Ida, are united at last, their happy end is undermined somewhat by Herrmann being elected as a member of the tribunal's opaque power structures. Naubert's original remained essentially a sentimental romance, very much along the lines of Sophia Lee's *The Recess* (1783–1785) or Anne Radcliffe's *Romance of the Forest* (1791).

The same cannot be said of Naubert's English afterlife. An anonymous English translation of the novel appeared in 1794, which seems to have been translated from French, as the misspelled title suggests.[31] The primary source of the English prose translation was Baron de Bock's two-volume French translation *Hermann d'Unna* (1792)[32] and there are numerous amendments in the English text that seem to have their origin in Bock's historical studies, all of which increase the importance of the secret tribunals in the novel. Whereas the episodes involving the *Vehmgericht* were merely one element of the two-volume German work, the English translation includes Bock's "Essay on the Secret Tribunal" as an extended foreword. Prefacing the novel with Bock's polemical study obviously emphasized the *Vehmgericht* and the conspiratorial elements of the plot for an English readership.[33] German dramatic adaptations and the French stage also play an important role in the transmission of Naubert's novel to Britain. Competing adaptations included Johann Nepomuk Komarek's *Ida oder Das Vehmgericht* (1792) and Ludwig Ferdinand Huber's *Das heimliche Gericht* (first published in Schiller's *Thalia* journal in 1790).[34] The latter play was also translated by Bock as *Le tribunal secret* in 1791,[35] and this melodramatic "historical" drama seems to have been the main source of Boaden's later version, as the similarity of his title, *The Secret Tribunal*, underlines.

Sensitive to the changing dramatic tastes among the wider audiences in late-eighteenth-century London, Boaden develops a form of suspense-driven melodrama in *The Secret Tribunal* that departs quite radically from the novel's more complex tale of female insecurity and maturation to develop a more worrying depiction of domestic secrecy and ominous violence. In keeping with the personalized plotlines of the melodrama, the play still pays lip service to the love story between Hermann and Ida, but as the title suggests, the plot immediately turns toward conspiracy and secrecy. Set in Swabia, the plot of rivalry in love between Hermann and his uncle Ratibor is only a loose framework for a tale of treason, with Ratibor plotting to murder his brother, the Duke, and to attribute the murder to the "Secret Tribunal" of judges known as the "Invincibles," which proves easy to infiltrate because its judges and servants constantly operate in disguise. This enables Boaden to develop a dramatic representation of hidden state apparatuses that seems less a genuine engagement with the German novel than a reflection of the political anxieties in Britain immediately prior to play's performance in 1795, including the London Corresponding Society Trials in 1794. Thus we hear that the Tribunal's "eyes are every where—unseen they hear— / Their agents mingle in the walks of life, / And even our servants are their secret spies."[36] Such imagery obviously draws on the fantasies surrounding Adam Weishaupt's *Illuminatenorden* in Germany (a radical secret society that did indeed exist, but whose small numbers and lack of meaningful political influence certainly did not merit the paranoia surrounding them in Germany, France, and Britain),[37] but it also references the images of revolutionary conspiracy in France made popular by the Abbé Barruel and mediated in Britain by public figures such as John Robison and Edmund Burke.[38] As I have discussed elsewhere,[39] Robison's *Proofs of a Conspiracy against all the Religions and Governments of Europe, carried on in the Secret Meetings of Free-Masons, Illuminati and Reading Societies, etc., collected from good authorities* (1798) was particularly influential in generating and disseminating this conspiracy theory, arguing that the Illuminati had infiltrated the Freemasons with their radical Enlightenment social and political agenda. Transported from Germany to Britain, *Herrmann von Unna* becomes barely recognizable, reduced to a plot of privately motivated insurrection against the state.

Given that these were adaptations of a pre-Revolutionary text set in a climate of political paranoia in 1794–1795, significant contextual factors color Naubert's reception. Already a corrupt institution in Naubert's original novel,[40] the *Vehmgericht* could scarcely not be associated by readers in the 1790s with conspiracy theories surrounding secret societies and the French Revolution under these conditions. The conspirators, secretive judiciary, and the social disorder represented in Naubert's novel, for example, were easily recoded as harbingers of radicalism and revolutionary politics. This was assisted by the novel's path to Britain via Paris, or from Naubert to Boaden, via Huber and Bock, adding weight to the claims of conspiratorial links between Germany, Paris, and political radicals in London made by the *Anti-Jacobins* and writers like Robison. In Bock's play Naubert's fictional marker in the novel's subtitle "*eine* Geschichte" (a story) became the less ambiguous "drame historique" (historical drama) thus suggesting a factual basis for the story of a secret society in a British context where an unhealthy fixation with conspiracy theories, concealment, and fears of radical political collusion was already rife. This was taken even further by Boaden's 1795 adaptation where the romance plot may indeed remain as the motor of his melodramatic version, but the title and the more visible role that the *Vehmgericht* plays in the plot unduly emphasizes its importance.[41] The often unclear authorial relations under which translations, adaptations, and redactions were produced led to German drama itself becoming associated with secret societies, conspiracy, and even the French Revolution itself. As Robison writes "we know that the enemy is working among us" in the "blackguard production of the German presses."[42] Monstrosity of melodramatic form and political monstrosity went hand in hand for British audiences viewing German drama for the first time.

FLUIDITY OF FORM IN POPULAR GERMAN FICTION

While the notoriety of Gothic drama in Britain was very much a homegrown phenomenon—the result of novels of various origins being turned into dramas and other forms of performances—the development of narrative fiction in eighteenth-century Germany suggests that there may be a more complex story of generic uncertainty to be told around the "German School" on British stages. Most accounts of German literature in British critical debates have focused on partisan politics and xenophobia, and while these are indeed central issues, there were also formal reasons in the source texts themselves that encouraged dramatic adaptations rather than prose translations.

The lack of suitably qualified translators in Britain hampered the transmission of German novels to Britain. Nevertheless, the comparatively late emergence of the novel as a central literary genre in Germany resulted in a wide range of formal experimentation being present well into the late eighteenth century, which seems to have lent itself readily to dramatic adaptation. This is not to say that Germany did not produce novels or shorter prose fiction in the Enlightenment: the novels of Christian Fürchtegott Gellert, Sophie von La Roche, Christoph Martin Wieland, or August Lafontaine were very popular in their own day and were also available in translation. But these works—particularly those of Lafontaine and other popular forms of novel production in the late 1780s and 1790s—betray a lack of formal stringency and coherency. Goethe's *Bildungsroman*, *Wilhelm Meisters Lehrjahre* (Wilhelm Meister's Apprenticeship, 1795–1796), may have subsequently established itself as the canonical novelistic mode in Germany, but for Romantic critics it was the generic hybridity of Goethe's novel—with its rich admixture of prose, poetry, and descriptions of the contemporary theater—that made Goethe's work the quintessential novel of the age. Friedrich Schlegel writes: "Wer Goethes 'Meister' gehörig charakterisierte, der hätte damit wohl eigentlich gesagt, was es jetzt an der Zeit ist in der Poesie" (If you were to write a proper critical appreciation of Goethe's "Wilhelm Meister" you would actually be defining what is right now the state of the art in literature),[43] and he praises in particular how it aims to mix and merge "Poesie und Prosa, Genialität und Kritik, Kunstpoesie und Naturpoesie" (poetry and prose, ingenuity and critique, nature poetry and poetry of art).[44] Prior to its transfer to Britain, the German novel was itself already a dynamic, but formally unstable genre.

As multiple studies of genre theory in the Enlightenment have shown, the novel had some difficulty in establishing itself within a traditional triadic model consisting of poetic, dramatic, and epic writing,[45] and these difficulties are visible in the few examples of late-Enlightenment genre theory that do focus on the novel, such as those of Johann Jakob Engel and Friedrich von Blanckenburg.[46] Martin Huber has outlined how, owing to theater's dominant cultural status, the German novel oriented itself primarily toward drama in the period of its generic gestation, and Huber develops the neologism of "theatrales Erzählen" (theatrical narration) to describe this formal structuring.[47] Of course there are significant differences between Blanckenburg and Engel, but they do share an interest in characters speaking for themselves as a means of generating interest on the part of the reader, hence Blanckenburg's advocacy of the epistolary novel in generating the maximum affective reception of a text.[48] Engel, on the other hand, advocated a form of the novel that deployed the use of dialogue in order to present the plot as *action*, rather than reporting events through the medium of a narrative perspective. As such it is little surprise that he advocates the *Dialogroman* (the dialogue novel), a French import now primarily associated with Wieland, as the preferred model of prose fiction.[49] This relative fluidity with regard to the form of the novel can be most clearly seen in the realm of popular fiction around 1800, however. Given that the *Ritter-, Räuber-, und Schauerromane* followed a poetics of shock, tension, and fear, it is not surprising to find these "dramatic" tendencies in broadly Gothic narratives.[50] In these works, extended passages of dialogue are often loosely linked together through sections of short narrative reports. Indeed, speakers are often identified almost as "roles" in paratextual directions in these texts. The case of *Herrmann von Unna* illustrates this formal openness effectively.

Naubert's novel is broadly episodic, consisting of various adventures that are interlinked by the background presence of the *Vehmgericht*. Although her novels are notable for their larger narrative passages, Naubert uses a dialogic technique at crucial junctures of the story, such as when Herrmann is being freed from captivity at the hands of Emperor Siegmund:

> Es ist schwer zu beschreiben, mit was für Gedanken und Empfindungen Herrmann die Zeit der fürchterlichen Stille, die auf dieses Trauergetös folgte, zubringen mochte.—Es war weit nach Mitternacht, als er aus seinen schrecklichen Träumereyen durch ein Geräusch an der Gefängnißthür geweckt wurde.
>
> Die Riegel öfneten sich. Eine weibliche Stimme rief, Ritter von Unna, ihr seyd frey!—
> Ich frey? auf wessen Befehl?—
> Durch Hülfe eines armen Mädchens, welches Mitleid mit euch hat, und ihre schweren Sünden gern durch eine gute That abbüßen wollte. Fliehet! Fliehet! ehe es zu spät wird!—
> Ich fliehen! Die Unschuld fliehet nie!—
> Gilt eure Unschuld hier etwas?—[51]

[It is difficult to describe the sorts of thoughts and feelings with which Herrmann spent the period of awful silence that followed the cries of mourning.—It was well past midnight when he was awoken from fearful dreams by a noise at the door of the prison.
 The bolts unfastened. A female voice called, Ritter von Unna, you are free!—
 Me, free? By whose command?—
 By the aid of a poor maiden who has pity on you and who would like to absolve herself from her sins through a good deed. Flee! Flee! before it is too late!—
 Me, flee! Innocence never flees!—
 Does your innocence matter here?—]

Passages like this one have a dual function: first, the immediacy and intimacy of this dialogic performance of character and their respective "unmediated" responses to the events immediately happening to them encourage a greater intensity in the reception of the texts and their action.[52] Second, they generate a form of characterization whereby the fictional figures (like Herrmann here) characterize themselves and their responses in their own words and actions (what contemporary theorists of the German novel like Engel term *Charaktergemälde*) and encourage an empathetic response.[53] As such, the dialogic immediacy in Naubert's novel generates a heightened sense of tension and action, while also offering the unmediated access to a character's consciousness and feelings demanded by the sentimental genre, all of which is heavily informed by dramatic form.

The original novel provided a welcome collection of dramatic scenarios from which British playwrights only needed to choose key moments in order to produce their stage versions. In *The Secret Tribunal* the already inherently visual, theatrical nature of Naubert's novel is clearest in Boaden's vivid depictions of the Tribunal itself, most notably in the spectacular, occult symbolism at the play's finale. Arguably the most chilling aspect of the play is the fact that the Tribunal is constituted as an arm of the state, making the survival of the Duke and established dynastic order ultimately dependent on a secret network of spies, opaque legal structures, and an anonymous executive. It is on the steps of the church that the Tribunal's "Minister of Vengeance" appears to Ida and her father. Set in the "place of subterraneous meeting" which is reached directly via a passageway from the market square, the scene draws on dramatic, hellish imagery: "The scene represents a spacious Crypt, or vaulted Court of Justice, underground, of Gothic Architecture. At the upper end is a luminous Cross of deep red, and over this, surrounded by Clouds, an Eye, radiated by points of fire."[54] The Tribunal ultimately finds in their favor, and the Duke agrees to sanction their marriage after Ratibor's plans have been discovered. With the happy ending of an impending marriage the play returns to the—only partially satisfactory—sentimentalizing plot of the novel.

FROM *RÄUBERROMAN* TO MELODRAMATIC CONSPIRACY: ZSCHOKKE AND LEWIS

The fluidity of generic borders between prose and drama that can be identified in German popular fiction generates novelistic pretexts in which the immediacy of dialogic performances of action, character, and their respective responses to events already exert a powerful presence prior to being adapted for stage, whether in German or in English.[55] Following on from the success of the various incarnations of Naubert's *Herrmann von Unna*, Zschokke's *Abaellino* is the next major example of a novel that is so dramatically structured that it is little wonder the author decided almost immediately to adapt it for the German stage himself.[56] Zschokke's novel tells the story of the Graf Obizzo of Naples who, having been betrayed by his family, escapes to Venice where he assumes a dual identity of a Florentine nobleman called Flodoard and a penniless beggar who, because of being mistreated by the Venetian aristocrat he helped to save from the robbers, himself becomes a feared robber and murderer known as Abaellino. However, he longs to serve Venice and he surfaces simultaneously in the Doge's court under the name Flodoard, where he becomes besotted with the Doge's niece, Rosamunde. As a doppelgänger, he is able to plot against the bandits to have them arrested, giving Abaellino a criminal monopoly. At this stage, a group of conspirator politicians engage his services to bring down the Doge, but Abaellino is able to hide the intended victims and then reveal his dual identity, thus showing the plotters' activities in a spectacular scene before the court. When he brings the Doge's friends out of hiding, Abaellino wins back the court's favor, and hence ultimately Rosamunde's hand in marriage.

Although the "Trauerspiel" (tragedy) is more stringently structured and the character profiles and their motivations more clearly developed—particularly those of the conspirators Grimaldi and Parozzi—the original novel was so strongly dialogic and visual at its central junctures that it lent itself to adaptation for the stage quite readily. In the grand finale, for example, we find a spectacular masque scene where Abaellino transforms his physiognomy into that of the handsome Flodoard:

> Ein schauerliches Stillschweigen wohnte im Saale. Jeder gehorchte der Stimme des großen Banditen, der mit der Majestät des höllischen Monarchen durch den Saal schritt, wenn anders der Teufel Majestät besizzen kann.
> *Rosamunde* schlug die Augen auf—ihr erster Blik haftete auf den verwandelten *Flodoard.*
> "O!" rief sie: "Allbarmherziger, ist es nicht möglich—es ist ein satanisches Blendwerk!"
> *Abaellino.* (zu ihr tretend) Nein, kein Blendwerk, Rosamunde; dieser Bandit Abaellino ist dein Flodoard von Florenz. . . .
> *Abaellino* riß das Pflaster vom Auge, rieb mit seinem Tuch im Gesicht umher, faltete die verzognen Mienen in ihre natürliche Ordnung zurük, strich die schwarzen Haare von der Stirn, und siehe da, der schöne Flodoard stand in Abaellinos Banditentracht vor den Augen der Versammlung.[57]

> [A terrible stillness lay in the room. Everyone obeyed the voice of the great bandit, who paced through the room with the majesty of a hellish monarch, if the devil can possess majesty.
> *Rosamunde* opened her eyes—her first glance landed upon the transformed *Flodoard.*
> "Oh!" she cried: "Oh most merciful, it is impossible—it is a satanic illusion!"
> *Abaellino.* (coming towards her) No, not an illusion, Rosamunde; this bandit Abaellino is your Flodoard of Florence. . . .
> *Abaellino* tore the band from his eyes, rubbed his face with his cloth, folded his contorted countenance back into its natural state, wiped the black hairs from his forehead, and look there, the handsome Flodoard stood in Abaellino's bandit clothing before the eyes of all assembled.]

This is a deliberate performance by Abaellino/Flodoard, staged for an audience waiting in great suspense for the spectacle. Abaellino/Flodoard reveals himself as a stage performer, his face mutating with the help of makeup and taping. As Gail K. Hart writes: "The book is dramatic in character, and also in form, since much of it consists of dialogue and the narrator's comments could often just as well be stage directions. . . . Like spectators in the theater, readers have to see and hear the action."[58] Hart does not trace this visual spectacle back to the insecure position of the novel form in Germany, however, but it is clear that Zschokke's novel is a prime example of the "theatrical narration" identified by Huber as characteristic of the popular novel around 1800.

Zschokke's own stage version, *Abällino der große Bandit. Ein Trauerspiel in 5 Aufzügen* borrows the novel's dialogue almost verbatim at times, although his adaptation curiously relies more heavily on monologue in places than did the novel. This is most notably the case where Abällino speaks at length about his actions, providing an immediate—but subjective—psychological justification for his development as a criminal character. A good example of the play's reliance on the dialogic nature of the novel is in the final scene:

> *Rosamunde.* (sich erholend) Albarmherziger, er ist es nicht! es ist ein satanisches Blendwerk!
>
> *Abällino.* (zu ihr tretend.) Nein, kein Blendwerk, schöne Rosamunde. Dein Flodoardo ist Abällino und Abällino Dein Flodoardo.
>
> *Rosamunde.* (ihn mit Abscheu zurückstoßend.) Geh, geh, entsetzlicher Lügner, es ist nicht möglich!—Du und Flodoardo! Seraph und Satan, wer schmilzt die zusammen?[59]

> [*Rosamunde.* (recovering) God almighty, it is not him! It is a satanic illusion!
>
> *Abaellino.* (approaching her) No, not an illusion, fair Rosamunde. Your Flodoardo is Abaellino and Abaellino is your Flodoardo.
>
> *Rosamunde.* (repelling him in disgust) Be gone, you horrific liar—that is impossible!—You and Flodoardo! Who can conjoin an Angel and Satan?]

Even purely orthographically both of Zschokke's texts have the appearance of dramatic texts, but the novel's focus on visuality and spectacle (formally) and on performance of identity (thematically) clearly lends itself readily to theatrical adaptation.

Given the theatricality of the original German novel and the international success of Zschokke's own adaptation, it is unsurprising that *Abaellino* enjoyed an equally multigeneric career in Britain. Lewis first translated Zschokke's novel in prose form as *The Bravo of Venice* in 1805, but it is notable that this version disappeared from critical view almost immediately following a series of five stage versions in German, English, French, and Italian between 1800 and 1810 alone, including Lewis's own *Rugantino* of 1805. Indeed Victor Sage has noted that both the original novel and its English translation are almost conspicuous by their complete absence in even the best-stocked academic libraries, whereas various versions of the play can be found relatively simply.[60] The success of *Rugantino* is also indicative of the unclear paths of transmission between Germany and Britain more generally. Having published his novel, Lewis wanted to bring *Rugantino* to the London stage in 1805, only to be beaten to it by versions by Robert Elliston and William Dunlap, named *The Venetian Outlaw* and *Abaellino*, respectively, in the same year. Elliston's version for the Drury Lane theater is clearly based on Pixérécourt's 1801 French adaptation, *L'homme à trois visages* already mentioned: *The Venetian Outlaw* reproduces the characters' names, most of the settings, and the main lines of the plot and dialogue in the French melodrama. Dunlap's New York version *Abaellino the Great Bandit* (1802) is likewise mediated through Paris: it is based on Jean-Henri-Ferdinand Lamartelière's 1799 version *Abelino, ou Le grand bandit*, and even repeats Lamartelière's mistake of attributing the play to Schiller.[61] Given his own command of German, Lewis will not have needed to consult either French version and indeed his *Rugantino* is markedly closer to the plot of *The Bravo of Venice* than either of the French plays. Lewis's version prevailed—most likely a result of his established reputation as a Gothic dramatist and of the excellent connections he had with the London theater world—running for over thirty nights at Covent Garden and then given repeat performances throughout the 1810s. This popularity even led to several chapbook versions, including *Rugantino, the Bravo of Venice*, an undated version published by the London firm Dean & Munday. Zschokke's *Räuberroman* becomes little more than a ghostly presence in Anglo-German cultural transfer.

The plot of *Rugantino* is simple and reproduces Zschokke's own dramatic version more clearly: prior to the play's opening, Rosabella, daughter of Andreas, Duke of Venice, has fallen in love with a handsome, noble, but poor young man, Flodoardo, though the Duke has arranged a marriage between her and the Prince of Milan. At Rosabella's request, Flodoardo has left Venice. The play opens as a group of bravos conspire against Andreas and Rosabella, fueled by the thwarted lust of their leader, Parozzi, for Rosabella. These bravos are actually the henchmen of a secret group within the Venetian Council that is plotting an insurrection against the Doge, thus introducing a familiar theme of the secret society into the *Räuberroman*. Rugantino, a horrifyingly ugly thief who is the terror of the city, saves Rosabella from Parozzi's bravos before menacingly telling her she will marry him. Flodoardo returns at the beginning of the second act, when the audience becomes aware that he and Rugantino are the same person. The Duke agrees to let Rosabella marry Flodoardo if he can capture Rugantino. Flodoardo agrees and on the night of a masque he reveals himself to be Rugantino in a metatheatrical extravaganza. He delivers the bravos to the Duke, explains how he carried out the deception, returns the Duke's friends, who have been in hiding, to the court, and confirms his love for Rosabella. The play ends with a tableau confirming the aversion toward insurrection and the return of order to Venice.

Given its orderly conclusion, *Rugantino* is designed to be a politically reassuring play among post-Revolutionary tensions, moving through violence, monstrosity, and confusion to safe closure. That said, the dramatic devices of role-playing, dissimulation, and resorting to an outlaw figure as a means of restoring order, no matter how noble he turns out to be, must surely raise questions about the legality of this restored political order. For an English audience painfully aware of the suspension of Habeas Corpus in 1794, the fact that the status quo is only maintained through criminal activities must have been particularly unsettling. Rugantino is a questionable beacon of hope for Venice: he achieves order through collusion with criminals, and his activities are those of an undercover vigilante who takes it upon himself to spy on, capture, and imprison political conspirators, thieves, and murderers alike. In his lecture "On the German Drama," Hazlitt associated such plots of conspiracy with radical politics. Recalling how the "loud trampling of the German Pegasus on the English stage" had caused anxieties through its supposed "overturning all the established maxims of society," he interprets dramatic works such as *Rugantino* as a worrying aesthetic articulation of the unspeakable horrors of the Age of Revolution.[62] In an age of paranoia, secret tribunals, and secret societies across continental Europe, it is easy to see how Rugantino's acts of dissimulation were interpreted as an attempt—in an admittedly extravagant form—to visualize radical politics.

While the content of novels such as *Abaellino* or *Herrmann von Unna*, with their tales of secret societies, collusion between power-hungry parvenus and decrepit legal institutions, and unmotivated violence fueled these theories, the predilection for such texts and their interpretation in relation to the French Revolution may say more about homegrown British tastes than actual German literary tastes. The popularity of Naubert, Zschokke, Boaden, and Lewis seems to respond to an urgent need to make manifest the complex structures of social organization, communication, and intersubjective interactions of a culture on the brink of modernity that appeared increasingly opaque, incomprehensible, and threatening. In both its guises, Zschokke's work is ultimately the story of a noble criminal in the mode of Schiller's Karl Moor in *Die Räuber* (1781); Abaellino is a good man who resorts to criminal activity because of the society around him, and he does so in order to uncover and prevent greater crimes, and thereby save the established social order. There is a deeper, more troubling question behind this contemporary political issue, however. If the text indicates that social order can only be maintained through spectacle, performed identities, and ultimately collusion with criminals, then *Abaellino* casts a shadow on the very workings of social order itself. Contrary to what writers as different as Hazlitt and Robison suggest, the morals, values, and laws of society no longer appear as a natural given, but are rather products of individual social performance. In helping to fictionalize this problem for mass audiences, perhaps conservative critics were correct to view these plays with suspicion—just not on the polemical grounds which they themselves articulated.

CROSSING BORDERS AND CREATING SPECTERS: GOTHIC PERMEABILITY

While it may seem logical to recognize Gothic dramas by virtue of obviously fantastic or supernatural elements, the German Gothic works that were most successful on British stages actually suggest an interest in dramatic verisimilitude. While we may find a catalog of atmospheric devices and objects—from ruined castles and monasteries to gloomy forests and underground dungeons; from suits of armor to bloody weapons—in these dramas, with the exception of "The Bleeding Nun," all three dramas betray an interest in domestic scenarios. Notwithstanding this domestic focus, given the widespread contemporary criticisms of spectacle and phantasmagoria, it was rather secret tribunals and bands of brigands in German plays that seem to have interested British audiences in particular. Although certainly spectacular, these would have appeared realistic to an audience brought up on the notoriety of German secret societies and a staple diet of accounts of Jacobinical secret plotting.

The Gothic that emerges through Anglo-German cultural transfer is a multigeneric mode of cultural expression: texts move across generic borders just as easily as they move across national and cultural borders. What each of the plays discussed here shows is that Gothic drama moved rather freely between tragic and comic-romance trajectories from play to play, adaptation to adaptation, and even within individual plays. In their happy resolutions, the three plays analyzed here underline the basic melodramatic structuring in the Gothic drama as a whole; all three offer a broadly personalized narrative that is used as the motor of a sentimental plot, ending in marriage and closure. While, on the one hand, this range of plot options enabled the Gothic drama to engage particularly effectively with the tensions of the post-Revolutionary 1790s, this generic ambivalence was one of the key points of criticism by

Romantic writers who demanded less permeability of generic borders. On the other hand, the permeability of German Gothic texts across genres was a crucial means of achieving popularity and maximum cultural reach in Britain, with German, Gothic, and drama becoming almost synonymous around 1800. Wordsworth speaks openly of the "German" drama as a spectral formation, its popularity haunting both him and English society. But on the evidence of the plays discussed here, perhaps we should say that these specters are doubly ghostly. Indeed, with these palimpsestic, transmedial, melodramatic versions of German texts eliding the original prose texts from view, Wordsworth's dramatic specters are in actual fact the spectacular afterlife of German prose on the British stage—the British ghosts of the German Gothic novel.

NOTES

1. Originally published across five issues of *The Courier* in 1816; reprinted (in amended form) as chapter 23 of Samuel Taylor Coleridge, *Biographia Literaria*, *The Collected Works of Samuel Taylor Coleridge*, ed. James Engell and W. Jackson Bate, sixteen volumes (Princeton: Princeton University Press, 1973–2017), volume 7.2, 221. See Alethea Hayter, "Coleridge, Maturin's *Bertram*, and Drury Lane," in *New Approaches to Coleridge. Biographical and Critical Essays*, ed. Donald Sultana (London: Barnes & Noble, 1981), 17–37.

2. *The Anti-Jacobin Review, or Weekly Examiner* 30 (June 4, 1798), in *The Anti-Jacobin Review, or Weekly Examiner In Two Volumes* (London: J. Wright, 1799), volume 2, 415–16.

3. The role of drama within the formation of the Gothic more generally has also been a blind spot in research until relatively recently. Those scholars who have addressed Gothic drama at length are Jeffrey Cox, *In the Shadows of Romance* (Athens, OH: Ohio University Press, 1987); Paul Ranger, *Gothic Drama in the London Patent Theatres* (London: Society for Theatre Research, 1991); Michael Gamer, *Romanticism and the Gothic* (Cambridge: Cambridge University Press, 2000); Diego Saglia, "Gothic Theatre," in *The Gothic World*, ed. Glennis Byron and Dale Townshend (Abingdon: Routledge, 2014), 354–65; and Francesca Saggini, *The Gothic Novel and the Stage* (London: Pickering & Chatto, 2015). I have profited greatly from these studies far more than the individual references suggest, even if the focus of the chapter diverges from their primarily English focus.

4. Juvenis, "Letter to the Editor," *The Anti-Jacobin Review and Magazine* 7 (1801), 516. See David Simpson, *Romanticism, Nationalism, and the Revolt against Theory* (Chicago and London: University of Chicago Press, 1993), 89–94.

5. Anon, "Review of Joanna Baillie's *Plays on the Passions*," *Monthly Review* 27 (1798): 66. See Gamer, *Romanticism*, 129–38.

6. On the relationship between Musäus and Lewis, see Karl S. Guthke, *Englische Vorromantik und deutscher Sturm und Drang* (Göttingen: Vandenhoeck & Ruprecht, 1958), 176–83; and Syndy M. Conger, *Matthew G. Lewis, Charles Robert Maturin*

and the Germans (Salzburg: Institut für englische Sprache und Literatur, 1977), 93–105.

7. Johann Karl August Musäus, *Volksmärchen der Deutschen*, five volumes (Gotha: Ettinger, 1782–1787), volume 5, 271.

8. Matthew G. Lewis, *The Monk* (Oxford: Oxford University Press, 1995), 124.

9. Musäus, *Volksmärchen*, volume 5, 272.

10. Lewis, *The Monk*, 133.

11. On these differences, see Dan Hall, *French and German Gothic Fiction in the Late Eighteenth Century* (Bern: Lang, 2005), 109–10.

12. See Saggini, *The Gothic Novel*, 151–54.

13. Matthew G. Lewis, *The Castle Spectre* (London: Bell, 1798), 79.

14. Montague Summers seems to think it more likely that Henry William Grosette was the author. See Montague Summers, *The Gothic Quest* (London: Fortune, 1838), 228.

15. James Boaden, *Aurelio and Miranda* (London: Bell, 1799).

16. Boaden, *Aurelio*, unpaginated preface.

17. See David Christopher, "Matthew Lewis's *The Monk* and James Boaden's *Aurelio and Miranda*—From Text to Stage," *Theatre Notebook* 65 (2011): 152–70.

18. See Gamer, *Romanticism*, 129–38.

19. Hester Lynch Piozzi, *Retrospection: Or a Review of the Most Striking and Important Events*, two volumes (London: Stockdale, 1801), volume 2, 511–12. Emphasis in the original.

20. "I am perfectly easy about the theatre, if I had no other method of employing myself Mr. Lewis's success would have thrown me into despair. *The Castle Spectre* is a Spectre indeed. Clothed with the flesh and blood of £400 received from the treasury of the theatre it may in the eyes of the author and his friend appear very lovely." William Wordsworth to James Tobin, March 6, 1798, in *The Early Years, 1797–1805*, volume 1 of *The Letters of William and Dorothy Wordsworth*, ed. Ernest de Selincourt and Chester L. Shaver, five volumes (Oxford: Clarendon Press, 1967–79), 210.

21. This is William Hazlitt's recollection; see William Hazlitt, "On my First Acquaintance with Poets," in *Uncollected Essays*, ed. P.P. Howe, volume 17 of *The Complete Works of William Hazlitt*, ed. P.P. Howe et al, twenty-one volumes (London: Dent, 1930–34), 118. See also Michael Gamer, "Authors in Effect: Lewis, Scott, and the Gothic Drama," *ELH* 66, no. 4 (1990): 834–36.

22. Walter Scott, *The House of Aspen: A Tragedy*, in *The Keepsake for MDCCCXXX*, ed. Frederic Mansel Reynolds (London: Hurst, 1830), 1–2.

23. James Boaden, *The Secret Tribunal* (London: Longman, 1795), n.p.

24. Jane Moody, *The Illegitimate Theatre in London, 1770–1840* (Cambridge: Cambridge University Press, 2000) offers an excellent overview of these debates; De Wilde's satirical illustration is reproduced on page 26.

25. For historical overviews, see Paula Backschneider, *Spectacular Politics: Theatrical Power and Mass Culture in Early Modern England* (Baltimore: Johns Hopkins University Press, 1993); and Matthew S. Buckley, "The Formation of Melodrama," in *The Oxford Handbook of the Georgian Theatre, 1737–1832*, ed. Julia Swindells and David F. Taylor (Oxford: Oxford University Press, 2014), 457–75.

26. See Lionel Field Thompson, *Kotzebue, a Survey of his Progress in France and England* (Paris: Champion, 1928), 137–38, 157–58.

27. Johann Heinrich Daniel Zschokke, *Abaellino der große Bandit*, ed. Josef Morlo (St. Ingbert: Röhrig, 1994); *Aballino der große Bandit. Ein Trauerspiel in fünf Aufzügen, nach der Geschichte dieses Namens von demselben Autor* (Leipzig, Frankfurt a.d. Oder: Opitz, 1795); René Charles Pixérécourt, *L'homme à trois visages* (Paris: n.p. 1801). Zschokke's spelling changes between different editions and adaptations; I have reproduced the original spelling from each version as appropriate, even if this appears confusing.

28. Jennifer Willenberg's study, *Distribution und Übersetzung englischen Schrifttums im Deutschland des 18. Jahrhunderts* (Munich: Saur, 2008) offers a very useful survey of what is too large a field of study to fully reference here; see especially pages 132–40 on French journals and chapter four, pages 157–74, on paths of transmission and translation.

29. [Benedikte Naubert], *Herrmann von Unna. Eine Geschichte aus den Zeiten der Vehmgerichte* (Leipzig: Weygand, 1788).

30. See, however, Hilary Brown, *Benedikte Naubert (1756–1819) and her Relations to English Culture* (Leeds: Maney, 2005).

31. [Benedikte Naubert,], *Hermann of Unna. A Series of Adventures of the Fifteenth Century, in which the Proceedings of the Secret Tribunal under the Emperors Winceslaus and Sigismond are Delineated. In Three Volumes. Written in German by Professor Kramer* (London: G.G. and J. Robinson, 1794).

32. *Herman d'Unna, ou Aventures arrivées au commencement du quinzieme siècle [Texte imprimé], dans le temps où le tribunal secret avoit sa plus grande influence*, trans. Baron de Bock (Paris: Metz, 1791).

33. See Silke Arnold-de Simine, "'Lost in Translation'? Die englische Übersetzung von Benedikte Nauberts *Herrmann von Unna*," in *Populäre Erscheinungen. Der deutsche Schauerroman um 1800*, ed. Barry Murnane and Andrew Cusack (Munich: Fink, 2011), 130–31.

34. Johann Nepomuk Komarek, *Ida oder Das Vehmgericht* (Pilsen and Leipzig: Morgensäuler, 1792); Ludwig Ferdinand Huber, "Das heimliche Gericht," in *Schauspiele* (Berlin: Vossische Buchhandlung, 1795).

35. [Ludwig Ferdinand Huber], *Le tribunal secret, drame historique, en cinque actes*, trans. Jean-Nicolas-Etienne de Bock (Metz: Claude Lamort, 1791).

36. Boaden, *Secret Tribunal*, 27.

37. On the *Illuminaten* and their legacy in popular and literary culture, see especially Ralf Klausnitzer, *Poesie und Konspiration: Beziehungssinn und Zeichenökonomie von Verschwörungsszenarien in Publizistik, Literatur und Wissenschaft 1750–1850* (Berlin: de Gruyter, 2007); a slightly older but still highly informative account is Richard van Dülmen, *Der Geheimbund der Illuminaten: Darstellung, Analyse, Dokumentation* (Stuttgart: Frommann-Holzboog, 1975).

38. See especially Nigel Aston, "Burke and the conspiratorial origins of the French Revolution: some Anglo-French resemblances," in *Conspiracies and Conspiracy Theories in Early Modern Europe*, ed. Barry Coward and Julian Swann (Aldershot: Ashgate, 2004), 213–33.

39. Barry Murnane, "Radical Translations: Dubious Anglo-German Cultural Transfer in the 1790s," in *(Re-)Writing the Radical: Enlightenment, Revolution and Cultural Transfer*, ed. Maike Oergel (Berlin and Boston, MA: de Gruyter, 2012), 44–60.

40. See Barry Murnane, "Heterotopien. Gedanken zum historischen Ritterroman als Variante des Schauerromans," in Murnane and Cusack, *Populäre Erscheinungen*, 101–20.

41. Boaden, *The Secret Tribunal*.

42. John Robison, *Proofs of a Conspiracy against all Religions and Governments of Europe* (New York: Forgotten Books, 2004 [reprint of fourth edition of 1797]), 246–47.

43. Friedrich Schlegel, "[Athenäums-Fragment 116]," in *Charakteristiken und Kritiken I (1796–1801)* ed. Hans Eichner, vol. 2.1 of *Kritische Friedrich-Schlegel-Ausgabe*, ed. Ernst Behler et al (Paderborn and Zurich: Schoeningh, 1958–2018), 162.

44. Schlegel, "Athenäums-Fragment," 162.

45. See, for example, Stefan Trappen, *Gattungspoetik. Studien zur Poetik des 16. bis 19. Jahrhunderts und zur Geschichte der triadischen Gattungslehre* (Heidelberg: Winter, 2001).

46. Johann Jakob Engel, *Über Handlung, Gespräch und Erzählung* (Stuttgart: Metzler, 1964 [1774]); Friedrich von Blanckenburg, *Versuch über den Roman* (Leipzig: Siegert, 1774).

47. Martin Huber, *Der Text als Bühne. Theatrales Erzählen um 1800* (Göttingen: Vandenhoeck & Ruprecht, 2003).

48. Huber, *Text als Bühne*, 98–100.

49. On this term and on the tradition more generally, see Hans-Gerd Winter, *Dialog und Dialogroman in der Aufklärung. Mit einer Analyse von J. J. Engels Gesprächstheorie* (Darmstadt: Thesen Verlag, 1974).

50. Huber, *Text als Bühne*, 131–33.

51. Naubert, *Herrmann von Unna*, 326–27.

52. Winter, *Dialog*, 181–85.

53. Engel, *Über Handlung*, 171–77; see Peter Hasubek, *"wer am meisten red't, ist der reinste Mensch." Das Gespräch in Theodor Fontanes Roman "Der Stechlin"* (Berlin: Schmidt, 1998), 88–89.

54. Boaden, *Secret Tribunal*, 59.

55. Winter, *Dialog*, 181–85.

56. Johann Heinrich Zschokke, *Eine Selbstschau* (Aarau: Sauerländer, 1842), 47–48.

57. Zschokke, *Abaellino*, 72–73.

58. Gail K. Hart, "Good Bad Men: Familiarity, Security, and the Robber Novels of Zschokke and Vulpius," *Colloquia Germanica* 39 (2006): 286.

59. Zschokke, *Abällino*, 181–82.

60. Victor Sage, "Black Venice: Conspiracy and Narrative Masquerade in Schiller, Zschokke, Lewis, and Hoffmann," *Gothic Studies* 8 (2006): 52–72.

61. Matthew G. Lewis, *Rugantino. The Bravo of Venice* (London: Cumberland, 1830 [1806]); René Charles Pixérécourt, *L'homme à trois visages* (Paris: 1801);

Robert Elliston, *The Venetian Outlaw* (London: Baldwin, 1805); William Dunlap, *Abaellino the Great Bandit* (Boston: Russel & Cutler, 1802): J.H.F. Lamartelière, *Abelino, ou Le grand bandit*, in *Théatre de Schiller*, two volumes (Paris: Renouard, 1799), volume 2, 331–524.

62. William Hazlitt, "Lectures on the Dramatic Literature of the Age of Elizabeth. Lecture 7 [On the German Drama]," in *Lectures on the English Comic Writers and Lectures on the Age of Elizabeth*, ed. P.P. Howe, volume 6, *Complete Works*, 360.

Chapter Two

"From Scotland New Come Home"

Scottish Ghosts and Afterlives of Bürger's "Lenore"

Lucy Wood

Writing in his 1830 "Essay on Imitations of the Ancient Ballad," Walter Scott states that "during the last ten years of the eighteenth century, the art of poetry was at a remarkably low ebb in Britain."[1] In the wake of Hayley, Rogers, Campbell, and Cowper yet before the days of Southey, Wordsworth, and Coleridge, the field of British poetry "seemed to lie open to the first bold invader" ("Imitations," 23–24). Looking back on the 1790s, however, Scott saw that the ballad was ultimately resuscitated by the example of contemporary German literature. Scott described a "new species of literature" that "might be easily employed as a formidable auxiliary to renewing the spirit of our own, upon the same system as when medical persons attempt, by the transfusion of blood, to pass into the veins of an aged and exhausted patient, the vivacity of the circulation and liveliness of sensation which distinguish a young patient" ("Imitations," 29). It seems appropriate that Scott should pick the modern medical comparison of a blood transfusion—a potentially life-saving procedure—when discussing the requirements of the "aged and exhausted" British poetry: Scott's comment emerges in a cultural context in which ancient British ballads and poems were acknowledged to be a dying species, if not already dead; they were therefore being preserved in literary repositories by a scholarly movement that has been identified, albeit problematically, as marking both the "death of orality" and "the ballad revival."[2] Furthermore, in light of this apparent need for a *transfusion*, it is fitting that one of the works Scott credits in his essay with the relevant powers of revitalization was a ballad concerned with a revenant.[3]

According to Scott, Gottfried August Bürger's Gothic ballad "Lenore" (1774) should be credited as one of the several German works that offered a lifeline to British poetry and indeed inspired the first productions of his own poetic pen. In the years following its publication, Bürger's ballad, depicting the wild midnight ride of a skeleton horseman and his blasphemous paramour, enjoyed extraordinary success. First published in the *Göttinger Musen-almanach* (Göttingen Almanach of the Muses) for 1774, the ballad quickly became popular throughout Germany and across Europe, where it was swiftly translated into several languages. In Britain in one year alone no fewer than five versions of the ballad appeared in translations by William Taylor of Norwich, Scott himself, John Thomas Stanley, William Robert Spencer, and Henry James Pye. By 1904 the number of translations and adaptations of this ballad had reached a total of well over forty, even before we include parodies in our count.[4] Such was the popularity of the ballad among the poets and public alike that Scott quipped that the ballad held supernatural powers: "as if there had been a charm in the ballad, no one seemed to cast his eyes upon it without a desire to make it known by translation to his own countrymen" ("Imitations," 37).

As even this brief account shows, the originality of Bürger's ballad meant that "Lenore" experienced a number of afterlives. Yet it was certainly not without its ghosts. Ghosts and the dead are, of course, common to ballads from a number of national traditions.[5] But Bürger's ballad also contained the ghosts of older ballads—ballads taken from precisely that tradition whose death Scott was later to bemoan and which ended up being rejuvenated by it. Scott and other translators late in the eighteenth century turned to Bürger's ballad as a means to reviving their work, but "Lenore" had itself been part of a process in which Bürger had sought to reanimate aspects of the British ballad tradition for carving out new directions in German poetry. By examining the ghosts and afterlives of Bürger's "Lenore," this contribution will trace the circular movement of poetical currents that flowed freely between Scotland and Germany in the latter half of the eighteenth century. Previous critical accounts suggest, often in passing, that Bürger's ballad owed much to the relics of British ballad poetry. This is beyond doubt, but I shall demonstrate that a particularly Scottish inheritance can be found in "Lenore" by considering two early translations of the ballad: one by William Taylor of Norwich and another by Scott. Of the many translations that emerged in Britain at the end of the eighteenth century, Taylor's and Scott's are particularly significant: their translators sought not only to replicate the innovative and exciting ballad composed by Bürger but also to emphasize and enhance what the German poet had borrowed from British ballads. In the final section, I shall consider Scott's revisiting of the revenant-lover theme in his first original ballad imitation, "The Eve of St. John" (1799). I shall argue that in the same way that Bürger, according to the *Analytical Review* of 1796, took "liberty with the English ballads which he ... *germanized*,"[6] in "The Eve of St. John" Scott re-appropriates Bürger's *German* ballad, eventually recontextualizing it within a Scottish landscape and Scottish history. Thus in its composition and immediate reception Bürger's "Lenore" undertakes a complex journey from, and back to, Scotland.

HERDER, TAYLOR, AND THE SCOTTISH GHOSTS OF "LENORE"

As Scott observed, at the end of the eighteenth century German literature presented a stimulating resource for both British poets and the reading public alike. German poems, plays, and novels were in great demand across Britain, and William Taylor was one of the first "propagandists"[7] to meet this demand by producing English translations. Unlike several of the other translators of "Lenore," Taylor's engagement with German literature began before and continued after his translation of Bürger's ballad. At the age of just sixteen Taylor traveled to Detmold in Germany, where he spent eighteen months learning the German language. His translating career began shortly afterwards in 1791 with Gotthold Ephraim Lessing's *Nathan der Weise* (Nathan the Wise, 1779), followed in 1793 by a translation of Johann Wolfgang Goethe's *Iphigenie auf Tauris* (Iphegenia on Tauris, 1787). It was perhaps during his time in Detmold that Taylor first discovered the ballad "Lenore." He had certainly translated the ballad many years before he first published it in the *Monthly Magazine* for March 1796 as "Lenora," and in a separate publication as "Ellenore." Though Taylor's translation was one of a host of versions that appeared 1796, several of the other British translators acknowledged the prior existence and tremendous influence of Taylor's translation, which had been circulating in manuscript form for some years before print publication.

Given his fluency in the German language and his previous experience in translation, Taylor was well placed to be able to put forward an accurate and authoritative translation of "Lenore" for a British readership. It is therefore notable that in his translation Taylor introduced some of the most significant deviations from the German original. Perhaps the most fundamental of these changes is Taylor's decision to relocate the scene of Bürger's overtly German ballad to Britain. Taylor himself admitted that in "shifting the scene of adventure to Great Britain," he had taken considerable poetic license with a work that claimed to be a translation.[8] Taylor's relocation was not restricted to the spatial location of the ballad; he also relocated the ballad in a temporal sense. While in Bürger's ballad William had fought in a modern, German war, in Taylor's translation William is a knight of the twelfth century, fighting for the King of England during the Crusades: "with Richard's host / The paynim foes to quell."[9] Alongside these fundamental changes, Taylor's language is archaic and imitative of ancient ballad meter and phrase; an alteration that Taylor once again openly admitted, expressing his hope that "a version in the dialect of the old English ballad may . . . find favourers."[10] These considerable alterations, coupled with Taylor's justifications for them, suggest that Taylor's translation was made with his British readers in mind. His translation strategy appears to signal that he still holds German culture to be too alien for a readership in Britain and therefore attempts to render the German text more akin to something from the older English tradition. His readership was, however, at this time more keenly attuned to the "new species of literature" offered by German poets and dramatists. Moreover, Taylor was aware all along that he was bringing a text back to British culture after it had been appropriated and incorporated into an emerging German tradition.

Despite his claims that an "English" version of "Lenore" might "find favourers" in his readership, Taylor's motives in shifting the geography and temporality of Bürger's ballad were arguably more complex than this seemingly humble concession might suggest. Writing in the *Monthly Magazine* for March 1796, the same issue in which his translation of "Lenore" first appeared, Taylor also published "Some Account of the Poems of G. A. Bürger," an article reviewing a selection of the poet's works. In this article, which was printed considerably earlier on in this issue than his translation of "Lenore," Taylor made a strong claim for the German poet's indebtedness to British ballads. Taylor stated that in collections of poetry published by Bürger in 1779 and 1789, many of the ballads were "translated, with improvements, from English originals."[11] Among these works, Taylor pointed in particular to the ballads "The Child of Elle" and "The Friar of Orders Gray," both of which had appeared in Thomas Percy's seminal ballad anthology *Reliques of Ancient English Poetry* in 1765. Taylor's decision to draw attention to these ballads by name in the same publication in which he would offer his translation of "Lenore" is telling. Both "The Child of Elle" and "The Friar of Orders Gray" contain themes similar to Bürger's ballad: the former features a knight's nocturnal visit to his lover and their subsequent escape together on horseback, and the latter consists of an impassioned exchange between a lady mourning for her deceased lover and a holy man, eventually revealed to be her lover in disguise. More notable still is Taylor's observation that in Bürger's translations of these British ballads "the scene of adventure has been uniformly transferred to Germany."[12] Taylor's article therefore leads his readers' attention to Bürger's engagement with British ballads, and in illuminating the fact that the poet had relocated the scene of the ballads to his own national land, it indicates that Bürger's knowledge of British ballads was an essential factor in the composition of "Lenore." This article lays the groundwork for what he hopes will be the ballad's smooth passage between cultures as a result of its emergence from the traditions of its receiving culture. Taylor's own heavily adapted and domesticated translation of "Lenore"—complete with British locations and ballad references and appearing just a few pages later in the *Monthly Magazine*—would then support his thesis. He would later go on to make this claim in a more forthright manner in his *Historic Survey of German Poetry* (1828–1830). Here he states that Bürger's acquaintance with British ballads "decided forever the character of his excellence. From a free translation of 'The Friar of the Orders Gray' [*sic*] (Bruder Graurock), and 'The Child of Elle' (Die Entführung) . . . he rapidly passed on to the production of 'The Wild Huntsman,' The Parson's Daughter,' and 'Lenore.'"[13] Through such claims, Taylor alleged that Bürger had moved beyond translation and into the realm of poetical appropriation—appropriation that Taylor's own translation of "Lenore" could point out, albeit with the help of some editoral licenses.

Taylor was certainly not wrong to suggest that Bürger was indebted to British balladry. In the summer of 1773 when he was writing "Lenore," Bürger's reading material was predominantly British ballad collections. He came to such material through the direction of Johann Gottfried Herder, in particular through Herder's 1773 essay "Auszug aus einem Briefwechsel über Ossian und die Lieder alter Völker" (Extract from a Correspondence on Ossian and the Songs of Ancient Peoples). It was this essay that Bürger read enthusiastically during the summer of 1773, identifying in Herder's thinking an ethos similar to his own. While for Scott the field of British poetry at the end of the eighteenth century "seemed to lie open to the first bold invader," only a few decades before it was German poetry that seemed to require revitalization. For Herder, German poetry was in need of liberation from the prescriptive models of classicist literature and from the cultural and societal preference for the French language and literature. Poetry, Herder suggested, was both more natural and more effective when composed in the mother' tongue of the nation, and this voice itself was to be found in ancient songs and poetry.[14] By engaging with and imitating this rich folk tradition, Herder suggested that modern German poets could revitalize traditional ballads and songs while also infusing their own works with the same simplicity and energy, thus renewing their own poetic culture. This plan was realized most fully in his *Volkslieder* (1778–1779), an anthology of almost two hundred ballads and songs old and new from around the world.

In Herder's essay, however, Bürger found not only a call to action for German poets to write modern German ballads. He also found a steady course of recommended reading material consisting of British ballad collections published earlier in the century and especially Percy's *Reliques*, which Herder pointed to as a rich and instructive compendium from which German poets might draw inspiration. Indeed Taylor himself noted Bürger's reliance on Percy's anthology: in his *Historic Survey*, he states that Bürger diligently followed Herder's advice and refers to Percy's *Reliques* as Bürger's "manual."[15] The *Historic Survey* was written over thirty years after Taylor produced his translation of "Lenore," but even at that earlier point in time, Bürger's debt to Percy cannot have escaped him. Herder's scheme was markedly similar to and certainly took inspiration from the ballad revival in Britain earlier in the century, when ancient poetry and ballads in particular began to gain admiration for simplicity, beauty, and the natural outpouring of emotion. British ballad collectors and literary antiquarians gathered songs and poems in collections and presented them as the precious relics of a previous cultural moment to be admired and preserved. Yet, as Murray Pittock notes,[16] Herder's project of mixing ancient preservation with modern production particularly resembles the ballad culture of eighteenth-century Scotland. Printed ballad collections had begun to flourish in Scotland early in the century, notably in the wake of the 1707 Act of Union when the political and geographical unification of England and Scotland seemed to menace the latter nation's cultural independence. Though neither explicitly nor uniformly resistant to this political union, Scottish ballad collectors were almost universally eager to preserve the cultural independence of their nation. Just as Herder saw the potential for a German ballad tradition to reinvigorate and protect German culture, so too did ballad collections in Scotland provide a way in which Scottish culture, both past and present, might flourish.[17]

Given the ideological correspondences between the early Scottish ballad collections and Herder's *Volkslieder*, it is worth noting that in the very essay Bürger was reading in the summer of 1773 Herder considered several Scottish works to be most truly representative of the "Lieder alter Völker." As indicated in its title, a portion of Herder's essay was devoted to James Macpherson's Ossian works, presented to the reading public as fragments of ancient poetry discovered in the Highlands of Scotland. The influence of Ossian across Europe, most notably in the German states, cannot be overestimated.[18] Perceived by many contemporary eighteenth-century critics as a fraudulent publication, Macpherson's works are now more commonly accepted as the creative work of an editor, piecing together and liberally contributing to the fragments of ancient poetry in order to assemble "auld sangs . . . designed to reanimate a Scottish nationalism and an oral tradition on the wane since the 'spirit-breaking' '45."[19] For Herder, it was precisely due to this combination of ancient fragments and modern composition that Ossian offered an excellent example for German poets to follow. Yet in lieu of fashioning "den deutschen Ossian,"[20] Ossian himself was adopted as the national bard in mid-eighteenth-century Germany.[21] More notable still is that in "Lieder alter Völker," Bürger also found two British ballads taken from Percy's *Reliques*, translated by Herder in full. Of the almost two hundred ballads in Percy's collection, the two reproduced by Herder and subsequently read by Bürger were the Scottish ballads "Sweet William's Ghost" and "Edward, Edward."[22] And as a closer examination of these ballads alongside "Lenore" indicates, "Lenore" was itself an attempt on Bürger's part to move a Scottish ballad from its cultural and historical context into a context that might have more to say to a German readership as well as to the specific national and cultural aspirations of the *Göttinger Hain* poets of which Bürger himself was a member.

Scholarship has long contested the source of Bürger's "Lenore." No older German ballad has been identified in this capacity, but its similarities to "Sweet William's Ghost" from Percy's *Reliques* are more than a little conspicuous.[23] "Sweet William's Ghost" is proffered in Percy's *Reliques* as having precise national origins as "A *Scottish* Ballad."[24] Its plot is as follows: Margaret, the living lover, waits to hear the fate of William (the deceased soldier), returning to Scotland from battle. Perhaps problematically, the battle also took place in Scotland, as Willie is by his own insistence "from Scotland new come home" (*Reliques*, 3:129). Thus, Willie has the difficult task of both returning to and from Scotland—a geographical complexity that occurs in this and in later incarnations of the ballad. While this complexity may itself be a mistake that has arisen through oral transmission, it perhaps questions Percy's certainty about its origins: "Sweet William's Ghost" may have been sung in response to a number of different battles and had possibly already traveled before it became this particular incarnation of a Scottish ballad. Sweet William's visit to his love takes the form of a sad yet peaceful pilgrimage to request that Margaret release him from his promise to marry her, so that his soul might rest. Margaret is reluctant to relinquish this "troth," and instead insists that William take her "to yon kirk yard" to marry; William replies that he cannot, as his "bones are *buried* in a kirk yard, / Afar beyond the sea" (*Reliques*, 3:129–30, emphasis added). This exchange not only raises once more the geographical complexity of a region that is both local and distant, but also demonstrates the frequent oscillation between the marriage, death, and burial of lovers common in ballads. This oscillation features prominently in Bürger's ballad. Following a series of piteous appeals to William, Margaret eventually concedes and sadly relinquishes her troth-plight:

She stretched out her lilly-white hand,
As for to do her best:
Hae there your faith and troth, Willie,
God send your soul good rest. (*Reliques*, 3:130)

The final exchange of the lovers is tender; hearing the cock-crow, William caringly observes "Tis time, tis time, my dear Margaret, / That you were gane away" (*Reliques*, 3:130). Likewise, Margaret's "O stay, my only true love, stay" is a heartfelt appeal to her once beloved (*Reliques*, 3:131). When William vanished "in a cloud of mist," "the constant Margret" also perishes: "Wan grew her cheeks, she clos'd her een, / Stretch'd her saft limbs, and died"—a tragic yet peaceful unity of lovers, united in death (*Reliques*, 3:131).

Though Robert Lawson-Peebles has suggested that Bürger's ballad is a "translation" of "Sweet William's Ghost," such a statement both considerably overestimates the similarities between the ballads and grossly underestimates Bürger's innovation and the extent to which he adapts his source material to arrive at "Lenore."[25] Like "Sweet William's Ghost," "Lenore" also begins with lovers separated by war. Yet, rather than replicating tragic romance of unspecified war in a medieval setting, Bürger situates the ballad within the recent context of the Seven Years' War (1756–1763), with William a soldier in the army of Frederick the Great. Bürger's "Lenore," as Lawson-Peebles has suggested, therefore dramatically updates the ballad, replacing "Scots vernacular and . . . sentimental Jacobitism" with an oral German vernacular.[26] Bürger exchanges the sentimental treatment of tragic romance found in "Sweet William's Ghost" with an anger directed at senseless loss of life, bringing the ballad into a German present.[27] What had previously appeared in "Sweet William's Ghost" as desperate pleas to a tragic lover translates in Bürger's ballad into a vehement interrogation of God himself, as Bürger's ballad begins with Lenore's anguish at William's failure to return home after battle. A student of theology, Bürger was able to construct a series of hard-hitting heresies delivered by Lenore, and a series of religious remedies, delivered with an equal passion by Lenore's anxious mother. To her mother's pious suggestion that "Das hochgelobte Sakrament / Wird deinen Jammer lindern" (The honoured holy Sacrament / Will ease thy misery), Lenore exclaims:

"O Mutter, Mutter! was mich brennt,
Das lindert mir kein Sakrament!
Kein Sakrament mag Leben
Den Todten wiedergeben."[28]

["Mother, mother! no sacrament
Will ease my burning breast.
No sacrament brings back
Life to the dead and gone"]

This theological section of the ballad represents a thematic departure from "Sweet William's Ghost," but the refrain of "Mother, Mother" used across five stanzas and the question-and-answer format are similarly found in "Edward, Edward," the Scottish patricide ballad which had also appeared in translation in Herder's "Lieder alter Völker":

Quhy dois zour brand sae drap wi' bluid,
        Edward, Edward?
Quhy dois zour brand sae drap wi' bluid?
        And quhy sae sad gang zee, O?

O, I hae killed my hauke sae guid,
        Mither, mither:
O, I hae killed my hauke sae guid;
And I had nae mair bot hee, O. (*Reliques*, 1:53–55)

There are several further similarities between "Lenore" and "Sweet William's Ghost" in the scene in which William appears to his living lover. Upon her lover's return, rather than fearing this apparition, Lenore—like Margaret before her—pleads with William, asking him to enter her bower. In an unusual reversal of sensibility, Bürger's text is the more conservative at this moment: Lenore wishes to take her lover "in meinen Armen, / Herzliebste, zu erwarmen!" ("Lenore," 219; 57: Heart of my heart, come in / To warmth within my arms); in stark contrast, Margaret asks William to come in first to "kiss my cheek and chin," and secondly to "wed me with a ring" (*Reliques*, 3:129). Ultimately, the visit of the sad specter in "Sweet William's Ghost" is intended to regain his troth-plight, where Bürger's phantom has a greater conquest in mind, physically taking Lenore away from her home and with him to their mutual grave. Despite the differences in these encounters, the manners in which Margaret and Lenore concede to their lovers' requests are strikingly similar. Just as Margaret eventually stretches out "her lilly-white hand" (*Reliques*, 3:130) and returns the troth-plight, so too does Lenore yield to William's proposed midnight journey by mounting the horse and holding on to her lover with "ihre Lilienhände" ("Lenore," 221). When their respective requests for their lovers to enter are denied, both Margaret and Lenore ask William whether they might accompany them outside of the bower. Margaret, in full knowledge of her lover's status as "no earthly man," asks openly for admission to his grave:

Is there any room at your head, Willie?
Or any room at your feet?
Or any room at your side, Willie,
Wherein that I may creep? (*Reliques*, 3:130)

In Bürger's ballad, referring to the bridal bed, Lenore asks "Hat's Raum für mich?" (Is room for me?), replicating the phraseology of the earlier ballad though in simpler form ("Lenore," 221; 59).

Contrasting the simple sadness of "Sweet William's Ghost," "Lenore" offers what Walter Wilson Greg has described as a "continuous crescendo" of emotion that builds to a dramatic climax when William's unearthly guise is revealed.[29] As in "Sweet William's Ghost," "Lenore" culminates in a graveyard scene and with the disappearance of the revenant-lover, yet the horror offered in Bürger's ballad departs dramatically from the tragic pathos of the earlier ballad, as his William does not gently disappear but is revealed in his unearthly form appearing as Death himself: "Sein Körper zum Gerippe / Mit Stundeglas und Hippe" ("Lenore," 225; 63: A skeleton his frame, / Holding Time's reaping hook). Margaret's act of accompanying William to his grave—and ultimately the place of her own death—had been tragically resigned: "wan grew her cheeks, she clos'd her een, / Stretch'd her saft limbs, and died" (*Reliques*, 3:131). In contrast, there is a carnality and even subversive sexuality implicit in Bürger's ballad, as Lenore is thrown violently upon the ground amidst the graves, surrounded by howling, her "Herz, mit Beben, / Rang zwischen Tod und Leben" ("Lenore," 226; 65: quivering heart / Struggled twixt life and death) as phantoms dance around her "forfeit" body. Her blasphemy rather than her faithfulness has issued an invitation to the sinister and supernatural; she has ridden one hundred miles with a skeleton, and the terror of her undefined fate brings the ballad to a close. In all, Bürger's ballad goes beyond replicating the words and ideas of "Sweet William's Ghost"; instead, it appeals to Gothic and sentimental mores in updating this older Scottish ballad for a late-eighteenth-century German readership that was just beginning to encounter a new poetical tradition.

As we can see from both his commentary upon the ballad in the *Monthly Magazine* and also in the way he goes about his translation, Taylor was aware of the borrowings from British ballads in Bürger's "Lenore," including the similarities between it and "Sweet William's Ghost" and "Edward, Edward." And as his translation illustrates, Taylor was eager to demonstrate these similarities to his readers. As mentioned previously, Taylor moves the temporal and spatial setting of the ballad to medieval England. Beyond this, however, Taylor retained several of the phrases and references Bürger had incorporated into "Lenore," for example the refrain "O mother, mother," taken from the Scottish ballad "Edward, Edward:"

"O mother, mother! William's gone
What's all besyde to me?
There is no mercie, sure, above!
All, all were spar'd but he!"[30]

Of the 1796 translations, only Taylor and Scott chose to replicate the "mother, mother" refrain; Spencer's, Pye's, and Stanley's translations departed from the repeated phrasing of Bürger's ballad, suggesting that they were unaware of Bürger's source. Taylor, by contrast, demonstrably enjoys expanding upon and accentuating the borrowings he identified within Bürger's ballad—even those that did not appear as explicit quotations in "Lenore." One such example lies in Ellenore's innocent inquiry to her lover, regarding his "house, and home, / And bridal bed."[31] Taylor's choice of phrase, "And is there any room for me, / Wherein that I may creepe?"[32] closely resembles but also expands upon Bürger's "'Hat's Raum für mich?'—'Für dich und mich!'" ("Lenore," 221; 59: "Is room for me?"—"For thee and me!"), while clearly quoting from the passage of "Sweet William's Ghost" cited previously. By replicating the older Scottish ballad in his translation of "Lenore," Taylor nods to his knowledge of Bürger's sources for this composition. As a scholar of German literature, Taylor was well placed to provide an accurate translation of Bürger's ballad for his British readership. However, he chose to depart widely in several details—including shifting the scene of the ballad—and to enhance the paraphrases of British ballads found in Bürger's "Lenore." These alterations themselves indicate that Taylor's ballad represented an exercise in bringing "Sweet William's Ghost" home from its place in an emerging German tradition and inserting it into a rejuvenated British tradition—a tradition that was to be reawakened through a particularly circular case of poetic exchange. Yet Taylor's ballad was to play yet another part in an even more convoluted and complex pattern of exchange when it was brought to the attention of a very young Walter Scott.

"AN OLD FRIEND IN A FOREIGN LAND": SCOTT'S "WILLIAM AND HELEN"

It was not Bürger's "original" ballad "Lenore," but Taylor's geographically and temporally relocated ballad "Ellenore" that Scott heard "about the summer of 1793 or 1794" ("Imitations," 37). Anna Laetitia Barbauld, Taylor's close friend, had recited the translation at a meeting of the Edinburgh Literature Society, held at the home of Scott's tutor, Dugald Stewart. Scott did not attend the meeting, yet the rapturous reports he received by those who had been present were sufficient to fuel his curiosity, and he immediately attempted to acquire a copy of the ballad ("Imitations," 38). He eventually obtained a German copy of the work from his aunt, Harriet Scott of Harden, and set about the task of translating the work, describing his almost feverish enthusiasm: "I began my task after supper, and finished it about daybreak the next morning, by which time the ideas which the task had a tendency to summon up were rather of an uncomfortable character" ("Imitations," 39). The work was promptly published in 1796 as "William and Helen" in a small, closely circulated and privately published pamphlet entitled *The Chase; and William and Helen* (also including a translation of another of Bürger's ballads, "Der wilde Jäger," published by Scott as "The Chase").

In many ways, Scott's translation of "Lenore" followed Bürger's very closely, replicating not only the theme and dramatic crescendo of the ballad, but also the verse structure and rhyme. Early on in the ballad, for example, during the passionate exchange between mother and daughter, Lenore protests the religiosity of her love for William: "Bey ihm, bey ihm ist Seligkeit! / Und ohne Wilhelm, hölle!" ("Lenore," 218; 57: With him alone is Paradise, / And without William, Hell). In Scott's ballad, Helen closely mirrors Lenore's phrasing in her declaration: "My William's love was heaven on earth, / Without it earth is hell."[33] Furthermore, Scott endeavours to retain the word order and sound of Bürger's ballad:

"O mother, what is gone, is gone,
What's lost for ever lorn:
Death, death alone can comfort me;
O had I ne'er been born!" (WH, 22)

This closely resembles Bürger's phrasing, subtly altering it in order to retain an effective rhyming structure:

"O Mutter! Mutter! Hin ist hin!
Verloren ist verloren!
Der Tod, der Tod ist mein Gewinn!
O wär ich nie geboren!" ("Lenore," 217)

Translating the ballad Scott noticed with no small degree of pleasure that the Scottish and German languages were closely connected, and that the poetry of each nation might therefore easily be replicated without too great an alteration to its aesthetic quality. He reported this phenomenon later in life, using the example of "Sir Patrick Spence," which is translated in Herder's *Volkslieder*:

The King sits in Dunfermling town,
Drinking the blood red wine;
"Where will I get a good skipper
To sail this ship of mine?"

Der Kœnig sitzt in Dunfermling Schloss,
Er trinkt blutrothen Wein;
"O wo treff' ich einen Segler gut
Dies Schiff zu seglen mein?" ("Imitations," 43n1)

Reflecting upon this easy transfer, Scott notes: "It requires only a smattering of both languages to see at what cheap expense, even of vocables and rhymes, the popular poetry of the one may be transferred to the other. Hardly anything is more flattering to a Scottish student of German; it resembles the unexpected discovery of an old friend in a foreign land" ("Imitations," 43n1).

Yet, as with Taylor's translation, Scott's translation of "Lenore" was not based solely upon the text before him. Rather, this composition was mediated first of all through Scott's initial experience of the ballad as translated work, in Taylor's "Lenora" and second of all through his own extensive knowledge of Scottish ballads. Scott prided himself upon having been a master of Scottish ballads since his infancy, when his Aunt Janet would read to him from Allan Ramsay's *Tea-Table Miscellany* (1724–1750), and his grandmother would sing the ballads and songs of the Scottish Borders. Reading "Lenore" might therefore have meant for Scott the discovery of "an old friend in a foreign land" in quite another manner. As Greg writes, Scott's ballad is also "the one that departs most widely from the German text," departing, as I shall argue, only to consciously harken back to earlier, Scottish incarnations of the ballad.[34] Matthew Gregory Lewis, one of Scott's first publishers and ballad collaborator in the German-inspired *Tales of Wonder* (1801), articulated his concerns about the considerable distance between Scott's "William and Helen" and Bürger's original ballad "Lenore." On January 6, 1799, Lewis wrote to Scott: "in order that I may bring it nearer the original title, pray introduce, in the first stanza, the name Ellenora, instead of Ellen" ("Imitations," 55). Scott's was the only one of the six 1796 translations to considerably alter the ballad's title: Taylor's first version was titled "Lenora," the second "Ellenore"; Stanley's and Spencer's ballads were titled "Leonora"; and Pye chose to preserve the original "Lenore." Through his choice of title Scott not only anglicized the ballad, making Lenore *Helen*, but he also brought his ballad in line with a 1724 rewriting of "Sweet William's Ghost" by Scottish poet David Mallet, titled "William and Margaret." So too may Scott have chosen "Helen" as a reference to "Fair Helen of Kirconnell," a Scottish ballad of ill-fated lovers that had appeared in *Scots Musical Museum* and Joseph Ritson's *Scottish Songs* (1794) and would later appear as a "Romantic" ballad in Scott's *Minstrelsy of the Scottish Border* (1802–1803). Scott further nods to this Scottish ballad by beginning his "translation" of "Lenore" with the words: "From heavy dreams *fair Helen* rose."

Like Taylor before him, Scott temporally relocates the ballad to the conventional, medieval ballad time. A knight of the twelfth century, Scott's William fights not for Frederick the Great but for "gallant Fred'rick" in "the bold Crusade" (WH, 19). Unlike Bürger's modern battle for his modern ballad, Scott antiquated both battle and ballad, situating them as components of archaic romance. In his "Preface to the First Edition" of *The Lay of the Last Minstrel* (1805), Scott suggests that, had *The Lay* not been written in the form of the "Ancient Metrical Romance," the "manners" and "machinery" described "would have seemed puerile."[35] Scott approached his ballad "translation"—or rather rearticulation—of "Lenore" with a similar sentiment. For Scott, modernizing the ballad was to miss the point. Thus Scott's language, like Taylor's, is decidedly archaic, using old English phraseology, such as in the refrain of "full fast I ween we ride" (WH, 30). Furthermore, that Scott's ballad belongs not to a real modern world but to a "romantic" past is emphasized in the description of Helen's home as a medieval castle, full with "lonely tower" and "glimmering lattice," and the "heavy drawbridge," "moat," and "winding stair" through which William must pass (WH, 26–27). Notably, perhaps already demonstrating his interest in German plays of chivalry and works of Gothic fiction, Scott's William has not died fighting for an English or Scottish king, but for Holy Roman Emperor Frederick I; like Bürger's William, he is a German. Indeed, in moving the temporal setting of Bürger's ballad to the crusades, Scott was drawing an association between the Gothic, the supernatural, and the new German literature that he was in the process of discovering. But in order to make this seemingly new German literary culture accessible, he saw fit to alter Bürger's text to fit the expectations of a contemporary British readership. And while signaling the ballad's Germanness, he simultaneously casts it as the product of an affiliated culture—of "an old friend in a foreign land."

Like Taylor's, Scott's ballad illustrates Bürger's borrowings from the British ballad tradition. One ballad Scott evokes is William Hamilton of Bangour's "The Braes of Yarrow," an imitation ballad first published in 1724 and then again in Percy's *Reliques*.[36] In Hamilton's ballad, a man who has murdered a woman's lover takes the woman by force from the scene of the murder to be his bride. This "barbarous man" addresses his conquest as they ride away together:

Busk ye, busk ye, my bonny bonny bride,
Busk ye, busk ye, my winsome marrow,
Busk ye, busk ye, my bonny bonny bride,
And think nae mair on the Braes of Yarrow. (*Reliques*, 2:361)

Scott recalls Hamilton's lines in "William and Helen" in William's appeal to Helen to "Busk, busk, and bourne! Thou mount'st behind / Upon my black barb steed," with two further appeals for Helen to "busk, and bourne" further on in the ballad (WH, 29). Like "Sweet William's Ghost," "Lenore," and "William and Helen," Hamilton's ballad ends with a spectral visitation in the form of "the expected husband lover"; this is the murdered youth in his "pale shroud, bleeding after" (*Reliques*, 2:366).

For all of his incorporation of the British ballad tradition into his text, the supernatural spirit, descriptive intensity, and moral questionability of Bürger's ballad remain in Scott's translation. Scott closely replicates the crucial phrases of the ballad, retaining William's refrain of "Hurrah! Die Toten reiten schnell!" ("Lenore," 221; 63: Hurrah! The dead ride fast!), which Scott translates as "Hurrah! Hurrah! The dead can ride" (WH, 35). Scott even makes additions to the band of sinister and supernatural figures that are summoned by William to follow in the couple's unhallowed bridal entourage, including a "shrouded corpse," and "Gibbet and steel, th' accursed wheel; / A murderer in his chain" (WH, 33 and 35). In Scott's, as in Bürger's ballad, William himself belongs to this unearthly populace. Fully transformed from the piteous lover of earlier ballads, Scott's William reveals his identity as a vision of unnatural horror:

The eyes desert the naked skull,
The mould'ring flesh the bone,
Till Helen's lily arms entwine
A ghastly skeleton. (WH, 40)

This description is strikingly similar to Bürger's version:

Des Reiters Koller, Stück für Stück,
Fiel ab, wie müber Zunder.
Zum Schädel, ohne Zopf und Schopf,
Zum nackten Schädel ward sein Kopf.

[The rider's jerkin, piece by piece
Fell off like brittle tinder.
His head became a naked skull
Skull shorn of hair and hide.] ("Lenore," 225; 63)

Further still, however, Scott rejects any notion of his female protagonist suffering as a result of her chastity and faithfulness, as we saw in "Sweet William's Ghost." Instead, as in "Lenore," Scott's ballad indicates that Helen, through her acts of transgression and moral abandon, will join the supernatural afterlife of her lover. Helen is cast upon the ground amid a circle of specters that "wheel around the maid in dismal dance, / And howl the funeral song," as her "soul is from her body reft" (WH, 40–41). This frantic dance of death and eerie dirge is similar to that by Bürger's phantoms at the ballad's close; yet it also recalls the "warlocks and witches in a dance" of Robert

Burns's "Tam o' Shanter" (1791). "William and Helen," then, contains strategies clearly intended to play up the affinities between the new German culture and older British traditions while still keeping Bürger's text and its national context at arm's length. Yet Scott's approach to his materials illustrates that German culture provides a less sober and more daring intermediary between a past and a future for British balladry.

THE AFTERLIFE OF "LENORE": "THE EVE OF ST. JOHN"

The differences between Bürger's ballad and Scott's translation were sufficient to prevent Lewis from adding the latter to his *Tales of Wonder*, choosing instead the more conventional translation by Taylor. Scott did, however, contribute several other ballads for the collection—ballads that are based on supernatural themes from Germanic or Scottish sources.[37] As well as his translation of Bürger's "Der wilde Jäger," Scott contributed an imaginative translation of a ballad sung in Goethe's *Claudine von Villa Bella* (1776) that he titled "Frederick and Alice," a German-inspired ballad named "The Fire-King," and two original Scottish ballads, "Glenfinlas, or, Lord Ronald's Coronach" and "The Eve of St. John." All but "The Fire-King" share the theme of an unearthly visitant; in all but "The Wild Huntsman," the visitant is a deceased lover. Yet of the *Tales of Wonder* ballads, it is "The Eve of St. John"—one of Scott's "original" ballads for this collection—that stands out as the descendent of "Lenore." If, as Shields asserts, Scott's "William and Helen" might be considered as a "re-writing in a personal style" of "Lenore," then I suggest that "The Eve of St. John" is a continuation of this personal approach to rewriting and the first example we have of Scott's implementation of the rejuvinating forces of German culture on a deceased British ballad tradition.[38]

"The Eve of St. John" begins with the line "the baron of Smaylho'me rose with day,"[39] and therefore offers an immediate point of similarity to the ballads discussed previously. The aforementioned ballads also begin with a wakening from slumber: "Lenore fuhr um's Morgenroth / Empor aus schweren Träumen" ("Lenore," 214; or, in Scott's version, "From heavy dreams fair Helen rose" [WH, 19]). Like these ballads too, "The Eve of St. John" opens with a knight returning from battle (or rather two knights, as the Baron returns bodily, and Coldinghame returns as a ghost). Scott names the battle as Ancrum Moor, fought in the Scottish Borders in 1545; thus, the battle of the ballad is aligned to a precise moment in Scottish history and located in a Scottish setting. Indeed, much of the dramatic action of the ballad takes place at Smailholm Tower in Roxburghshire, home of Scott's paternal grandparents and location of his childhood. Much like the death of William in Bürger's and Scott's ballads, Sir Richard of Coldinghame's death has taken place before the ballad has begun; however, this time the death did not occur in battle. Rather, we are told that the Baron's axe and dagger were stained with blood, though "it was not English gore." In other words, the Baron has murdered Coldinghame, a knight fighting on his own side ("Eve," 139). His motives for doing so are swiftly revealed in the ballad, as we learn that Coldinghame and Baroness Smailholme had been having an affair; and so the central, spectral figure of the ballad is, once again, a revenant lover.

Undeterred by the small matter that he is in fact dead, Coldinghame visits his living lover and treats his posthumous status with grim irony. The Baroness, unaware that he is a revenant, reveals her plot to bring him to her bower in secret on the eve of St. John. Again, like Lenore and Helen before her, even when in conversation with her deceased lover the Baroness does not notice his spectral status. Attempting to persuade him to visit her at night, she assures him that "the priest who sleepeth to the east" of her chamber will not disturb their tryst, for he had journeyed to nearby Dryburgh Abbey "to say mass, till three days do pass, / For the soul of a knight that is slayne" ("Eve," 142). At these words, her lover

turn'd him around, and grimly he frown'd;
Then he laugh'd right scornfully—
"He who says the mass-rite for the soul of that knight,
Might as well say mass for me." ("Eve," 142)

When Coldinghame later communicates his predicament to his lover—"By the Baron's brand, near Tweed's fair strand, / Most foully slain I fell"—like Margaret of "Sweet William's Ghost," the Baroness does not fear her lover ("Eve," 146). Instead, she accepts his status, and asks for details: "Love mastered fear—her brow she crossed: / 'How, Richard, hast thou sped?'" ("Eve," 146). In "The Eve of St. John" it is the murderer, not the living lover, who fears the revenant. As Coldinghame's murderer, the Baron is troubled by his page's account that Coldingham is at Smailhome Tower, though he believes that the man is safely dead by his own hand: "the worms around him creep, and his bloody grave is deep . . . / It cannot give up the dead!" ("Eve," 145). Coldinghame's ghost, however, does not regard seeking his murderer to be his priority; like William before him, his principal interest lies in his former lover. The ghost visits the Baroness in order to share his guilty burden with her, as their "lawless love" in life dictates his restlessness in death ("Eve," 147). Furthermore, Coldinghame notes that the Baroness has herself to blame, having initiated this visit. He notes that he "had not the power to come to thy bower / Had'st thou not conjured me so": just as Lenore's blasphemy invited William, the living-dead lover to return to her, so too does the Baroness' "lawlessness"—that is, outside of the sacred bonds of marriage—invite the supernatural figure of the knight to visit her ("Eve," 146).

Correspondences with Bürger's ballad continue as the Baroness asks Coldinghame, "art thou saved, or art thou lost?" ("Eve," 146), resembling Lenore's question: "Bist untreu, Wilhelm, oder todt" ("Lenore," 214). Even amid these numerous similarities and thematic borrowings from Bürger's ballad, there are several similarities that specifically hark back to the Scottish ballad variants of "Sweet William's Ghost." Not least, Scott borrows the distinctly Scottish setting of the latter: Coldinghame and the Baron are "from Scotland new come home," having been at battle on Scottish soil at Ancrum Moor. Therefore, Scott gives both Scottish historical context and real geographical and architectural locations. He also replicates the significance of touch that is present in older Scottish ballads such as "Sweet William's Ghost." In this ballad, William warns his lover of the dangers of becoming too close:

If I shou'd come within thy bower,
I am no earthly man;
And I shou'd kiss thy rosy lips,
Thy days will not be lang. (*Reliques*, 3:129)

In Scott's ballad, Coldinghame warns the Baroness of the danger of his visitation:

I cannot come; I must not come;
I dare not come to thee:
On the eve of Saint John I must wander alone:
In thy bower I may not be. ("Eve," 141)

Still, despite this danger, Margaret of "Sweet William's Ghost" must physically touch her lover in order to return the troth she once conferred:

O sweet *Marg'ret*! O dear *Marg'ret*!
I pray thee speak to me!
Give me my faith and troth, *Marg'ret*,
As I gave it to thee.
. . .
She stretch'd out her lilly-white hand,
And for to do her best,
Hae there's your faith and troth, Willie,
God send your soul good rest. (*Reliques*, 3:130)

"The Eve of St. John," however, reverses this touch. Coldinghame must touch the living lover in order to communicate the severity of their mutual punishment for adultery:

"Who spilleth life shall forfeit life;
So bid thy lord believe:
That lawless love is guilt above,
This awful sign receive."

He laid his left palm on an oaken beam,
His right upon her hand;
The lady shrunk and fainting sunk,
For it scorched like a fiery brand.

The sable score of fingers four
Remains on that board impressed;
And forevermore that lady wore
A covering on her wrist. ("Eve," 147)

In retaining this central detail of the importance of touch between living and dead lover, Scott once more refers to the Scottish ballad "Sweet William's Ghost." For Scott, it was the act of returning the "troth-plight" of the dead by the living that gave the ballad its narrative appeal, and also perhaps its national credentials. Furthermore, this tradition was one in which Scott had a particular interest and of which he claims to have had some first-hand experience. He confirms this superstition in his diary of his 1814 voyage to Orkney, Shetland, and Fair Isle with the Commissioners of the Northern Lights, and later writes about it in his advertisement to the 1822 novel, *The Pirate*. Upon his voyage, Scott had heard the tale of a Miss Gordon, betrothed by troth-plight in the form of a handshake to Orkney pirate John Gow. Upon his execution the lady traveled to London to seek its return by shaking hands with his corpse. Scott describes how this was a necessary ritual "according to the superstition of the country," without which the living lover "could not have escaped a visit from the ghost of her departed lover, in the event of her bestowing upon any living suitor, the faith which she had plighted to the dead." "This part of the legend," he writes, "may serve as a curious commentary on the beautiful tale of the fine Scottish ballad which begins, There came a ghost to Margaret's door, &c."[40]

Scott's modern ballad "The Eve of St. John" may be considered as a personal rewriting of the German ballad "Lenore," or as an imitation of the ancient Scottish ballad "Sweet William's Ghost." However, the thematic similarities between "The Eve of St. John" and "William and Helen" suggest that his rewriting of the Scottish ballad was crucially mediated through his knowledge of the German ballad, "Lenore." "Lenore" itself was, however, distinctly indebted to "Sweet William's Ghost." "The Eve of St. John" might be described as an imitation of an ancient Scottish ballad, from Germany new come home. In all, however, it is Scott's original ballad in which he was attempting to write in the new, promising vein that he had just been discovering through Bürger and Goethe. When Scott was drawn to German balladry and saw in it the potential to renew British poetic culture, therefore, he was participating in a form of cultural change that could be best facilitated by works that repackaged something historically similar in the guise of something ostensibly very alien.

NOTES

1. Walter Scott, "Essay on Imitations of the Ancient Ballad," in *The Minstrelsy of the Scottish Border*, ed. T.F. Henderson, four volumes (Edinburgh: Blackwood, 1902), volume 4, 23. Hereafter referred to in the body of the text with the abbreviation "Imitations."

2. For further discussion, see Penny Fielding, *Writing and Orality: Nationality, Culture, and Nineteenth-Century Scottish Fiction* (Oxford: Oxford University Press, 1996); Maureen McLane, *Balladeering, Minstrelsy, and the Making of British Romantic Poetry* (Cambridge Cambridge University Press, 2008); and Ruth Finnegan, *Oral Poetry: Its Nature, Significance, and Social Context* (Cambridge: Cambridge University Press, 1980).

3. Following the definitions offered by the Oxford English Dictionary, I understand the term "Revenant" in the following to refer to: "A person who returns from the dead; a reanimated corpse; a ghost," and a person "[t]hat has returned from, or as if from, the dead; resembling or reminiscent of a ghost.". "revenant, n. and adj.2". Oxford English Dictionary Online. June 2017. Oxford University Press [accessed 23 June 2017].

4. See Hugh Shields, "The Dead Lover's Return in Modern English Ballad Tradition," *Jahrbuch für Volksliedforschung* 17 (1972): 98–114.

5. David Buchan, "Tale Roles and Revenants: A Morphology of Ghosts," *Western Folklore* 45, no. 2 (1986): 143–60; and Lowry C. Wimberly, *Folklore in English and Scottish Ballads* (New York: Ungar: 1959), 225.

6. "ART. XII. Lenore, a Tale: From the German of Gottfried Augustus Bürger," *The Analytical Review; Or, History of Literature* 24, no. 5 (November 1796): 479. Emphasis in original.

7. F.W. Stokoe, *German Influence in the English Romantic Period 1788-1818, with Special Reference to Scott, Coleridge, Shelley and Byron* (Cambridge: Cambridge University Press, 1926), 33.

8. William Taylor, *Ellenore, A Ballad Originally Written in German by G.A. Bürger* (Norwich: John March, 1796), n.p.

9. Taylor, *Ellenore*, 1.

10. Taylor, *Ellenore*, n.p.

11. William Taylor, "Some Account of the Poems of G.A. Bürger," *Monthly Magazine, and British Register* 1, no. 2 (March 1796): 117.

12. Taylor, "Some Account," 118.

13. William Taylor, *Historic Survey of German Poetry, Interspersed with Various Translations*, three volumes (London: Treuttel and Würtz, 1830), volume 3, 169.

14. Stokoe, *German Influence*, 4.

15. Taylor, *Historic Survey*, Volume 3, 169.

16. Murray Pittock, "Allan Ramsay and the Decolonisation of Genre," *The Review of English Studies* 58, no. 235 (2007): 318.

17. See Janet Sorensen, "Alternative Antiquarianisms of Scotland and the North," *Modern Language Quarterly* 70, no. 4 (2009): 415–44; Leith Davies, "At 'sang about': Scottish Song and the Challenge to British Culture," in *Scotland and the Borders of Romanticism*, ed. Leith Davis, Ian Duncan, and Janet Sorensen (Cambridge University Press, 2004), 188–224; Paula McDowell, "'The Art of Printing was Fatal': Print Commerce and the Idea of Oral Tradition in Long Eighteenth-Century Ballad Discourse," *Ballads and Broadsides in Britain, 1500–1800*, ed. Patricia Fumerton, Anita Guerrini, and Kris McAbee (Farnham: Ashgate, 2010), 35–56.

18. See, for example, Howard Gaskill, ed., *The Reception of Ossian in Europe* (London: Continuum, 2004).

19. Katie Trumpener, *Bardic Nationalism: The Romantic Novel and the British Empire*. (Princeton, NJ: Princeton University Press, 1997), 75.

20. Johann Gottfried Herder, "Auszug aus einem Briefwechsel über Ossian und die Lieder alter Völker," in *Von deutscher Art und Kunst, Einige fliegende Blätter*, Johann Gottfried Herder, Johann Wolfgang von Goethe, Paolo Frisi, and Justus Möser (Leipzig: Göschen, 1892), 6.

21. See, for example, Paul Barnaby and Tom Hubbard, "The International Reception and Literary Impact of Scottish Literature of the Period 1707-1918," in *The Edinburgh History of Scottish Literature, Volume Two: Enlightenment, Britain and Empire (1707–1918)*, ed. Ian Brown and Susan Manning (Edinburgh: Edinburgh University Press, 2007), 35.

22. Herder, "Ossian und die Lieder alter Völker," 18–20. For a recent discussion of Herder's translation of "Edward, Edward," see Michael White, "Herder and Fontane as Translators of Percy's *Reliques of Ancient English Poetry*: The Ballad 'Edward, Edward,'" in *Fontane and Cultural Mediation: Translation and Reception in Nineteenth-Century German Literature*, ed. Ritchie Robertson and Michael White (Cambridge/Leeds: Modern Humanities Research Association/Maney, 2015), 107–19.

23. For further discussion of possible sources, see, for example, Francis James Child, *The English and Scottish Popular Ballads*, five volumes (New York: Cooper Square, 1965), volume 5, 60; and John G. Robertson, *A History of German Literature* (Edinburgh and London: Blackwood, 1970), 246.

24. Thomas Percy, *Reliques of Ancient English Poetry; Consisting of Old Heroic Ballads, Songs, and Other Pieces of our Earlier Poets, (Chiefly of the Lyric Kind.) Together with some few of later Date*, three volumes (London: J. Dodsley, 1765),

volume 3, 128. Emphasis added. Hereafter referred to in the main body of the text with the abbreviation "*Reliques*," followed by volume and page number.

25. Robert Lawson-Peebles, "Translation in Uncertain Times: The Case of Bürger's 'Lenore,'" in *Revolutions and Watersheds: Transatlantic Dialogues, 1775–1815*, ed. W.M. Verhoeven and Beth Dolan Kautz (Rodopi: Amsterdam, 1999), 9.

26. Lawson-Peebles, "Translation in Uncertain Times," 8.

27. Lawson-Peebles, "Translation in Uncertain Times," 10.

28. Gottfried August Bürger, "Lenore," in *Göttinger Musenalmanach auf das Jahr 1774*, ed. Albrecht Schöne (Göttingen: Vandenhoeck & Ruprecht, 1962), 216. English translation in: E.S. Blenkinsop. *A Poet's Feelings* (Sherbourne: The Abbey Press, 1970), 55. Page numbers to this edition of Bürger's poem are referred to in the body of the text in parentheses containing "Lenore," immediately followed by the page number of the translation in Blenkinsop's edition.

29. Walter Wilson Greg, "English Translations of 'Lenore': A Contribution to the History of the Literary Relations of the Romantic Revival," *The Modern Quarterly of Language and Literature* 2, no. 5 (1899): 15.

30. Taylor, *Ellenore*, 2.

31. Taylor, *Ellenore*, 7.

32. Taylor, *Ellenore*, 8.

33. Walter Scott, trans., "William and Helen," in *The Chase and William and Helen: Two Ballads, from the German of Gottfried August Bürger* (Edinburgh and London: Mundell and Son for Manners and Miller, 1796), 23. Subsequent page references to this ballad will be given in parentheses in the body of the text with the abbreviation "WH."

34. Greg, "English Translations of 'Lenore,'" 18.

35. Walter Scott, "Preface to *The Lay of the Last Minstrel*," in *The Poetical Works of Sir Walter Scott*, Bart., twelve volumes (Edinburgh: Robert Cadell & Whittaker, 1833–1834), volume 6, 39.

36. The "ancient" ballad upon which it was based, "The Dowie Dens of Yarrow," was first published by Scott himself, in his 1803 edition of the *Minstrelsy*.

37. See Susan Oliver, *Scott, Byron and the Poetics of Cultural Encounter* (Basingstoke: Palgrave Macmillan, 2005), 35.

38. Shields, "The Dead Lover's Return," 101.

39. Walter Scott, "The Eve of St. John," in *Tales of Wonder*, ed. Matthew Gregory Lewis, two volumes (London: Printed by W. Bulmer and Co. Cleveland Row, for the author; and sold by J. Bell, No.148 Oxford Street , opposite New Bond Street, 1801), volume 1, 137. Hereafter referred to in the body of the text as "Eve."

40. Walter Scott, "Advertisement," in *The Pirate* (Edinburgh: Edinburgh University Press, 2001), 4.

Chapter Three

Of German Genres and Scottish Sentiments
Henry Mackenzie, Walter Scott, *and the* Schauspiel

Michael Wood

In his 1819 "Essay on the Drama," Walter Scott looks back at the end of the eighteenth century as a turning point in the history of British theater. After describing the rise of British drama and performance in Elizabethan England and its decline thereafter, he cites David Garrick as having promised the renewal of the British dramatic tradition in the eighteenth century: Garrick brought natural, passionate acting back to the stage and paved the way for a new appreciation of Shakespeare.[1] Yet the predominance of French neo-classical rules was strangling British dramatic writers and performers. With the benefit of hindsight, Scott writes that by the end of the century

> the French model had been wrought upon till it was altogether worn out; and a new impulse from some other quarter—a fresh turning up of the soil, and awakening of its latent energies by a new mode of culture, was become absolutely necessary to the renovation of our dramatic literature. England was destined to receive this impulse from Germany, where literature was in the first luxuriant glow of vegetation, with all its crop of flowers and weeds rushing up together. There was good and evil in the importation derived from this superabundant source. But the evil was of a nature so contrary to that which had long palsied our dramatic literature, that, like the hot poison mingling with the cold, it may in the issue bring us nearer to a state of health. ("Essay," 380–81)

Twenty years later, Scott finds that although the tragedies of *Douglas* (1756) by John Home and *The Mysterious Mother* (1768) by Horace Walpole had gone some way to restoring "truth and passion" ("Essay," 378) to the British stage, the ailing British theatrical tradition needed treatment from an external source *other* than France. This new source—Germany—was far from perfect. Scott goes on to describe August von Kotzebue's plays, for example, as full of "demoralizing falsehood" and "wretched" ("Essay," 385–86). He also specifically takes issue with the genre of "the pathetic comedy, which might be rather called domestic tragedy" ("Essay," 385), which he associates with the works of Kotzebue, above others. Yet what he applauds about German drama is that it was never subjected to the "arbitrary forms" of rigid genre categories and Aristotelian unities that French dramatists had followed: "And there can be no doubt that the license thus given to the poet . . . left them at liberty to exert the full efforts of their genius" ("Essay," 383–84). Scott identifies in German drama a role model for rejecting French "pedantry," and he believes that, in pointing in this direction, German plays are able to draw on the "latent energies" already *within* British drama so that British drama might renew itself.

Scott's comments on the role of German drama in the rejuvenation of British theater are, of course, presented in hindsight. But they attest to his belief that foreign literary innovation was central to domestic cultural development. They also reflect on a period in which Scott was at the forefront of the British reception of German drama and composed his very own play as a result of his study, *The House of Aspen*, written in 1799–1800. When scholarship examines the state of British drama in the 1790s and looks to its relationship with German drama, scholars tend to agree with Scott that native dramatic talent was at an all-time low,[2] but research has traditionally only paid attention to the status of Kotzebue's works in England and their impact on the emergence of melodrama on the English stage in response to the public's predilection for overwrought sentimentalism.[3] Rather than being regarded as a force for renewal, German drama tends to be treated as an episode that was soon to be overcome. The likes of Charles Maturin's *Bertram* (1816) and Lord Byron's *Manfred* (1817) are, perhaps conveniently, seen as the results of a later encounter with German Romanticism and are not usually traced back to this period of alleged "Kotzebue-mania." Original works that emerged directly as a result of reading and studying new plays from Germany in the late 1790s—such as Scott's *House of Aspen*—are written off altogether as youthful folly partaking in the latest craze for melodrama in medieval settings; at the same time, Samuel Taylor Coleridge's reception of German Idealism appears to place his reading, interpreting, and translating of works by Friedrich Schiller high above the efforts of other seeming hack translators making their living translating melodrama.[4]

In the following, therefore, I want to offer another perspective on German drama in Britain and its role in helping to rejuvenate British culture. I shall focus on two things that have not been given sufficient attention thus far. First of all, while scholarship has hitherto dedicated much attention to German drama in England in the 1790s and the early years of the nineteenth century, it has barely studied the specific context of Scotland. As I hope to demonstrate, an understanding of the particular philosophical context of late-eighteenth-century Edinburgh highlights that Scottish–German exchange in the period operated on a set of terms different to elsewhere in Britain—terms that had a great effect on *what* would be taken up from German drama at the time and *how*. Moreover, I want to argue that genre categories and ways of making sense of the genre of dramatic texts play a central role in how German drama was received in Scotland. While German plays helped to fuel the development of the melodrama south of the border, it was precisely the approach of German playwrights to dramatic genres that drove the interest of both Henry Mackenzie and Scott and then fed into Scott's creative output. The role of genre in intercultural exchange has remained relatively understudied to date and only recently has research begun to pay heed to genre as a means by which literary forms are recognized by different cultures.[5] As Stephen Heath writes, genres constitute "stabilizations of relations of communication," but insofar as "they depend on the reworking of recognized ways of making sense," they can be reformulated by looking at them through different lenses.[6] Emily Apter claims that "[o]ccidental genre categories invariably function as program settings" when Western literary criticism studies World Literature,[7] expressing that one culture might find it difficult to put the finger on and identify what constitutes a genre in the works of another.

As I shall argue, however, it is precisely this difficulty in tying down another culture's genre categories that features at the forefront of the Scottish reception of German drama in the late eighteenth century. In finding what they thought to be a set of plays that question generic forms, both Mackenzie's and Scott's attention came to rest on the *Schauspiel* (drama or play) as an intermediary genre; the *Schauspiel* was attractive because it stands somewhere *between* tragedy and comedy, but with each text consisting of a different mixture of the ingredients of these two more established genres. Mackenzie was guided to this intermediary genre by the philosophical inheritance of the Scottish Enlightenment that he appeared to recognize in it: the degree to which German dramatists questioned and overturned neo-classical categories was seen through the lens of the discourse of the passions and their role in civil society. Peter Garside has argued that Scott needs to be read within the intellectual context of the Scottish Enlightenment,[8] and this context is itself illuminating with regard to what Scott takes from German drama. I shall therefore discuss how Mackenzie received German drama at the tail end of the Scottish Enlightenment before turning to Scott's reception and translations of German plays in 1796–1798; this will help us in understanding how Scott came to writing his first full-length work *The House of Aspen*. Lastly, I shall suggest how these innovations inform the structural basis of Scott's work as a novelist. In all, this chapter will demonstrate that genres—or indeed the difficulties in tying them down—play an integral part in intercultural exchange that must not be taken for granted, and it will argue that the philosophical developments underlying how genres come into being establish the very conditions under which strange genres can be picked up by foreign cultures and—in the case under discussion at least—recognized as not so alien at all.

MACKENZIE AND THE DRAMA OF FEELING: "ACCOUNT OF THE GERMAN THEATRE"

The starting point of the popular reception of German drama in England can be identified in 1789 to 1790. Richard Brinsley Sheridan's translation of Kotzebue's *Menschenhaß und Reue* (Misanthropy and Repentance, 1788) as *The Stranger* "took the English stage by storm" in 1789, then a production of Thomas Holcroft's *The German Hotel*—itself an adaptation of the 1767 comedy *Der Gasthof; oder trau, schau, wem!* (The Guesthouse; or: Take Care in Whom You Trust) by Johann Christian Brandes served to further awaken the public's desire for German plays.[9] In Scotland, however, the watershed came on April 21, 1788, when Henry Mackenzie delivered his "Account of the German Theatre" to the Royal Society of Edinburgh. In this lecture, Mackenzie described what he saw as general characteristics of German drama, based on his study of two French anthologies of recent German plays. Mackenzie's lecture is notable for introducing its Edinburgh audience to a novel subject; beyond that, it reveals Scottish receptivity to German dramatic innovation, and it provides a focus for what the much younger Scott came to gain from German plays later on.

Mackenzie, born in 1745, was already one of Edinburgh's leading *literati* at the time he gave his lecture on German theater. His status owed in large part to the tremendous success of his sentimental novel *The Man of Feeling* (1771). This novel is written in the sentimental vein of Samuel Richardson, and it plays with genre, presenting itself as a fragment of a longer (fictional) manuscript, consisting of scenes that focus on the feelings of its protagonist, Harley, and their relationship to his surroundings. *The Man of Feeling* did not merely tap into the current craze for sentimentalism; it also figured within the eighteenth-century Scottish Enlightenment discourses on the passions and morality. Scott himself later described Mackenzie as "the last link in the chain which connects the Scottish literature of the present age with the period when there were giants in the land—the days of Robertson, and Hume, and Smith, and Home, and Clerk, and Fergusson [*sic*]."[10] At the time of delivering his lecture in 1788, he was a living remnant of a philosophical tradition that sought to carve out a place for the passions in both epistemology and in the functioning and progress of civil society, including in its *belles lettres*.[11]

It is perhaps no surprise that, when Mackenzie looks to German plays, therefore, his attention repeatedly turns to the passions. He writes, for example, that he finds a "deep impassioned sensibility" manifested in these plays,[12] and he places the emotional force depicted in and elicited by them at the forefront of his recipients' concerns. Early on, in a way reminiscent of the Speculative Historians of the Scottish Enlightenment, Mackenzie deduces that socio-economic and linguistic structures had impeded the growth of a particularly German drama until now. A fortunate result of the lack of a single courtly center with hierarchies of patronage, however, is that, unlike French drama, German plays appear to be "[d]ramas that rouse the passions, that shake the soul, afford pleasure only to the body of the people" ("Account," 157). After providing a lengthy discussion of the presentation of heightened emotional states in Schiller's *Die Räuber* (The Robbers, 1781), he calls this work "one of the most uncommon productions of untutored genius that modern times can boast." He recognizes that it may have its faults, but, he states, "its power over the heart and the imagination must be acknowledged" ("Account," 191). As he later writes, looking back on the discovery of German theater in Britain, it introduced "a new Stile of Poetry of passion tutored by metaphysics, & sentiment mixing its refinement with every day [*sic*] occupations."[13]

Mackenzie's remarks on the passions in German drama are worth dwelling on as they are telling with respect to the Scottish context in which Mackenzie was reading and propagandizing on behalf of German playwrights. English and Irish critics tended to view Schiller's play as a moral aberration for its depiction of criminals and largely felt that the German plays took too many liberties "to write in direct opposition" to the rules of dramatic composition.[14] As is well known, Coleridge had spoken favorably about the pathos of *Die Räuber*, referring to Schiller in a letter to Robert Southey in 1794 as a "convulser of the heart."[15] Yet the final chapter of his *Biographia Literaria* (1817) attests to a conviction that Schiller's more iconoclastic plays from the *Sturm und Drang* (Storm and Stress) period were formally defective; this points to one reason why Coleridge was to admire Schiller's works from the period that began with the *Wallenstein* trilogy. Mackenzie, however, applauds the depiction of passions in German plays and links this depiction *directly* to formal innovation. He cites the beginning of the awakening of German drama as when "the taste for sentimental and pathetic writing began to be wonderfully prevalent in Germany. The works of Sterne, and several other English authors of the same class, were read with the greatest avidity" ("Account," 158). He can therefore forgive some of the faults of German drama in breaking the rules of neo-classical decorum:

> We are not therefore to wonder, if, amidst what we might be apt to term refinement in point of sentiment and expression, we should find in those German dramas, a disregard for the regularities and the decorum of the stage, which is considered as marking a very rude state of the dramatic art. Such disregard, in effect, some of those dramas exhibit in a remarkable degree. . . .
>   This disregard of rule, and this licence [sic] of the scene, are attended with many unfavourable, and yet perhaps with some fortunate effects. The rules of sound criticism certainly produce, in the hands of great ability and genius, the most exquisite and delightful performances. Yet there is a certain reach of genius, which they may restrain from exertions that might sometimes accomplish very valuable productions. ("Account," 158–59)

From his own theatrical tastes and his experiences of theater in Paris, we know that Mackenzie was not necessarily disposed to rejecting neo-classical rules, but capable of recognizing the limits of adhering to them.[16] But he not only permits of infringements to them where the presentation and eliciting of passions are concerned—he welcomes these infringements of dramatic rules and goes on to outline the ways in which German plays disband the unities of action, time, and place to varying degrees, on top of breaking with classical decorum.

Mackenzie grants British sentimental literature a firm position in the founding of this new German dramatic tradition, thus placing this alien cultural product in a narrative of domestic literary traditions. It is, however, notable that he presents Gotthold Ephraim Lessing as the father of modern German drama and emphasizes the role of sentimentalism in it. Lessing was, after all, a reader of British sentimental literature,[17] and so Mackenzie was correct in that assertion. For his knowledge of the history of German drama and Lessing's place within it, he seems to lean on the introductory essay in Adrien Chrétien Friedel and Nicolas de Bonneville's anthology, *Nouveau Théatre* [sic] *Allemand* (1782–1785). Friedel and de Bonneville's "Histoire abrégée du théatre [sic] allemande" (Abridged History of German Theater) starts with a scathing criticism of Johann Christoph Gottsched as an "homme de beaucoup d'érudition, mais sans genie, vain & pedant" (a man of much erudition, but without genius, vain and pedantic),[18] and Mackenzie follows suit in denigrating Gottsched's *Sterbender Cato* (Dying Cato, 1732). He also follows their lead in citing Lessing's reforms of the theater and his reappraisal of Aristotelian rules as the force that established "the theatrical taste of Germany" ("Account," 157).[19]

But beyond being pointed in the direction of Lessing's reforms to German drama by a French intermediary, Mackenzie is drawn to Lessing's achievements as a playwright and particularly his treatment of generic categories. In his analysis of *Emilia Galotti* (1771), he highlights that Lessing's works stay fairly close to the standards of Aristotelianism; he remarks, however, that they depart from it in their depiction of characters and "in genuine expression of passion, and pointed force of dialogue" ("Account," 176–77). He is intrigued by a breed of plays that he seems to have encountered for the very first time, denoted in the French translations as *drames* (dramas),

> containing a delineation of the affections and passions of ordinary life, more allied to tragedy than to comedy, being only related to comedy in its persons, but to tragedy in its sentiments and its sufferings. . . . The situation and distress of the persons represented in it, are but little removed from the situation in which that class of readers are placed, or those distresses which they often feel. Hence perhaps no species of the drama may be supposed to have a stronger effect on actual life and conduct. . . . In general, I think we may venture to pronounce these dramas favourable both to moral principle and to the practice of virtue. ("Account," 172–73)

In looking at a selection of foreign plays, Mackenzie focuses on the role of the rule-breaking and irregularity of German drama. He believes the most morally edifying type of play to be one in which decorum is breached and the boundaries between tragedy and comedy are broken down. Indeed, the term he uses, *drame*, is the French equivalent of the German term *Schauspiel*. He focuses on a term that had been used by Goethe to subtitle his first play *Götz von Berlichingen* (1773) in order to signal a rejection of those neo-classical Aristotelian rules that Goethe felt had been strangling German dramatic genius. By the time Mackenzie was delivering his lecture in 1788, the term *Schauspiel* had merely come to refer to a play that contained tragic distress but had a happy ending—and was therefore an increasingly common term in use in Germany's growing theater industry,[20] but this questioning of the rules of genre in Lessing's thought and practice emerges as a result of his concerns for the moral import of the theater and was drawn from Lessing's own readings in and lessons from the moral philosophy of Scottish Enlightenment philosophers Francis Hutcheson and Adam Ferguson.[21]

For Lessing, if tragedy was to be able to fulfill its function of awakening pity and fear in an audience, it needed to do away with seemingly arbitrary generic distinctions that had been introduced as a result of misinterpretations of Aristotle. The so-called *Ständeklausel* of neo-classical drama—whereby tragedy should feature high-born characters with noble, lofty sentiments, and comedy was the reserve of low-born, everyday people with private concerns—was in the way of allowing audience members to take a sympathetic interest in characters and their demise. In the fourteenth entry to the *Hamburgische Dramaturgie* (Hamburg Dramaturgy, 1767–1768), Lessing writes: "Das Unglück derjenigen, deren Umstände den unsrigen am nächsten kommen, muß natürlicher Weise am tiefsten in unsere Seele dringen; und wenn wir mit Königen Mitleid haben, so haben wir es mit ihnen als mit Menschen, und nicht als mit Königen" (The misfortune of those whose conditions are most like ours must naturally affect the depths of our souls the most profoundly; and if we have pity for kings, then we have it with them as people and not as kings).[22] That is, for Lessing, presenting a king as an alien, noble entity is going to be ineffective as a means of arousing pity in an audience and thereby causing moral improvement in the theater; if, however, the very *situation* in which that king finds himself is one with which an audience can identify, it is possible for pity to be felt. As Lessing puts it in the nineteenth number of the *Hamburgische Dramaturgie*: "Auf dem Theater sollen wir nicht lernen, was dieser oder jeder einzelne Mensch getan hat, sondern was ein jeder Mensch von einem gewissen Charakter unter gewissen gegebenen Umständen tun werde" (in the theater we should not learn what this or that particular person did, but what a particular person of a certain character under certain given circumstances will do).[23]

Lessing arrives at the importance of "Umstände" (circumstances) partially through his reading of Denis Diderot, who writes in his 1757 *Entretiens sur Le Fils naturel* (Treatise on the Natural Son) that theater should foreground "conditions" rather than characters.[24] And it is the focus on the primacy of conditions over and above presenting particular characters that leads Lessing—as Diderot had proposed before him—to innovate with genre, casting the rigid rules of tragedy and comedy to one side to write in the form of the *bürgerliche Trauerspiel* (bourgeois tragedy); here, the conditions under which private individuals live are placed in the spotlight, mixing people from different classes and disrupting simple psychological depictions of characters so that audience members can take pity on these characters. Moreover, Lessing throws off the restriction that tragedy should be in verse; he further muddies the distinctions between tragedy and comedy by casting his characters' speech in life-like prose, accompanied by gestural language and punctuation to signal it. In *Emilia Galotti*, for example, when we meet the Prince at the beginning of the play, his speech is intended to be a realistic depiction of a character driven by his obsession with the title figure:

Emilia? (*indem er noch eine von den Bittschriften aufschlägt, und nach dem unterschriebenen Namen sieht.*) Eine Emilia?—Aber eine Emilia Bruneschi—nicht Galotti. Nicht Emilia Galotti! Was will sie, diese Emilia Bruneschi? (*er lieset*) Viel gefordert; sehr viel.—Doch sie heißt Emilia![25]

[Emilia? (*in opening another one of the supplications and looking for the name signed on it.*) An Emilia?—But an Emilia Bruneschi—not Galotti. Not Emilia

Galotti! What does she want, this Emilia Bruneschi? (*he reads*) Quite a lot; very much, in fact.—But she is called Emilia!]

This realism of emotion clearly appealed to Mackenzie, who states in his lecture that the writing in Lessing's play, "in genuine expression of passion, and pointed force of dialogue, may be compared to some of the best which the modern stage can boast." This opening scene contains "some of those little incidents that mark an intimacy with human nature, which genius alone can claim" ("Account," 177). And, tellingly, Mackenzie interprets *Emilia Galotti* as a play about "a prince tyrannised over" by his passion ("Account," 163).

But while the dramatic impetus for Lessing's generic innovation came from Diderot (and George Lillo's *London Merchant* of 1731),[26] the philosophical underpinning came from the Scottish Enlightenment tradition that regarded the awakening of sympathetic interest as integral in the functioning of civil society and emphasized the role of socio-economic conditions in guiding the possibilities for action. Considering the German plays he had read, Mackenzie declares that "[m]ost of the pieces of which [the anthologies] consist are plays of situation, rather than of character" ("Account," 163). He has therefore grasped a fundamental aspect not only in Lessing's drama, but in Lessing's contribution to the history of German drama. The surroundings in which individuals find themselves have led to the growth and channeling of their passions. Rather than presenting static characters drawn from tragedy or potentially laughable characters drawn from comedy, here the generic playfulness of German playwrights has caused a breakdown of standard genre rules, leading to a breed of plays that were to forsake the categories of tragedy and comedy altogether; these plays opt, instead, for the term *Schauspiel* and follow Lessing's lead in presenting dialogue through prose rather than verse. Indeed, as Peter Szondi notes, the traits of Lessing's bourgeois tragedy map neatly on to the later term *Schauspiel*.[27]

Moreover, Mackenzie, like Lessing, was concerned about the moral import of the theater, and given the proximity that the characters and situation of *Schauspiel* might have to everyday life, it is most likely a more effective force in executing the theater's ethical duties than works of drama aimed merely to please the tastes of the court. Mackenzie's "Account of the German Theatre" therefore introduced his audience to a product of a culture that seemed strange. But given its philosophical underpinnings, it was eminently marketable to an Edinburgh audience steeped in the teachings of the Scottish Enlightenment. Rejecting neo-classical decorum and challenging the rules of genre were a fundamental aspect in forming an in-between genre of the *Schauspiel* that would present passions on stage in order to arouse pity and fear in an audience. Indeed, drawing on their shared basis in the Scottish Enlightenment, both Scottish and German concerns about the moral role of theater in evoking pity went far beyond improving individual subjects. In his *Treatise of Human Nature* (1739), David Hume had drawn attention to the "great uniformity we may observe in the humours and turn of thinking of those of the same nation." As Hume goes on, "'tis much more probable, that this resemblance arises from sympathy, than from any influence of the soil and climate, which, tho' they continue invariably the same, are not able to preserve the character of a nation the same for a century together."[28] A truly Scottish-German tone, possibly even an echo of Hume and Lessing, can be detected in Schiller's famous 1784 essay on the moral import of the theater. Here, Schiller writes of the benefits to an audience that is "durch *eine* allwebende Sympathie verbrüdert" (joined through *one* all-encompassing sympathy),[29] and writing in 1792 about the experience of impassioned emotion in the theater, Dugald Stewart—a close compatriot of Mackenzie's and Professor at the University of Edinburgh—writes, that "[i]t is in situations of this kind, that we most completely forget ourselves as individuals, and feel the most sensibly the existence of those moral ties, by which Heaven has been pleased to bind mankind together."[30] In both Scottish and German discourses at the time, that is, sympathy in the theater promised the building of a collective entity of moral subjects.

READING GERMAN DRAMA IN SCOTLAND: SCOTT AND SIX GERMAN PLAYS

When Mackenzie introduced German drama into Scotland in 1788, his lecture pin-pointed those aspects of German drama that we might expect appealed to an individual who had emerged from the tradition of the Scottish Enlightenment and had maintained an interest in the function of the passions. He was drawn to the ways in which genre rules might be broken in German plays and tried to make sense of a genre that, in his eyes at least, did not represent a stable genre: the *Schauspiel*, for Mackenzie, was a morally edifying work that broke with rules to present situations, but he included works labeled both comedies and tragedies within his observations. No doubt, Mackenzie could count on his audience being able to pick up on his references to Scottish Enlightenment ethical discourses. Commenting on *Die Räuber*, he states that it poses a potential moral danger: "It covers the natural deformity of criminal actions with the veil of high sentiment and virtuous feeling, and thus separates (if I may be pardoned the expression) the *moral sense* from that morality which it ought to produce" ("Account," 192; emphasis in the original). The expression for which Mackenzie seeks a pardon is explicitly borrowed from Hutchesonian ethics. Mackenzie accepts passionate exchanges and the excitement of the passions in the audience, but not if they contradict what should naturally be deemed vice or virtue in ourselves or others.

Mackenzie's lecture is not, however, purely of interest for the way in which it points to a circle of Scottish-German philosophical exchange through which Scottish philosophy formed the basis for German dramatic innovations that were in turn received in Scotland. It is also remarkable because it aids in gaining an impression of how people in Edinburgh encountered German culture in the first place—among them, the young Walter Scott. As Scott writes in 1830, Mackenzie's lecture "made much noise, and produced a powerful effect,"[31] and this is certainly borne out in the increase of interest in German drama amongst private individuals, societies, and within institutions such as the library of the Faculty of Advocates. Scott recollects in 1830 that Mackenzie's lecture introduced its Edinburgh audience to

> dramatists, who, disclaiming the pedantry of the unities, sought, at the expense of occasional improbabilities and extravagancies, to present life in its scenes of wildest contrast, and in all its boundless variety of character, mingling, without hesitation, livelier with more serious incidents, and exchanging scenes of tragic distress, as they occur in common life, with those of a comic tendency. This emancipation from the rules so servilely adhered to by the French school, and particularly by their dramatic poets ... was the means of giving free scope to the genius of Goethé, Schiller, and others, which, thus relieved from the shackles, was not long in soaring to the highest pitch of poetic sublimity.[32]

Given Scott's own account of the impact of Mackenzie's lecture—and the fact that he was able to recall it some forty-two years later—his own reception of German drama was clearly impacted by Mackenzie's focus on the passions, the rejection of genre rules, and the beginning of a seemingly new genre altogether in these plays.[33] From 1796 to 1798, Scott read a number of German plays, translating six in total before writing his first original creative work drawing on the lessons learned from his study of German drama, *The House of Aspen*. As I shall argue in the following, Mackenzie's particularly Scottish Enlightenment take on genre in German drama left its mark on Scott, fueling his interest in the *Schauspiel* as a form and enabling him to see how the lessons learned from this genre might transcend the context of the drama altogether.

In 1796, Scott turned to reading and translating German plays. Only one, his translation of Goethe's *Götz von Berlichingen*, was ever published (in 1799). His translations of August Wilhelm Iffland's *Die Mündel* (The Wards, 1784), Jacob Maier's *Fust von Stromberg* (1782), and Karl Franz Guolfinger von Steinsberg's adaptation of *Otto von Wittelsbach* (1783) by Joseph Marius von Babo are still accessible as manuscripts. His translation of Schiller's *Die*

Verschwörung des Fiesco zu Genua (Fiesco's Conspiracy at Genoa, 1783) was, however, "given away or lost,"[34] and his alleged translation of *Emilia Galotti* has vanished without a trace. While Scott's library is filled with German volumes that were published early enough for him to have read them in 1796 to 1798,[35] it is hard to tell which ones were in his possession at that time. John Gibson Lockhart's *Life of Scott* usefully cites Scott's notebook from June to July 1797 to show that he was reading Lessing's *Nathan der Weise* (Nathan the Wise, 1779) at the time,[36] but such information regarding whether and when he read further works of German drama is lacking.

The six translations were to constitute the first two volumes of a twelve-volume "compendium of the Chefs d oeuvres [sic] of the German stage" that Scott proposed to the publishers Cadell and Davies in May 1798.[37] Counting the six plays mentioned here as masterworks may sound odd to modern ears. While it is true to say that Goethe, Schiller, and Lessing are considered three of the most important figures in German literature—let alone German drama—Babo, Steinsberg, and Maier tend to have been forgotten by literary history and Iffland's one-time status as the second-most performed German playwright (second only to Kotzebue) is now well and truly lost; even *Fiesco* is certainly not the most highly regarded of Schiller's plays. Scott may, of course, have been over-selling the significance of these plays in order to increase his chances of having his translations published.

If we look for what unites the six plays Scott translated and therefore dedicated significant amounts of time to reading and studying, however, we find that they are tied together by a departure from neo-classical norms and decorum (albeit in varying degrees and with respect to different aspects of formal construction); they also strive for an intensification of subject matter that leads to outpourings of emotions from characters and seek to evoke an emotional response from the audience. Furthermore, they foreground situation over character and are written in prose as opposed to verse. *Otto von Wittelsbach*, for one, presents the passing of five years and not once does it acknowledge this passage of time; the action of *Fust von Stromberg* occurs in various different cities and countries, involving a cast of twenty named characters and even more unnamed ones. Whatever *Die Mündel* makes up for by adhering to the unity of time and only using two settings, it does away with by breaking with classical decorum in its repudiation of the *Ständeklausel* and in its presentation of excessively emotional scenes. Where immoral deeds are committed by the protagonist (as in the cases of Otto von Wittelsbach, Fiesco, and—at least in Scott's and Mackenzie's reading—the Prince of *Emilia Galotti*), this is as a result of the perversion of the passions through the situation in which the character has found himself.[38] It is no small coincidence that Scott comments to his friend, Mrs. Hughes, in 1827 that his translation of *Götz* used to reduce his listeners to "sobbing and weeping" when he read it to them.[39] Yet not only do the plays described break generic rules in striving to depict passions and elicit emotions, but three of the six plays identify themselves as *Schauspiele*, and a further three plays that he likely acquired at the time are subtitled *Schauspiele*. Thus Scott was clearly on the look-out for this type of play in which Mackenzie had previously put so much store. And that the young Scott was interested in the morality of sensibility in the theater is clear from his avoidance of translating any works by Kotzebue. He owned a copy of *Bruder Moritz* (Brother Moritz, 1790), and editions of other plays by Kotzebue were also available in the collection of the Library of the Faculty of Advocates in Edinburgh at the time; there is good reason to think that he held the low opinion of Kotzebue that we have noted in his "Essay on the Drama" already in the 1790s and therefore avoided aiding in the dissemination of his works.[40]

WRITING GERMAN DRAMA IN SCOTLAND: *THE HOUSE OF ASPEN*

One test of the degree to which Scott learned from the innovative approaches to genre and generic rules that he found in German drama is the extent to which these same things can be traced in Scott's first attempt to implement what he had been studying. Scott's *House of Aspen*, as he describes it in 1829, is a "rifacimento" of *Die heilige Vehme* (The Sacred Tribunal, 1795) by Leonhard Wächter (writing under the pseudonym of Veit Weber), adapting this material because Scott admired the original and could not "trust . . . to his own efforts" of imagination.[41] The details of Scott's treatment of Wächter's text have been almost entirely overlooked by scholarship to date and the work tends to be cast off as youthful folly or viewed purely for the presence of the secret tribunal in it (which later features in his 1829 novel, *Anne of Geierstein*).[42] But when we give closer attention to the alterations and supplementations that Scott makes to his source material, we recognize that *The House of Aspen* is based on much more than just one German drama; it is a composite text, crafted from what Scott has learned from the passionate, genre-busting plays he had been reading.

Die heilige Vehme appeared as the sixth volume of Wächter's seven-volume work *Sagen der Vorzeit* (Legends of a Bygone Age), originally published in 1787–1798. These volumes contain fourteen stories of secret societies, bandits, marauding and gallant knights, supernatural prophesies, and the like, all set against the backdrop of medieval Europe, quite as the late eighteenth-century German "consumer" of literature had come to expect from a literary marketplace dominated by writers such as Benedikte Naubert, Carl Gottlob Cramer, and Christian August Vulpius.[43] At a first glance, *Die heilige Vehme* is an unperformable play: the first edition consists of 392 pages of text and features an enormous cast of thirty named characters with further unnamed soldiers and knights of various kinds.[44] Rather than obeying a five-act structure, Wächter opts for fourteen long scenes. The play is set in Westphalia in the year 1438, takes place in various different locations, and has seemingly impossible stage directions. Along with its huge cast and elaborate demands for stage design, *Die heilige Vehme* has a diffuse plot that consists of jealousy, plotting, revenge, remorse, conflicting senses of duty, and more. The central thread consists of the gradual destruction of the once powerful Aspenaus through the malicious scheming of Rüdiger von Maltingen.

Formally, there are many respects in which, in Scott's eyes at least, *Die heilige Vehme* would have resembled some of the other German plays he had been studying. Not least, the scale of Wächter's *dramatis personae* is only matched by that of *Götz von Berlichingen*, with the likes of *Fust von Stromberg* coming a close second. Wächter's changes in settings would have posed challenges to late-eighteenth-century stagecraft on a par with those posed by *Götz*, *Die Räuber*, *Fust von Stromberg*, and *Otto von Wittelsbach*. *Die heilige Vehme*'s rejection of the unity of action is reminiscent of *Götz*, *Otto von Wittelsbach*, and *Die Mündel*. Furthermore, he mixes characters of all social classes from the baronial families to criminals and torturers, casting their dialogue in prose. If Scott was drawn to plays that rejected the dramatic unities, he certainly found one in *Die heilige Vehme*.

Scott makes changes to Wächter's material. The year 1438 in Westphalia is important in *Die heilige Vehme*, being the year in which the Holy Roman Emperor reformed Westphalia's corrupt secret tribunals; the action of *Die heilige Vehme* is a result of these exact historical circumstances. Scott's play is, however, set in an indistinct time perhaps in the early twelfth century, somewhere in Bavaria. Scott also makes a number of sweeping formal changes to Wächter's text. He condenses an unwieldy text consisting of fourteen sections over 392 pages into a sixty-six-page, five-act play. This may, at first, appear like a conservative measure on Scott's part. But keeping to five acts seemed sufficiently sacred to even the most radical *Sturm und Drang* playwrights that they followed Shakespeare's lead in maintaining that structure. Scott also significantly reduces the *dramatis personae* to sixteen named characters and additional "Soldiers, Judges of the Invisible Tribunal, &c. &c." (*HoA*, 3).

With this reduction in the cast comes a streamlining of the action. Scott expunges many threads of Wächter's plot: for example, there is no longer a subplot about Otto von Herborn lusting after Katharine von Hohenwart, and instead of introducing a character who (like Berthold von Aspenau) has been tasked with cleaning up the secret tribunals, in Scott's play the impetus for change comes from George of Aspen. Yet Scott keeps much of the plot of *Die heilige Vehme*: the action still revolves around a central family (the Aspens), who are brought to their downfall through a combination of the scheming of their enemies—here Roderic of Maltingen—and a son's duty to uphold his word as a sworn member of the sacred tribunal. Even Maltingen's method for discovering Adelgunde's/Isabella's secret—that is, that she murdered her first husband—is the same: in both plays, the wounded servant Martin accidentally tells this to Maltingen, thinking him to be an Aspenau/Aspen. Indeed, the bloodbath at the end of both plays is astonishingly similar. Fewer people die in Scott's play than in *Die heilige Vehme*, but the deaths are achieved in both in the form of off-stage stabbings in a sacristy. While Scott reduces the plot, cast, incidents, and length of *Die heilige Vehme*, he also adds to it at the same time. Quite in keeping with both British and German theater of the time, *The House of Aspen* contains songs that are sung as diegetic music. And aside from the bulk of the main story, Scott maintains Wächter's preference for detailed, unstageable stage directions.

Die heilige Vehme contains the pathos that Scott had come to expect from German drama, and much like many of the German plays Scott had been reading, the sentiment of the characters of *Die heilige Vehme* is more like the sentiment of late-eighteenth-century Germans than like that of people living in the middle ages. Toward the end of the second section of *Die heilige Vehme*, Georg reports Martin's death to Veit, Adelgunde, and Katharine; Adelgunde is insistent on learning whether Martin died with a clean conscience, and the following dialogue ensues in realistic dialogue:

G. v. Asp. Martin Bleyer ist todt.

Adelg. *freudig, doch äußert sich die Freude nur im schnellen Herausstoßen der Worte:* Martin todt?

G. v. Asp. *vor sich.* Schuldig!

Kathar. Der arme Mann!

Herrm. v. Asp. Freylich; denn nun kann er sein Ursel nicht mehr küßen.

Adelg. Er starb in der Schlacht?

G. v. Asp. Während der Schlacht, zu meinen Füßen.

Adelg. Bey ungeschwächtem Bewußtseyn?

G. v. Asp. Ja.

Adelg. Trug er dir nicht auf, mich zu bitten, Seellösungen für ihn—?

G. v. Asp. Nein.

Adelg. Vielleicht war seine Zunge schon gelähmt?

G. v. Asp. Das nicht.

Adelg. Nun, ich werde meine Christenpflicht doch nicht vernachläßigen.

Herrm. v. Asp. Georg hat schon Meßen für Martin auf der Wahlstatt gelesen, dürfft also keinen Pfaffen drum bemühen, Frau Adelgunde.

Adelg. Er starb ruhig, mein Sohn?

Herrm. v. Asp. Wie Kriegsleute pflegen, ohne Zweifel. Ein Stoßseufzer, die Hände über's Schwerdt kreuz zusammengefaltet und die Augen vest zugedrückt; dann stirbt sich's wohl.—

Adelg. Starb er ruhig, Georg?

G. v. Asp. Eine Herzenswunde schmerze ihn sehr, klagte er.

Adelg. *fährt zusammen und verstummt,*

G. v. Asp. *der seine Mutter immer scharf beobachtet hat, wendet sich von ihr, beißt die Zähne zusammen, schaut gen Himmel und ballt die Hände, welche er zur Erde niederstößt, vor sich.* Schuldig! Schuldig!! (*hV*, 82–83)

[G. v. Asp. Martin Bleyer is dead.

Adelg. (*joyful, but her joy is only expressed in her quickly blurting out her words.*) Martin dead?

G. v. Asp. (*to himself.*) Guilty!

Kathar. The poor man!

Herrm. v. Asp. Indeed, for now he can kiss his Ursel no more.

Adelg. He died in battle?

G. v. Asp. During the battle, at my feet.

Adelg. With a clear conscience?

G. v. Asp. Yes.

Adelg. Did he not task you with asking me to pray that his soul—?

G. v. Asp. No.

Adelg. Maybe his tongue was already numb?

G. v. Asp. Not that.

Adelg. Now, I shall not neglect to discharge my Christian duties.

HERRM. V. ASP. Georg has already said masses for Martin on the battlefield, so you need not bother a priest with it, Frau Adelgunde.

ADELG. He died in peace, my son?

HERRM. V. ASP. Just as anyone at war, without a doubt. A deep sigh, his hands crossed over his sword, and his eyes closed tightly. Then he died to be sure.—

ADELG. Did he die in peace, Georg?

G. V. ASP. He complained that a wound in his heart was causing him much pain.

ADELG. (*starts and falls silent.*)

G. V. ASP. *(who has always been observing his mother closely, turns from her, bites his teeth together, looks up to the sky and clenches his fists, which he thrusts down to the ground; to himself.)* Guilty! Guilty!!]

Throughout this scene, Wächter layers details upon one another in Adelgunde's reaction, depicting the exact processes of people trying to hide their emotional response to a situation in working out the degree to which they have been implicated. Georg's blunt answers represent his outrage at the situation in contrast to the longer, detailed responses of Hermann that illustrate his ignorance in the situation. Once Georg can be sure of his mother's guilt, Wächter has Georg produce physical representations of his anger.

The passage from *Die heilige Vehme* cited previously ends up being extended in *The House of Aspen*. Already at the beginning, however, we can note Scott's approach to writing passions:

ISA. Perhaps some friend lost?

GEO. It must be.—*Martin is dead.*—(*He regards her with apprehension, but steadily, as he pronounces these words.*)

ISA. (*starts, then shows a ghastly expression of joy.*) Dead!

GEO. (*almost overcome by his feelings.*) Guilty! Guilty!—(*apart.*)

ISA. (*without observing his emotion.*) Didst thou say dead?

GEO. Did I—no—I only said mortally wounded. (*HA*, 31; emphasis in the original)

Scott's foremost concern here appears to be for the physicality of this scene. He describes the reasons for George and his mother saying what they have said, intricately plotting a process whereby George discovers his mother's guilt for himself. Emotions become how the two read each other; these are not any old feelings, but ones that "overcome" them or are "ghastly." As this scene develops, however, Scott focuses less on gesture and gradually more on the pathos of the situation as presented in language:

Isa. (*almost speechless.*) Alas! what did he do?

Geo. He did (*turning his head from her, and with clasped hands*) what I can never do: —he did his duty.

Isa. My son! My son!—Mercy! Mercy! (*Clings to him.*)

Geo. Is it then true?

Isa. What?

Geo. What Martin said? (Isabella *hides her face.*) It is true!

Isa. (*looks up with an air of dignity.*) Hear, Framer of the laws of nature! the mother is judged by the child—(*Turns towards him*). Yes, it is true—true that, fearful of my own life, I secured it by the murder of my tyrant. Mistaken coward! I little knew on what terrors I ran, to avoid one moment's agony.—Thou hast the secret!

Geo. Knowest thou to whom thou has told it?

Isa. To my son.

Geo. No! No! to an executioner.

Isa. Be it so—go, proclaim my crime, and forget not my punishment. Forget not that the murderess of her husband has dragged out years of hidden remorse, to be brought at last to the scaffold by her own cherished son—thou art silent.

Geo. The language of Nature is no more! How shall I learn another? (*HA*, 33–34)

The two lattermost citations from *The House of Aspen* are taken from what Scott refers to in a letter to Lady Abercorn in 1811 as "the only good scene" in the play (*HA*, 30–36).[45] In this scene we recognize Scott's use of gesture that both depicts emotion and helps us understand the motivations for actions and feelings. The situation in which the two find themselves results in a passionate exchange. The language and the tone in which it is delivered are hyperbolic and, with some nod to Lessing and Schiller, attempt to recreate the speech of a mind at work, full of false starts, incomplete ideas, and hesitations. Scott has recreated not the emotional heights of *Die heilige Vehme*, but of the despairing characters of *Die Mündel*, *Emilia Galotti*, *Die Räuber*, and *Fiesco*. He recognizes the particularly German pathos of his play, telling Lady Abercorn in 1811 that *The House of Aspen* had been written "when my taste was very green and when like the rest of the world I was taken in with the bombast of Schiller."[46] This statement is further testament to the lasting impact that Mackenzie's discussion of Schiller in his 1788 lecture was to leave on the young Walter Scott.

In making the aforementioned changes to Wächter's text, Scott did not just adapt *Die heilige Vehme*. As a result of his experience of German drama, he has written a formally challenging piece of theater, guided by a desire to reproduce human suffering and feeling and based on a text that is more likely to be a particularly rigid case of a dramatic novel rather than a text intended for realization on a stage. And this new piece of drama is one that bears the marks of its multiple German sources on its sleeve. Moreover, in his changes to the plot, Scott has removed any ambiguity surrounding the morality of Wächter's Adelgunde: Isabella in *The House of Aspen* is wracked with guilt about having murdered her husband, but she was driven to do so by her despair at being constantly brutalized by him; Isabella, however, merely loved another. Responding to the ethical demands of his context, therefore, Scott has cleaned up Wächter's work so that we see how Isabella's moral sense has been perverted by the passions into which she has been worked up by her particular situation. The version of this text that ends up being published in the *Keepsake* in 1829 is subtitled "A Tragedy," and, given that the protagonists die in their efforts to overcome endemic corruption, this seems an appropriate generic description for the play. Yet, tellingly, the earliest known manuscript version of *The House of Aspen*, dated to the period in which Scott composed the play itself, labels the play "A Drama of Chivalry."[47] *The House of Aspen* does indeed represent chivalry to some degree and has much in common with the plays Scott had been reading that based their action in the Middle Ages. Scott was not, however, subtitling *The House of Aspen* "A Drama of Chivalry" as a translation of the German term *Ritterstück* or *Ritterschauspiel*: these two terms are not used as subtitles of any of the plays we know him to have read. Rather, in opting to designate the genre of his work with the term "drama," Scott was nodding in the direction of the *drames* or *Schauspiele* to which Mackenzie had drawn his attention, and he signaled his own play's affinities with its German forebears.

AFTER THE GERMAN: FROM THE *SCHAUSPIEL* TO THE NOVEL

As early as 1801, Scott recognized that his play had been of limited success. In a letter to his friend, George Ellis, he states that "the Plays of the Passions have put me entirely out of conceit with my Germanized brat; and should I ever again attempt dramatic composition, I would endeavour after the genuine old English model."[48] In 1808, Scott calls his first play a tragedy "upon the vile German plan which was then the rage,"⁴⁹ and in his correspondence with Lady Abercorn in 1811, he describes *The House of Aspen* as his "half-mad German tragedy."⁵⁰ Where he notes deficiencies in *The House of Aspen*, he speaks of the Germanness of this work and sees it as a failed attempt to write "tragedy." His reason for moving on from German plays and instead opting for "the genuine old English model" is the example set by the first series of Joanna Baillie's *Plays on the Passions* (1798). Scott had seemingly gone too far in adopting the formal innovations that he found in German dramatists: where *The House of Aspen* is a prose drama featuring an enormous cast of characters, all pulled in various directions by their passions, Baillie's tragedies *Count Basil* and *De Monfort* are written in blank verse, and each focuses primarily on the development of the passions in the protagonist. Baillie's work emerged from the same philosophical tradition as Lessing, as she too was interested primarily in how theatergoers might be improved by a "sympathetick interest" in a character. Baillie therefore attempted to present mental activity via an early psychological realism whereby the situations into which characters are placed enables an audience to pity the protagonist in his demise.⁵¹ Scott's works, however, pushed their infringements of genre rules too far and, in so doing, failed to meet the Shakespearean standards of Baillie. This goes some way in helping us understand Scott's later rejection of the bourgeois tragedy and the sentimental comedy, which was to roll together into one in his 1819 essay.

If Scott recognized that he had taken the lessons of the *Schauspiel* too far in his first piece of dramatic writing, however, we can see German drama's legacy in Scott's novels. Just as Mackenzie had drawn Scott's attention to rule-breaking in German plays, Scott is later to actively shirk the conventions of the structure of the novel. As his fictional author responds to Captain Clutterbuck in the "Introductory Epistle" to *The Fortunes of Nigel* (1822), he has no interest in writing a novel that takes a measured approach to developing a plot in which "every step brings us closer to the point of catastrophe." The rules of genre, he writes, are purely arbitrary: "These great masters have been satisfied if they amused the reader upon the road; though the conclusion only arrived because the tale must have an end—just as the traveller alights at the inn, because it is evening."⁵² In his novels, Scott is much less interested in developing character psychologies than in throwing average characters into situations in which they are at the whim of their conditions. We see a striking similarity between Scott's own assessment from 1817 of what had so far been published of his *Tales of My Landlord* series and Mackenzie's remarks about German plays as "plays of situation." Scott's "chief characters are never actors, but always acted upon by the spur of circumstances, and have their fates uniformly determined by the agency of subordinate persons."⁵³ Not only does

Scott give primacy to situation over character, but, as he himself notes in the same review, he also puts the action "as much as possible, into a dramatic shape."[54] Both the dramatic shape of his novels and the primacy of the situation in which his characters find themselves bear remarkable resemblances to the formal innovations of Lessing and the traits of the German *Schauspiele* Scott had been reading in the late 1790s.

As this chapter has argued, when German drama came to Scotland in the 1790s, Mackenzie was well equipped to make sense of this seemingly alien culture and its artistic offerings. In the context of late eighteenth-century Edinburgh, German plays appealed to a way of thinking about human activity that stemmed from the Scottish Enlightenment. These German plays themselves were part of a German cultural inheritance that led back to the Scottish discourse on the passions via Lessing, and, taking their lead from Lessing's repudiation of neo-classical genre rules, German playwrights rejected the genre distinctions of tragedy and comedy in fashioning an in-between genre, the *Schauspiel*. This genre itself is hard to tie down, allowing for a great deal of internal variation. But Mackenzie's attention seized upon it as a means of presenting and eliciting the passions and showing human activity as bound to specific situations. Mackenzie's lecture guided Scott's interest in German drama, which, in *The House of Aspen*, resulted in Scott's first attempt to write something as a direct consequence of learning from German playwrights; yet while this play, in Scott's eyes at least, signaled that his own Germanic dramatic innovation had gone too far, the traits of this imprecise genre of the *Schauspiel* helped to form the structural basis for his later novels. Thus this one genre-busting descriptor both set the stage for its reception in another culture as a result of a shared philosophical heritage; in looking at the movement of dramatic genre from culture to culture, we have also recognized the way in which specific elements of that genre can be harnessed for an entirely different purpose and different form of creative work altogether. While German drama may not have rejuvenated British theater at the turn of the century, as Scott was later to pronounce, it did, however, lay the foundations for one of British literature's greatest cultural exports in the nineteenth century.

NOTES

1. Walter Scott, "Essay on the Drama," in *The Miscellaneous Prose Works of Sir Walter Scott, Bart.*, twenty-eight volumes (Edinburgh: Cadell, 1834–1836), volume 6, 376–77. Hereafter, referred to in the body of this essay with the abbreviation "Essay."

2. See, for example, Violet Stockley, *German Literature as Known in England 1750–1830* (London: Routledge, 1929), 185–87.

3. On the topic of Kotzebue in England, see, for example, Julie Carlson, "Unsettled Territory: The Drama of English and German Romanticisms," *Modern Philology* 88, no. 1 (1990): 45; Carlotta Farese, "The Strange Case of Herr von K: Further Reflections on the Reception of Kotzebue's Theatre in Britain," in *The Romantic Stage: A Many-Sided Mirror*, ed. Lilla Maria Crisafulli and Fabio Liberto (Amsterdam and New York: Rodopi, 2014), 71–84; John Mander, *Our German Cousins: Anglo-German Relations in the 19th and 20th Centuries* (London: John Murray, 1974), 26–30; Allardyce Nicholl, *A History of Late Eighteenth Century Drama 1750–1800* (Cambridge: Cambridge University Press, 1927), 61–73; and Walter Sellier, *Kotzebue in England. Ein Beitrag zur Geschichte der englischen Bühne und der Beziehungen der deutschen Litteratur [sic] zur englischen* (Leipzig: Oswald Schmidt, 1901).

4. See, for example, Julie A. Carlson, *In the Theatre of Romanticism: Coleridge, Nationalism, Women* (Cambridge: Cambridge University Press, 1994), 63–93.

5. Jernej Halbjan, for, example, writes in 2016, that "if we want to approach the historical dimension of literature, we might as well start with genre." Jernej Halbjan, "Introduction: Globalizing Literary Genres," in *Globalizing Literary Genres: Literature, History, Modernity*, ed. Jernej Halbjan and Fabienne Imlinger (London and New York: Routledge, 2016), 3.

6. Stephen Heath, "The Politics of Genre," in *Debating World Literature*, ed. Christopher Prendergast (London and New York: Verso, 2004), 169, 172.

7. Emily Apter, *Against World Literature: On the Politics of Untranslatability* (London and New York: Verso, 2013), 59.

8. See Peter D. Garside, "Scott and the 'Philosophical' Historians," *Journal of the History of Ideas* 36, no. 3 (1975): 497–512.

9. See Farese, "The Strange Case of Herr von K," 75–76; and Theodor Grieder, "The German Drama in England, 1790–1800," *Restoration and 18th Century Theatre Research* 3, no. 2 (1964): 39.

10. Walter Scott, *Lives of the Novelists* (London, New York, and Toronto: Oxford University Press, 1906), 167.

11. For a concise account of sympathy and the passions in the Scottish Enlightenment, see John Dwyer, *The Age of the Passions: An Interpretation of Adam Smith and Scottish Enlightenment Culture* (East Linton: Tuckwell, 1998).

12. Henry Mackenzie, "Account of the German Theatre," *Transactions of the Royal Society of Edinburgh* 2 (1790): 169. Hereafter cited in the body of the text with the abbreviation "Account."

13. Henry Mackenzie, "Poetry in Briatin about 1763," in *Literature and Literati: The Literary Correspondence and Notebooks of Henry Mackenzie*, ed. Horst Drescher, two volumes (Frankfurt a.M.: Lang, 1989–1999), volume 2, 205.

14. See Hannah More, *Strictures on the Modern System of Female Education*, in two volumes (London: Cadell and Davies, 1799), volume 1, 48; and William Preston, "Reflections on the Peculiarities of Style and Manner in the Late German Writers Whose Works Have Appeared in English, and on the Tendency of Their Productions," *The Transactions of the Royal Irish Academy* 8 (1802): 15–79. For further literature on conservative reactions to German drama at the time and accounts of "Europhobia" in general, see, for example, Jeffrey N. Cox, "Ideology and Genre in

the British Antirevolutionary Drama of the 1790s," *ELH* 58, no. 3 (1991): 579–610; Peter Mortensen, *British Romanticism and Continental Influences. Writing in an Age of Europhobia* (Basingstoke: Palgrave Macmillan, 2004); G. Waterhouse, "Schiller's *Räuber* in England Before 1800," *Modern Language Review* 30, no. 3 (1935): 355–57; and L.A. Willoughby, "English Translations and Adaptations of Schiller's *Robbers*," *Modern Language Review* 16, no. 3/4 (1921): 297–315.

15. Samuel Taylor Coleridge to Robert Southey, November 1794, in *Collected Letters*, ed. Earl Leslie Griggs, six volumes (Oxford: Clarendon, 1956), volume 1, 122.

16. See Henry Mackenzie, "Diary of a Journey to Paris in 1784," in *Literature and Literati*, volume 2, 232, 239.

17. For a recent account of Lessing's role in the transmission of British sentimental novels in the German-speaking world, see Till Kinzel, "Gotthold Ephraim Lessing und Johann Joachim Eschenburg als Leser und Vermittler Samuel Richardsons. Wege der deutschen Anglophilie im achtzehnten Jahrhundert," in *Britisch-deutscher Literaturtransfer 1756–1832*, ed. Lore Knapp and Eike Kronshage (Berlin and Boston, MA: de Gruyter, 2016), 39–52.

18. Adrien Chrétien Friedel and Nicolas de Bonneville, "Histoire abrégée du theatre [sic] allemand," in *Nouveau Théatre [sic] Allemand, ou Recueil des pieces qui ont paru avec succès sur les Théatres des Capitales de l'Allemagne*, twelve volumes (Paris: Caron, 1782–85), volume 1, 9.

19. Compare with Friedel and de Bonneville, "Histoire abrégée," 17–34. The subject of French intermediaries in the British reception of German literature is a vast one, but for some research on this topic, see, for example, Robert Alan Charles, "French Mediation and Intermediaries, 1750–1815," in *Anglo-German and American-German Crosscurrents*, ed. Philip Allison Shelley, Arthur O. Lewis Jr, and William W. Betts Jr (Chapel Hill, NC: University of North Carolina Press, 1957), 1–38; Robert Alan Charles, *French Intermediaries in the transmission of German literature and culture to England, 1750–1815* (PhD dissertation, Pennsylvania State College, 1952); and Stefanie Stockhorst, "Introduction. Cultural transfer through translation: a current perspective in Enlightenment studies," in *Cultural Transfer through Translation: The Circulation of Enlightened Thought in Europe by Means of Translation*, ed. Stefanie Stockhorst (Amsterdam and New York: Rodopi, 2010), 7–26.

20. This can be seen very clearly in the differences between the *Schauspiel* and *Trauerspiel* versions of Schiller's early plays when they were adapted for audiences at Mannheim. See, for example, Lesley Sharpe, *Schiller and the Historical Character: Presentation and Interpretation in the Historiographical Works and in the Historical Drama* (Oxford: Oxford University Press, 1982), 9–12; and Ursula Wertheim, *Schillers "Fiesko" und "Don Carlos": Zu Problemen des historischen Stoffes* (Berlin and Weimar: Aufbau, 1967), 68–113.

21. See Fania Oz-Salzberger, *Translating the Enlightenment: Scottish Civic Discourse in Eighteenth-Century Germany* (Oxford: Clarendon Press, 1995), 217–28; Benjamin W. Redekop, *Enlightenment and Community: Lessing, Abbt, Herder, and the Quest for a German Public* (Montreal and Kingston: McGill-Queen's University Press, 2000), 58–122; Hans-Jürgen Schings, *Der mitleidigste Mensch ist der beste*

Mensch: Poetik des Mitleids von Lessing bis Büchner, second edition (Würzburg: Königshausen & Neumann, 2012); and Norbert Waszek, "The Scottish Enlightenment in Germany, and its Translator, Christian Garve (1742–98)," in *Scotland in Europe*, ed. Tom Hubbard and R.D.S. Jack (Amsterdam and New York: Rodopi, 2006), 55–57.

22. Gotthold Ephraim Lessing, *Hamburgische Dramaturgie*, in *Minna von Barnhelm. Hamburgische Dramaturgie. Werke 1767–69*, ed. Klaus Bohnen (Berlin: Deutscher Klassiker, 2010), 251.

23. Lessing, *Hamburgische Dramaturgie*, 276.

24. Denis Diderot, *Entretiens sur Le Fils naturel*, in *Entretiens sur Le Fils naturel. De la poésie dramatique. Paradoxe sur le comédien* (Paris: Flammarion, 2005), 135. Here, Diderot writes, "il ne sont plus, á proprement parler, les caractères qu'il faut mettre sur la scène, mais les conditions" (properly speaking, it is no longer characters that we must put on stage, but conditions).

25. Gotthold Ephraim Lessing, *Emilia Galotti*, in *Gotthold Ephraim Lessings Sämtliche Schriften*, ed. Karl Lachmann, twenty-three volumes, third edition, ed. Franz Muncker (Stuttgart: Göschen, 1886–1924), volume 1, 379.

26. For a full treatment of the place of Lillo's play in the development of the bourgeois tragedy, see Peter Szondi, *Die Theorie des bürgerlichen Trauerspiels im 18. Jahrhundert* (Frankfurt a.M.: Suhrkamp, 1973), 15–90.

27. Szondi, *Theorie*, 181.

28. David Hume, *A Treatise of Human Nature*, ed. L.A. Selby-Bigge, second edition (Oxford: Oxford University Press, 1978), 316–17.

29. Friedrich Schiller, "Was kann eine gute stehende Schaubühne eigentlich wirken?" in *Sämtliche Werke*, ed. Wolfgang Riedel, five volumes (Munich: Deutscher Taschenbuch, 2004), volume 5: *Erzählungen. Theoretische Schriften*, 830–31. Emphasis in the original.

30. Dugald Stewart, *Elements of the Philosophy of the Human Mind*, in *The Works of Dugald Stewart*, seven volumes (Cambridge: Hilliard and Brown, 1829), volume 3, 161.

31. Walter Scott, "Essay on Imitations of the Ancient Ballad," in *The Minstrelsy of the Scottish Border*, four volumes (Edinburgh: Cadell, 1849), volume 4, 40.

32. Scott, "Essay on Imitations," 39.

33. Critical literature on the subject of Scott's reception of German drama in the 1790s, however, repeatedly places his interest in either medieval subject matter or depictions of history. See, for example, Ruth Adams, "A Letter by Sir Walter Scott," *Modern Philology* 54, no. 2 (1956): 122; Christopher Johnson, "Scott and the German Historical Drama," *Archiv für das Stuidium der neueren Sprachen und Literaturen* 233, no. 1 (1996): 2–36; Georg Lukács, *The Historical Novel*, trans. Hannah and Stanley Mitchell (London: Merlin, 1962), 22; Duncan Mennie, "Walter Scott's Unpublished Translations of German Plays," *Modern Language Review* 33, no. 2 (1938): 238–39; G.H. Needler, *Goethe and Scott* (Toronto: Oxford University Press, 1950), 22; Paul M. Ochojski, "Sir Walter Scott's Continuous Interest in Germany," *Studies in Scottish Literature* 3, no. 3 (1966): 166; F.W. Stokoe, *German Influence in the English Romantic Period 1788–1818, with Special Reference to Scott, Coleridge,*

Shelley and Byron (Cambridge: Cambridge University Press, 1926), 28, 71; and E.H. Harvey Wood, "Scott's Foreign Contacts," in *Scott Bicentenary Essays: Selected Papers read at the Sir Walter Scott Bicentenary Conference*, ed. Alan Bell (Edinburgh and London: Scottish Academic Press, 1973), 245.

34. Walter Scott to Mrs Hughes, Edinburgh, December 13, 1827, in *The Letters of Sir Walter Scott*, ed. Herbert Grierson, twelve volumes (London: Constable, 1932–37), volume 10, 331.

35. See *Catalogue of the Library at Abbotsford* (Edinburgh: Constable, 1838). This collection is searchable online via the Advocates Library Catalogue, housed within the online main catalogue of the National Library of Scotland.

36. John Gibson Lockhart, *The Life of Sir Walter Scott*, ten volumes (Edinburgh: Constable and Jack, 1902), volume 1, 302.

37. Walter Scott to Cadell and Davies, Edinburgh, May 5, 1798, printed in: Adams, "A Letter by Sir Walter Scott," 121.

38. For a detailed exploration of what brings together the six texts that Scott translated and a more detailed account of his interpretation of them, see Michael Wood, "On Form and Feeling: German Drama and the Young Walter Scott," *German Life and Letters* 71, no. 4 (2018): 395–414.

39. Walter Scott to Mrs Hughes, September 20, 1827, in *Letters*, volume 10, 283.

40. For discussion of the status of Kotzebue and his works in Scotland at the time, see David W. Lindsay, "Kotzebue in Scotland, 1792–1813," *Publications of the English Goethe Society* 33 (1963): 56–74; and Michael Wood, "Notes on a Scandal: Robison, Scott, and the Reception of Kotzebue in Scotland," *Notes and Queries* 65, no. 3 (2018): 314–16.

41. Walter Scott, *The House of Aspen, A Tragedy*, in *The Keepsake for MDCCCXXX*, ed. Frederic Mansel Reynolds (London: Hurst, Chance & Co.: 1829), 1. Hereafter referred to as *HoA*.

42. See, for example, Arthur Melville Clark, *Sir Walter Scott: The Formative Years* (Edinburgh and London: Blackwood, 1969), 266; and Paul M. Ochojski, *Walter Scott and Germany: A Study in Literary Cross-Currents* (PhD dissertation, Columbia University, 1960), 61. Christopher Johnson writes the play off altogether as being full of "platitudinous and high-flown sentiment": Johnson, "Scott and the German Historical Drama," 23. See also Wilman Brewer, *Shakespeare's Influence on Sir Walter Scott* (Boston, MA: Cornhill, 1925); William Gordon Dustan, *Sir Walter Scott and the Drama* (PhD dissertation, University of Edinburgh, 1933); and Needler, *Goethe and Scott*, none of which even mentions the play, even though *The House of Aspen* would recommend itself for their studies.

43. See Michael Hadley, *The Undiscovered Genre: A Search for the German Gothic Novel* (Bern: Lang, 1978), 9.

44. Veit Weber [i.e. Leonhard Wächter], *Die heilige Vehme*, volume 6 of *Sagen der Vorzeit*, seven volumes (Berlin: Maurer, 1787–98), 3–4. Hereafter referred to as *hV*.

45. Walter Scott to Lady Abercorn, Ashestiel, July 25, 1811, in *Letters*, volume 2, 520.

46. Walter Scott to Lady Abercorn, Edinburgh, May 17, 1811, in *Letters*, volume 2, 495.

47. For discussion about the status of three extant manuscripts of *The House of Aspen*, see Michael Wood, "An Elusive Manuscript of Scott's *House of Aspen* at the National Library of Scotland," *Notes and Queries* 66, no. 2 (forthcoming, 2019). It is also worth noting in this context that, like *The House of Aspen*, *Götz von Berlichingen* ended up shifting genre when Scott's translation of it was published in March 1799 as *Goetz of Berlichingen, with the Iron Hand: A tragedy* (London: Bell, 1799). I suggest that the term "tragedy" was used in the latter case as a result of the market conditions of Britain (where marketing a play as a "play" or a "drama" would have been uncommon), and both Scott's later appraisal of Joanna Baillie's tragedies and his love of Shakespeare, combined with domestic understandings of genre had a part to play in *The House of Aspen* ending up designated a "tragedy."

48. Walter Scott to George Ellis, Edinburgh, December 8, 1801, in *Letters*, volume 1, 124.

49. Walter Scott to Miss Smith, Ashestiel, September 17, 1808, in *Letters*, volume 2, 89.

50. Scott to Abercorn, May 17, 1811, 495.

51. Joanna Baillie, *Plays on the Passions (1798 Edition)*, ed. Peter Duthie (Peterborough, ON: Broadview, 2001), 81.

52. Walter Scott, *The Fortunes of Nigel*, ed. Frank Johnson (Edinburgh: Edinburgh University Press, 2004), 7.

53. Walter Scott, "*Tales of My Landlord*, 1817," in *Sir Walter Scott on Novelists ad Fiction*, ed. Ioan Williams (New York; Barnes & Noble, 1968), 240.

54. Scott, "*Tales of My Landlord*, 1817," 239.

Chapter Four

Kotzebue's Adaptations of English Comedies

Colman, Cumberland, and Conservatism after 1815

Johannes Birgfeld

When we think of August von Kotzebue, two aspects of his life and work tend to spring to mind: first, that he was the most successful German-speaking dramatist of the end of the eighteenth and the beginning of the nineteenth centuries both at home and abroad; secondly, we may think of the enormous number of plays he published under his name, which current estimates place at 227,[1] although more may have existed. If we add historical, autobiographical, and journalistic writings—all remarkable in their number and often also in their volume and scope—to the count, along with a number of poems, it seems unlikely that Kotzebue did anything at all besides write. Kotzebue's tremendous output for the stage, however, was not as surprising back in his day as it might seem today. In fact, it was in part a result of the sudden and unprecedented need for plays in Germany in the late eighteenth century, triggered by the national theater movement and the erection of many new theaters since the 1770s, not to mention the Vienna *Spektakelfreiheit*, Joseph II's surprising permission for the unrestricted opening of theaters in Vienna in 1776.[2] Around 1800, German theaters everywhere were facing the same challenge: to create a playing schedule that would offer an attractive diversity and consist of plays capable of repeatedly drawing in paying audiences in large quantities.

One consequence of this situation was an exponential growth in the number of male and female authors writing for the stage. A second lay in the rise of writers with a profound understanding of dramaturgy and the audience's current interests. Often their name alone drew in crowds, and in most cases their dramatic efforts pleased the predominantly middle-class spectators. Hence, the *Goethezeit* (Age of Goethe) was also an age of the so-called *Vielschreiber* (prolific writers)[3]: Joseph Felix von Kurz is said to have written more than three hundred comedies,[4] August Wilhelm Iffland produced no fewer than seventy plays,[5] Alois Gleich about 225, Karl Meisl approximately two hundred, Adolf Bäuerle an estimated number of eighty dramatic works,[6] and Johann Nepomuk Nestroy left behind around ninety plays. Most of these writers, like Kotzebue, subscribed to what one might call an aesthetic of professionalism: they willingly put their individual writing impulses second to the theaters' needs to be financially successful; they therefore aimed to strike a balance between literary ambition and the limited ability of large audiences to follow complex, intellectually avant-garde debates and concepts on the stage.[7] Kotzebue himself is explicit in stating that his work seeks to strike just this balance. In his 1797 *Fragmente über Recensenten-Unfug* (Fragments on Reviewers' Nonsense), for example, he writes:

> Man werfe doch einen Blick auf die Zuschauer: hier ein Geschäftsmann, der Erholung, dort eine Dame, die Zerstreuung sucht; hier ein guter Bürger mit träger Fassungskraft, dort ein flüchtiger Jüngling, dessen Aufmerksamkeit schwer zu fesseln ist; hier ein Hofmann, der ein paar Stunden tödten will, dort ein Mädgen, zu dessen Kopfe der Weg nur durch das Herz führt u. s. w. welcher von Allen, ich bitte euch, wird (wenn auch seine Bildung dazu hinreichte), dem Verfasser dasjenige in Einer Minute nachdenken, wozu Jener vielleicht eine Stunde brauchte, es hervorzubringen?—Man will unterhalten und belehrt seyn, aber ohne große Anstrengung, und nur unter der Bedingung, daß es unmerklich geschehe, erlaubt man dem Volksdichter, auch die Köpfe seiner Zuhörer in Thätigkeit zu setzen. Sie dürfen gleichsam nicht gewahr werden, daß sie denken.[8]

[One should take a closer look at the spectators: here's a businessman, hoping for recreation, there a lady, looking for distraction; here a moral citizen of slow apprehension, there a flighty youngster, whose attention is hard to catch; here a member of the court killing a few hours, there a girl whose head can only be reached through her heart, and so forth. Which one of all these, I ask you, will (providing that her or she has a sufficient education) reflect on within a minute what the dramatist might have taken an hour to write?—The audience does want to be entertained and educated, but without great effort. And the popular poet is permitted to set the audience's mind in motion only on the condition that it all happens imperceptibly. The spectators should never realize that they are made to think.]

What Kotzebue proposes is not easy to achieve. As his comment makes abundantly clear, his project had to also take into account the diversity of the large audiences that had started flocking to the theaters of the German-speaking world. Yet he developed strategies to succeed nonetheless. In many of his plays, he uses well-established dramatic forms like that of the marriage-initiation play (the *Eheanbahnungsstück*), employed stock characters, and drew on the familiar tropes of "entertaining" plays as a means to present solutions to both new and old conflicts. In addition, most of his plays were conceived so that they would not overstrain the majority of spectators intellectually. Instead they used familiar plots to engage with current (social) issues and problems and to address newly arisen challenges: *Die Spardose* (The Saving Box, 1804), for example, discreetly introduces audiences to basic rules of a capitalist market,[9] and *Der Educations-Rath* (The Education Counsel, 1815) promotes sympathy for the new salon culture, pitting modern urban reality against the humdrum existence and narrow-mindedness of small-town life.[10] *Das zugemauerte Fenster* (The Blocked Window, 1810) focuses on the brutality of war by using a marriage-initiation plot to invoke and engage with the audience's frustrations about Prussia's recent military defeat against Napoleon; at the same time, it encourages patriotic acts in defense of the beleaguered German Fatherland.[11] Thus not only did Kotzebue make use of familiar plots and forms in an effort to communicate with his audiences, but his plays also avoided the sort of alienation that might occur had he made aesthetic choices unfamiliar to his audiences.

Also crucial to Kotzebue's attempt to provide audiences and theaters with a constant stream of plays that met his standards of an aesthetic of professionalism was his regular adaptation and appropriation of plays by foreign writers. Around 1800, a large number of French and English (popular) plays were responding to similar social conflicts using similar plots and dramatic concepts as German playwrights, so adapting foreign plays became common practice for the latter. Like many of his contemporaries, Kotzebue turned to foreign plays that either had already been successful on stage elsewhere or that he felt could easily be adapted to German audiences' tastes and his own dramatic concepts. When turning to the works of others, French writers were Kotzebue's favored source: anecdotes, tales, and plays of Jean-Nicolas Bouilly were "used" in at least seven of Kotzebue's plays[12]; others were based on works by Alexandre Duval,[13] Molière, Louis-Benoît Picard, Auguste Creuzé de Lesser, Alain-René Lesage, Joseph-Marie Pain, and Pierre-Ange Vieillard. While in the case of his adaptation of Molière a long time span separated the original from Kotzebue's version, the majority of his interactions with French drama were impressively up to date. Sometimes, as in the case of Pain and Vieillard's *Le Père d'occasion* (The Second-Hand Father, 1803), only eight months lay between the first French performance and the premiere of Kotzebue's translation *Der Vater von ungefähr* (The Father with No Intent).[14] Kotzebue even became acquainted with a number of the French writers whose works he adapted. During his second stay in Paris in 1804, for example, he met with Bouilly, Picard, Duval, and Andrieux.[15] And in some cases the exchange of ideas and texts went both ways: Kotzebue's *Graf Benjowsky* became the model for Alexandre Duval's and Adrien Boïeldieu's opera *Béniowski ou les exilés du Kamchattka* (Beniovski; or, the exiles of Kamchatka, 1800), whereas Kotzebue's *Der Verschwiegene wider Willen* (The Reluctant Secretive) inspired Georges Duval's *Une Journée à Versailles* (A Day at Versailles, 1814).[16]

Kotzebue's relation to English writers and plays, however, was far from being similarly close or intense. Although a lot of his plays were translated into English—most famously *Menschenhaß und Reue* (Misanthropy and Repentance, 1788) as *The Stranger*, *Das Kind der Liebe* (The Child of Love, 1790) as *Lovers' Vows*, and *Die Spanier in Peru* (The Spaniards in Peru, 1794) as *Pizarro*—making Kotzebue an enormous success on the English stage,[17] only two were based on English comedies: *Der Westindier* (1815)[18] on Richard Cumberland's *The West Indian* (1771)[19] and *Die eifersüchtige Frau* (1818)[20] on George Colman's *The Jealous Wife* (1761).[21] Again, in marked contrast to Kotzebue's strong interest in contemporary French drama, these two English plays were more than four decades old when he reworked them and had already been translated into German many years before.[22] What is more, at the time Kotzebue adapted Cumberland's and Colman's comedies in 1815 and 1818, Cumberland, born in 1732, had been dead since 1811 and Colman, also born in 1732, since 1794. Drawing on older French or English plays for inspiration was not uncommon for the German theater of the time.[23] But those few cases in which Kotzebue adopted and adapted English drama are conspicuous in their rarity and yet have been overlooked by scholarship to date. Notably, too, both adaptations were made after 1815 and therefore during a period in which Kotzebue assumed a decidedly conservative position with regard to the social and political issues of the day. Hence, turning to Kotzebue's treatment of English texts provides us with new insights into the later works of Germany's most successful playwright at the time and helps us to identify how he gave voice to his conservatism in this period. In the following, therefore, I shall analyze Kotzebue's approach to translating these two plays by Colman and Cumberland, illustrating the ways in which he harnesses certain aspects of the English comedies to his own conservative ends while radically effacing much of what he finds in the original texts. Indeed, the plays in their original forms both provided him with means to entertain his audiences, but any social or political progressiveness within them is undercut by his desire that his audiences are to be "belehrt . . . aber ohne große Anstrengung" (educated, but without great effort). Kotzebue's entire adult dramatic output—even discounting his translations and adaptations—demonstrates his awareness that theater can be used to political ends, and his adaptations and translations of French plays had provided him with means of doing so that would be fairly familiar to his diverse German public. Turning to these older, English comedies, however, presented him with ideas and contexts largely inaccessible to his German audiences and served his increased conservatism within the political landscape of Europe after 1815.

EMBRACING OLD-FASHIONED VALUES: *DER WESTINDIER*

The West Indian was one of Richard Cumberland's earlier plays. It was produced at Drury Lane, directed by David Garrick, and its first performance on January 19, 1771, was so successful that it ran for twenty-eight nights. According to Arthur Sherbo, Cumberland made £150 through the sale of the copyright and allegedly sold twelve thousand copies of it.[24] It was also, as Stanley T. Williams has pointed out, "the most discussed eighteenth century [*sic*] comedy of the sentimental school," with the main character Belcour being "at once one of the most censured and most popular of dramatic characters."[25] According to Williams, in the period from December 1779 to January 1805, it was performed another forty-eight times.[26] By turning to Cumberland and *The West Indian*, Kotzebue not only chose a writer with an extensive oeuvre of nearly fifty plays, but also—and probably more importantly—a comedy that had long proven its ability to attract and engage an audience.

Cumberland was no stranger to Germany—or to Kotzebue, for that matter: a handful of his plays had been translated into German between 1772 and 1798.[27] On February 29, 1776, the Weimar *Liebhabertheater* (private theater) under Goethe's directorship put on *The West Indian* with Goethe as Belfour and Charlotte von Stein as Miss Rusport in one of the earliest German performances of the piece, and it is likely that Kotzebue was a member of the audience. Aged only fifteen, Kotzebue visited as many theater performances in Weimar as possible; he and his family received regular visits by Goethe, and he had access to the performances of the *Liebhabertheater* in which not only his mother but, on November 21, 1776, he himself acted alongside Goethe in the very first performance of *Die Geschwister* (The Siblings).[28]

While the relationship between *Der Westindier* and Cumberland's original is to be considered in the following, it is worth noting that, long before 1815, Kotzebue may have drawn on Cumberland as a source for his own work. Lionel F. Thompson, for example, gives good reason to believe that a number of Kotzebue's English characters are based on or inspired by those of Cumberland's plays available in German at the time.[29] Kotzebue also may have been aware of the debate surrounding the first performance of Cumberland's *The Wheel of Fortune* on February 28, 1795, when Cumberland was accused of having pilfered his plot from Kotzebue's *Menschenhaß und Reue*, which was apparently in the manager's possession when *The Wheel of Fortune* was in production.[30] As the British writer, translator, and critic William Mudford observed at the time:

> The striking similarity between the chief incidents of the two plays, justified, indeed, this suspicion, and the author of the translation from Kotzebue openly accused Cumberland of having unfairly pirated from his work. This charge Cumberland has openly denied, and professed, I believe, that he took the hint of his own play from a review of the German one which he accidentally saw.[31]

Later, in 1800, Cumberland created an English version of Kotzebue's *Johanna von Montfaucon* (1799) for the London stage, relying on an English translation commissioned for him by the owners of the Covent Garden Theatre.[32] And when London reviews were not favorable, Kotzebue "hastened to disavow the trash grafted upon his stock, by a public address in the newspapers signed with his name," declaring that all parts that shocked the audience were additions by Cumberland.[33] This intervention may have been triggered by the fact that Kotzebue had just negotiated a contract with London theaters "for a regular supply of his newest manuscripts"[34] if and when he felt they could become successful in England.[35]

Cumberland's *The West Indian* focuses on the fate of two families: the Rusports and the Stockwells. In its "geradezu romanhaft verwickelte[r] Handlung" (utterly novel-like entangled plot) as Leonhard Herrmann describes it,[36] the successful merchant Mr. Stockwell is expecting a visit from Mr. Belcour—his secret son raised in Jamaica who is unaware of the identity of his real father—on a matter of business. Belcour, who has only recently inherited a significant fortune from his (surrogate) father, plans to settle in London. Here he accidentally runs into Louisa Dudley whose beauty instantly inflames Belcour with his first ever feelings of love. In addition, Belcour is not familiar with the conventions governing the interaction between members of the opposite sex: when he first encounters Louisa, for example, he follows her through the streets of London up to her home where he interviews her landlady about her; at the first opportunity, he confronts Louisa with a declaration of his love for her. In contrast to Belcour's wealthy background, Louisa is the daughter of Captain Dudley and sister of Charles Dudley, both honorable but poor men. They are related to the rich Lady Rusport, a hard-hearted woman with no inclination to provide Louisa's father with the two hundred pounds he urgently needs to return to military service in order to support himself and his two grown-up children. At the end of the play, the discovery of the hitherto unknown will of Lady Rusport's father, Sir Oliver Roundhead, awarding "his whole estate" not to Lady Rusport, as an earlier will had stated, but to her late sister's son, his "grandson, Charles Dudley," clears the way for a happy ending (*TWI*, IV, vi; 61): Charles is now able to marry his sweetheart Charlotte (a daughter from the first marriage of Lady Rusport's late husband), Belcour and Louisa get engaged, while Lady Rusport is duly punished for her lack of humanity and compassion when the will that she tries to destroy strips her of most of her wealth. Within this plot, there are three more characters that need to be mentioned: Mr. and Mrs. Fulmer, a couple of villains with a long history of fraud and deception, trying to take advantage of the fact that Belcour is caught wholly unprepared by their dishonesty; and the Irish Major Dennis O'Flaherty, constructed as a funny stock character, who has been a soldier for the last thirty years and is coarse but good-hearted.

Cumberland's play is characterized by its complicated plot structure. As Johann Jakob Engel derided it at the time: "Es hat zu viel Personen, zu viel Verwickelung, einen zu schwerfälligen Gang" (It has too many characters, is too entangled, moves too slowly).[37] That has as much to do with the fact that most of the characters are in one way or another related to each other, as with the accumulation of multiple character faults, misunderstandings, and the inability to listen to one another. Beyond that, the sentimental comedy punishes the immoral, rewards the decent and humble, and offers the audience many an occasion to laugh, be appalled, and be moved. If there is a unique element in this play, it lies with the character of Belfour and with the portrayal of the Irishman O'Flaherty. Tellingly, in terms of the play's relationship with its London audiences, Joseph Keenan describes what might have been exceptional about Belfour and O'Flaherty:

> The play has a serious moral purpose: to dispel the prejudice that existed against those British who lived in the West Indies and the long-standing prejudice against the Irish. Belcour is the most engaging of West Indians; although impetuous and improvident, he is never cruel. His blood may run too warm from the island sun, but his heart is open and sensitive to human virtue and suffering. Not only is he a man of feeling, but he is a laughable one. His fight with the customs officials over his menagerie proves funny because it illustrates Belcour's naiveté as well as the oversophistication of Londoners.[38]

In Keenan's eyes at least, Cumberland's play was politically fairly progressive in its original context. One might add that the portrayal of Belcour comes close to invoking the concept of the noble savage. As a man of best intentions and a naïve trust in his fellow men, to some extent at least Belcour resembles the idealized indigene, outsider, or "other" who has not been "corrupted" by civilization, and therefore symbolizes humanity's innate goodness. Any potentially radical political agenda on Cumberland's part is, however, undercut by one small detail: the noble savage in Cumberland's comedy is white, being the son of London businessman Stockwell and the daughter of an English "planter" (*TWI*, I, i; 8). His whiteness might have made him even more appealing to the English audiences, as in all his naiveté, in the end he is one of them: the politics of skin color could not therefore threaten his integration into society and thus preclude the final aim of this and most comedies. In addition, on a purely economic level, Cumberland exploited the attraction of English audiences to the exotic, something promised by Belcour's upbringing in the Caribbean.

For a German audience in 1815—the year Kotzebue adapted the play—the West Indies, life in a remote colony, and the world of overseas trade were as far away from their everyday reality as in 1771, when Cumberland's original premiered in London. Nevertheless, Kotzebue decided to settle for a close adaptation with changes mainly in detail, and hardly in substance or structure. He retained the five acts, kept all *dramatis personae* with their original names, and did not reduce the number of locations. The most visible alteration consisted in subdividing the five acts into a total of sixty-nine scenes where Cumberland only needed forty-five; with Kotzebue—and the German-speaking drama of the period in general—whenever a character leaves or enters the stage, one scene ends and the next begins. The alterations in Kotzebue's adaptation concern the streamlining of the conversations, abbreviating individual statements in order to create more dynamism in the dialogue. Cumberland opens the first act with the following scene:

> STUKLEY. He seems disordered: something in that letter; and I'm afraid of an unpleasant sort. He has many ventures of great account at sea; a ship richly freighted for Barcelona; another for Lisbon; and others expected from Cadiz of still greater value. Besides these, I know he has many deep concerns in foreign bottoms, and underwritings to a vast amount. I'll accost him. Sir! Mr. Stockwell!
>
> STOCK[WELL]. Stukely!—Well, have you ship'd the cloths?
>
> STUKLEY. I have, Sir; here's the bill of lading, and copy of the invoice: the assortments are all compared: Mr. Traffic will give you the policy upon 'Change.
>
> STOCK. 'Tis very well; lay these papers by; and no more of business for a while. Shut the door, Stukley; I have had long proof of your friendship and fidelity to me. A matter of most intimate concern lies on my mind, and 'twill be a sensible relief to unbosom myself to you. (*TWI*, I, i; 7)

Kotzebue transforms this into a livelier version:

> *Stockwell, in großer Bewegung einen Brief öffnend, Stuckley tritt ein.*
>
> STOCKW. (*ihn erblickend*) Sind Sie es, Stuckley? Das ist mir lieb, denn ich muß mein Herz erleichtern.
>
> STUCKL. Sie sind doch nicht in Unruhe wegen der gestrigen Börsennachrichten?

Stockw. Ganz und gar nicht.

Stuckl. Die waren falsch. Unsere reiche Ladung ist in Barcellona glücklich angelangt.

Stockw. Sehr wohl. —

Stuckl. Und das Schiff, welches wir nach Lissabon abgefertigt haben—

Stockw. Wird auch wohl glücklich anlangen.

Stuckl. Erlauben Sie, das hat conträren Wind gehabt.

Stockw. Lieber Stuckley! in meinem Leben segelt' ich noch nie mit so günstigem Winde.

Stuckl. Ei, ich dächte —

Stockw. Lassen wir jetzt unsere kaufmännischen Geschäfte. Denn fürwahr, Sie möchten Gewinn oder Verlust von Millionen mir zu melden haben, in diesem Augenblick könnte ich darüber mich weder freuen noch betrüben. (*DW*, I, i; 3–4)[39]

[*Stockwell, agitated, opens a letter. Stuckley enters.*

Stockw. (*catching sight of him*) Is that you, Stuckley? Oh, I am glad, I need to unburden my mind.

Stuckl. Surely, you are not still agitated over yesterday's stock exchange news?

Stockw. Not at all.

Stuckl. They were wrong. Our rich cargo has landed safely in Barcelona.

Stockw. Very well.—

Stuckl. And the ship, that we dispatched for Lisbon—

Stockw. It surely will also reach its destination.

Stuckl. Excuse me, it met with a headwind.

Stockw. Dear Stuckley! Never in my life have I sailed with such favourable a wind.

Stuckl. Well, I thought—

Stockw. Let's now put our commercial business aside. For in truth, you might have to report profits or losses by the millions, but at this very moment I would be neither able to celebrate nor to be saddened.]

Aside from making the dialogue more lively and dynamic, Kotzebue also occasionally adds references to specifics of German life. When Lady Rusport condemns her niece's education, for example, she remarks: "according to the modern stile of education you was brought up. It was not so in my young days; there was then some decorum in the world, some subordination, as the great Locke expresses it" (*TWI*, I, v; 14). Kotzebue has her say instead:

> Die Frau Mutter war eine Modedame, ließ das Töchterchen nach der neuesten Mode erziehn; ich glaube gar, Gott verzeih' mir die Sünde; sie nannten es elementarisch. Das ist nun auch wieder vorbei: jetzt werden die Kinder in die Schweiz geschickt, zu einem Manne, der die Pest in seinem Namen führt. Nein, das war es zu meiner Zeit ganz anders, da gab es noch Subordination und Decoration in der Welt, wie der große Locke es nennt. (*DW*, I, vi; 21).

> [Your mother was a lady of fashion, wanted her daughter educated according to the latest fashion. I even do believe, God may have mercy on me, that they called it elementary. But all that has passed. Nowadays children are sent to Switzerland to a man carrying the plague in his name. No, it was very different in my time: there was still subordination and decoration in the world, as the great Locke calls it.]

The allusions to German and Swiss educational reformers Johann Bernhard Basedow and his famous *Elementarwerk* (Elementary Work) from 1774 and Johann Heinrich Pestalozzi are obvious and mark—beyond the attempt to "Germanize" or "nationalize" the English text—Kotzebue's specifically conservative stance in the European Restoration following the Vienna Congress of 1814–1815. What might seem just a joke at the expense of heroes of the bygone age of reason by the author Kotzebue himself[40] also works to highlight ignorance as a character flaw of Lady Rusport. We must assume that Kotzebue knew earlier German translations of Cumberland's play, as he characterizes his translation on its title page: "aufs neue für die deutsche Bühne bearbeitet" (newly adapted for the German stage). In the scene quoted previously, for example, Kotzebue mistranslates Lady Rusport's educated reference to Locke and a lack of "decorum" in the present day with a lack of "Dekoration" (decoration); in the first German translation of *The West Indian* in 1772, however, Johann Joachim Christoph Bode had translated "decorum" correctly as "Decorum."[41] Yet Kotzebue's (obviously intended) "mistake" highlights a profound lack of understanding on Lady Rusport's part of the very issue she is grumbling about. Here two attitudes overlap: one that stands diametrically opposed to all that Kotzebue regards as too extreme or too exaggerated (here: educational reformers); the other against those people that violate his (predominantly Enlightenment) values.[42]

While Kotzebue makes some occasional changes to *The West Indian* to enliven the dialogue and to heighten the deficiencies of many of its characters, he rarely strays far from Cumberland's original. When translating Belcour's attempt to explain why his passion for Louisa arose so suddenly, for example, Kotzebue opts for presenting the selfsame vivid imagery of the original:

> BELCOUR: Oh, Sir, if this is folly in me, you must rail at Nature: you must chide the sun, that was vertical at my birth, and would not wink upon my nakedness, but swaddled me in the broadest, hottest glare of the meridian beams. (*TWI*, III, ii; 39)

In Kotzebue's version, this appears as:

> BELCOUR: Bin ich ein Narr, so ist's nicht meine Schuld, es ist die Schuld der Sonne, die bei meiner Geburt mir senkrecht auf den Kopf brannte und mich in das heiße Bad ihrer Mittagsstralen tauchte. (*DW*, III, iii; 82)
>
> [BELCOUR: If I am a fool, then it is not my fault but the fault of the sun, that burned vertically upon my head at my birth and immersed me in the warm bath of her midday rays.]

Here, Kotzebue favors a strategy of conveying the exact images depicted in Belcour's speech. One result of this is that Belcour's inability to restrain his passions is firmly credited to circumstances of nature that cannot be undone by nurture. No doubt, maintaining this presentation of Belcour in *Der Westindier* served Kotzebue's ambition to keep his version of the play entertaining and keep his characters clear-cut and unambiguous. To this extent, it is notable that one scene Kotzebue eliminated showed Dudley as a man of books, praising Laurence Sterne's *Tristram Shandy* (1759–1767) (*TWI*, II, ii; 20–21). As Kotzebue had quarreled with so many of his colleagues over the years, it is surprising that he passed on this opportunity to offer his audience yet another bit of his wisdom as a literary critic (cf. *DW*, II, ii; 38–42). But then again, as the moral hero of this work, Kotzebue apparently did not wish for Dudley to be even slightly comparable with Sterne's comical protagonist lest his moral integrity—and therefore the social stance of *Der Westindier*—be questioned by the audience.

As previously shown, with a few exceptions Kotzebue stays very close to Cumberland's English, with the result that his *Westindier* largely turns out to be a close translation. Yet it still has much to tell us about Kotzebue's work for the theater, his use of foreign (English) plays for his own political ends, and the treatment of foreign plays on the German stage in general. First of all, in 1815 the need for new plays had not diminished. Kotzebue would not have undertaken the translation had there not been a market for it. More importantly, though, Cumberland's *The West Indian* might have appeared to Kotzebue an appropriate play for his time: it is rich in funny and distinctive characters and uses long-established techniques to keep the audience attentive throughout every twist and turn of its complex plot. But if Cumberland had indeed attempted to "dispel the prejudice that existed against those British who lived in the West Indies," this attempt was no more relevant to German spectators in 1815 than it would have been for them when the play had been written in 1771. With its lack of colonial interests and possessions, German society was a far cry from that of Britain. Cumberland's politically progressive stance of accepting strange, exotic, and seemingly savage people was therefore bound to be lost on a German audience. One must assume that it was rather the appeal of the exotic[43] and the noble savage[44] that Kotzebue assumed would attract German audiences, and therefore partly guided his interest in the play. Above all, the old-fashionedness of Cumberland's play fitted Kotzebue's politically conservative agenda. At the end of *The West Indian* all villains receive "proper" punishment, "unnatural" family structures (e.g., the secret son) and all forms of "unnatural" behavior (e.g., the cold-hearted aunt) stand corrected, two couples become engaged, and central Enlightenment virtues prevail.[45] In short, order—of a very conservative, traditionalist sort—is restored on all levels, and even Belcour, who tries to blame his uncontrolled passion on nature, is disciplined in a most conservative way. Stockwell chides him, saying: "the libertine's familiar plea—Nature made us, 'tis true, but we are the responsible creators of our own faults and follies" (*TWI*, III, i; 39); later Belcour himself claims to be in need of a woman to keep him in line. In the final scenes of the play, he exclaims: "I beseech you, amiable Louisa, for the time to come, whenever you perceive me deviating into error or offence, bring only to my mind the Providence of this night, and I will turn to reason and obey" (*TWI*, V, viii; 83). These correctives and sentiments are reproduced in Kotzbue's translation.[46]

After years in which he had enthusiastically spoken about the need for freedom of the press, the constitution, and democracy, the Kotzebue of the years following the Napoleonic Wars acknowledged that he had been wrong all along, that in fact the monarchy had proven to be the most natural and benevolent form of government.[47] Thus we may not be wrong to read Kotzebue's translation of Cumberland's *The West Indian* as an expression of his new, post-1815 political beliefs as much as of his unchanged concepts of a popular theater to serve the best interest of his audiences as he defined it.

RE-APPROPRIATING OLD-FASHIONED FORM: *DIE EIFERSÜCHTIGE FRAU*

When Kotzebue was assassinated in Mannheim on March 23, 1819, by liberal student Karl Ludwig Sand, he was still leading the life of an active writer.

He regularly involved himself in the political debate of the day, not least through the medium of the Weimar-based *Literarisches Wochenblatt* (Literary Weekly) he had founded in 1818 and had been editing since. In its first issue he programmatically declared the socially conservative intentions of his didactic theater in an address "An den Leser" (To the Reader):

> Wer von diesem Blatte Erzählungen, Gedichte, gewöhnliche Theater-Nachrichten und dergl. sucht, der wird sie nicht finden; denn es ist blos bestimmt, Gedanken und Begebenheiten mitzutheilen, die der Zeitgeist gebahr; es soll dem gesunden Menschenverstande dienen; es soll die literarischen Gaukeleyen beleuchten, das Gute überall hervor heben, das Wunderliche verspotten, das Böse entlarven, es soll die Religion ehren, den Aberglauben bekämpfen; Vernunft und Redlichkeit in Schutz nehmen, doch den Anstand nicht verletzen.[48]

> [He who expects short stories, poems, trivial theater news, and suchlike, will not find it here; for this [weekly paper] aims only to communicate ideas and occurrences born by the Zeitgeist. Its purpose is to serve common sense, to shed light on literary shenanigans, to foreground the good everywhere, to ridicule the fantastic, to unmask the evil. It intends to honour religion, fight superstition; to come to reason's and honesty's defence, without doing harm to decency.]

Beside his journalistic undertakings, Kotzebue kept writing and publishing for the stage. In particular he continued his *Almanach Dramatischer Spiele zur geselligen Unterhaltung auf dem Lande* (Almanac of Dramatic Plays Designed for the Convivial Entertainment in the Countryside): the seventeenth volume had just been released near the end of 1818. And Kotzebue was already writing and collecting texts for the eighteenth edition at the time he was murdered.

The first of the three plays that were published in the posthumous eighteenth volume of the *Almanach*—the *Almanach* often contained up to six pieces in each edition—was *Die eifersüchtige Frau*, a comedy in two acts based, as Kotzebue points out in the subheading, on an English play. *Die eifersüchtige Frau*, as Kotzebues publisher Paul Gotthelf Kummer notes, had premiered, still in its author's lifetime and even in his presence, to great acclaim at the national theater at Mannheim.[49] Kummer, the editor of this last *Almanach,* insists that *Die eifersüchtige Frau* will prove a lively and therefore most welcome acquisition for every private and public stage.[50] Such a prediction, however, seems remarkable considering that Kotzebue's source, Colman's *The Jealous Wife*, had had its first performance more than fifty years before in 1761. George Colman, a London theater manager and a playwright, had only just seen the publication and performance of his first play in 1760, when one year later his *Jealous Wife* became a success at London's Drury Lane theater. Despite finding its way to the stage over half way through the 1760–1761 theater season, it achieved a run of nineteen performances in its first season and a further fifty-four before Garrick's departure in 1776; between 1776 and 1800, it was performed another seventy times.[51]

In an advertisement for his play, Colman revealed that in writing the play he had relied heavily on the literary works of others, just as Kotzebue would later rely on Colman:

> The Use that has been made in this Comedy of *Fielding*'s admirable Novel of *Tom Jones*, must be obvious to the most ordinary Reader. Some Hints have also been taken from the Account of Mr. and Mrs. *Freeman*, in N°. 212, and N°. 216, of the *Spectator*; and the short Scene of *Charles*'s Intoxication, at the End fo the Thrid Act, is partly an Imitation of the Behaviour of *Syrus*, much in the same Circumstances, in the *Adelphi* of *Terence*. There are also some Traces of the Character of the Jealous Wife, in one of thee latter Papers of the *Connoisseur*.[52]

Colman expresses his gratitude to Garrick, who, as Colman points out, inspected the comedy "in its first rude State" and offered detailed advice "relating both to the Fable and Characters."[53] Both—Garrick's involvement and the play's success—one may surmise, could have been a reason for Kotzebue to want to subject this play to a closer reading. After all, it was clearly able to draw in audiences. And there were more similarities between Cumberland's *The West Indian* and Colman's *The Jealous Wife*: Colman, like Cumberland, constructed his comedy as a five-act play set in London—again, both are *Eheanbahnungsstücke*—and although Colman restricted himself to three locations, the plot structure had at least as many strands and was at least as multilayered as Cumberland's, if not more complex.

In Colman's play Harriot Russet, daughter of Mr. Russet, is about to be married by her father to Sir Harry Beagle, "the richest man in the county" (*TJW*, VI, ii; 69). However, she is determined not to obey, not least because she is in love with young Charles Oakly whom she met at the countryside residence of Major Oakly, Charles's uncle. She secretly escapes to London where Charles is living and triggers a complex chain of events. In fact, Colman's comedy not so much combines one main plot with a number of subplots, but rather interweaves a number of equally significant plots and stories. First there is Mrs. Oakly, the jealous wife, whose doubts regarding her husband's fidelity have long since bordered on the pathological and turned Mr. Oakly's life into living hell. Secondly, we have Lady Freelove, a puffed-up representative of what she calls "Persons of Fashion" (*TJW*, II, iii; 33), "Men of Quality" (*TJW*, II, iii; 33), and "Persons of Quality" (*TJW*, II, iii; 35), acquainted with "the World" (*TJW*, II, iii; 31), rich enough—as the play illustrates—to be beyond the law, but naturally immoral and "mischievous as a Monkey" (*TJW*, I, i; 20). Lady Freelove is accompanied by Lord

Trinket, again a "person of fashion" and "quality," introducing French in his speech wherever he can (*TJW*, II, iii; 34–35). But he does more than just plot like Lady Freelove; he, in fact, attempts to rape Harriot on stage (*TJW*, II, iii; 37–38). Only marginally less disagreeable is Sir Harry Beagle, an exaggerated caricature of a racehorse lover, whose motivation to marry Harriot is basically an ambition to get his hands on more money and therefore more racehorses (*TJW*, II, i; 24). Consequently, he compares everything (including women) to horses (*TJW*, II, i; 24–26 and IV, ii; 67). Finally, we have Charles Oakly, Harriot's lover whom, in the end, she marries. While he does indeed save her from Trinket's attempted rape (*TJW*, II, ii; 38), he twice disappoints her severely by drinking so heavily as to lose control over himself (*TJW* I, i; 18–19 and III, ii; 57–58), raising serious doubts as to whether he is proper marriage material after all.

Alcoholism, rape, arrogance, and the immorality of the upper classes, as well as the single-mindedness of the racehorse lover, are serious issues brought to the stage in Colman's play. Only one among the many issues addressed in it is that of the overly jealous wife. At the end, the play suggests that Charles and Mrs. Oakly have learned from their mistakes and will no longer be prone to jealousy or alcoholism. The other morally dubious characters are simply banished from the Oakly family's life.

Given the moral depravity depicted within it, we might ask what could have attracted Kotzebue to *The Jealous Wife* to the degree that he would produce a German version of it. We find some answer in Kotzebue's introduction to the play, published in Kummer's posthumous edition of *Die eifersüchtige Frau*:

Das alte englische Lustspiel, aus welchem ich die Scene der Eifersucht, und sonst nichts, entlehnt habe, und dessen Verfasser mir unbekannt ist, hat fünf Acte und nicht weniger als siebzehn Personen, wimmelt von Abgeschmacktheiten und nicht selten auch von Unanständigkeiten; wovon deutsche Leser sich überzeugen können, wenn sie den achten Band der Wiener Schaubühne (1770) nachzuschlagen sich bemühen wollen. Die lebendige, wiewohl übertriebene, Schilderung des Hauptcharacters verdiente wohl gerettet und gesichtet zu werden. Uebrigens hat das Einschmelzen in zwei Acte große Veränderungen nöthig gemacht. So wie es nun ist, schmeichle ich mir, daß es unterhalten werde, zumal es sich ganz zu einem Gesellschaftsspiel im Zimmer eignet, indem es gar keiner scenischen Vorbereitungen bedarf (*DEF*, 3).

[The old English comedy, from which I have taken the jealousy scene only and nothing else, and whose author is unknown to me, has five acts and no less than seventeen *dramatis personae*. It abounds with tastelessness and not seldom of indecencies too, of which German readers can assure themselves by making the effort to look up the eighth volume of the Viennese Playhouse from 1770. The vivid, albeit exaggerated portrayal of the main character deserved to be saved and inspected. By the bye, reducing it all to two acts made comprehensive changes necessary. The way it is now, I dare flatter myself, it will entertain, especially since it is perfectly suited for a parlour-game in the sitting room where no stage setting is needed.]

Seemingly serving the ends of entertainment and making the play performable in one space, Kotzebue condensed Colman's play in a number of respects. He reduced it to two acts set in only one location—a sitting room—with eight instead of eighteen characters, and he eliminated every element of the play beyond the plot of the excessively jealous wife and her reform. He also changed the remaining characters' names. While Colman had used telling names (Sir Harry Beagle, Lady Freelove, the French servant named Paris, Captain O'Culler, Lord Trinket), Kotzebue gives his characters uninformative names: Herr and Frau von Uhlen meet family von Bosen. As far as the plot concerned with matrimonial jealousy is concerned, however, Kotzebue stays true to his original. Even the intensity of Mrs. von Uhlen's jealousy—so intense to involve "Thränen, Krämpfe, Ohnmachten" (*DEF*, I, iv; 19; tears, fits, and fainting)—has been adopted from the original.

The changes Kotzebue made to Colman's play were clearly designed to render it both easier to play and easier to follow. But in his sweeping changes to the plot structures of *The Jealous Wife*, we can also recognize his political and social conservatism asserting itself. Indeed, once stripped of its "Abgeschmacktheiten" and "Unanständigkeiten" (tastelessness and obscenities) what Kotzebue saw and liked in Colman's play and what he then formed into his *Die eifersüchtige Frau* is that at its heart it is both structurally and morally an old-fashioned *Besserungsstück* (play of improvement). Strongly promoted by Johann Christoph Gottsched in 1730 in his *Versuch einer critischen Dichtkunst vor die Deutschen* (Essay on a Critical Poetics for the Germans), the *Besserungsstück* had its first heyday in the 1730s and 1740s. Distinguishing Kotzebue's *Eifersüchtige Frau* from these predecessors, however, are numerous specific allusions and references to the European Restoration era, often expressing Kotzebue's own conservative convictions. Mr. von Uhlen for example, reacting to his wife's irrationality and—alluding to Franz Anton Mesmer's highly controversial theories of animal magnetism that were, however, popular with the romantics Kotzebue liked to polemize against—moans: "Wenn ich nur magnetisiren könnte, ich wollte sie calmiren" (*DEF*, I, i; 7: If only I could magnetize her, I would surely calm her). Mrs. von Uhlen ponders publishing a harmless letter to her husband as proof of his infidelity: "Diesen Brief lass' ich drucken! . . . ins Morgenblatt, ins Abendblatt, in die Zeitung für die elegante Welt!" (*DEF*, I, i; 13: I'll have this letter published! In the morning paper, in the evening paper, in the Weekly for the Elegant World), a direct reference to the Leipzig-based *Zeitung für die elegante Welt*, against which Kotzebue had fought one of his many private feuds in 1803.[54] *Die eifersüchtige Frau* also includes invectives against a "Wunderdoktor in Schlesien" (a quack in Silesia) named Richter (*DEF*, I, ix; 36–37) and the *Turnerbewegung* (*DEF* I, ix; 38), the nationalistic gymnastics movement most popular among the student movement Kotzebue fought against. Other allusions—to (false) rumors that Wellington had been shot at in Paris (*DEF*, I, ix; 43) or to the famous "Eau de Cologne" (*DEF*, II, v; 63)—served no further purpose than to give this comedy a contemporary feel.

RESTORING THE PUBLIC AND PRIVATE SPACE AFTER 1815

The two English plays that Kotzebue adapted for the German stage have, in some respects, much in common. When we consider Kotzebue's desire to write plays that would both entertain and discreetly educate his audiences, it is not surprising that the two plays he chose from Colman and Cumberland had already proven their box office success. Added to that, as Kotzebue himself became ever firmer in his social and political conservatism, he selected two older English plays that, being of their time, expressed a traditional worldview. Both promised to entice audiences into the theater without encouraging radical views. Kotzebue could, in fact, eradicate Cumberland's politically progressive message through bringing this play to a culture in which the exotic figure of the British colonialist was bound to be alien (and certainly comical) to a German audience; and his alterations (albeit minor) to Cumberland's text demonstrate just how he considered himself able to draw his audiences to the German social context of the European Restoration and to focus them on what constitutes morally—and therefore politically—good or bad behavior. In the case of Colman's even older play, Kotzebue shows himself to be a tried and tested master of dramatic adaptation: his work on *The Jealous Wife* boils Colman's complex play down to a simple, digestible whole, again with a socially and politically conservative agenda. As both of these adaptations were undertaken in the years between 1815 and 1819, they serve as examples of Kotzebue's use of foreign plays to engage his German audiences in the turmoil of their day: in his view, eighteenth-century English values and dramatic forms therefore had a place—once suitably adapted—in a conservative conception of Germany.

As the example of Kotzebue's adaptation of Colman's *The Jealous Wife* shows, however, Kotzebue's own political agenda was to be all-pervading. He decided that *Die eifersüchtige Frau* should appear in his *Almanach Dramatischer Spiele zur geselligen Unterhaltung auf dem Lande,* in which he published plays meant to be presented without actors: these were plays to be performed by ordinary citizens in their free time and in their sitting room in front of friends and family as a pastime, or in other words, as theater on location and without actors.[55] There was, of course, a clear economic drive behind this, as Kotzebue wanted his *Almanach* to find its way into any number of homes and for any number of occasions. He poses the rhetorical question in his general preface to the *Almanach*:

> Wie nun, wenn ich dem Publikum nach und nach eine Anzahl kleiner Stücke oder Scenen lieferte, bald rührend, bald lustig oder possenhaft? Stücke, zu welchen man nur vier oder fünf Personen und ein paar spanische Wände nöthig hätte? die man in zwei Tagen vertheilen, lernen und aufführen könnte? die zum Theil auch von Kindern an Geburtstagen ihrer Eltern gespielt werden möchten?[56]

> [What now, if I offered the audience little by little a number of minor plays or scenes, sometimes sentimental, sometimes amusing or farcical? Plays, easily staged with just four or five individuals and a few folding screens? Where parts could be assigned, learned and performed within two days? Which in part could be presented by children at their parents' birthdays?]

These were plays for every occasion and every private person. That rape, alcoholism, or crimes by the upper classes remained unpunished in Colman's original play was obviously not suited for this specific model of private theater, where otherwise a father might have ended up acting out the attempted rape of his daughter. Indeed, it would appear that the form of theater Kotzebue had chosen for his adaptation of *The Jealous Wife* necessitated the changes he was to make to it. If, as we see in *Der Westindier*, the right and traditional relationships between members of a family—like those between members of a state—were to prevail, then dramatic decorum was required just as much as moral probity.

NOTES

1. See, for details, Johannes Birgfeld, Julia Bohnengel, and Alexander Košenina, eds., *Kotzebues Dramen: Ein Lexikon* (Hannover: Wehrhahn, 2011).

2. See Franz Hadamowsky, *Die Josefinische Theaterreform und das Spieljahr 1776/77 des Burgtheaters: Eine Dokumentation* (Wien: Verband der Wissenschaftlichen Gesellschaften Österreichs, 1978), 14–15.

3. It is perhaps interesting to note that the phenomenon of the *Vielschreiber* was so well established that the term itself was also common currency at the time.

4. See Gero von Wilpert, "Kurz, Joseph Felix von," in *Deutsches Dichterlexikon*, Gero von Wilpert, third edition (Stuttgart: Kröner, 1988), 472.

5. See Mark-Georg Dehrmann and Alexander Košenina, eds., *Ifflands Dramen: Ein Lexikon* (Hannover: Wehrhahn, 2009).

6. The estimates regarding the scale of Gleich's, Meisl's, and Bäuerle's dramatic production follow Jürgen Hein, *Das Wiener Volkstheater*, third ed. (Darmstadt: Wissenschaftliche Buchgesellschaft, 1997), 44–45.

7. For a more detailed exploration of the concept of an "aesthetic of professionalism" as opposed to an "aesthetic of autonomy and originality," see Johannes Birgfeld and Claude D. Conter, "Das Unterhaltungsstück um 1800: Funktionsgeschichtliche und gattungstheoretische Vorüberlegungen," in *Das Unterhaltungsstück um 1800. Literaturhistorische Konfigurationen—Signaturen der Moderne*, ed. Johannes Birgfeld and Claude D. Conter (Hannover: Wehrhahn, 2007), vii–xxiv, (especially xvii); and Johannes Birgfeld, "Medienrevolution und gesellschaftlicher Wandel: Das Unterhaltungstheater als Reflexionsmedium von Modernisierungsprozessen," in Birgfeld and Conter, *Das Unterhaltungsstück*, 81–117.

8. August von Kotzebue, *Fragmente über den Recensenten-Unfug: Eine Beylage zu der Jenaer Literaturzeitung* (Leipzig: Kummer, 1797), 69–70.

9. See, for a more detailed account, Julia Bohnengel, "Die Sparbüchse," in Birgfeld, Bohnengel, and Košenina, *Kotzebues Dramen*, 202–03.

10. See, for more details, Johannes Birgfeld, "Der Educations-Rath," in Birgfeld, Bohnengel, and Košenina, *Kotzebues Dramen*, 54–55.

11. See, for more details, Johannes Birgfeld, "Das zugemauerte Fenster," in Birgfeld, Bohnengel, and Košenina, *Kotzebues Dramen*, 251–52.

12. This is the case with his plays *Fanchon, das Leyermädchen, Die hübsche kleine Putzmacherin, Die Sparbüchse, Der Taubstumme, Die beiden kleinen Auvergnaten, Die Rosen des Herrn von Malesherbes*, and *Der fürstliche Wildfang oder Fehler und Lehre*. For details, see the corresponding entries in Birgfeld, Bohnengel, and Košenina, *Kotzebues Dramen*.

13. These plays are *Eduard in Schottland, oder die Nacht eines Flüchtlings* and *Der Gefangene*.

14. See Julia Bohnengel, "Der Vater von ungefähr," in Birgfeld, Bohnengel, and Košenina, *Kotzebues Dramen*, 230–31.

15. See August von Kotzebue, *Erinnerungen aus Paris im Jahre 1804. Zwey Abtheilungen*, two volumes (Karlsruhe: [no publisher], 1804), volume 1, 231–32, and volume 2, 260–61.

16. See, for details, Ulrike Leuschner, "Graf Benjowski," and Johannes Birgfeld, "Der Verschwiegene wider Willen," both in Birgfeld, Bohnengel, and Košenina, *Kotzebues Dramen*, 87–89 and 237–38, respectively.

17. For a survey of research on the "*Kotzebue-mania* that spread across England" after 1798, see Carlotta Farese, "The Strange Case of Herr von K: Further Reflections on the Reception of Kotzebue's Theatre in Britain," in *The Romantic Stage: A Many-Sided Mirror*, ed. Lilla Maria Crisafulli and Fabio Liberto (Amsterdam: Rodopi, 2014), 74 and 75n10. A list of studies dealing with Kotzebue's success in other European countries is provided by Bärbel Fritz, "Kotzebue in Wien: Eine Erfolgsgeschichte mit Hindernissen," in *Theaterinstitution und Kulturtransfer II: Fremdkulturelles Repertoire am Gothaer Hoftheater und an anderen Bühnen*, ed. Anke

Detken, Brigitte Schultze, Horst Turk, and Thorsten Unger (Tübingen: Narr, 1998), 135n2. A list of the thirty-six plays that were translated into English "in the course of 46 years" of which "22 were produced" is given by Lionel F. Thompson in *Kotzebue: A survey of his progress in France, and England, preceded by a consideration of the critical attitude to him in Germany* (Paris: Champion, 1928), 58.

18. August von Kotzebue, *Der Westindier: Ein Lustspiel in fünf Akten von Cumberland. Aufs neue für die deutsche Bühne bearbeitet* (Leipzig: Kummer, 1815), hereafter quoted in the body of the text as "*DW.*" Act and scene numbers are followed by page number.

19. Because it is unknown which edition of Cumberland's play Kotzebue might have used, I shall be referring to what apparently is the first edition: [Richard Cumberland], *The West Indian: A Comedy. As it is performed at the Theatre Royal in Drury-Lane.* A new edition (London: [no publisher], 1771), henceforth cited in the body of this essay as "*TWI.*"

20. August von Kotzebue, *Die eifersüchtige Frau*, in: August von Kotzbue, *Almanach Dramatischer Spiele zur geselligen Unterhaltung auf dem Lande*, eighteen volumes (Leipzig: Kummer, 1803–1820), volume 18, 1–94, henceforth quoted in the body of the text as "*DEF.*"

21. Because it is unknown which edition of the play Kotzebue used, I shall quote from one of the first editions: George Colman, *The Jealous Wife. A Comedy: As it is Acted at the Theatre Royal in Drury Lane* (Dublin: Printed for A. Leathly, G. and A. Ewing, [. . .], 1761), henceforth quoted in the body of the text as "*TJW.*"

22. The earliest translations in both cases appear to have been by Johan Joachim Christoph Bode: Richard Cumberland, *Die eifersüchtige Ehefrau, ein Lustspiel in 5 Aufz., aus dem Engl. durch B.—* (Hamburg: Bohn, 1764); and Richard Cumberland, *Der Westindier ein Lustspiel in fünf Handlungen aus dem Englischen des Herrn Cumberland.* (Hamburg: Bode, 1772).

23. As Germany for most of the eighteenth century trailed England and France in a number of economic and social areas, plays from France and England often focused on issues years and sometimes decades before they became relevant to a German audience. Hence in 1784 Friedrich Ludwig Schröder, to name but one instance, could very successfully stage his farce *Die Heurath durch ein Wochenblatt*, an adaptation of Edmé Boursaults's *Le Mercure Galant* (The Gallant Mercury) from 1683. See, for more details, Birgfeld, "Medienrevolution und gesellschaftlicher Wandel."

24. Arthur Sherbo, "Cumberland, Richard (1732–1811)," in *Oxford Dictionary of National Biography*, online edition May 2006, accessed June 18, 2016, http://www.oxforddnb.com/view/article/6888.

25. Stanley T. Williams, "Richard Cumberland's West Indian," *Modern Language Notes* 35, no. 7 (1920): 413–14.

26. Williams, "Richard Cumberland's West Indian," 417.

27. See Thompson, *Kotzebue*, 83n1.

28. See Peter Kaeding, *August von Kotzebue: Auch ein deutsches Dichterleben* (Berlin: Union Verlag, 1985), 12–22; and Gisela Sichardt, *Das Weimarer Liebhabertheater unter Goethes Leitung* (Weimar: Arion, 1957), 135, 140.

29. See Thompson, *Kotzebue*, 82–84.

30. Thomas Joseph Campbell, *Richard Cumberland's The Wheel of Fortune. A Critical Edition* (London and New York: Garland, 1987), 25.

31. William Mudford, *The Life of Richard Cumberland, Esq. Embracing a critical examination of his various writings* (London: Squire, 1812), 553. Regarding the mutual influences Kotzebue and Cumberland might have had on each other, see also Campbell, *Richard Cumberland's The Wheel of Fortune*, 79–81.

32. Walter Sellier, *Kotzebue in England: Ein Beitrag zur Geschichte der englischen Bühne und der Beziehungen der deutschen Litteratur zur englischen* (Leipzig: Schmidt, 1901), 65.

33. Cf. Sellier, *Kotzebue in England*, 71.

34. Thomas Dutton, *The Wise Man of the East, or, The Apparition of Zoroaster, the Son of Oromases to the Theatrical Midwife of Leicester Fields. A Satirical Poem, in Four Parts*, second edition (London: J. Fricker 1800), III.

35. Cf. Sellier, *Kotzebue in England*, 63. This deal also explains why *Das Schreibepult* was first performed not in German but in London in Elizabeth Inchbald's English translation as *The Wise Man of the East*. See Sellier, *Kotzebue in England*, 60.

36. Leonhard Herrmann, "Der Westinidier," in Birgfeld, Bohnengel, and Košenina, *Kotzebues Dramen*, 246.

37. See Johann Jakob Engel, "Der Westindier. Ein Lustspiel in fünf Handlungen," in *Allgemeine deutsche Bibliothek: Anhang zu dem dreyzehnten bis vier und zwanzigsten Bande der allgemeinen deutschen Bibliothek. Zweyte Abtheilung* (Berlin and Stettin: Friedrich Nicolai, 1777), 1144.

38. Joseph J. Keenan Jr., "Richard Cumberland," in *Restoration and Eighteenth-Century Dramatists: Third Series (Dictionary of Literary Biography* 89), ed. Paula R. Backschneider (Detroit: Gale, 1989), 106–26.

39. In contrast to Kotzebue's adaptation, Bode's 1772 translation followed Cumberland's text closely (cf. in this case: Cumberland, *Der Westindier*, 1–2).

40. See for another humorous reckoning of the education revolutions of the late eighteenth century, associated with names like Basedow, Salzmann, and Pestalozzi, Kotzebue's *Der Educations-Rath*, also first performed in 1815 only a few weeks after *Der Westindier*. (Cf. for details: Birgfeld, *Der Educations-Rath*).

41. Cumberland, *Der Westindier*, 20.

42. It seems quite typical for the solitary position Kotzebue chose on most issues for most of his life, that he engaged to defend those educational reformers—he otherwise liked to ridicule—when they came under attack by those Kotzebue himself disliked, like the members of student patriotic fraternities or the *Turnerbewegung*—as in the first issue of 1818 of his *Literarisches Wochenblatt* (August von Kotzebue, "Die edle Turnerkunst," *Literarisches Wochenblatt* 2, no. 1 (1818): 1.

43. Bärbel Fritz has emphasized Kotzebue's tendency to include elements of foreign, "exotic" cultures (Fritz, "Erfolgsgeschichte," 137, 142, 145–46), suggesting that he appreciated in particular their potential as a projection screen to his audiences' suppressed desires as much as a means to generate moments of irritation among his spectators (137).

44. Kotzebue more than once uses the concept of the noble savage. See Fritz, "Erfolgsgeschichte," 146.

45. Quite telling in this regard is Bode's introduction to his 1772 translation of *The West Indian*, in which he praises, how "der Major, und auch Andre, das so heraus sagten, was der liebe Gott in den Grund der Herzen gelegt hat, ich meyne, Menschlichkeit und Mitleiden mit seinen Nebengeschöpfen, und Unwillen über Boßheit" (the major and others spoke bluntly what dear God had laid on the ground of their hearts, I mean: humanity and empathy with one's fellow beings, and dislike of cursedness). Cumberland, *Der Westindier*, unpaginated dedication.

46. Kotzebue's translation of the latter, for example, reads: "nur Sie können mich heilen! erbarmen Sie sich meiner! vertrauen Sie mir! es ist unmöglich, in Ihren Armen ein schlechter Mensch zu seyn" (*DW*, V, vi; 178: Only you can cure me! Have mercy on me! Have trust in me! In your arms, it is impossible to be wretched).

47. Cf., for example, Kaeding, *Kotzebue*, 275–81.

48. August von Kotzebue, "An die Leser," *Literarisches Wochenblatt* 1, no. 1 (1818): 1.

49. Paul Gotthelf Kummer, "Vorrede," in Kotzebue, *Almanach*, volume 18, vi. This claim, however, cannot be verified based on the surviving records. Oscar Fambach instead gives January 15, 1822, as the first performance at the Mannheim Hof- and Nationaltheater: cf. Oscar Fambach, *Das Repertorium des Hof- und Nationaltheaters in Mannheim 1804–1832* (Bonn: Bouvier, 1980), 308.

50. Kummer, "Vorrede," vi: "Die zwei ersten Stücke, von denen No. I. noch bei des Verfassers Leben und in dessen Gegenwart, mit großem Beifalle zu Mannheim aufgeführt worden ist, werden für jede Privat- und öffentliche Bühne in ihrer Lebendigkeit eine sehr willkommene Acquisition seyn" (The first two plays—of which the first gained great applause when it was performed in Mannheim, when the author was still alive and was present at the performance—will be a very welcome acquisition for every private and public theater for their spiritedness).

51. "The Jealous wife," in *British Dramatists from Dryden to Sheridan*, ed. Arthur E. Case, George G. Nettelton, and George Winchester Stone, second edition (Carbondale, IL: Southern Illinois University Press, 1975), 669.

52. Case, Nettelton, and Stone, *British Dramatists*, 670.

53. Case, Nettelton, and Stone, *British Dramatists*, 670.

54. Cf. Kaeding, *Kotzebue*, 224.

55. For further detail, see Johannes Birgfeld, "Theater ohne Schauspieler? Theatre on location? Kotzebues Konzept dramatischer Spiele zur geselligen Unterhaltung auf dem Lande mit Blick auf sein Verhältnis zum Publikum," in *"Das Theater glich einem Irrenhause". Das Publikum im Theater des 18. und 19. Jahrhunderts*, ed. Hermann Korte (Heidelberg: Winter 2012), 193–214.

56. August von Kotzebue, "Vorrede zu dem Almanache dramatischer Spiele" in August von Kotzbue, *Theater*, volume 14 (Leipzig and Vienna: Kummer and Klang, 1841), 177–78.

Chapter Five

Surveying Shakespeare's Impact on German Drama

Taking a Computational Approach to an Epoch

Nils Reiter and Marcus Willand

In this chapter, we study formal similarities between the plays of William Shakespeare and plays written by German authors between 1731 and 1804, with a focus on the playwrights of the *Sturm und Drang* (Storm and Stress).[1] The aim of this examination is to achieve a better understanding of the structural composition of a large number of plays. Even though Shakespeare's influence on German playwriting might be one of the most widely studied areas of Anglo-German literary studies,[2] thus far, very few quantitative analyses have been conducted in this field. Early quantitative studies were based on statistical material about the frequency and course of translations.[3] Yet not only metadata can be subjected to quantitative analysis. More recently, scholars such as Tom Cheeseman have turned their attention to quantitative analysis of translations of Shakespeare's plays. In his project "Visualising Version Variation: Case Study on Translations of Shakespeare's Othello," Cheeseman shows how large quantities of translations reflect cultural changes and individual intentions.[4]

In this chapter, we want to illustrate that content-related information such as poetological claims about playwriting (e.g., by German playwrights themselves) equally can be identified and operationalized as measurable aspects that testify to Shakespeare's influence. Through this, we seek to demonstrate that quantitative analysis offers approaches to this seminal moment in Anglo-German cultural exchange throughout the Sattelzeit, which undermine or challenge some of the central claims about the poetics of the period. Specifically, as we will show, our computational analysis questions the degree to which the dramatists of the *Sturm und Drang* really were the innovative iconoclasts of the age: judging by the structural criteria we have operationalized here, they come off as arguably more conservative than some of their peers with respect to their adherence to a particular set of rules. In turn, perhaps a computational approach might have further insights for us when studying the impact of single authors in intercultural dialogue at the time.

Generally, the question of the influence and impact of an author, a genre, or a nation's literature of a specific time span gave rise to a larger number of scholarly works that we would consider as early results of the growing discipline now known as Digital Humanities. Much of this scholarship follows ideas popularized by Franco Moretti, whereby large numbers of literary texts can be analyzed quantitatively, and graphs and diagrams drawn using these data are understood to disclose new insights about the developments of literary forms.[5] Moretti's form of so-called distant reading replaces the practice of close reading by selecting a number of characteristics that are then sought out in a corpus of possibly thousands of texts. And this necessarily very distant perspective that a scholar has to take when studying the system(s) of World Literature and/or unreadably large numbers of digitized books also resulted in methodological innovations.[6] This paper combines the methodologies of literary studies and digital humanities to enrich the critical discourse about Shakespeare's influence on German playwrights by studying a large corpus of plays. The ongoing discussion in the digital humanities about appropriate computational methods will be amplified and contextualized in terms of controversies involving historical concepts of dramatic form and function. We aim to make use of the new methodologies of computational literary studies while maintaining a critical attitude with regard to these tools. This entails not putting blind trust in statistical methods but inspecting findings critically and validating them against reasonable expectations that are often derived by conventionalized knowledge in a certain field of studies. In order to be transparent about methodological limitations and potential error sources, we include discussion about relevant methodological issues and considerations. Results will therefore mostly be presented in the form of visualizations with accompanying discussions. While it might take time to get used to this kind of visualization, it allows readers to follow and to be critical about the findings we highlight in the discussions.

Specifically, this chapter compares Shakespeare's plays with sixty-eight plays from four distinct phases of the history of German drama, some of which are allegedly influenced by Shakespeare while others are not (see Table 5.1). The 104 plays of our corpus are therefore divided into five subcorpora:

1. Shakespeare's own writings: thirty-eight plays, translated by Friedrich Schlegel and Ludwig Tieck[7]
2. *Frühaufklärung*: twenty-two plays from the Early Enlightenment, written between 1730 and 1749

3. *Populäre Stücke*: twelve popular plays, mainly by August von Kotzebue and August Wilhelm Iffland, from 1784 to 1802
4. *Sturm und Drang*: twenty-three plays by Johann Wolfgang von Goethe, Heinrich Wilhelm von Gerstenberg, Friedrich Maximilian Klinger, Johann Anton Leisewitz, Jakob Michael Reinhold Lenz, Friedrich Schiller, and Heinrich Leopold Wagner, written between 1768 and 1787
5. *Weimarer Klassik*: eleven plays written by Goethe and Schiller between 1776 and 1804 that are viewed as being part of Weimar Classicism

In choosing these subcorpora, we set out to have sufficient cases and categories to visualize the assumed influence of Shakespeare on *Sturm und Drang* playwrights. We therefore set up a corpus of plays written and published earlier (*Frühaufklärung*) and one written and published later (*Weimarer Klassik*) than the period in question. The subcorpus of popular plays functions as a corrective in many ways: it includes well-known and often-performed plays in the period from 1784 to 1802, which means that they are contemporary to both the plays of *Sturm und Drang* and *Weimarer Klassik*. Those popular plays are less canonical and represent different dramatic genres. While most plays in our subcorpora of German plays are tragedies (*Tragödien, Trauerspiele*), the popular plays are comedies (six out of twelve are *Lustspiele*) or neither (*Schauspiele*, i.e., simply "dramas," or *Familien-* and *Sittengemälde*, i.e., portraits of families or manners). Table 5.1 at the end of this chapter provides a complete list of the texts in question. We will extract a number of formal, structural, and linguistic properties for each play in each subcorpus and look at the overall position of the selected property as well as its spread within the subcorpus.

POETICS FROM GOTTSCHED TO GOETHE

Before examining the corpus itself, it is worth outlining the poetological basis against which it is to be tested. It is well established in scholarship that Shakespeare was rejected in the first half of the eighteenth century because his work did not meet the requirements of rule-based drama. It is equally well known that this rejection was reversed with the emergence of the poets and playwrights associated with the *Sturm und Drang*.[8] Gotthold Ephraim Lessing is usually understood to be one of the most important influences in this process of reorientation, but positive references to Shakespeare can already be found even earlier than in Lessing's writings. Significantly, these references aim at precisely those aspects of Shakespeare's dramatic conception that end up becoming central arguments in *Sturm and Drang* poetics but which are then explicated with much more emphasis and pathos. The account given in the following focuses on references to Shakespeare in this period that allow us to pick out and define quantifiable properties of Shakespeare's plays that were subsequently implemented by German dramatists. By this we mean poetological conceptualizations of character and composition that can be formalized and subsequently analyzed as measurable properties of dramatic texts. We also focus on authors of literary treatises who also produced dramatic texts. Although there are more than thirty authors that match this criterion,[9] this overview is limited to five of some of the most significant authors to write about Shakespeare in the eighteenth century: Johann Christoph Gottsched, Johann Elias Schlegel, Lessing, Gerstenberg, and Goethe.

Gottsched's *Versuch einer Critischen Dichtkunst vor die Deutschen* (Essay on a Critical Poetics for the Germans, 1730)—as well as sticking to the tenets of classical French criticism, which was decisive for Gottsched—followed the ideas of the courtly poetic tradition, and was, at least in part, still bound to the medieval concept of Ordo.[10] Consequently, his poetological writings focus on regulative principles and can be understood as attempts to set structural features as preconditions for the definition of good dramatic practice. That his claim is not always rooted in plot-related reasoning can be illustrated by the five-act rule. Gottsched defines and defends the five-act rule functionally by the avoidance of boredom: "Die Ursache dieser fünffachen Eintheilung ist wohl freylich willkührlich gewesen: Indessen ist diese Zahl sehr bequem, damit dem Zuschauer nicht die Zeit gar zu lang würde. Denn wenn jede Handlung eine halbe Stunde daurete, so ... konnte das Spiel nicht viel länger als drey Stunden dauren" (The cause of this five-fold division was, of course, probably arbitrary: yet this number is very convenient, so that the viewer does not get tired of the time. For if every action were to last half an hour ... the play could not last much longer than three hours).[11] The fact that the definition of the five-act rule is external to the dramatic action devalues this rule as an irrelevant category for everything that occurs in the fictional world of the play. This is implicitly confirmed by the fact that Gottsched writes little about this rule, even though its tradition leads back to Menander's Greek comedies and Seneca's Latin tragedies. Considering the popularity of five-act dramatic production in almost all literary periods and theatrical genres since then, it is worthwhile to reflect on the pervasive presence of this model, not only among those adhering to classical or French poetics, but also among their opponents. As Shakespeare's plays abide by the five-act rule, the "Unordnung" (disorder) and "Hindansetzung der Regeln" (disregard for the rules) that Gottsched still claims to find in his works must refer to something else.[12] For Gottsched, Shakespeare's most flagrant breaches of the rules of dramatic writing are found in his disregard for the unities of time and place as well as in his disbanding of the so-called *Ständeklausel*: Shakespeare includes both high-born and low-born characters in his plays and does not always distinguish them through their language.

Gottsched's position on the specific characteristics of Shakespeare's dramatic figures gained significant prominence in the following fifty years of poetological thinking.[13] It was adopted early by Gottsched's pupil, Johann Elias Schlegel, who was particularly responsible for Shakespeare's fame in the German-speaking world.[14] Schlegel's *Vergleichung Shakespears und Andreas Gryphs* (Comparison of Shakespeare and Andreas Gryphius, 1741) also seems to point forward to the much later *Sturm und Drang* poetics.[15] For him, Shakespeare's pieces were, in a strictly anti-Aristotelian sense, "mehr Nachahmungen der Personen, als Nachahmungen einer gewissen Handlung" (more so imitations of people as opposed to imitations of a particular action).[16] In contrast to Gottsched, however, he concedes these "selber gemacht[en] Menschen als] Vergnügen" (556; fictitious people as enjoyment) and a "Stärke des Engelländers" (552; strength of the Englishman), but not without complaining about the violation of decorum: "[E]s mag so gut nachgeahmet seyn, als es will. ... Die Natur dient also nicht zur Entschuldigung, wenn man großen Herren schlechte Redensarten und Schimpfwörter in den Mund leget" (569; It may be as well imitated as it wants to be. . . . Nature does not serve as an excuse for putting bad forms of speech and cursing in the mouths of great men). All in all, Schlegel cannot help assessing Shakespeare from the viewpoint of rule-based poetics. He criticizes those tragedies, "wo die Eröffnung mit einem Haufen Pöbel und mit einigen gemeinen und niedrigen Scherzreden geschieht, wo die Zeit der Handlung nicht nach Stunden, auch nicht nach Tagen, sondern nach Monathen und Jahren gemessen werden muß, und wo der Anfang zu Rom, und das Ende zu Philippis ist" (561; which opens with a heap from the common rabble and with some vulgar and cheap jokes, in which the time of the action must be measured not by hours, nor by days, but by months and years, and which begin in Rome and end in Philippis).

The fact that many literary studies of *Sturm und Drang* poetics begin with Lessing seems odd, given J.E. Schlegel's different and not entirely negative reconstruction of Shakespeare's figures almost two decades earlier. Lessing, of course, praises Shakespeare with much more verve, not least by demonstrating, on the basis of the German *Doctor Faust*, that even "unsre alten Stücke wirklich sehr viel Englisches gehabt haben," which "nur ein Shakespearesches Genie zu denken vermögend gewesen" (our old pieces have really had a lot of English about them, that only a Shakespearean genius could think up).[17]

However, the "Magerkeit" (meagerness)[18] of his content-related statements on Shakespeare can be explained by his one-sided functionalization.

Lessing does not integrate Shakespeare into his own poetology or his dramatic output. As Friedrich Gundolf writes: "Als Dichter hatte Lessing Shakespeare nicht nötig und machte keinen Gebrauch von ihm . . . weil er das vernünftige Prinzip höher stellte als das Leben woran es sich offenbarte" (As a poet Lessing did not need Shakespeare and made no use of him . . . because he placed the rational principle higher than the life in which it manifested itself).[19] On the contrary, Lessing adheres to the rules, especially to the classical unities, and deals with Shakespeare only as a "Stock, mit dem er auf die Franzosen einschlägt" (stick with which to batter the French).[20]

Today's appreciation of Lessing cannot conceal the fact that—at the beginning of the second half of the eighteenth century—other voices of Shakespeare's advocates such as Gerstenberg were heard quite clearly. The impact of his *Briefe über Merkwürdigkeiten der Litteratur* (Letters on Literary Curiosities, 1766) can hardly be underestimated. Letters 14 to 18 are configured as a poetological *Versuch über Shakespears Werke und Genie* (Essay on Shakespeare's Works and Genius), which is barely in line with Aristotelian rules anymore. Gerstenberg praises Shakespeare's skills of shaping figures naturally:[21] "Der Mensch! die Welt! Alles! . . . Weg mit der Claßification des Drama! Nennen Sie diese *plays* mit Wielanden, oder mit der Gottschedischen Schule, . . . wie Sie wollen: ich nenne sie lebendige Bilder der sittlichen Natur" (Man! The world! Everything! . . . Away with the classification of drama! Call these plays with Wieland, or with Gottschedian school . . . as you like: I call them living pictures of moral nature).[22] A change in tone is audible here. It directly affected Johann Gottfried Herder and, via Herder, influenced Goethe and thus echoed right into the core of *Sturm und Drang* poetics; as Goethe writes in his *Rede zum Schäkespears Tag* (Address on Shakespeare's Birthday): "Und ich rufe Natur! Natur! Nichts so Natur als Shäkespears Menschen" (And I cry nature! Nature! Nothing so natural as Shakespeare's people).[23] Goethe's appraisal of Shakespeare raises the tone once again, this time up to humility and shame, but it adds nothing to the matter, except pathos. A central part of the rhetoric of this speech, delivered at his parents' house in October 1771, is the promise of his poetological submission to Shakespeare. Whether Goethe obeys this promise and thus draws very practical conclusions for the design of his plays, the subsequent analyses will aim to show. The core of Goethe's speech seems to come down to the following assertion:

> Ich zweifelte keinen Augenblick dem regelmäsigen Theater zu entsagen. Es schien mir die Einheit des Orts so kerkermäsig ängstlich, die Einheiten der Handlung und der Zeit lästige Fesseln unserer Einbildungskrafft. . . . Und ietzo da ich sahe, wieviel Unrecht mir die Herrn der Regeln in ihrem Loch angethan haben, . . . so wäre mir mein Herz geborsten, wenn ich ihnen nicht Fehde angekündigt hätte, und nicht täglich suchte ihre Türne zusammen zu schlagen.[24]

[I never had my doubts for a moment about renouncing regular theatre. The unity of place seemed to have the anxiety of a prison, the unities of action and time burdensome annoying fetters on our imagination. . . . And now that I saw how much injustice the Lords of the Rules have done to me in their dungeon . . . my heart would have burst if I had not declared a feud with them, and not tried daily to smash down their towers.]

Differing from Goethe, Herder does not solely think of "die sogenannten Theaterregeln" (the so-called rules of theater) and demands—according to his generic method—the historical-cultural appropriateness of the representation of figures in drama.[25] In this respect, Lenz's well-known *Anmerkungen übers Theater nebst angehängten übersetzten Stück Shakespears* (Comments on the Theater Printed Alongside a Translated Play by Shakespeare) were more in line with Goethe's criticism of the classical unities:

Was heissen die drey Einheiten? hundert Einheiten will ich euch angeben, die alle immer doch die eine bleiben. Einheit der Nation, Einheit der Sprache, Einheit der Religion, Einheit der Sitten—ja was wirds denn nun? Immer dasselbe, immer und ewig dasselbe. Der Dichter und das Publikum müssen die eine Einheit fühlen aber nicht klassifiziren.[26]

[What are these three units? I will give you a hundred unities, all of which will always remain one. Unity of nation, unity of language, unity of religion, unity of customs—what will it be now? Always the same, always and eternally the same. The poet and the audience must feel the one unity but not classify it.]

In addition to dramatic rules and structure, poetological discussions of Shakespeare made reference to a number of properties of Shakespeare's plays: the make-up of individual figures as well as the size of the *dramatis personae*, length of the overall play, and artificiality of plot and figures, to name just a few features. In the following, we will pick up on some of these properties and show how they can be analyzed quantitatively. Throughout, we are guided by the hypothesis that surely the increasingly positive reception of Shakespeare in poetical treatises would mean that new drama would be gradually less aligned with neo-classical rules and would strive to follow Shakespeare's lead in disregarding them.

CORPUS PREPARATION

Quantitative analyses of texts generally rely on the availability of digital corpora. In the case of German dramatic texts, many texts up to the beginning of the twentieth century have been digitized in the TextGrid project and are now available in the TextGrid repository.[27] As dramatic texts are a highly structured text genre, an adequate digital representation of these texts is of the utmost importance. TEI (Text Encoding Initiative) XML has been established as the quasi-standard for the digital, machine-readable representation of printed texts, in particular in the digital humanities community. The plays in the TextGrid repository are encoded in such a way that the spoken words of an individual figure within a specific scene or act can be accessed directly. As it represents a ready and usable source, all texts in our corpus are taken from the TextGrid repository. Before being ready for analysis, the texts are preprocessed to add a number of linguistic and non-linguistic annotations to each text. Preprocessing is undertaken automatically, with some exceptions noted in the following, using the software package DramaNLP.[28] One crucial aspect when processing dramatic texts is to treat the different text elements (stage directions, spoken text, act/scene headings, speaker attributions) in an adequate way. We rely on the TEI XML mark-up for detecting this text structure and apply tools for natural language processing (NLP) separately to the text elements.

While speaker attributions are machine-readable, their assignment to the figure declaration in the *dramatis personae* is not. It is often the case that figures are introduced in the *dramatis personae* with a certain name but subsequently named differently in the text.[29] In addition, there are a certain number of seemingly unimportant figures (e.g., "first watch") that appear as speakers during the play, but these are not mentioned in the *dramatis personae* or only as a group (e.g., "watchmen"). These phenomena make the correct identification of speakers non-trivial (for computers). Although it is possible to define heuristics to automatically match these names (e.g., a maximal difference of one character), we opted for a more controlled, rule-based approach, in which we manually specified the correct figure assignment for each speaker. The reason for this is that we currently focus on the high-precision analysis of the texts. By using heuristics that are too simple, one risks introducing false-positives that are difficult to detect later on. Tokenization and sentence splitting of the spoken text was performed using Java's built-in BreakIterator.

Part of Speech Tagging and Lemmatization

A part of speech tagger (PoS-tagger) detects parts of speech in texts, that is, it assigns word categories like "noun," "verb," and "adjective" to words. Modern PoS-taggers are based on probabilistic models and trained on large corpora, typically from the news domain (often considered the standard domain in NLP). On this domain, PoS-taggers achieve performances of well over 95 percent accuracy on unseen test data. We have employed the Stanford

PoS-tagger[30] for tagging the dramatic texts and used the standard model for German. This model has been trained on the Negra corpus[31] and includes distributional similarity features from the Huge German Corpus.[32] According to the accompanying description, it achieved an accuracy of 96.9 percent on unseen texts. We employed the Mate Lemmatizer[33] to detect inflectional variants of the same word (e.g., past tense forms of verbs or plural forms of nouns). It is reported to have an accuracy of 98.28 percent (on news text). It can be expected that the performance of both the PoS-tagger and the lemmatizer on dramatic texts is lower than on news texts, although the exact loss of quality is impossible to determine without an annotated corpus. Manual inspection of some of the PoS-tagged texts shows that the error rate is in acceptable margins.

ANALYSIS

Having outlined how we prepared the texts, we will now turn to how some of the claims about the influence of Shakespeare on German drama can be operationalized. This consists of studying a number of quantified properties of the subcorpora of dramatic texts and comparing them with each other and with Shakespeare's plays, albeit in German translation. We will first discuss and explain the numerical findings and then relate these to drama-theoretical claims.

Acts and Scenes

As discussed previously, the number of acts and scenes is an important concept in eighteenth-century poetological discussions of Shakespeare. It is sometimes addressed under the notion of overall drama "length." Figure 5.1 shows the number of acts and scenes per drama, averaged over each subcorpus. The corpus contains a few texts without explicit act markings, like plays "in einem Aufzuge" (in one act). In these cases, we assume the texts to be composed of a single act, such as Lessing's 1747 play *Damon*.

Without exception, Shakespeare's plays are comprised of five acts. Plays from the *Frühaufklärung* contain either five (45%), three (36%), or one act (18%). This results in an average number of 3.6 acts per play. The spectrum expands in the subcorpus of popular plays, with a higher average, but also some plays containing four acts (25%). The majority of plays from the *Sturm und Drang* period contains five acts (83%), but there is a single play featuring six acts (4%). Plays from the *Weimarer Klassik* contain either five acts (75%) or none at all, without exception.

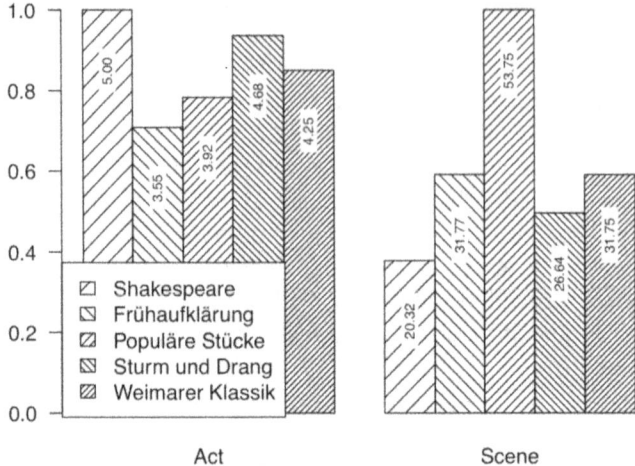

Figure 5.1. Average number of acts and scenes. All values have been scaled, so that the maximum value in each category is 1. Unscaled values are shown inside the bars.

The analysis of the number of acts leads to a notable result: bearing in mind that Shakespeare is used by the *Stürmer und Dränger* to declare rule-based poetics as obsolete, it is revealing that the plays in both subcorpora adhere to the classical five-act scheme much more than the others. Because deviations from this structure are clearly less common in the *Sturm und Drang* than in other periods, one could infer that they, in fact, follow Shakespeare, yet they follow him in a non-innovative aspect of his plays. So, this aspect can hardly be the intended outcome of Gerstenberg's revolutionary doing away with classification and Goethe's renunciation of regular theater ("regelmäsigen Theater"). It is much more likely that acts are a fairly overlooked category in both poetology and playwriting. Besides the ubiquitous five- and the still common three- and one-act plays, there are only very few deviations from this convention, in particular in the upper scale, such as the six-act plays *Die Kindermörderin* (The Infanticide, 1776) by Wagner and *Prinz Zerbino* (Prine Zerbino, 1799) by Tieck. These exceptions have to be understood as intended deviations from established norms.

The analysis of the average number of scenes per play yields similar results. The proportions between the different subcorpora are highly similar for acts and scenes: Shakespeare's plays contain on average 20.3 scenes (the fewest), *Sturm und Drang* plays only contain several more scenes (26.6), and the subsequent *Weimarer Klassik* contains over thirty scenes (31.8).

If we look at the variation within each subcorpus, we notice interesting differences, however. Apparently, Shakespeare's plays have a relatively low standard deviation (6.9): many plays have a similar number of scenes. The variation increases over time. Plays from the *Frühaufklärung* show a deviation of 11.8, *Populäre Stücke, Sturm und Drang,* and *Weimarer Klassik* between 18.4 and 20.5.

Scenes in Acts

According to Gottsched's understanding of the five-act rule, each act in a play has to be roughly of equal length. Because we cannot measure passed time directly (Gottsched pinpoints half an hour per act), we rely on the number of scenes as a proxy for passed time. As we want to study their uniformity over the acts, we measure the standard deviation of the scenes. If all acts contain the same number of scenes, the standard deviation becomes zero. Generally, a low standard deviation indicates that the number of scenes in an act is close to the mean number of scenes in all acts. The higher the standard deviation, the more spread are the numbers of scenes in all acts.

Figure 5.2 shows the standard deviations for all plays in a subcorpus as a box plot. In a box plot, the individual data points (plays in this case) are ranked and then split into quartiles (each quartile contains 25 percent of the data plays). The plays with less than 25 percent and more than 75 percent of the maximal deviation are shown as individual points, whereas the plays between 25 percent and 75 percent are displayed as boxes. The strong bar

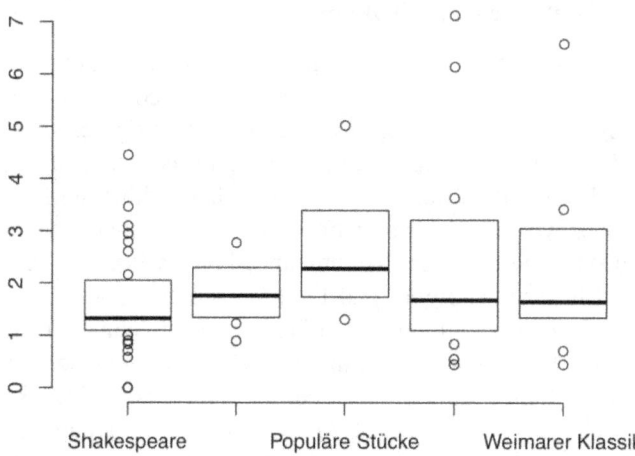

Figure 5.2. Standard deviations of scenes per act, restricted to plays with five acts.

in each box represents the median. In essence, box plots allow a sense of both the position and the spread of a number of data points: we not only see a single value as a result, but also gain insight into how distributed the data points are.

Plays by Shakespeare show the lowest median: 50 percent of the plays have a standard deviation of 1.3. By contrast, *Sturm und Drang* plays show a median standard deviation of 2.8. For the vast majority of his plays, Shakespeare follows the rule of equally long acts and includes only minor variation in act length. This is remarkable because it is not known whether Shakespeare was acquainted with the classical poetic rules or just followed established practices of contemporary playwrights.[34] In any case, in the extreme case of *A Midsummer Night's Dream*, every single act contains two scenes (resulting in standard deviation of zero). The poetics of the *Sturm und Drang*, however, allow much more variation. In the play with the widest distribution, *Götz von Berlichingen*, in the first printed version from 1773, the number of scenes per act varies from 5 to 22 (standard deviation = 7.1).

Although *Sturm und Drang* playwrights follow Shakespeare in some aspects, the number of scenes per act is not one of them. Instead, *Sturm und Drang* features a lot of variation in this metric. This fact also holds true for *Populäre Stücke* and, to a lesser degree, for the *Weimarer Klassik* and *Frühaufklärung* (which includes a play by Gottsched). This suggests that the rule of equally long acts, as mentioned by Gottsched, has generally been used less frequently after Gottsched. But, again, as in the case of the more conventionalized five-act structure, Shakespeare is the strictest practitioner of this rule.

Utterances, Sentences, and Tokens

Measuring acts and scenes is but one aspect of dramatic length; others include utterances, sentences, and tokens. For utterances, we count every moment of speech that is delivered by one or more figures. If two figures share an utterance by saying the same words simultaneously, it is counted only once. Stage directions and act/scene headings are not included; neither are footnotes. To count sentences, we rely on automatically detected sentence boundaries. In our setup, a sentence never crosses utterance boundaries, that is, if a figure is interrupted by another figure and the sentence continues into their next utterance, two sentences are created. While this is a technical necessity, we expect it to be a rare occurrence in these plays. In addition, some utterances do not contain full grammatical sentences (e.g., there is no finite verb in *Romeo: "Um neun Uhr." / Romeo: "At the hour of nine."*), but are considered a sentence anyway. The counting of tokens measures every spoken token, that is, every word that is part of an utterance.

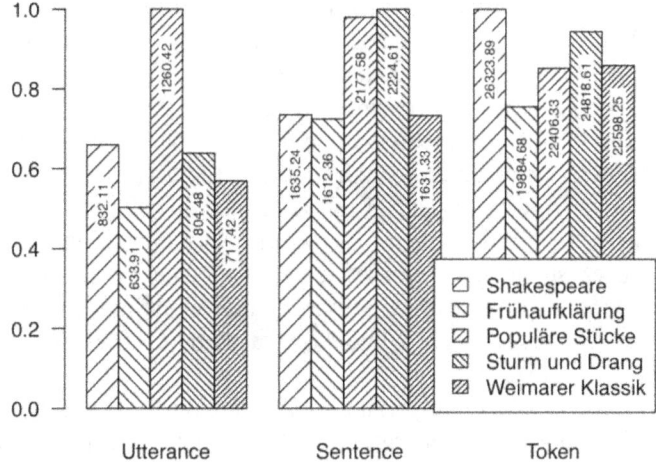

Figure 5.3. Average number of utterances, sentences, and tokens. All values have been scaled so that the maximum value in each category is 1. Unscaled values are shown inside the bars.

Looking at average numbers of utterances, sentences, and tokens (Figure 5.3), we find that plays from the *Frühaufklärung* are the shortest. For the succeeding measurements, however, we can find some interesting differences: on the level of the number of tokens, we observe that *Populäre Stücke* and plays of the *Weimarer Klassik* have roughly the same length. Measured as sentences, however, their lengths are quite different: the number of sentences in *Weimarer Klassik* is much lower than in *Populäre Stücke*. Except for the number of sentences, we can confirm our initial observation about similarities between *Shakespeare* and *Sturm und Drang*: in terms of utterances and tokens, *Sturm und Drang* plays are the most similar to *Shakespeare* among the subcorpora under discussion.

If we turn to the ratio of tokens and sentences, we can make some observations about the average *sentence length*. Shakespeare's plays contain the longest sentence (16.1 token/sentence), followed by the *Weimarer Klassik* (13.8) and *Frühaufklärung* (12.3). Playwrights in the *Sturm und Drang* do not seem to follow Shakespeare in this respect, with an average sentence length of only 11.2. It should be noted that the Schlegel/Tieck translations of Shakespeare's plays are written in verse, which makes the average sentence length difficult to compare.

Another observation concerns the number of utterances: while the subcorpus *Populäre Stücke* is ranked second and third in number of tokens and sentences, these plays have by far the highest number of utterances: these utterances are just much shorter than in the plays of other subcorpora. This can be explained with the cast and genre of these plays. In six *Lustspiele* and six *Schauspiele, Familien-*, and *Sittengemälde* the social setting of the plays is—with few exceptions—the chamber instead of the court.[35] The intended audience of middle-class comedies, along with their plots and intended effect, explains why the language of comedies clearly represents social interaction and attributes of figures instead of existential conflicts, as the language of tragedies does.[36] And this is therefore reflected in the length and number of utterances: because the language used to negotiate those different subjects on stage should imitate how real people speak, an average utterance in popular plays is only 17.8 tokens long, while they reach about 31 tokens in all other subcorpora.

We will briefly look not only at the average number, but also at the spread of the distribution in each subcorpus. The distribution of the number of utterances was very similar for all subcorpora. For tokens (Figure 5.4) and sentences (not shown), however, the *Sturm und Drang* plays show a much wider distribution (consider the vertical size of the boxes and the outliers in Figure 5.4), as well as a single text that is over fifty thousand tokens long: Friedrich Müller's *Golo und Genovefa* (1775–1781). As it would appear, some of the rules that traditionally apply for writing dramas no longer apply for *Sturm und Drang*, thus allowing both much longer, but also shorter dramatic texts.

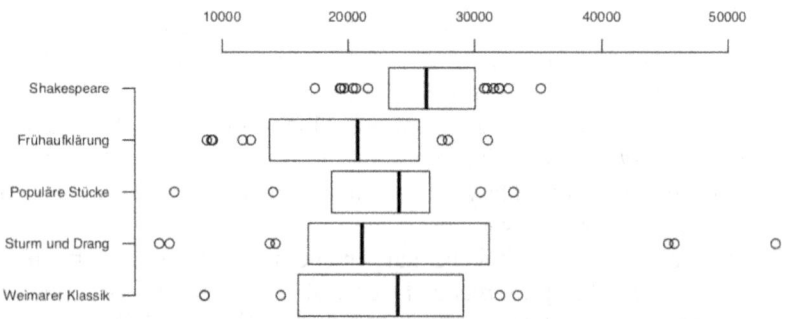

Figure 5.4. Distribution of number of tokens per subcorpus.

Number of Figures

We stressed at the beginning that the conception of figures is discussed numerous times in drama poetics. Those ideas and functions that a dramatic figure represents are manifold and vary over time. That makes the computational analysis of dramatic figures challenging. One very basic approximation to the "statistical understanding" of a figure is to measure the number of all figures in a play (as mentioned in the *dramatis personae*). This metric might be able to serve as a proxy for figure conception. The underlying assumption in rejecting the rules of neo-classical decorum is that, for example, a cast of figures that forsakes the *Ständeklausel* in including and mixing figures from different social backgrounds, drawn by an innate *Halbgott* (demi-god),[37] should represent the world as a whole and therefore needs a much larger (and more varied) cast than *Rührstücke* (melodramas) would.

Figure 5.5 shows the distribution of the number of figures in the *dramatis personae*; the four plays without *dramatis personae*—all from the *Sturm und Drang*—are excluded from this analysis. Shakespeare's plays feature the largest ensemble, and there is relatively little variation in the sizes of casts called for in his plays. Half of the plays include between twenty and twenty-eight figures. None of the other subcorpora reaches this cast size. The median for *Sturm und Drang* pieces, for instance, is very close to the median for *Populäre Stücke*, with a slightly higher variation. In fact, some plays feature significantly more or fewer figures, but the overall distribution of figures in *Sturm und Drang* is surprisingly conventionalized. Even the play with the largest cast group still contains fewer figures than the longest Shakespeare play.

This changes only in the *Weimarer Klassik*. The median (nineteen) is still quite a bit lower than for Shakespeare's plays, but the maximal number of figures (found in Schiller's *Wilhelm Tell* from 1804) is higher than that of

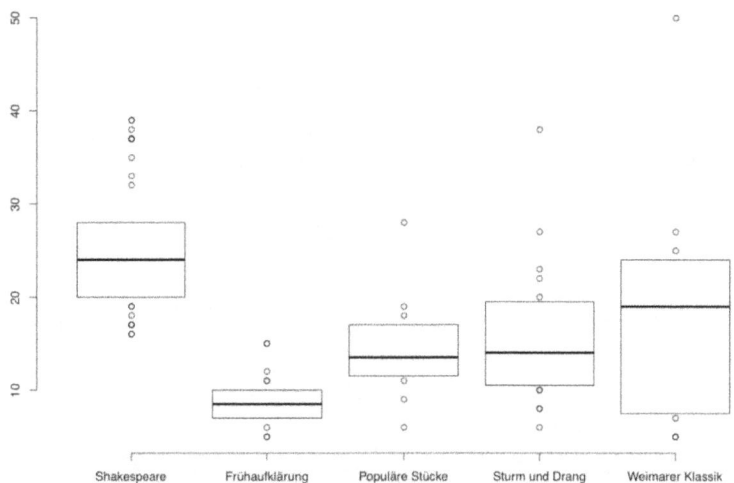

Figure 5.5. Distribution of the number of figures in the *dramatis personae* per subcorpus. Plays without a printed list of *dramatis personae* are excluded.

Shakespeare plays. By contrast, a large variation occurs toward the lower end of the spectrum. *Weimarer Klassik* also allows plays with a much smaller cast size. We find, for example, only five figures in Goethe's *Iphigenie auf Tauris* (Iphigenia on Tauris, 1786).

First Appearances

One major rule of dramatic composition in the period is still to be considered. The rule that no major figure should appear on stage that has not been present or at least been mentioned by others in the first act was introduced by pierre Corneille and subsequently popularized in Germany.[38] We will examine the act in which figures have their first appearance. To this end, we select from each text the five figures that speak the most words, as it is highly likely that those figures are central in Corneille's sense. Then, we extract the act number of the first appearance of each of the five figures. Figure 5.6 displays the result as a stacked bar chart: Among the plays in our subcorpus of Shakespeare's plays, for instance, 78 percent of the top five figures have their first appearance in the first act and another 15 percent of the figures first appear in the second act.

As can be seen from the chart, most of the figures in all subcorpora have their first appearance in the first act. However, every subcorpus features a number of figures that have their first appearance in the second, third, and sometimes even the fourth and fifth acts. Again, we can identify similarities between Shakespeare plays and *Sturm und Drang* plays: the two subcorpora

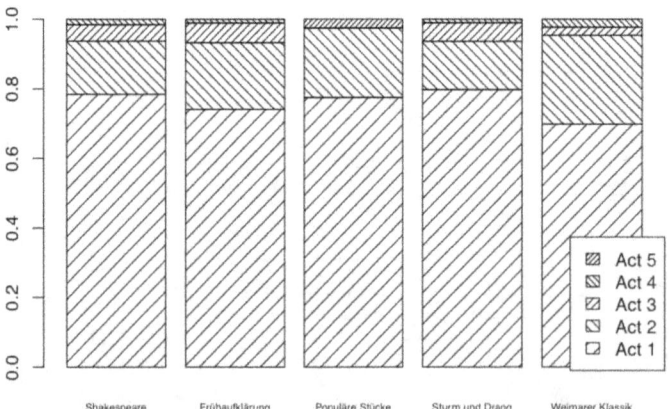

Figure 5.6. First appearances of the five most speaking figures per play.

feature the highest portion of figures that first appear in the first act (Shakespeare: 78 percent, *Sturm und Drang*: 79 percent). This similarity continues to the second act, with 15 percent and 14 percent of the figures, respectively, having their first appearance in the second act.

The most liberal interpretation of this "first appearance" rule can be discerned for *Populäre Stücke* (first act: 71 percent) and *Weimarer Klassik* (first act: 70 percent). The findings in the latter case are surprising, given the self-description of playwrights in the *Weimarer Klassik* as following classical dramatic traditions.

Figure Ranking

Next to the raw number and the act of the first appearance, the ranking of figures is another aspect of the conception of a play. In this analysis, we compare the ranking given by the *dramatis personae*, that is, the order in which figures are listed, with the ranking given by their appearance, meaning the order in which figures appear on stage. Figure 5.7 plots data for the figures that appear in a certain position in the *dramatis personae* and in a certain order within the text. The size of each dot indicates how many figures share this characteristic. One technical caveat: the plot contains only figures for which

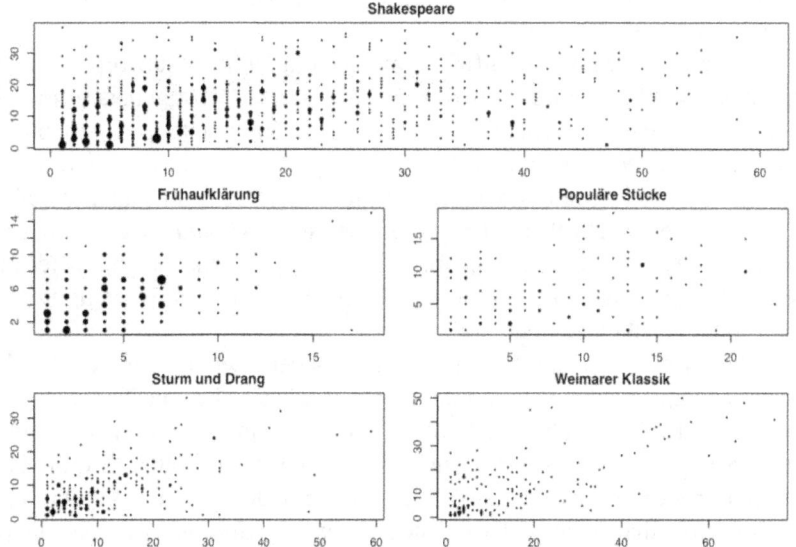

Figure 5.7. Figure ranks according to first appearance (x axis) and *dramatis personae* (y axis). Dots are scaled according to the number of figures at this rank.

we have a correct assignment of speaker tags in the play to figure mention in the *dramatis personae*. Karl von Moor, for example, appears in the *dramatis personae* of Schillers *Die Räuber* (1781) as "Karl" but, in the course of the play, the speaker tag (indicating his speech) varies with the dramatic contexts from KARL VON MOOR to RÄUBER MOOR to only MOOR. For the most important figures of each play in our corpus, this identification is done, but there may be some missing assignments for minor figures.

The fact that Shakespeare not only created a lot of figures but also wrote a lot of plays leads to the result that the Shakespeare plot is generally more populated with dots than the others. In all subcorpora, except the *Populäre Stücke*, many dots are concentrated in the bottom left corner: figures that appear early in the text (x axis) tend to be ranked highly in the *dramatis personae* (y axis) and vice versa. The plays from the *Frühaufklärung* show a relatively strong concentration within the 7×7 mark, and very few figures outside of this rectangle. Obviously, the low number of figures in this subcorpus is relevant here. The records for *Sturm und Drang* and *Weimarer Klassik* show an approximate linear relation between ranking in *dramatis personae*. In addition, *Weimarer Klassik* plays are different from the others in that they do not contain the exceptional cases that we find in the other subcorpora. Most subcorpora contain dots in the bottom right or top left corner, indicating figures that appear late but are ranked highly in the *dramatis personae* or vice versa. Plays from *Weimarer Klassik* lack these cases. In this respect, authors from *Weimarer Klassik* seem to adhere more strictly to the rules of dramatic composition.

That the *Populäre Stücke* differ so much from all other subcorpora can be explained by the structure of the *dramatis personae*. Most genres follow the regulatory principle of social rank (or, less common, first appearance), but the genres represented in the popular plays do not. As mentioned earlier, the action mainly takes place in bourgeois and middle-class realms and, therefore, it is the (tender) father that is first mentioned in the *dramatis personae*, as in Iffland's *Die Jäger* (The Huntsmen, 1785); rarely is it the daughter. Because the whole family has to be subordinated, relatively insignificant figures are likely to be listed close to the top.

As discussed, the average number of tokens per utterance can be related to the social status of the cast. But another factor has to be considered as well: Lessing's attempt to subordinate the dramatic diction to the law of naturalness.[39] Starting with Lessing, a shorter sentence length—as a discriminator between spoken and written language—can be understood as an imitation of persons rather than actions. This is most likely why *Sturm und Drang* authors use relatively short sentences in their plays: they imitate the linguistic characteristics of spoken language.

Typically, when it is written down, spoken language also contains a lot of verbalizations of emotion and hesitation, such as "um" or "er" in English, or, in German, "ach." In terms of part of speech, these are grouped as interjections in the STTS tagset.[40] Figure 5.8 shows the relative frequency of interjections per drama per subcorpus. Overall, interjections are uncommon. Under 1 percent of the dramatic text consists of interjections. There are, however, substantial differences between the subcorpora. *Populäre Stücke* contain the highest number of interjections per play (50 percent of the plays consist between 0.25 percent and 0.35 percent of interjections), which is to be expected, given the middle-class settings and the expected audience of those plays. The subcorpus of Shakespeare's plays is relatively modest with respect to interjections, although it has to be taken into account that we are dealing with translations of his works. An explanation for the seemingly low number of interjections in his plays is that Wieland explicitly disliked translating Shakespeare's partially vulgar language, and therefore went to some efforts to clean it up.[41]

The *Sturm und Drang* again allowed experimentation in both directions. But in contrast to previous findings, the range of interjections is even larger in the plays of the *Frühaufklärung*. The most striking finding in our analysis concerns the *Weimarer Klassik*. Interjections are not used anymore, with only a few exceptions, such as Schiller's *Wallensteins Lager* (1798), and even those that make use of them do so only sparingly.

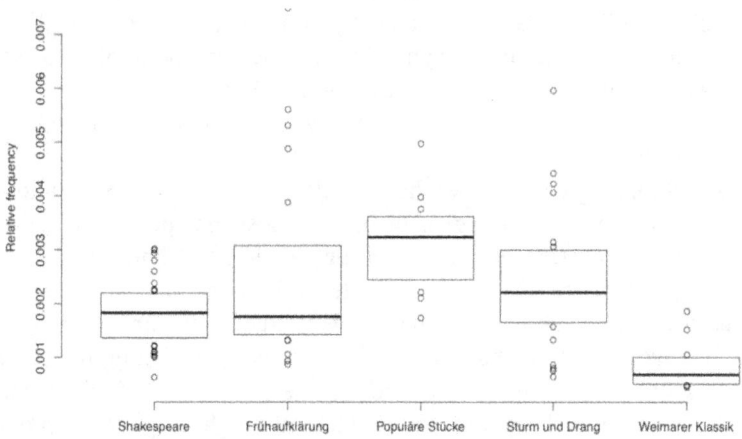

Figure 5.8. Relative frequency of interjections per play.

CONCLUSION

It is, of course, nothing new to state that the drama of the *Sturm und Drang* exhibits more varied and less strict range of styles of plays.[42] This is in line with the poetological claims and demands of the authors in this period. We can add to this discussion not only the confirmation of existing hypotheses but point out experimentation and dramatic rule-breaking in the *Sturm und Drang*. Yet some of the findings we have presented in this chapter about the plays of the *Sturm und Drang* turn out to be surprisingly conservative: most of the plays are five-act plays, and most of the figures have their first appearance in the first act. In addition, *Sturm und Drang* playwrights appear to follow Shakespeare in these aspects closely, testifying to the English dramatist's influence, but in following Shakespeare's example closely, this subcorpus shows a stricter adherence to rules and therefore less variation than the other subcorpora. Yet this is surely not what their poetics aimed at in looking to Shakespeare. So it is more likely that those structural aspects to which *Sturm und Drang* playwrights so strictly adhere either go unnoticed by them or are considered as irrelevant, even though they were explicitly stated as dramatic rules. In any case, the plays illustrate that neither Shakespeare nor the *Stürmer und Dränger* rejected rules and conventions completely.

In other cases, such as the number of scenes per act or the length measured in tokens, playwrights from *Sturm und Drang* break with traditions that Shakespeare himself followed. This can be interpreted as an overgeneralization of Shakespeare's rule-breaking poetics: he disregarded mainly figure-related rules of classical drama, a practice that was not, initially, well received among German playwrights. In turn, the perception of Shakespeare as a breaker of rules and shunner of tradition allowed playwrights to explore more options in dramatic composition and thus led to more variation than in other subcorpora.

On a methodological level, we have confirmed our initial expectation that there is a gap between poetological claims and possible operationalizations of them. We see two major reasons for this gap: one of a technical and the other of a conceptual nature. On the technical level, it is obvious that the ability of computers to cope with natural language is limited. This limits our ability to operationalize certain claims directly. Quantitatively analyzing references to figures exactly, for instance, would require us to be able to include and account for references to figures that are made through anaphora or pronouns that do not obviously refer to them. This difficulty has not been resolved in the quantitative study of dramatic texts, and is considered a hard problem even for the analysis of news texts. While there has been significant progress in recent years in developing the technology needed for such quantitative research, fictional and literary texts have only recently become a subject of interest in the NLP methodological community. It can be expected that similar performance numbers on literary texts as we see them on news texts can be reached in the not-so-distant future, at least on core NLP tasks like PoS-tagging. Other potential text analysis tasks (such as judging naturalness of the figure speech) are more difficult to study from an engineering perspective, and this is related to the more conceptual aspect. Claims about the naturalness of Shakespeare's figures might seem to be intuitively comprehensible, but actually they remain relatively vague. Poetics typically do not specify in detail what naturalness of figures is (their language? their composition? their behavior?). This impression of vagueness is a result of the extreme context-dependence of these claims. Unclear contexts typically give rise to a number of differing or even contradicting interpretations, both for literary and poetological writings.

For these reasons, it will remain very difficult to operationalize poetological claims directly. Yet we have shown in a number of examples how related, more simplified operationalizations can serve as a proxy toward more complex phenomena and lead to findings that are concrete and traceable: Empirical methods thus aid in uncovering supporting and contradicting evidence related to claims made in the discussion about the influence of Shakespeare on the German drama, and about the relation between poetological and dramatic writing. And perhaps the empirical methods applied in this chapter will have more to show us about the impact of further central figures, works, and genres in the intercultural development of both German and British drama in the period. Using computational methods to read across hundreds or even thousands of texts promises to test, add to, and even challenge our understanding of literary exchange.

Table 5.1. List of texts with assignments to subcorpus.

Title	Author	Subcorpus
Romeo und Julietta	Shakespeare, William	Shakespeare
Julius Cäsar	Shakespeare, William	Shakespeare
König Richard II	Shakespeare, William	Shakespeare
König Heinrich VI Dritter Teil	Shakespeare, William	Shakespeare
Was ihr wollt	Shakespeare, William	Shakespeare
Viel Lärmen um nichts	Shakespeare, William	Shakespeare
König Heinrich VI Erster Teil	Shakespeare, William	Shakespeare
Der Sturm	Shakespeare, William	Shakespeare
Titus Andronicus	Shakespeare, William	Shakespeare
Ein Sommernachtstraum	Shakespeare, William	Shakespeare
Wie es euch gefällt	Shakespeare, William	Shakespeare
Timon von Athen	Shakespeare, William	Shakespeare
Der Kaufmann von Venedig	Shakespeare, William	Shakespeare

(continued)

Table 5.1. *(continued)*

Title	Author	Subcorpus
Das Wintermärchen	Shakespeare, William	Shakespeare
Coriolanus	Shakespeare, William	Shakespeare
Macbeth	Shakespeare, William	Shakespeare
Die lustigen Weiber von Windsor	Shakespeare, William	Shakespeare
Ende gut, alles gut	Shakespeare, William	Shakespeare
König Heinrich IV Zweiter Teil	Shakespeare, William	Shakespeare
Cymbeline	Shakespeare, William	Shakespeare
Der Widerspenstigen Zähmung	Shakespeare, William	Shakespeare
Troilus und Cressida	Shakespeare, William	Shakespeare
König Heinrich VIII	Shakespeare, William	Shakespeare
Perikles	Shakespeare, William	Shakespeare
Die beiden Veroneser	Shakespeare, William	Shakespeare
Othello	Shakespeare, William	Shakespeare
Die Komödie der Irrungen	Shakespeare, William	Shakespeare
Maß für Maß	Shakespeare, William	Shakespeare
Hamlet. Prinz von Dänemark	Shakespeare, William	Shakespeare
Liebes Leid und Lust	Shakespeare, William	Shakespeare
Romeo und Julia	Shakespeare, William	Shakespeare
König Heinrich V	Shakespeare, William	Shakespeare
König Richard III	Shakespeare, William	Shakespeare
Antonius und Cleopatra	Shakespeare, William	Shakespeare
König Lear	Shakespeare, William	Shakespeare
König Heinrich VI Zweiter Teil	Shakespeare, William	Shakespeare
König Heinrich IV Erster Teil	Shakespeare, William	Shakespeare
König Johann	Shakespeare, William	Shakespeare
Der Bookesbeutel	Borkenstein, Hinrich	Frühaufklärung
Die zärtlichen Schwestern	Gellert, Christian Fürchtegott	Frühaufklärung
Die Betschwester	Gellert, Christian Fürchtegott	Frühaufklärung
Der sterbende Cato	Gottsched, Johann Christoph	Frühaufklärung
Atalanta oder die bezwungene Sprödigkeit	Gottsched, Johann Christoph	Frühaufklärung
Das Testament	Gottsched, Luise Adelgunde Victorie	Frühaufklärung
Der Witzling	Gottsched, Luise Adelgunde Victorie	Frühaufklärung
Die Pietisterey im Fischbein-Rocke	Gottsched, Luise Adelgunde Victorie	Frühaufklärung
Die Candidaten oder Die Mittel zu einem Amte zu gelangen	Krüger, Johann Christian	Frühaufklärung
Die Geistlichen auf dem Lande	Krüger, Johann Christian	Frühaufklärung
Die alte Jungfer	Lessing, Gotthold Ephraim	Frühaufklärung
Der Freigeist	Lessing, Gotthold Ephraim	Frühaufklärung
Der junge Gelehrte	Lessing, Gotthold Ephraim	Frühaufklärung
Der Misogyn	Lessing, Gotthold Ephraim	Frühaufklärung
Die Juden	Lessing, Gotthold Ephraim	Frühaufklärung

Title	Author	Subcorpus
Damon, oder die wahre Freundschaft	Lessing, Gotthold Ephraim	Frühaufklärung
Die Schäferinsel	Mylius, Christlob	Frühaufklärung
Der Hypochondrist	Quistorp, Theodor Johann	Frühaufklärung
Canut	Schlegel, Johann Elias	Frühaufklärung
Die stumme Schönheit	Schlegel, Johann Elias	Frühaufklärung
Der geschäftige Müßiggänger	Schlegel, Johann Elias	Frühaufklärung
Der Triumph der guten Frauen	Schlegel, Johann Elias	Frühaufklärung
Das Erbtheil des Vaters	Iffland, August Wilhelm	Populäre Stücke
Die Jäger	Iffland, August Wilhelm	Populäre Stücke
Figaro in Deutschland	Iffland, August Wilhelm	Populäre Stücke
Verbrechen aus Ehrsucht	Iffland, August Wilhelm	Populäre Stücke
Der Spieler	Iffland, August Wilhelm	Populäre Stücke
Die deutschen Kleinstädter	Kotzebue, August von	Populäre Stücke
Der Wildschütz oder Die Stimme der Natur	Kotzebue, August von	Populäre Stücke
Menschenhaß und Reue	Kotzebue, August von	Populäre Stücke
Der Hyperboreische Esel, oder Die heutige Bildung	Kotzebue, August von	Populäre Stücke
Die Indianer in England	Kotzebue, August von	Populäre Stücke
Die beiden Klingsberg	Kotzebue, August von	Populäre Stücke
Der Vetter in Lissabon	Schröder, Friedrich Ludwig	Populäre Stücke
Faust [in ursprünglicher Gestalt]	Goethe, Johann Wolfgang	Sturm und Drang
Clavigo	Goethe, Johann Wolfgang	Sturm und Drang
Götz von Berlichingen mit der eisernen Hand	Goethe, Johann Wolfgang	Sturm und Drang
Das Jahrmarktsfest zu Plundersweilern	Goethe, Johann Wolfgang	Sturm und Drang
Egmont	Goethe, Johann Wolfgang	Sturm und Drang
Stella	Goethe, Johann Wolfgang	Sturm und Drang
Ugolino	Gerstenberg, Heinrich Wilhelm von	Sturm und Drang
Sturm und Drang	Klinger, Friedrich Maximilian	Sturm und Drang
Die Zwillinge	Klinger, Friedrich Maximilian	Sturm und Drang
Die neue Arria	Klinger, Friedrich Maximilian	Sturm und Drang
Das leidende Weib	Klinger, Friedrich Maximilian	Sturm und Drang
Simsone Grisaldo	Klinger, Friedrich Maximilian	Sturm und Drang
Julius von Tarent	Leisewitz, Johann Anton	Sturm und Drang
Pandämonium Germanicum	Lenz, Jakob Michael Reinhold	Sturm und Drang
Die Soldaten	Lenz, Jakob Michael Reinhold	Sturm und Drang
Der Hofmeister oder Vorteile der Privaterziehung	Lenz, Jakob Michael Reinhold	Sturm und Drang
Der neue Menoza	Lenz, Jakob Michael Reinhold	Sturm und Drang
Golo und Genovefa	Müller, Friedrich (Maler Müller)	Sturm und Drang
Don Carlos, Infant von Spanien	Schiller, Friedrich	Sturm und Drang

(continued)

Table 5.1. (continued)

Title	Author	Subcorpus
Kabale und Liebe	Schiller, Friedrich	Sturm und Drang
Die Verschwörung des Fiesco zu Genua	Schiller, Friedrich	Sturm und Drang
Die Räuber	Schiller, Friedrich	Sturm und Drang
Die Kindermörderin	Wagner, Heinrich Leopold	Sturm und Drang
Torquato Tasso	Goethe, Johann Wolfgang	Weimarer Klassik
Die Aufgeregten	Goethe, Johann Wolfgang	Weimarer Klassik
Iphigenie auf Tauris	Goethe, Johann Wolfgang	Weimarer Klassik
Der Bürgergeneral	Goethe, Johann Wolfgang	Weimarer Klassik
Der Großkophta	Goethe, Johann Wolfgang	Weimarer Klassik
Maria Stuart	Schiller, Friedrich	Weimarer Klassik
Wallensteins Lager	Schiller, Friedrich	Weimarer Klassik
Wilhelm Tell	Schiller, Friedrich	Weimarer Klassik
Die Piccolomini	Schiller, Friedrich	Weimarer Klassik
Die Jungfrau von Orleans	Schiller, Friedrich	Weimarer Klassik
Die Braut von Messina oder die feindlichen Brüder	Schiller, Friedrich	Weimarer Klassik
Wallensteins Tod	Schiller, Friedrich	Weimarer Klassik

NOTES

1. This paper was written as part of the mixed-methods project *QuaDramA: Quantitative Drama Analytics* (https://quadrama.github.io/), which is funded by Volkswagen Stiftung.

2. See Lawrence M. Price, *Die Aufnahme englischer Literatur in Deutschland, 1500–1960* (Bern and Munich: Francke, 1961), 223. Price's book itself is testament to the focus that has traditionally been given to the German reception of Shakespeare over the years. And this subject continues to occupy a central position in research to this day. For some recent volumes dealing with this subject, see, for example, Günther Erken, "Deutschland," in *Shakespeare-Handbuch: Die Zeit—Der Mensch—Das Werk—Die Nachwelt*, ed. Ina Schabert, fourth edition (Stuttgart: Kröner, 2000), 635–60; Kira Liebert, "Die kreative Aneignung Shakespeares im Werk von Karl Philipp Moritz," in *Britisch-deutscher Literaturtransfer 1756–1832*, ed. Lore Knapp and Eike Kronshage (Berlin and Boston, MA: de Gruyter, 2016), 171–91; Roger Paulin, *The Critical Reception of Shakespeare in Germany 1682–1914: Native Literature and Foreign Genius* (Hildesheim: Olms, 2003); and Roger Paulin, ed., *Shakespeare im 18. Jahrhundert* (Göttingen: Wallstein, 2007).

3. Cf. Bayard Quincey Morgan and A.R. Hohlfeld, eds., *German Literature in British Magazines: 1750–1860* (Madison, WI: University of Wisconsin Press, 1949).

4. See, for example, Zhao Geng, Robert S. Laramee, Tom Cheeseman, Alison Ehrmann, and David M. Berry, "Visualizing Translation Variation: Shakespeare's Othello," in *Advances in Visual Computing*, ed. George Bebis et al., Part I (Berlin and Heidelberg: Springer, 2011), 653–63.

5. See, for example, Franco Moretti, "Conjectures on World Literature," *New Left Review* 1 (2000): 54–68.

6. See, for example, Gregory Crane, "What Do You Do with a Million Books?," *D-Lib Magazine* 12, no. 3 (2006); and Martin Mueller, "Scalable Reading" https://scalablereading.northwestern.edu/?page_id=22 (accessed August 21, 2017).

7. We are using the translation by Schlegel and Tieck simply because Wieland's is not completely digitized yet. Although the playwrights of the *Sturm und Drang* emphasized their criticism of Wieland and his Shakespeare translation, they actually used this translation when they were quoting Shakespeare. See Sabine Kob, *Wielands Shakespeare-Übersetzung: Ihre Entstehung und ihre Rezeption im Sturm und Drang* (Frankfurt am Main: Lang, 2000).

8. The probably best-known representative of this thesis is Friedrich Gundolf, *Shakespeare und der deutsche Geist* (Berlin: Bondi, 1911), especially Book 2 (*Shakespeare als Form*) and Book 3 (*Shakespeare als Gehalt*). Carolin Steimer postulates, that "das von Shakespeare entwickelte Dramenverständnis in Theorie und Praxis eine neue Epoche einleitet" (the understanding of drama that Shakespeare introduces a new epoch in both theory and practice). Carolin Steimer, *"Der Mensch! die Welt! Alles"*: *Die Bedeutung Shakespeares für die Dramaturgie und das Drama des Sturm und Drang* (Frankfurt a.M.: Lang, 2012), 14.

9. Cf. the selection of Peter Langemeyer, ed. *Dramentheorie: Texte vom Barock bis zur Gegenwart* (Stuttgart: Reclam, 2011), esp. 77–274.

10. Cf. Juliane Vogel, "Aus dem Takt. Auftrittsstrukturen in Schillers *Don Carlos*," *Deutsche Vierteljahrsschrift für Literaturwissenschaft und Geistesgeschichte* 86, no. 4 (2012) for a different approach to the idea of Ordo and formal structure. She describes the interrelations between ceremonial and dramatic principles of court representation.

11. Johann Christoph Gottsched, *Versuch einer Critischen Dichtkunst vor die Deutschen* (Leipzig: Breitkopf, 1730), 570. We find a similar observation on page 26: "Die Neuern haben zwar zuweilen nur drey gemacht, aber alsdann bekommt jede Handlung gar zu viel Scenen oder Auftritte, so, daß dem Zuschauer Zeit und Weile darüber lang wird. Es ist also besser man bleibe bey dieser Regel Horatii, und folge lieber dem Exempel der alten Griechen nach, als den heutigen Jtalienern." (The moderns have at times only made a division into three, but because of that each act has too many scenes or entrances so that the time seems too long to the spectator. It is therefore better, regarding this rule, to remain as it were, Horatians and to follow the example of the ancient Greeks rather than that of the present day Italians.)

12. Johann Christoph Gottsched, *Anmerkungen über das 592. Stück des Zuschauers* [1742], in *Shakespeare-Rezeption: die Diskussion um Shakespeare in Deutschland. Band 1: Ausgewählte Texte von 1741 bis 1788*, ed. Hansjürgen Blinn (Berlin: Schmidt, 1982), 62.

13. Like Pfister we speak of dramatic *figure* instead of *character* "to establish a terminological counterweight to an equally common tendency to discuss dramatic figures as if they were people or characters from real life, and thus to emphasize the ontological difference between fictional figures and real characters." Manfred Pfister, *The Theory and Analysis of Drama* (Cambridge and New York: Cambridge University Press, 1988), 161.

14. See Hans Wolffheim, *Die Entdeckung Shakespeares: Deutsche Zeugnisse des 18. Jahrhunderts* (Hamburg: Hoffmann & Campe, 1959), 16. Borck's translation of Shakespeare's *Julius Caesar* is known to have had the same impact.

15. Ulfo, the antagonist of Schlegel's *Canut* was repeatedly read as a precursor of the *Kraftkerle* that became popular with the *Sturm und Drang*. This idea can be traced back to Johann von Antoniewicz's article on Johann Elias Schlegel in the *Allgemeine Deutsche Biographie*, 56 vols. (Leipzig: Duncker & Humboldt, 1875–1912), 31: 382. Here Antoniewicz writes: "Sicher erscheint mir eine tiefere Kenntniß Shakespeare's aus Schlegel's hervorragendstem Drama 'Canut' zu sprechen" (To be sure, it seems to me to be more fitting to talk of Schlegel's deeper understanding of Shakespeare in his greatest drama Canut).

16. Johann Elias Schlegel, *Vergleichung Shakespears und Andreas Gryphs bey Gelegenheit des Versuchs einer gebundenen Uebersetzung von dem Tode des Julius Cäsar, aus dem Englischen Werken des Shakespear*, in *Beyträge Zur Critischen Historie Der Deutschen Sprache, Poesie und Beredsamkeit*, hrsg. von einigen Liebhabern der deutschen Litteratur 7, no. 28 (1741): 550.

17. Gotthold Ephraim Lessing, "Siebzehnter Brief [Den 16. Februar 1759]," in *Gotthold Ephraim Lessings Sämtliche Schriften*, ed. Karl Lachmann, third edition by Franz Muncker, twenty-three volumes (Stuttgart: Göschen, 1886–1924), volume 8, 43.

18. Monika Fick, *Lessing-Handbuch: Leben—Werk—Wirkung*, second edition (Stuttgart: Metzler, 2004), 316.

19. Friedrich Gundolf, *Shakespeare und der deutsche Geist* (Berlin: Bondi, 1911), 128.

20. Hugh B. Nisbet, *Lessing: Eine Biographie*, trans. Karl S. Guthke (München: Beck, 2008), 516. One example related to Gottsched should be given: "Denn eben dieses, daß [Gottsched] den Addisonschen Cato für das beste Englische Trauerspiel hält, zeiget deutlich, daß er hier nur mit den Augen der Franzosen gesehen, und damals keinen Shakespeare, keinen Jonson, keinen Beaumont und Fletcher etc. gekannt hat, die er hernach aus Stolz auch nicht hat wollen kennen lernen" (Lessing, "Siebzehnter Brief," 42) (For even the fact that Gottsched held Addison's Cato to be the best English tragedy clearly shows that here he only saw with the eyes of a Frenchman and at that point did not know Shakespeare, Jonson, or Beaumont and Fletcher, which he did not want to know thereafter out of Pride.)

21. See Friedrich Sengle, "Der Umfang als ein Problem der Dichtungswissenschaft," in *Gestaltprobleme der Dichtung*, ed. Richard Alewyn, Hans-Egon Hass, and Clemens Heselhaus (Bonn: Bouvier, 1957), 299–306, especially 301–03; and Karl S. Guthke, "Themen der deutschen Shakespeare-Deutung von der Aufklärung bis zur Romantik," in *Wege zur Literatur: Studien zur deutschen Dichtungs- und Geistesgeschichte*, ed. Karl S. Guthke (Bern: Francke, 1967), 118. See also Norbert C. Wolf, *Streitbare Ästhetik: Goethes kunst- und literaturtheoretische Schriften 1771–1789* (Tübingen: Niemeyer, 2001).

22. Heinrich Wilhelm von Gerstenberg, *Briefe über Merkwürdigkeiten der Litteratur*, Zweyte Sammlung (Schleswig and Leipzig: Hansen, 1766), 220.

23. Johann Wolfgang von Goethe, "Rede zum Schäkespears Tag," in *Goethes Werke. Hrsg. im Auftrag der Großherzogin Sophie von Sachsen*, 143 volumes (Weimar: Böhlau, 1896) (*Weimarer Ausgabe*), I. Abt, volume 37, 133.

24. Goethe, "Rede zum Schäkespears Tage," 131.

25. Johann Gottfried Herder, *Von Deutscher Art und Kunst* (Hamburg: Bode 1773), 82.

26. Jakob Michael Reinhold Lenz, *Anmerkungen übers Theater nebst angehängten übersetzten Stück Shakespears* (Leipzig: Weygand, 1774), 29.

27. This resource is fully accessible at https://textgridrep.org.

28. Nils Reiter, "DramaNLP 0.4.2," https://doi.org/10.5281/zenodo.214846 (accessed January 18, 2017).

29. A prominent example for this is Juliet in the Wieland translation of Shakespeare's *Romeo and Juliet* (called *Romeo und Juliette* in German). In the *dramatis personae*, she is introduced as *Julietta, Capulets Tochter*, whereas her speech within the text is always marked with *Juliette* (note the "e" at the end).

30. Kristina Toutanova, Dan Klein, Christopher Manning, and Yoram Singer, "Feature-Rich Part-of-Speech Tagging with a Cyclic Dependency Network." Paper presented at the Human Language Technology Conference of the North American Chapter of the Association for Computational Linguistics, Edmonton, Canada, May–June 2003.

31. Wojciech Skut, Brigitte Krenn, Thorsten Brants, and Hans Uszkoreit, "An annotation scheme for free word order languages." Paper presented at the Fifth Conference on Applied Natural Language Processing, Washington, DC, 1997.

32. Institut für Maschinelle Sprachverarbeitung, "Huge German Corpus," http://hdl.handle.net/11858/00-247C-0000-0022-6265-2 (accessed January 18, 2017).

33. Anders Björkelund, Bernd Bohnet, Hafdell Love, and Pierre Nugues, "A high-performance syntactic and semantic dependency parser." Paper presented at the 23rd International Conference on Computational Linguistics, Beijing, China, August 2010.

34. This question is addressed in Hans-Peter Eyink, *Zum Einfluß von Shakespeares Tragödien und Historien auf Puskins Drama "Boris Godunov": Einteilungsprobleme des Dramas in Puškins Gesamtwerk* (PhD dissertation, Munster, 1987), 236.

35. Indeed, there are mainly comedies in the *Frühaufklärung*-subcorpus, but yet, the language in drama orientates not as strictly to natural language as it does a few decades later. See for example Walter Jens, *Von deutscher Rede* (Munich: Piper, 1969).

36. The top fifteen words associated with comedy are "gut," "frauenzimmer," "machen," "sagen," "herr," "verstehen," "wissen," "sache," "leute," "lieber," "hübsch," "dumm," "fein," "bekommen," "nehmen." The fifteen most prevalent words in tragedy are "abgrund," "haupt," "aug," "mörder," "brust," "tod," "blut," "lebend," "fluch," "mord," "heil," "antlitz," "beugen," "schmach," "empor." See Nils Reiter and Marcus Willand, "Geschlecht und Gattung. Digitale Analysen von Kleists *Familie Schroffenstein*," *Kleist-Jahrbuch* (2017), 177–95. The word lists are also discussed in a shorter online-version of this paper: "Ottokar Capulet & Julia Schroffenstein? Liebeskonflikte und Gattungskontexte bei Kleist und Shakespeare," https://quadrama.github.io/blog/2016/10/07/ottokar-capulet.

37. Johann Wolfgang von Goethe, "Von deutscher Baukunst," in *Goethes Werke*, ed. Erich Trunz, fourteen volumes (Hamburg: Wegner, 1960), volume 12, 116.

38. See Bernhard Asmuth, *Einführung in die Dramenanalyse*, fifth edition (Stuttgart: Metzler, 1997), 42.

39. See Jens, *Von deutscher Rede*.

40. See http://www.ims.uni-stuttgart.de/forschung/ressourcen/lexika/GermanTagsets.html for an overview of the tag set as well as annotation guidelines.

41. See Kob, *Wielands Shakespeare-Übersetzung*.

42. See Francis Lamport, "'Shakespeare has quite spoilt you': The Drama of the Sturm und Drang," in *Literature of the Sturm und Drang*, ed. David Hill (Rochester, NY: Camden House, 2003), 117–39.

Chapter Six

Milton in Germany
Translation and Creative Response
John Guthrie

Shakespeare today in Germany is a household name, but John Milton is known only to the few, despite the existence of a modern translation of *Paradise Lost* published by Reclam Verlag.[1] If we return to the beginning of the eighteenth century, we see a different picture. Long before the presence of Ossian, Milton was in the process of becoming the first great English poet to be discovered and paving the way for the flood of English writing into Germany. By the end of the century Johann Gottfried Herder could justly maintain: "Wo ist dem Milton und Oßian wärmer gehuldigt worden, als in Deutschland?" (Where are Milton and Ossian paid greater homage than in Germany?)[2] Looking back at the century before Herder asked this—albeit rhetorical—question helps us to make sense of just how Milton acquired this status. And it aids us in appreciating his diminishing status afterwards.

Translation is not the only route by which cultural transfer takes place. But in Milton's case it was the most important. When examining how far Milton's ideas penetrated into Germany, it is illuminating to consider them firstly in relation to developments in translation. The first translations can be seen largely as only having qualified success, but as the century moved on, further translations enabled readers to come closer to the core of Milton's ideas. The translations in turn were a trigger for debates on language and aesthetics. Here Milton played a key role and changed the course of German literature. Lawrence Marsden Price, in his pioneering work on Anglo-German literary relations in the eighteenth century,[3] argued that the "Miltonian wave" in Germany (represented by Milton, Edward Young, author of *Night-Thoughts*, and Samuel Richardson) lasted from 1740 to 1770. The transition to the "Miltonian" wave was created by James Thomson, following on from the "Augustan" wave (1720–1750); after it came the "Shakespearean" wave (1760–1780). As Price notes, the definition of "waves" itself is problematic. Moreover, Milton's influence in Germany, as I shall show, begins earlier and ends later than Price suggests. It certainly does not end in 1770 and indeed its long history sheds light on the effects the reception of Milton had upon German literature and culture at the end of the eighteenth century and into the nineteenth. It paves the way for Shakespeare's reception in Germany and even continues into that. The reception of Milton in Germany is more complex and diverse than Price's idea of a "Miltonian wave" suggests, having several different strands: it is the source of debates in aesthetics and stimulates the writing of religious verse, idyllic and pastoral poetry, and rapturous prose writing. And while it is a commonplace that Milton was the major stimulus for Klopstock's religious poetry, what is still to be appreciated is the emergence of the Satanic strand that materializes in the prose, poetry, and drama of the *Sturm und Drang* (Storm and Stress). This chapter, therefore, takes a long view of the reception of Milton in the German-speaking world from the end of the seventeenth century right to the beginning of the nineteenth. In so doing, I not only challenge Price's characterization of a "Miltonian" wave being brought to an end upon a "Shakespearean" wave, but I sketch the developments of the literary and cultural context in which Milton was being received, demonstrating too that Milton was a central figure in guiding those same changes. Indeed, Milton's own impact on German culture helped to steer the various traditions that would seek to both align themselves with and distance themselves from him. Moreover, by looking as far back as the seventeenth century, we can chart the development of traditions that begin with interpersonal exchange between Milton and his German counterparts. The changing fate of Milton in Germany in eighteenth century therefore serves as a complex case study of how one poetic persona can figure within cultural transfer.

BODMER'S MILTON: LANGUAGE AND "DAS WUNDERBARE"

The beginning was difficult. The ground for cultural transfer between England and Germany during Milton's lifetime was not fertile. Few people knew English and bilingual dictionaries were non-existent. In addition, there was Milton's reputation as a radical and writer of political tracts: he was a defender of regicide, of arguments for divorce, and of freedom of the press, all of which were dangerous ideas. It was not until a German theologian, Theodore Haak, had been to England, studied, worked, and befriended Milton that a route for the poetry began to be established. Haak was the first translator of Milton into German, indeed into any language—that is, even before Milton was translated into Latin, which began with William Hog's translation in

1690, providing confirmation that the work had attained the status of a classic. Haak, a theologian, a member of the clergy, and founding member of the Royal Society, began his translation of *Paradise Lost* around 1680. He was keen to convey the religious message of the poem and sensed the power of Milton's poetic language. He evidently thought of the poem as political.[4] He translates into unrhymed iambic pentameter and frequently uses enjambment, syncope, and apocope in an effort to imitate the original. But in Haak's hands the style becomes monotonous and un-Miltonic. Pamela Barnett's close study of Haak's translation shows that it imitates the literary style of the seventeenth century and trivializes the grandeur of the original through oversimplification and changes of emphasis. It fails to create the halftones that enliven Milton's poem: Heaven and Hell are painted solidly in blacks and whites, characterization is affected, and Satan in particular is robbed of his lofty expressions and therefore of a way of expressing his pride and dignity.[5]

Haak translated only Books I to III and fifty lines of Book IV of *Paradise Lost*. His translation reached Germany in manuscript form. When Haak showed it to his friend, Ernst Gottlieb von Berge, the latter used it as a source for his own translation, which became the first published translation in German eight years after Milton's death in 1682.[6] Of some interest is the three-page dedication to Dorothea, Marggräffin und ChurFürstin zu Brandenburg, second cousin of the Great Elector. Here Dorothea is described as being not without influence in political matters and very probably responsible for Haak's appointment to the post of the Elector's translator and private secretary in autumn 1682. The exaggerated submissiveness of the dedication and its praise of God's omnipotence highlight the role of patronage and suggest the courtly elite readership for which the translation was destined; at the same time, this submissiveness deflects from the poem's political message—if indeed von Berge was aware of it. In his preface, von Berge shows he is keen to endorse the advantages of Milton's English style (such as its freedom and profusion of shorter words) and imitate them in German. But he does not improve on Haak in any way. His style is even more strained than Haak's and exaggerates the latter's defects. By the time Johann Jakob Bodmer came to do his translation in the 1720s, von Berge's translation was considered to be unsatisfactory; Bodmer found it had obscured Milton's meaning.[7] Johann Christoph Gottsched was equally critical, particularly of the frequent use of enjambment, which von Berge had imitated and which Gottsched believed must be equally unpleasant in English.[8]

A curiosity on the way to Bodmer is a translation by Christoph Wegleiter, who was stimulated by his friend Haak, whom he visited in England, to translate the first 195 lines of *Paradise Lost* into Alexandrines in 1687.[9] Wegleiter saw *Paradise Lost* as a poetic devotional book in the Puritan sense.[10]

His translation avoids the syncope and apocope of his predecessors, in effect reclassicizing Milton and producing smoother lines; it lacks the plasticity and color of the original and barely involves the narrator in the action. Milton is watered down; this is particularly apparent in the treatment of Satan, whom Wegleiter takes against from a theological point of view. It is an adaptation rather than a translation, and it has in common with its predecessors that it gives little sense of the original.[11]

Several more translations into Latin had appeared by the beginning of the eighteenth century that were available in Germany, and in 1727 a French prose translation came out that found a German readership. A French version of *The Spectator* had also begun to appear from 1714, though it did not include Joseph Addison's papers on *Paradise Lost*. But while Milton was to lose popularity in France with the help of Voltaire, Germans were gaining deeper insight into his work. By 1724, Bodmer and Johann Jakob Breitinger were familiar with the English version of *The Spectator*, and Bodmer set about translating Milton with the help of a Latin-English dictionary. Bodmer was well aware of the shortcomings of von Berge's translation; he solved the problem of how to translate Milton by relinquishing any pretensions to poetry and choosing prose. The translation was published in 1732. Bodmer revised it time and again and published no fewer than six different versions (keeping him occupied until the 1780s).

Just as important as opting for prose to convey Milton's meaning was what motivated Bodmer to do so. His interest in Milton was aroused by his Italian friends Lodovico Antonio Muratori, who argued for the rights of the imagination, and Count Pietro Calepio, who defended (up to a point) Milton's depiction of angels; the Italians went on to do their own translations of Milton, which, according to John K. Hale, are the best in any language.[12] Bodmer's reading of Milton was an experience connected with nature; in a letter to his friend Laurenz Zellweger of January 28, 1724, he describes Satan's entry into Paradise (quoting the pastoral description that occurs in Book IX, ll. 445–53, which Bodmer translates).[13] The theological argument was undoubtedly important, and Bodmer wished to convey it in his translation. He states later that Adam is the hero of the poem, not Satan. Yet it is Satan's perspective on nature that he first adopts and which triggers his desire to translate the whole poem.

With Bodmer the idea of "Nature" was expanded to include both the real world as experienced by the individual *and* the realm of the possible that could be justified in rationalist terms: what was conceivable in terms of the imagination must be given freedom to express itself. Milton had brought the possible into the real. The most controversial aspect of *Paradise Lost*, that is, the appearance of the Christian supernatural in human form, is defended in

terms of "das Wunderbare"—the marvellous, the miraculous, the sublime—
which is the "new" and justifiable in the realm of the imagination. The contours of the debate that ensued, mainly with Gottsched in Leipzig, have been
sketched often enough and its importance for the course of German literature
well recognized. Less well recognized, however, has been the importance of
language in the debate. From Bodmer's and Breitinger's preoccupation with
the language of the original and his translation into German emerges the
theory that the marvellous, which, as Breitinger states in his *Critische Dichtkunst* (Critical Poetics, 1740), is the "äusserste Staffel des Neuen" (uttermost
stage of the new), also applies to language.[14] Indeed, it was the newness of
Paradise Lost ("things unattempted yet in prose or rhyme") that appealed to
Bodmer.

Although Bodmer's *Critische Abhandlung von dem Wunderbaren in der
Poesie* (Critical Treatise on the Marvellous in Poetry, 1740) has usually been
the focus of attention when discussing his ideas, it is in the shorter essay
Abhandlung von der Schreibart in Miltons verlohrnen Paradiese (Treatise on
Style in Milton's Paradise Lost, 1742) that we find his ideas on language.[15]
He addresses what he sees as the key features of Milton's language, from the
finer linguistic points of the lengthening and shortening of words through to
syntax and the nature of metaphor. Milton took advantage of the capacity
of English to absorb features of other languages. One such feature was the
shortening and lengthening of individual words. Bodmer follows Addison
in believing that Milton consciously chose forms of words less commonly
known, such as Beelzebub over Belzebub, or Uriel pronounced as two syllables instead of three, which added or subtracted a syllable to poetic effect.[16]
This could be viewed either as damaging the language by deviating from
convention or as creating something new and arresting. For Bodmer, Milton's
much discussed use of metaphor was characteristic of the freedom to invent.
He revived metaphors from an earlier stage in the language and put archaisms
to a new use. This can be compared with the more rigorous and purist attitude
of French poets and grammarians that prohibited them. German shared with
English the capacity to absorb features from other languages and to revive
earlier forms.

The most important feature of language that Bodmer singles out as significant is inversion and the placing of the epithet after the noun. This is a
device that he believed Milton had borrowed from Homer. English poetic
language had the capacity to allow this, as did German. Inversion arrests the
reader and creates expectation. Bodmer gives as an example the beginning of
Virgil's *Eclogue IV*, where the main verb is delayed after the object by five
lines. The similarity with the opening of *Paradise Lost* is striking. The technique of delay, Bodmer states, creates hope of something new, hope of "das

Wunderbare." In this way language has the capacity to create something new. Ellipsis can have a similar effect and there is a link between grammar, the form of individual words, and metaphor: metaphor compresses and connects things previously seen as belonging to different spheres, such as elements of different cultures like Christian and heathen myths (a controversial aspect of *Paradise Lost*). Gottsched had condemned Milton's use of "seltsame Metaphoren," whereas Bodmer defended them in poetic as well as in broader cultural terms.[17] The use of inversion and delay and the creation of new metaphors are analogous to a religious meaning being found in language; it is in effect the hope of salvation through language. For Bodmer as translator, the role of language as epiphany is just as important, if not more so, than the theological import of the poem in the didactic sense. It relies for its impact on the receptivity of the reading public, which can only occur when that public is ready to receive it, that is, when it has become educated and receptive to the poetic qualities of its own language.

Bodmer offered his readers a translation that was readable and conveyed much of the sense of Milton's poem. In particular, by translating into prose, Bodmer preserves the length of Milton's periods, one of the poem's outstanding stylistic features and crucial for its conceptual content. Though much is conveyed, Bodmer's style is less forceful and provocative than Milton's. "Who first seduced them to that foul revolt? / Th'infernal Serpent" (Bk I, l. 33), for example, becomes: "Wer beredete sie zu dem schändlichen Aufstand. Der höllische Wurm" (Who talked them into this shameful revolt? The hellish serpent). Bodmer finds it necessary to include a relatively large number of explanatory footnotes (some taken over from Addison and Richard Bentley), with his own interpretation of characters or comparisons with German poets (including reference to Albrecht von Haller's conventional view of the hierarchy of angels). Footnotes giving reference to German writers are features of many eighteenth-century translations from English to German that reveal the gap between the two cultures and bear witness to Bodmer's aim of bringing the essence of Milton's art closer to the German reader. Bodmer's is in effect a translation and an annotated edition, which like Breitinger's edition of the works of Martin Opitz, has the makings of a "historisch-kritische Ausgabe" (historical-critical edition).[18]

RESPONSES TO BODMER'S MILTON: FROM GOTTSCHED TO KLOPSTOCK AND LESSING

It was through Bodmer's translation that Milton entered German literature: first, through the translation itself, which was widely read, and second, through his debate with Gottsched. This debate is the most famous, protracted, polemical, and far-reaching literary debate of the eighteenth century in Germany. Rather than rehearsing all of its features here, in the following I shall draw attention to some features of the debate that bear on language and those that ultimately went on to color the reception of Milton by Klopstock, Lessing, and the *Stürmer und Dränger*.

Gottsched secured a copy of Bodmer's translation in 1732 and reacted positively. He gives it the ultimate accolade that it was better than the original: "Bodmer [hat] eine solche Stärke unsrer Sprache gewiesen, daß man sagen könnte, daß Milton durch diese Verdolmetschung noch mehr Kraft und Nachdruck gewonnen habe, als er in seiner Muttersprache besitzt" (Bodmer has shown such strength in our language that one could say that through this translation Milton has gained more force and vigour than he possesses in his own language).[19] He believed a prose translation was the best way to introduce Milton to German readers. However, he is also rather guarded in his praise. He singles out words and phrases that he deems poorly translated, beginning with the title of Bodmer's translation: this should have been "Das verlohrne Paradies" (Paradise Lost) rather than "Verlust des Paradieses" (Loss of Paradise). His criticisms range from those based around trivial grammatical points to castigating Bodmer for the use of unfamiliar words and regionalisms. He disapproves of the neologisms that Bodmer created: the poet was not entitled to create anything new, only to imitate.[20] What shines through above all is Gottsched's objections to Milton's style. Although Gottsched allowed for the fact that what was depicted in literature did not always have to correspond with what was experienced in reality, his conception of the possible in the realm of the imagination was much narrower than Bodmer's. He believed that Milton's style and the depiction of the supernatural were exaggerated and contradictory, and he finds in Milton absurdity taken to the highest degree.[21] The combination of paganism and Christianity disturbs him because it is inconsistent, and he rejects the Satanic because he considers it repulsive and barbaric.[22] Thus his objections to Milton are aesthetic and stylistic rather than primarily theological.

Further objections were laid at Milton's door relating to style: his use of metaphor and allegory, the digressions in which the poet talks from his own point of view, and the qualities of Milton's language itself. For Gottsched, Milton takes too much freedom and uses stylistic devices such as inversion that would create only barbarisms in German. His style is declared to be florid, reminiscent of the lofty and pompous style of Daniel Casper von Lohenstein and Christian Hoffmann von Hoffmannswaldau. What beauties there are in Milton's language—Gottsched has this on the authority of a learned Englishman—are based on grammatical errors. This is a curious argument, because Gottsched admits that there are beauties in Milton's lines even as there appear to be no such beauties to him. It is clear from his citation of an English critic that Gottsched's familiarity with the original is limited. In short, Milton's style cannot and should not be imitated in German. We find here arguments diametrically opposed to those of Bodmer and indeed to Milton's, for both of whom openness to the foreign was axiomatic and stylistic freedom fundamental. The German translations are condemned: if they are accurate they reflect the roughness and wildness of the original, if they are inaccurate they are rough and wild too, in comparison with a French verse translation. It is not surprising to find that the German version of *The Spectator* by Gottsched and his wife Luise Gottsched, which includes translations of the papers on Milton with excerpts from *Paradise Lost*, adds an additional beat to each line. This both brings it close to the formality of the French Alexandrine and robs Milton's poetry of its flexibility and thus of its atmosphere and power.[23]

It is one of the paradoxes of Milton's impact on the language of German poetry that the least poetic of translations (Bodmer's) gave rise to the most innovative and influential poetry (Klopstock's). Friedrich Gottlieb Klopstock was deeply affected by his reading of Milton in Bodmer's translation, and it became the direct and immediate inspiration for his twenty-canto epic poem *Der Messias*, the first three cantos of which appeared in 1748. In his own lifetime Klopstock was dubbed "the German Milton," but even Bodmer, who helped to create this legend, was aware of the distinctiveness of both poets and qualified his assertion by adding that Klopstock's *Messias* would better help its readers to appreciate Milton's inventiveness and ideas. To begin with, Klopstock's theological perspective is different to Milton's: he is not interested in Satan's rebellion and the Fall but in the possibility of redemption and the salvation of mankind. His poem has none of the subversive political content and attack on the Church that Milton's does; it is a tamer, more inward, and lyrical poem. A further point can be made about Klopstock's language. Using Bodmer's prose translation, Klopstock was not tempted to imitate Milton's iambic pentameters. He chooses the hexameter, the meter considered the most appropriate for epic, and thereby uses language more distant from his contemporaries than Milton's language was from that of *his* contemporaries. Readers had difficulty with Klopstock's hexameters. His style lacked the immediacy and directness of Milton's grand style. Others, however, appreciated what Klopstock was doing with the German language: reinventing it from within with the help of foreign models. Christian Fürchtegott Gellert summed up the paradoxes when he said that Klopstock's language was "stark; aber hart; kühn aber auch zuweilen fremd" (strong but hard, bold but at times strange).[24] The irony of this is that strangeness, hardness, roughness, and boldness were also qualities that could be found in Milton's language.

Klopstock was reinventing German poetic language by using foreign models and going beyond the accepted norm.

Although by mid-century Bodmer's prose translation had acquired enormous influence and fired the most significant debate in aesthetics, this did not deter another writer from attempting a new verse translation. The first volume of Friedrich Wilhelm Zachariae's translation appeared in 1760, followed by the second in 1763. Like Bodmer, Zachariae made changes to his first version and defended himself against criticisms. There is much to praise in Zachariae's translation: he builds on the literal accuracy of Bodmer's translation and is clearly attempting to convey the sense and some of the grandeur of Milton's style by using verse. But with the attempt at elevation through the hexameter comes watering down and wordiness. Zachariae translates the beginning of *Paradise Lost* thus: "Von dem ersten Vergehen des ungehorsamen Menschen, / Und dem verderblichen Essen der Frucht des verbotenen Baumes, / Welches den Tod auf die Erde gebracht, und alles ihr Elend, / Mit dem Verlust von Eden" (Of the first crime of disobedient man/ And the pernicious eating of the fruit of the forbidden tree / Which brought death onto earth and all its misery / With the loss of Eden).[25] The number of syllables in the opening phrase is doubled in German; the rhythm becomes dactylic; the style more abstract and bland ("mortal taste," for example, becomes "verderblichen Essen")[26]; the argument more categorical, thus "Or *if* Sion hill / Delight thee more [emphasis added]" becomes "doch gefällt dir der Hügel / Sions mehr" (but Sion's hill pleases you more), or simply more wordy. The wordiness of the translation is clear when Milton's words "Things unattempted yet in prose or rhyme" become "Und die geheiligte Spur von großen Dingen verfolget, / Die sonst niemand vor mir in Prosa noch Reimen versucht hat" (And followed the sacred path of great things which no one has attempted in prose or rhyme). Indeed, the first reference to Satan "Who first seduced them to that foul revolt?" is rendered as: "Sage, wer war es, der sie zuerst von ihrem Gehorsam / Zu dem schändlichen Auffstand verleitet?" (Tell me who it was who first led them from their obedience to the shameful revolt?). In this latter case, eight words become fifteen, and a relative clause is added. Similarly Satan, "the infernal serpent," becomes in Zachariae's translation a melodramatic character "der Drache der Hölle" (the dragon of hell).

Zachariae defends his translation in the preface to the second edition. The problem was that Milton's Satan is male. In German a serpent is feminine ("die Schlange"). Zachariae could have chosen "der höllische Wurm" (hellish serpent) as Bodmer did (indeed Satan is called at one point "that false worm," Bk IX, l. 1068); But that loses the feeling of snakiness, and, as Neil Forsyth writes, what "Eve really likes about the serpent after all, is that he is a talking snake."[27] Zachariae chooses a dragon, which makes the presence of evil more melodramatic, less insidious, and psychologically less plausible, whereas the real animal in nature becomes allegorical and mythological. The same watering down is evident in Zachariae's translation of the depreciative sense of "mate" in Satan's "mates," who become his "Gefährte" (companions).

Gotthold Ephraim Lessing provides the link between what we may call the first phase of Milton's reception in Germany and the next generation of writers of the *Geniezeit* (Age of Genius). He stands largely outside the acrimonious debate between Leipzig and Zurich and although he would have agreed with Bodmer on most points, he places Milton in the context of a broader aesthetics. There are two points that Lessing makes about Milton in *Laokoon: oder über die Grenzen der Malerei und Poesie* (Laocoön: or An Essay on the Limits of Painting and Poetry, 1766) and its drafts.[28] The first (in §XIV) is the pictorial quality of Milton's imagination and his ability to create a succession of images by the most sparing of means, his only equal in this being Homer. The second (in §XX) refers to the building of the Pandemonium, where Milton enters the poem saying: "the work some praise, and some the architect" (Bk I, l. 731–32). Lessing sees the poet's perspective as part of the aesthetic totality of the work. This deals implicitly with the charge (made by Gottsched) that *Paradise Lost* was full of digressions and the poet's intrusion. In the drafts to *Laokoon*, Lessing elaborates on the first point. It matters not that Milton depicts incorporeal spiritual beings, because they are visible to the imagination: the "inner eye" has precedence over the "bodily eye."

Lessing quotes from Jonathan Richardson's treatise on painting and endorses his view that after having read Milton one saw nature with different eyes.[29] Milton may use allegory, but does so sparingly to contribute to the sequence of progressive images rather than spinning out an allegory in the manner of an inferior author. Lessing gives the example of Satan's deception of Uriel (Bk III, ll. 681–93) and provides a further list of episodes to reinforce his point about progressive images. Most of these involve Satan (e.g., his emergence from the burning lake). He adds the example of the beauty of form in the description of Eve and Satan's attraction to her. Lessing recognizes that Satan's point of view, into which the poet enters, is essential to the poem's descriptive power. Thus where Satan transforms himself into the Serpent (an example of the miraculous) we experience the bodily movements as a series of "suczessive Gemälde" (successive pictures).[30] This is only possible if the poet shares his perspective with the character he has created. Lessing strongly endorses the narrative technique and the poetology of *Paradise Lost*. He further recognizes that Satan as a character is both the perpetrator of evil and the afflicted one.[31] He deals with other aspects that had aroused criticism, such as the fact that Adam is given a language he could not have used. For Lessing, this is one of Milton's necessary errors: it is aesthetically justified. With this,

Lessing confronts the other main strand of German aesthetics of this period: Lessing opposes the richness and strength of Milton's visual imagination to Johann Joachim Winckelmann's neo-Hellenism and its expectation of finding perfect moral beings and perfectly beautiful physical beings.

Lessing's insights were important. They emphasized the role of language and the descriptive power of the epic, and showed that, despite its controversial theology, the work could be a model for descriptive poetry. Lessing's reception of Milton is to some extent reminiscent of Bodmer's epiphany in nature. But for Lessing, unlike for earlier commentators, the appearance of the supernatural in human form was not a problem, and the theological issues of *Paradise Lost* were secondary to the aesthetic. He embraces Milton as both ancient and modern, and the ability of Milton's visual imagination to create the illusion of nature. The epic structure of the poem is of great interest to Lessing, and particularly the Satanic perspective which is the key to its descriptive power. Lessing's acclamation of Milton's descriptive powers paves the way for the reception of Milton in the final decades of the eighteenth century.

HERDER AND MORITZ:
FROM POET OF THE *VOLK* TO POET OF NATURE

Herder got to know Milton's work in the 1760s and read his work in the original. In his *Fragmente* of 1767 he deplores the translation into mediocre German hexameters of the poetry of Matthew Prior, Milton, and Young. He prefers Bodmer's prose translation of Milton to Zachariae's.[32] He believed that Milton could be translated into German better than into other languages because of the affinities between English and German. Herder is sensitive to the form of Milton's poetry, its euphony, meter, and the predominance of one-syllable words (producing what he calls its tuba-like tone).[33] At the same time as showing sensitivity to the form, Herder broadens the historical perspective on Milton. Gottsched rejected Milton's worldview and style as inappropriate to a rationalistic age. While expressing some reservations about Milton's theology (especially the depiction of Hell, the Satanic, the violent, and the terrible), Herder, however, saw Milton's poetry as a product of the cultural context of its time, that is, of the, "damalige Volksbegriffe." Milton is on the one hand a reflective, thinking poet at the beginning of a British tradition: "eine *denkende* ist die Britische Muse" (the British muse is a thinking one).[34] His poetry is at the same time organically related to a way of life. Like Lessing, Herder sees Milton together with Homer as the greatest of epic poets with unrivaled descriptive powers. He also compares him to Ossian and Shakespeare. Milton is, like Shakespeare, defended as a "Genie" (genius) against those who proclaim the importance of rules.[35] On the other hand, his poetry is also said to have achieved classical fullness and subtlety through Italian influences. And, by being a product of the Protestant Reformation in England, Milton's poetry had acquired a reflective element embodying a religious system that, however, damages the poem.[36] Milton is "der Chaosmaler ... der Angelo unter den Dichtern" (the painter of Chaos, the Angelo among the poets), whose powerful poetic depictions of darkness are comparable with Shakespearean tragedy.[37]

In his own translation of some passages from *Paradise Lost* it is clear that Herder attempts to make Milton into the type of folk poet and nature poet he sees as a model for German poets. On the first page of "Volkslieder, 1778/1779," we find:

- - Sind Blumen, nicht, die feine Kunst
Auf Beeten zog, in Sträußer zierlich band,
Sind Blumen, die Natur, die gute Mutter,
Auf Hügel, Tal und Ebnen ausgoß.[38]

[Flowers which nice art did not cause to grow in beds and daintily bind into bunches; flowers which nature, the good mother, poured onto hill, valley and plane.]

Milton's original, however, reads thus:

Flowers worthy of Paradise which not nice art
In beds and curious knots, but nature boon
Poured forth profuse on hill and dale and plain. (Bk IV, ll. 241–43)

Herder increases the number of lines but shortens them and makes them into end-stopped lines; he simplifies and domesticates the vocabulary so that overall his translation resembles a "Volkslied." The key word "Paradise" is omitted; the inversion with the prepositioning of "nicht" (not) works poorly in German, so that the first couplet yields its sense only with successive rereadings. "Zierlich band" for "curious knots" does little to suggest the roughness and strength of nature, whereas the sense in the second couplet is clearer, albeit at the cost of introducing a cliché: "die gute Mutter" is used for nature where Milton deploys the striking adjective "boon." Yet we can see in his use of one- and two-syllable words that Herder is attempting to imitate in German this same aspect of the original. He believed that no other poet apart from Milton so effectively combined single syllable words with words of more than one syllable.[39]

Herder viewed Milton as a folk poet and a spontaneous genius, like Klopstock. On the other hand, Klopstock and Milton should never have been compared. Milton's muse is masculine, like the iambic meter he uses, whereas Klopstock's is of a gentler kind and addresses the entire soul.[40] Herder thus locates the transformation that Milton's poetry undergoes in Germany with "Empfindsamkeit" (Sentimentalism). Herder embraces Milton's depiction of nature and Creation, especially the principle of Light. He is "der ungeheuermalende Milton" (Milton, the painter of the immense), a "Nachhall Göttlicher Stimme in Natur und Schrift" (echo of the divine voice in nature and the Word).[41] Milton's poems are powerful because they show God's voice in nature. In his treatise on Hebrew poetry Herder translated a substantial section, the opening of Book III ("Hail holy light"), where Milton powerfully evokes the inner light in his life.[42] Herder circumvents the controversial depiction of the Christian supernatural in *Paradise Lost* and concentrates instead on the human aspect of the poem. He focuses on the bower scene (i.e., the depiction of love in Paradise, though he is seemingly unaware that Adam and Eve have sex before the Fall as Milton implies).

Embracing Milton's religious message and showing his place in a British tradition of poetry, Herder acknowledges that Milton can be read in different ways. His own reading of Milton is selective and governed by what he is looking for. Because he senses the power of the darker aspects of the depiction of evil in *Paradise Lost*, Herder, strongly aware of his own religious beliefs, warns of the danger of misreading Milton (i.e., not accepting the religious message and allowing oneself to be swept away by the depiction of nature and the supernatural). His warning points to the ambiguity and the possibility of creative misreadings of *Paradise Lost*. Such creative misreadings become characteristic of the final phase of the reception of Milton in eighteenth-century Germany.

In the 1780s we find that Milton continued to be an inspiration in Germany. Karl Philipp Moritz saw Milton as the poet of England and the English, and experienced an epiphany *in loco*. Moritz read English literature enthusiastically in translation and in the original before going to England to visit London and tour parts of the country. His Milton experience is reminiscent of Christoph Wegleiter's *Reisetagebuch* (Travel Journal) but is deeper and broader and was reciprocated in England. When he arrived in London he aimed to experience the town as the English did. In the rotunda at Vauxhall on June 9, 1782, he found portraits of Shakespeare, Locke, Milton, and Dryden. "Selbst das Volk lernt diese Namen kennen und nennt sie mit Ehrfurcht" (Even the people get to know these names and mention them with reverence).[43] At Westminster Abbey on June 20, 1782, he admired the noble and tasteful simplicity of the busts in Poets' Corner. These have a sublime and stirring effect on the soul and evoke the memory of favorite passages in their works: "die edle und geschmackvolle Simplicität der Denkmäler, auf das Gemüth einen erhabenen und rührenden Eindruck machte, indeß ofte eine lebhafte Erinnerung an irgend eine Lieblingsstelle, aus den Werken eines Schakespear, oder Milton, in der Seele erwachte" (The noble and tasteful simplicity of the monuments had a sublime and stirring effect on the mind, while often a lively memory of some favorite passage from the works of a Shakespeare or Milton arose in the soul).[44] Milton is the English poet most frequently mentioned in his account of his travels. Moritz found the esteem in which national poets were held in England to be the most remarkable aspect of cultural life, and he compared this esteem to the lack of a comparable phenomenon of wide readership of a nationally revered poet in Germany. Further, he noted the availability of cheap duodecimo editions of the poets; he bought a pocket edition of Milton for two shillings before continuing on his travels. He broke his travels on foot by sitting down to read, especially Milton (June 13, 1782, and June 25, 1782; *Reisen*, 72–73, 80). He was reading *Paradise Lost*. It is the description of Eden that particularly moved him when he reached a river near Matlock on June 30 (*Reisen*, 111–12). Similarly, when he saw the mountains in the Peak District, he was reminded of the Angel appearing to Adam and "Immediately the Mountains huge appear / Emergent" (Bk VII, l. 285). He thought of the dispute among the Angels as he imagined seeing the Angel who plucks "the seated Hills with all their load" (Bk VI, l. 644; *Reisen*, 129–30). Moritz experienced the English landscape most intensely through his reading of Milton. He was not interested in the religious dogma or the "marvellous" as such and as with his reading of Pope at Windsor, he entered the poet's mind to relive the experience of the landscape at first hand. For Moritz, nature had the capacity to induce love or despair, to be idyllic or wild and grotesque. A comment in the preface of the English translation of Moritz's travels in 1808 reads:

> Our German does not deal in the marvellous; neither does he affect to be sentimental. On a fine prospect, it is to be owned, he loves to dwell, and describe, with some degree of rapture; but he does not bewilder either himself or his readers in the fairey scenes of picturesque beauty.[45]

With Moritz we find the fullest endorsement of Milton as the poet of England, the poet of nature and the attempt to imitate the experience of nature in rapturous prose.

Moritz first read Pope in Johann Jakob Dusch's translation (1758–1764), and then, while he was in England, he read it in the original. But he ends in the mid-1780s with translating (possibly with the assistance of his friend Karl Friedrich Klischnig) a handful of passages from *Paradise Lost* that were published in several numbers of his journal *Denkwürdigkeiten* (Memoirs, 1786), most of which are in prose, with one in verse. The modernizing translations make Milton's style accessible to readers in Moritz's times. The prose translations are generally accurate, strongly rhythmic, syntactically clear, and free of archaisms. Milton's archaisms, his inversions, and the use of rhetorical devices such as zeugma or the perversion of normal word stress in English (e.g., óbscure for obscúre) are not conveyed. And despite the overall accuracy of the translations, some poetic qualities conveyed by metaphor are ignored. Thus the olfactory sensations in the description of nature after Adam's first awakening in Book VIII (ll. 250–345) are omitted. Adam's words, "As new waked from soundest sleep / Soft on flow'ry herb I found me laid / In balmy sweat which with his beams the sun / Soon dried and on the reeking moisture fed," Moritz translates thus: "Als wie von tiefstem Schlaf erwacht, fand ich mich hingestreckt auf weichem Grase, das noch vom Thau befeuchtet war, den bald mit ihren Strahlen die Sonne wegsog—" (As if woken from deepest sleep I found myself stretched out on soft grass that was still damp with dew and which the sun soon sucked away with its rays).[46] There is nothing for "new" waked, which is arguably pleonastic, and the flowers are lost; again, anything expressing "balmy sweat" or "reeking moisture" is missing, but the grass is soft. The strong olfactory sensations have been transformed into visual ones and the impression of "flow'ry herb" is made purely tactile. In another passage, "fragrance" becomes the abstract "Erquicking" (refreshment), and the Creator's "nostrils," filled with "grateful smell," disappear from the translation altogether for the Creator merely being praised in silence. One suspects that some of the metaphors were considered too strong for the German reading public.

From the passages Moritz translated, it appears that he was keen to convey some of the poetic power of the description of nature and less directly the religious and didactic strand of the work. Thus, instead of translating the famous episode in Book IX in which Eve is tempted by the serpent, he translates the passage leading to it where Adam and Eve discuss the division of labor in the Garden of Eden; here, Eve indicates her desire to undertake her own work and Adam disagrees with her but eventually concedes, allowing her to leave his side. Seventeenth-century attitudes to marriage and gender emerge here alongside Milton's view that disagreement with patriarchal rule leads to sin. It is difficult to say whether Moritz, by choosing this passage, is endorsing Milton's view or, by highlighting it, trying to put it to the test. Another part of the poem that he chooses is that which concerns the origin of language. The passage describing Adam's first awakening has Adam saying, "To speak I tried and forthwith space: / My tongue obeyed and readily could name / Whate'er I saw" (Bk VIII, ll. 271–73), which became a classic statement of the Adamic theory of language whereby language is given to Man by God. Between Milton and Moritz this had been much debated and Moritz, like others, adhered to the belief that human invention and convention had a larger role to play in the development of language. Was he again trying to put Milton to the test here at the same time as trying to show his poetic power? At any rate, one side effect of the interest in the origins of language is that Adam no longer speaks archaic English, but modern German; Moritz, like others before him, is showing that German as a language also has the power to convey thoughts and feelings about the first and last things.

It is notable that Moritz—in parallel with his own interests and those of the 1780s—is interested in the psychology of evil and the power of poetry to convey it. This is apparent from the verse translation he includes in a fictitious letter "Noch etwas aus K . . . s Papieren" (Something else from K . . .'s Papers), dated "Wittenberg 3 May 1778ff.," which finds its place in the same journal as the prose translations. The first part of the letter, which precedes the translations, shows a mind engaged in an inner struggle: "Muß nicht der Mensch immer im Streit seyn auf Erden?" (Must not man on earth always be in conflict?); "Bin ich denn zwei Wesen, oder bin ich eins? Schrecklich! schrecklich!—" (Am I then two beings, or am I one? Horrible! Horrible!).[47] The inner struggle leads to the quotation of some passages from Book X (Sin's encouragement to Death to visit Satan's world and Death's reply; the arrival of Sin and Death in Paradise prior to God's curse of both: ll. 264–69, ll. 272–81, ll. 585–613). After the quotations, the writer comments that Sin lives within him and is to be followed by Death, who will bring about the destruction of his body; the endless turbulence of passion brings about inner destruction. The poem (both Milton's *Paradise Lost* and poetry in a general sense) becomes truth: "O das Gedicht ist zur Wahrheit geworden, und die Wahrheit zum Gedichte" (O the poem has become truth and truth the poem).[48] The theological framework has disappeared, and the consequences of the Fall have taken root in the mind of the individual. We do not know whether the individual can be considered guilty in the Christian sense; indeed, that is not the issue here. Here, literature itself fulfills a redemptive function insofar as the individual resorts to quotation, and to the archetype of the poem to alleviate his suffering. This is Moritz the moral doctor at work, and it represents the psychologizing that was to become the feature of the literature of his age. We find this accentuated in the last phase of Milton's influence in Germany.

THE FINAL PHASE: THE SATANIC AND MILTON'S DECLINE

Friedrich Schiller probably read Milton in Bodmer's translation while at the Hohe Karlsschule in Stuttgart in the late 1770s. His first play *Die Räuber* (The Robbers, 1781) and connected writings make several allusions to *Paradise Lost*. Like others, Schiller saw Satan as the most remarkable character in the poem. In his preface to the play he writes: "Miltons Satan folgen wir mit schauderndem Erstaunen durch das unwegsame Chaos" (We follow Milton's Satan with shuddering amazement through the pathless ways of Chaos).[49] In a supressed part of Scene 2 (*Dramen*, 166–76), Karl Moor condemns the law and defends the cause of freedom. He asks one robber whether he has read Milton, where he will find one character who cannot tolerate someone above himself and who challenges the Almighty with his sword—was Satan not, asks Moor, a "Genie?" He identifies Satan with the creative principle—with Prometheus—whose flame he intends to rekindle. In the poem "Monument Moors des Räubers" (A Monument for Moor the Robber, 1781),[50] Moor is the "Majestätischer Sünder" (majestical sinner), fallen from a pernicious height, rejected, fulfilling his terrible role, believing that he is climbing to fame and achieving admiration. In Karl Moor we find the combination of good qualities—that is, the rejection of the negative aspects of his own society and the impulse to seek freedom from bondage and tyranny—combined with an all-consuming aspiration towards greatness—that is, the rejection of authority at all costs while pursuing rebellion and overreaching himself. In his monologue in Act IV, scene 5 we find him (shortly after evoking Hamlet's death-wish) quoting Satan: "*Ich* bin mein Himmel und meine Hölle" (*Dramen*, 131, emphasis in original; *I* am my heaven and my hell; cf. Bk I, ll. 250–54).[51] With these words Karl Moor defends his rebellion and accepts the consequences as he becomes aware that his problem with the world is in fact the struggle he has with his own mind.

Unlike Satan, however, Karl Moor only has limited success implanting evil into the minds of his fellow men, and he ends in the world that Satan had created. He repents and submits to the rule of law, the very law that had reduced what might have risen to an eagle's flight to a snail's pace: "Das Gesetz hat zum Schneckengang verdorben, was Adlerflug geworden wäre" (*Dramen*, 32; What might have risen to eagle's flight has been reduced to a snail's pace by the law). But in contrast to *Paradise Lost*, redemption is impossible for the sinner. Karl Moor's rebellion is an experiment in free will in a world where God's authority has been questioned. Schiller has transposed the theological issues that underpin *Paradise Lost* into his own times and the mind of his youthful hero. Schiller's attitude to Milton changed and in later years and he was inclined to praise more the idyllic aspect of *Paradise Lost* and the poem's depiction of innocence in Paradise (see his 1795 *Über naïve und sentimentalische Dichtung* [On Naïve and Sentimental Poetry]) and to regard Milton as the embodiment of the sublime. There is nothing to equal the force of the impact of the figure of Satan on the young Schiller, which forms a bridge from the earlier Miltonic wave to the English Romantics. It is significant that, in another case of reciprocal influence, when Samuel Taylor

Coleridge read *The Robbers* and made his famous remark to Robert Southey, "*Who is this Schiller?* This convulser of the heart?" it is with Milton that he compares him.[52] Indeed, Coleridge was attracted to Schiller's hero by the "alcohol of egotism" that he had found in Milton's Satan.[53]

A further translation of *Paradise Lost* into verse by Samuel Gottlieb Bürde appeared in 1793. It is classicizing in tone, smoothing out Milton's rough style. Goethe ignored it and turned back to the earlier translation of Zachariae, which one may also characterize as classicizing through its use of hexameters, even though these were strongly criticized. The reasons for Goethe using Zachariae's translation may have to do not only with the poetic qualities of the translation itself. He had long since lost interest in Bodmer's poetic writings and in his autobiography concluded that Bodmer had remained, throughout his life, a child.[54] By contrast, with *Die Schöpfung der Hölle* (*The Creation of Hell*, 1760), Zachariae had written poetry inspired by Milton that focused on Satan's downfall.

Goethe had an interest in Milton that emerged several times during his long life. The appeal of Titanic figures to the *Sturm und Drang* has been noted, and it has been suggested that in Goethe's early poem "Mahomets Gesang" (Mahomet's Song) the key image of the river as "schlangewandelnd" (winding snake-like) derived from *Paradise Lost*.[55] In 1799, reading *Paradise Lost* in translation gave rise to some "wunderbare Betrachtungen" (wonderful observations) but Goethe is ambivalent about it, stating that it was "äußerlich scheinbar und innerlich wurmstichig und hohl" (outwardly splendid and inwardly rotten and hollow).[56] This was principally because of the poem's theology: Goethe did not believe that it was possible to depict the conflict between good and evil in the manner in which Milton had done so. This recalls Gottsched's rejection of Milton as the writer of fairy tales. But Goethe is not perturbed by the rationalist's rejection; he makes creative use of Milton's poetry and it was above all as a poet that Milton appealed strongly to him.[57] Goethe cannot accept Christian theology and the lack of free will that it implied, but he praises Milton, the failed revolutionary, and the fact that he fitted better into the role of devil than angel. *Paradise Lost* is a deeply personal poem into which the poet's persona enters directly, and the devil is central to it. Milton is, for Goethe, of the devil's party.

Like Milton's poem, Goethe's *Faust* was to become a deeply autobiographical work, and his devil Mephistopheles evokes sympathy. He does not transform himself into a serpent like Milton's Satan, but he claims him as kin, thus ironically evoking the biblical and Miltonic associations for a different age. Like Milton's Satan he is a master of persuasion and a wit; he experiences human emotions and adopts various human forms. Goethe's Mephistopheles, who is even more important in *Faust* than Satan is in *Paradise Lost*, is in essence a modern Satan and a hard-hitting critic of Church and society in Goethe's time. He is to some extent the essence of Evil that is linked to carnality: "Dort strömt die Menge zu dem Bösen" (l. 4039; There the crowd stream to the Evil One). His rebellion begins in heaven, but the spirit of negation is the starting point, not for the creation of evil, but for the creation of good. Faust is redeemed, not in Heaven, not by Christ, but by his own nature. It was necessary to endow evil with something and take something away from goodness. Goethe's Mephistopheles is famously "Ein Theil von jener Kraft, die stets das Böse will und stets das Gute schafft" (ll. 1336–37; A part of that force that always desires to do evil but always creates the good). This is the point at which Goethe's text comes closest to a verbal echo of Zachariae's translation: "O der unendlichen Huld, der unermäßlichen Güte, / Die soviel Gutes aus Bösem erzeugt, und selber das Böse / So in Gutes verwandelt" (Oh the infinite grace, the immeasurable goodness that produces so much good from evil and itself transforms evil into good).[58] Goethe's *Faust* is in one sense an attempt to rewrite *Paradise Lost* and *Paradise Regained* for his own age without the Christian theology. The debate about the depiction of the Christian supernatural was no longer relevant: Goethe frames his own worldview with the help of the abundant use of the supernatural, the transcendental, and the allegorical as well as the human, the realistic, and the ironical.[59]

By the time Goethe had completed his *Faust* in 1832, however, Milton's fame and his stimulus to creative writing in Germany had receded. He had been firmly rejected by the German Romantics. August Wilhelm Schlegel was initially positive about Satan—he calls him "gigantisch aber durchaus edel" (gigantic but thoroughly noble)[60]—comparing him with Catiline and quoting the same phrases as Schiller's Karl Moor. But after 1799 Schlegel preferred Dante's devils and decided that Milton's Satan lacked credibility.[61] In Milton's religion there was not enough mysticism or symbolism of nature, too much realism, too much dwelling on the depiction of nature and on the psychology of rebellion[62]—precisely those things that had attracted earlier writers to him. Ludwig Tieck admired certain aspects of Milton: the allegory and Sin and Death; the depiction of Paradise and of innocence; Satan's grand emotions; and God and his hierarchy. But for Tieck Christ's decision to die and everything connected to it was "höchst albern" (terribly silly).[63] In the meantime, some had recognized that there was a political side to Milton. A review in the South German periodical *Aurora* (1804–1805) stated, that "Milton hatte wirklich bei Verfertigung des verlornen Paradieses die verlorne Freiheit seines Vaterlandes im Auge" (In writing *Paradise Lost* Milton had the lost freedom of his fatherland in mind).[64] But perhaps even because of that political message, combined with what others saw as a religious didacticism that clashed with the inwardness of the Romantics in Germany, Milton's name was to resound no more in their age. It was left to the English Romantics and the French Romantics after them (for example, Germaine de Staël, then François-René de Chateaubriand) to mine his works for inspiration. The German reception of Milton therefore came full circle. After tentative beginnings in the late seventeenth century, when his work and opinions proved problematic and cultural transfer difficult, he was embraced in the early Enlightenment for liberating the imagination and providing religious inspiration for German "Empfindsamkeit": he embodied the English national spirit in poetry, exploring man's relation to nature and the psychology of evil. But he eventually found himself in a position in which, once again, German writers viewed his work as something alien and curiously English, inappropriate for their age.

NOTES

1. John Milton, *Das verlorene Paradies*, trans. Hans Heinrich Meier (Stuttgart: Reclam, 2008).
2. Johann Gottfried Herder, *Briefe zur Beförderung der Humanität*, in *Werke*, ed. Martin Bollacher et al, ten volumes (Frankfurt a.M.: Deutscher Klassiker Verlag, 1985–2000), volume 7, 557.
3. Lawrence Marsden Price, *English Literature in Germany* (Berkeley and Los Angeles: University of California Press, 1953), 48–49.
4. See Neil Forsyth, *The Satanic Epic* (Princeton: Princeton University Press, 2003), 63–64: "Benthem, at least gathered from talking to Haak, that Milton, 'dieser sehr schlau Politicus,' this wily politician, concealed under the story of the fall of our first parents a lament for the loss of Republican England at the Restoration."
5. Pamela Barnett, *Theodore Haak, F.R.S.: (1605–1690). The First German Translator of "Paradise Lost"* ('s-Gravenhage: Mouton, 1962), 183–86.
6. John Milton, *Das Verlustigte Paradeis*, trans. Ernst Gottlieb von Berge (Zerbst: Johann Ernst Bezel, 1782). Bodleian Library Oxford: 8o G 100 Linc. The Bodley copy of von Berge's translation from Haak's library has a small number of handwritten corrections that do not suggest Haak was unsatisfied with it.
7. See Johann Jakob Bodmer, "Vorrede," in *Johann Miltons Verlust des Paradieses*, trans. Johann Jakob Bodmer (Zurich: Marcus Rordorf 1732), n.p.
8. Johann Christoph Gottsched, "XI. Johann Miltons Verlust des Paradieses," in *Beyträge zur Critischen Historie der Deutschen Sprache, Poesie und Beredsamkeit*, Zweites Stück (Leipzig: Breitkopf, 1732), 290–303.
9. Christoph Wegleiter, "Johann Miltons Verlustigtes Paradies. Erstes Buch," in *Reisetagebuch*, unpublished manuscript, Germanisches Nationalmuseum Nürnberg Hs 40660.
10. Leoplold Magon, "Die drei ersten deutschen Versuche einer Übersetzung von Miltons Paradise Lost. Zur Geschichte der deutsch-englischen Literaturbeziehungen

im siebzehnten Jahrhundert," in *Gedenkschrift für Ferdinand Josef Schneider*, ed. Karl Bischoff (Weimar: Böhlau, 1956), 53.

11. See Hans-Dieter Kreuder, *Milton in Deutschland: Seine Rezeption im latein- und deutschsprachigen Schrifttum zwischen 1651 und 1752* (Berlin: de Gruyter, 1971), 114–18.

12. See John K. Hale, "The Significance of the Early Translations of Milton's *Paradise Lost*," *Philological Quarterly* 63 (1984): 31–53.

13. Quoted in Hans Bodmer, "Die Anfänge des zürerischen Milton," in *Studien zur Literaturgeschichte: Michael Bernays Gewidmet von Schülern und Freunden*, ed. L. Voss (Hamburg and Leipzig: Voss 1893), 190.

14. Johann Jakob Breitinger, *Critische Dichtkunst*, two volumes (Zurich: Orell, 1740), volume 1, 130.

15. Johann Jakob Bodmer, "Abhandlung von der Schreibart in Miltons verlohrnen Paradiese," in *Sammlung Critischer, Poetischer, und anderer geistvollen Schriften*, twelve volumes (Zurich: Orell and Comp., 1741–1744), volume 3, 75–133.

16. The other example Bodmer in *Von der Schreibart in Miltons verlohrnen Paradiese*, p. 119 is "Hessebon statt Heßbon." See Addison, *The Spectator* No. 285, p. 77.

17. Gottsched, *Versuch einer critischen Dichtkunst*, IX, §. 7.

18. See Max Wehrli, *Johann Jakob Bodmer und die Geschichte der Literatur* (Frauenfeld: Huber, 1936), 47.

19. Gottsched, *Beyträge zur critischen Historie*, 292.

20. Johann Christian Gottsched, *Auszug aus des Herrn Batteux Schönen Künsten* (Leipzig: Breitkopf, 1754).

21. Gottsched, *Versuch einer critischen Dichtkunst*, IV, §22.

22. Gottsched, *Versuch einer critischen Dichtkunst*, I.IV, §19.

23. Johann Christoph Gottsched, Luise Gottsched, and Johann Joachim Schwabe, trans. *Der Zuschauer*, eight volumes (Leipzig: Breitkopf, 1739–1743), volume 5, 16–19, 200–3. For a different view of Gottsched's translation see Hilary Brown, *Luise Gottsched the Translator* (Rochester, NY: Camden House, 2012), 90–91.

24. Klopstock, *Der Messias I–III*, 206.

25. *Das Verlohrne Paradies: mit Kupfern / aus dem Englischen Johann Miltons in Reimfreye Verse übersetzt, und mit eignen sowohl als andrer Anmerkungen begleitet*, trans. Friedrich Wilhelm Zachariae (Altona: Iversen, 1760), 3.

26. Cf. the Italian translation by Rolli (1730): "il Frutto / Di quell'Arbor vietato." *Del Paradiso Perduto. Poema Inglesi di Giovanni Milton*, trans. Paolo Rolli (London: 1736), 1.

27. Neil Forsyth, "'Evil' in the Bible and Milton. From 'Unimaginable' to 'Unspeakable,'" in *Colloquium Helveticum* 34 (2003): 121. One might compare this version of Satan with Richard Wagner's Fafner in the opera *Siegfried* who, as Wurm, is characterized by immobility.

28. Gotthold Ephraim Lessing, "Paralipomena" [to *Laokoon*], in *Werke und Briefe*, twelve volumes, ed. W. Barner (Frankfurt a.M.: Deutscher Klassiker Verlag, 1985–2003), volume 5/2 (1990).

29. Lessing "Paralipomena," 271. See also Jonathan Richardson, *An Essay on the Theory of Painting* (London: A. C., 1725).

30. Lessing, "Paralipomena," 283–88.
31. Lessing, "Paralipomena," 293.
32. Johann Gottfried Herder, *Fragmente I*, no. 18, in *Werke*, volume 1, 580.
33. Johann Gottfried Herder, *Briefe, das Studium der Theologie betreffend*, 20. Brief, in *Werke*, volume 9/1, 335.
34. Herder, *Briefe zur Beförderung der Humanität*, 97. Emphasis in the original.
35. Milton is compared with Shakespeare in 1778 in Johann Gottfried Herder, *Über die Würkung der Dichtkunst auf die Sitten der Völker in alten und neuen Zeiten*, in *Herders sämmtliche Werke*, ed. Bernhard Suphan, thirty-three volumes (Berlin: Weidmann, 1877–1913), volume 8, 429.
36. Herder, *Briefe zur Beförderung der Humanität*, 534.
37. Johann Gottfried Herder, *Über die ersten Urkunden des Menschlichen Geschlechts. Einige Anmerkungen*, in *Werke*, volume 5, 212.
38. Johann Gottfried Herder, *Volkslieder. Übertragungen. Dichtungen*, in *Werke*, volume 3, 71.
39. Herder, *Briefe zur Beförderung der Humanität*, 541.
40. Herder, *Briefe zur Beförderung der Humanität*, 556.
41. Johann Gottfried Herder, "An Prediger. Fünfzehn Provinzialblätter, in *Werke*, volume 9/1, 127.
42. Herder's translation of the first fifty-five lines of Book III is accurate, compact, and flowing, using the repetition of key words—for example, "des Ewigen mitewigen Strahl" for "Eternal coeternal beam"—that assist the rhythm. See Johann Gottfried Herder, *Geist der Ebräischen Poesie I, 3. Gespräch*, in *Werke*, volume 5, 732–34.
43. Karl Philipp Moritz, *Reisen eines Deutschen in England im Jahr 1782*, in *Sämtliche Werke*, ed. Anneliese Klingenberg et al. (Berlin: de Gruyter, 2005–), volume 5/1: *Reisebeschreibungen*, 31. Hereafter referred to in the body of the text with the abbreviation "Reisen."
44. Moritz, *Reisen eines Deutschen*, 64.
45. Quoted from the "Einleitung" to Karl Philipp Moritz, *Reisen eines Deutschen nach England im Jahr 1782*, ed. Otto zur Linde (Berlin: Behr's, 1903), xxii.
46. Karl Philipp Moritz, *Denkwürdigkeiten*, in *Sämtliche Werke*, volume 11, 163–65.
47. Karl Philipp Moritz, "Noch etwas aus K . . . s Papieren," in *Sämtliche Werke*, volume 11, 190–91.
48. Moritz, "Noch etwas aus K . . . s Papieren," volume 11, 194.
49. Friedrich Schiller, *Die Räuber*, in *Dramen I*, ed. G. Kluge (Frankfurt a.M.: Deutscher Klassiker Verlag, 1988), 17. Hereafter referred to in the body of the text with the abbreviation "*Dramen*."
50. Friedrich Schiller, "Monument Moors des Räubers," in *Sämtliche Gedichte*, ed. G. Kurscheidt (Frankfurt a.M.: Deutscher Klassiker Verlag, 1992), 532.
51. Compare with Milton's text in *Paradise Lost*: "Hail horrors, hail Infernal world, and thou profoundest Hell / Receive thy new possessor: One who brings / A mind not to be changed by place or time. / The mind is its own place, and in itself / Can make a Heaven of Hell, a Hell of Heaven."

52. Samuel Taylor Coleridge to Robert Southey, November 1794, in *Collected Letters*, ed. Earl Leslie Griggs, six volumes (Oxford: Clarendon, 1956), volume 1, 122. Emphasis in the original.

53. Coleridge, quoted in John Milton, *Paradise Lost*, ed. G. Teskey (NY: Norton 2005), 391.

54. To Johann Kaspar Lavater he writes on July 3, 1780, that he finds Bodmer's poetic works quite useless. Johann Wolfgang von Goethe, *Aus meinem Leben. Dichtung und Wahrheit*, in *Goethes Werke. Weimarer Ausgabe*, 143 volumes (Weimar: Hermann Böhlaus Nachfolger, 1887–1919), Section I, volume 27, 80.

55. Inka Mülder-Bach, "'Schlangewandelnd': Geschichten vom Fall bei Milton und Goethe," in *Von der Natur zur Kunst zurück. Neue Beiträge zur Goethe-Forschung: Gotthart Wunberg zum 65. Geburtstag*, ed. Moritz Baßler, Christoph Brecht, and Dirk Niefanger (Tübingen: Niemeyer, 1997), 79–94.

56. Johann Wolfgang von Goethe to Friedrich Schiller, July 31, 1799, in *Weimarer Ausgabe*, Section IV, volume 14 (1893), 138–39.

57. "Milton war in der Tat ein Poet und man muß vor ihm allen Respekt haben." Johann Wolfgang von Goethe to Johann Peter Eckermann, January 31, 1830, in *Weimarer Ausgabe*, Anhang: *Gespräche*, volume 7, 194.

58. For Milton's "Oh goodness infinite, goodness immense! / That all this good of evil shall produce" (Bk XII, ll. 469–70). Zachariae, *Das Verlohrne Paradies*, 240.

59. Karl Guthke has emphasized the role of humor and irony in the God of Goethe's *Faust*, which he compares with Milton's portrayal of god in *Paradise Lost*. I agree entirely with Guthke about the role of humor in Goethe's *Faust* but have emphasized the role of Mephistopheles here in order to show that Goethe, like others at this time, recognized the centrality of the figure of Satan in *Paradise Lost*. It is also significant that God in Goethe's *Faust* is seen partly through the eyes of Mephistopheles. See Karl S. Guthke, "Goethe, Milton und der humoristische Gott. Eine Studie zur poetischen Weltordnung im *Faust*," *Goethe* 22 (1960), 104–11.

60. August Wilhelm Schlegel, *Sämtliche Werke*, ed. E. Böcking, twelve volumes (Leipzig: 1846–47), volume 3, 290.

61. See Enrico Pizzo, *Miltons Verlorenes Paradies im deutschen Urteil des 18. Jahrhunderts* (Berlin: Felber, 1914), 138.

62. August Wilhelm Schlegel, "Geschichte der klassischen Litteratur," quoted in Pizzo, *Miltons Verlorenes Paradies*, 139.

63. Letter from Ludwig Tieck to Karl Wilhelm Ferdinand Solger, December 7, 1818, in *Solger's Nachgelassene Schriften und Briefwechsel*, ed. Ludwig Tieck and Friedrich von Raumer, two volumes (Leipzig: Brockhaus, 1826), volume 1, 695.

64. Anon., "Milton's verlornes Paradies, ein republikanisches Gedicht," *Aurora: eine Zeitschrift aus dem südlichen Deutschland*, 1 (1804–5): 128.

Chapter Seven

The Female Body in Text and Image

Amelia, Lavinia, and Musidora in the German Translations of Thomson's The Seasons *and Beyond*

Sandro Jung

In 1789 Ludwig Schubart published the fourth complete German-language translation of James Thomson's magnum opus, *The Seasons* (1730).[1] In an introductory note to the tragic-sentimental tale of the two lovers Celadon and Amelia appearing in *Sommer* (Summer), he states: "Diese Erzählung und die nachfolgende Bade-Idylle sind zu bekannt, als daß ich etwas über ihren anerkannten poetischen Werth sagen dürfte" (This tale and the subsequent bathing idyll are too well known for me to have to comment on their acknowledged poetic value).[2] The two tales were indeed widely known,[3] but not every reader would have agreed with Schubart's encomium on what he considered their generally acknowledged poetic value. The value, especially of the Damon and Musidora tale, which is the "Bade-Idyle" Schubart mentions, was questioned explicitly by at least one commentator in the period, the editor of the 1777 English edition of *The Seasons*, George Wright, who considered the interpolated story to be "disgustful." Wright held that "the too particular description of Musidora undressing herself" was morally hazardous, "raising indelicate and indecent ideas in the [male] breast." It failed to serve a purpose "for any beneficial instruction."[4] Thomson's tale contained a titillating scene in which Musidora, about to undress to bathe and cool down in the heat of the summer, is being observed by her lover, Damon. Rather than disrupting her bathing and articulating his passion verbally, he leaves a written testament of his having been in Musidora's proximity in which he expresses his love.

Wright's rejection of the episode needs to be understood in the context of Thomson's poem being widely cast as a moral work that was even used as a school book in both eighteenth-century Britain and Germany. To that end, translators and editors, while acknowledging the Damon and Musidora tale as a "berauschende . . . Idylle" (intoxicating idyll), at the same time sought to eliminate the "moral dubiety" of the tale and advance readings of the male lover as chaste and moral.⁵ The editors of the school edition of *Die Iahrszeiten* (The Seasons), I.P. und I. Horn, commented: "Wir schwindeln bei dem Gemählde der sich badenden Musidora, aber unser moralischer Sinn vergnügt sich an der Bescheidenheit des Damon" (We are made dizzy by the painting of the bathing Musidora but our moral sense delights in Damon's modesty).⁶ The bathing scene was arousing in its presentation of the nude Musidora, but also instructive as well as delightful in Damon's exemplary modesty and resistance to follow his desire. The Damon and Musidora tale had thus been reinscribed as a tale asserting moral orthodoxy and confirming models of self-control and self-regulation that fulfil a didactic function—especially in light of student readers encountering the scene through the editors' paratextual apparatus.

Criticism of the risqué display of an erotic scene feeding the male reader's desire and imagination was not confined to metatextual commentary as part of editors' annotation. Rather, at times, even illustrators, who had frequently visualized the two lovers since 1730, decided to censure this explicit eroticism by choosing to focus on Musidora as sole agent of the illustration. Alternatively, in one case—the illustration accompanying the 1814 Georgetown edition published by Richards and Mallory—manual force was applied to eliminate the offensive presence, at Musidora's bathing scene, of Damon. The male figure was eliminated from an engraving plate that had originally contained both lovers.⁷

This chapter will examine the ways in which eighteenth-century German translations of Thomson's tragic-sentimental tales of Celadon and Amelia (*Summer*, lines 1171–222), Damon and Musidora (*Summer*, 1269–370), and Palemon and Lavinia (*Autumn*, 177–310) conceive of the female body and its being loaded with eroticism. In Germany and beyond, these tales were singled out in a way no other passages from *The Seasons* were: they found their way into anthologies and affected the reception and a particular understanding of Thomson's work by inspiring a wide-ranging visual culture, including their being represented on objects of conspicuous consumption such as porcelain. As such, they constituted fashionable literary productions that, through their different medial incarnations, shaped both taste and the readerly understanding of modern British poetry of which the tales were considered representative. Next to the popularity of Alexander Pope's poetry in Germany, Thomson's tales were not only imitated but, in turn, affected the transnational development of genres, specifically through their impact on Christoph Martin Wieland (who until 1752 had known Thomson only through the German translations) and his own verse tales. This chapter aims to understand the adaptive mechanisms German mediators used in order to make Thomson's English original available for (and palatable to) readers from the German-speaking lands. I will explore how, in the interest of facilitating straightforward, unambiguous moral readings of the tales, different translators at times sought to defuse some of the sexual charge inherent to these tales. Particular attention will be paid to how Ludwig Schubart, above any other translator, succeeds in capturing the erotic ambiguity and moral complexity of Thomsonian characters like Amelia and Musidora.

The transmission of Thomson's work was effected not only by means of the typographic text, but also by an extensive visual culture that had fed demand for editions of *The Seasons* since 1730 and made English and French prints available in the German-speaking lands. These literary prints, as well as book illustrations deriving from Thomson's poem, promoted interpretive readings that, in turn, affected viewers' understanding of the work visualized. I shall therefore consider how book illustrations of Musidora negotiate the fine line between moral containment, on the one hand, and the explicit acknowledgment of desire and the voyeuristic gaze, on the other. Finally, I shall contextualize the male desire of Palemon as part of a reading that understands his gaze and (erotic) fantasizing as inherent to a dominant male social identity in which the upper-class male rarely experiences regulation of his desire—as long as this desire is focused on a female who is his social inferior, that is. The reception of the interpolated episodes via German-language translations will be shown to reflect their makers' cultural sensitivity. Both the print capital of *The Seasons* and the fact that Thomson's work as a whole and the interpolated episodes specifically were translated so frequently testify that the poem was marketable in a way few other modern texts were at the time. It was a modern classic and functioned as the cornerstone of a new genre of descriptive verse developing in Germany. Above all, the polyphony of Thomson's poem enabled readers to continuously identify it as current, even though its subjects—including its religion and morality—were contested. Because moral discourse was central to defining the functions of literature and social structures, its treatment by Thomson was paid special attention by German translators. In focusing on the interpolated tales, I shall contextualize their immersion in a moral discourse that, by the mid-1760s, was questioned by Wieland who, in his works, highlighted "the central value of sexual pleasure to men and women alike."[8] Attempting to elevate Thomson as moral paragon, and as distinct from any German poet, translators were, however, aware of the need to tone down or redact Thomson's explicit eroticism in order to domesticate it for consumption by morally conservative German readers.

Once the interpolated episodes were no longer exclusively available to readers with access to editions of complete translations of *The Seasons* only but appeared in miscellaneous collections of poems and in newspapers, the texts obtained a status as stand-alone productions. As such, they no longer functioned as part of the natural-descriptive framework of *The Seasons* but were instead considered moral(izing) vignettes. They exerted an influence on a range of poets, including Wieland, who departed from the moral paragon status assigned to Thomson's characters by adapting the Scottish poet's verse tales and imbuing his type of characters with a sensuality not articulated in *The Seasons*. The moral-religious inscription of Thomson's tales contrasted starkly with Wieland's *Erzaehlungen* (Tales, 1752), which reveal the extent to which the English episodes had operated on the German poet's imagination. Thomson, whom Wieland in his *Fryhling* (Spring, 1752) had termed "göttlichen Thomson" (divine Thomson), sought to foreground morality and render the characters of his tales largely abstract. By contrast, in poems such as "Balsora" and "Zemin und Gulhindy," but also in the remaining four poems of *Erzaehlungen*, Wieland highlights, with a high degree of particularity, how desire is enacted by the tactile means of embraces and kisses. Whereas "Balsora" is an oriental tale of two lovers (the beautiful titular heroine and Abdallah, the son of the lecherous tyrant of Persia) in which Balsora resists the despot's physical desire and advances, in "Zemin und Gulhindy" Wieland introduces two individuals that are formed for one another, brought up separately under the guidance of the good genius, Firnaz, but subsequently united to lead a life of tenderness and love. Central to Wieland's rhetoric of love and desire are the concepts of "Lust" (lust) und "Trieb" (drive). Instances of these terms abound in Wieland's poetry but are largely absent from Thomson's tales.[9] According to Simon Richter, Wieland is "breast-obsessed" and inclined "to the literal and the material," targeting primarily male readers with the erotic appeal he anchors in his evocation of the female body and the expression of desire.[10]

Whereas Thomson repeatedly implies passion, Wieland traces the workings of passion and desire in his characters' somatic responses. In "Zemin und Gulhindy," for example, Gulhindy describes her awakening of desire:

Welch ein bedeutend Zittern? Welche Wynsche?
Was heben dich, mein Herz, vor still Wynsche,
Vor unbefriedigte verborgene Seufzer,
Wenn du in S<small>IRMENS</small> Arme zärtlich sinkst?[11]

[What a meaningful trembling? What wishes? / What wishes, what unsatisfied sighs are affecting you, my heart / When you tenderly sink into Sirmen's arms?]

The speaker, realizing her unspecified "Wynsche" and the effect they have on both her body and mind, is self-reflexive in a way that Thomson's characters are not. In his *Erzaehlungen* Wieland still imitates Thomson, but his subsequent *Comische Erzählungen* (Comic Tales, 1764) would go significantly further in his eroticization of the body. His overt eroticism in *Erzaehlungen* offers an appropriate context for understanding the different attitudes to morality that underpin the Scottish and the German poets' works. At the same time, German appropriators sought to cast Thomson as an author of morality whose works possessed a status distinct from the modern productions of Wieland. By the mid-1780s, Thomson's works were even chosen by Sophie La Roche to feature in her instructing monthly journal for women, *Pomona für Teutschlands Töchter* (Pomona for Germany's Daughters).

CELADON AND AMELIA: THE HEAVING BOSOM AND THOMSON'S AMBIGUOUS NOTION OF LOVE

German translators approaching Thomson's poem confronted the cultural task of introducing a classic to those not able to read it in the original English while at the same time having to negotiate the Thomsonian understanding of the erotic body and corporeal love. Thomson endeavored to create abstract types of lovers—representing a complementary type of incarnations of the same essence but differentiated by biological sex ("With equal Virtue form'd, and equal Grace, / The same, distinguish'd by their Sex alone" [*S*, 1173–74][12]). Yet, as we see in the example of Celadon and Amelia, Thomson is at pains to negotiate the unmarried lovers' bodily presence and attraction toward one another in order to render them (morally) pure. In the Celadon and Amelia tale, the eponymous lovers are out on a walk and are overtaken by a thunderstorm. While Celadon trusts to God's protection and assures Amelia that no harm will come to her, it is his presumption that is swiftly punished by the latter being struck by lightning. The destruction of the female lover's body—the physical manifestation of Celadon's idolizing love—lastingly castrates the erotic desire the male lover projected onto the once living, mobile, and desiring body of Amelia.[13] Thomson terms the lovers "a matchless Pair" (*S*, 1172), for "Devoting all / To Love, each was to each a dearer Self; / Supremely happy in th' awaken'd Power / Of giving Joy" (*S*, 1182–85). This pair is punished in a physico-theological realm in which love must not be as exclusively centered in human beings as it is in the poet's characters. While *The Seasons* frequently introduces hymnal passages paying homage to the creator, it is the God of the Old Testament who chastises the lovers for their neglect of religious duty and their idolizing of one another.

That Celadon and Amelia are real characters that can be affected by the forces of the environment is demonstrated by Thomson's reference to contemporary discourse on the body. Their bodily existence relates them to human experience but also subjects them to the moral codes regulating interactions between different bodies. It is Amelia's "Bosom [that] heav'd / Unwonted sighs" (*S*, 1195–96) when she apprehensively observes the approaching thunderstorm. Thomson specifies the nature of the heaving bosom by using the abstract adjective "presageful" (*S*, 1193) in the 1727 and 1730 versions of *Summer*, whereas in 1744 he uses the adjectival phrase "Heavy with instant Fate" (*S*, 1195) for the same thing.[14] The combination of the abstract references to fate and the concrete movement of the physical breasts—which through the speaker's observation are represented in their associated bodily form in the readers' minds—results in a type of ambiguity typical of Thomson: the erotic charge of the body is relativized by attributes that are meant to reduce its corporeality. By adding adjectival characterization to the motion these body parts perform, the poet conceives of Amelia's breasts as media through which an ominous fate is channeled and made visible. And yet, despite this effort on Thomson's part to reduce erotic charge, the bosom remains closely associated with the female's physical breasts, functioning as metonymical placeholders for Amelia's own sexual identity.

The personified bosom is not calmed by the (rational) religious serenity that Celadon wants to instill in his lover; rather, it defies the reassurances of the lover through its assertive heaving, which parallels the last flickering of Amelia's flame of life before it is extinguished by the stroke of lightning. In Celadon's view, the bodily heaving of Amelia's bosom requires another bodily act: that of an embrace, termed by him the "clasp[ing] [of] Perfection" (*S*, 1214). Yet this physical encounter with his deified idol makes evident the male lover's hubris, which results in the death of Amelia and the monumentalization of Celadon as eternal mourner on his lover's tomb:

From his void Embrace,
(Mysterious Heaven!) that moment, to the Ground,
A blacken'd Corse, was struck the beauteous Maid.
But who can paint the Lover, as he stood
Pierc'd by severe Amazement, hating Life,
Speechless, and fix'd in all the Death of Woe!
So, faint Resemblance, on the Marble-Tomb,
The well-dissembled Mourner stooping stands,
For ever silent, and for ever sad. (*S*, 1214–22)

The embrace, which was meant to contain Amelia's anxiety and transform it into a more positive somatic response, once the lightning strikes the female, becomes "void." The living body has been transformed into something else and been torn from Celadon's tangible control.

Thomson's characterization of Amelia's bosom, in his revision for the 1744 variant of *The Seasons*, as "Heavy with instant Fate" seeks to reduce the semantic agency assigned to the female's breast.[15] The translator Heinrich Harries, who published his translation of *The Seasons* in iambic hexameters in 1796, retained the grammatical active—"Des Mädchens Busen, nahes Unheil ahnend, / stieg schwer empor, in ungewohnten Seufzern" (The maid's breast, boding nearing disaster, rose heavily in unaccustomed sighs).[16] By contrast, Johann Jakob Bodmer and Barthold Heinrich Brockes had respectively adopted passive constructions and assigned grammatical agency to the sighs. Thus Bodmer renders these lines as "Ihr Busen, dem das Unglück ahnte, war / Von ungewohnten Seufzern schwer" ("Celadon und Amalia," 29–30; Her breast, which foreboded disaster, was heavy with unaccustomed sighs),[17] whereas Brockes had opted for an active construction: "Mit ungewohnter Angst befangen, / Stieg aus der Brust ein ahnend Seufzen" (*Br*, 918–19; Possessed with unaccustomed fear, a foreboding sigh issued from her breast).[18] Brockes's translation had introduced Thomson's poem in its entirety to German readers in 1745, whereas Bodmer's translations of the three tragic-sentimental episodes had featured as "Erzehlungen aus Thomsons Englischem" (Tales from the English of Thomson), "Lavinia," "Damon," and "Celadon und Amalia," added to the second edition of Jacob Immanuel Pyra's collection of *Thirsis und Damons freundschaftliche Lieder* (Thirsis's and Damon's Amicable Songs).[19] These early translations offer resolutions to questions related to the moral-erotic fabric of Thomson's poem. However, subsequent translations would reject these in favor of a more explicit ambiguity of association in which the erotic charge of the human body would be implied if not directly described. In this respect, the shift from active to passive voice in Bodmer's rendering and Brockes's grammatical reordering of relationships between the "bosom," the action of heaving, and the "sighs" are indicative of translators' non-literal adoption of Thomson's original in the interest of moderating the prominence of the female body. In either case, the animatedness of the bosom, which underpinned its eroticism, is suppressed.

Each of the six translations of the Celadon and Amelia tale, which Christian Heinrich Schmid termed "eine moralische Erzählung" (a moral tale) in 1781,[20] approached the final act of Amelia's dissolution differently—Ludwig Schubart rendering the transformation scene in the following words:

In diesem Augenblick—geheimnisvolle Gottheit! wird das schuldlose Mädchen eine schwärzliche Leiche,—vom Blitz aus seiner leeren Umarmung zu Boden geschlagen.[21]

[At that moment—mysterious deity! the guiltless maid becomes a blackened corpse,—struck to the ground from his void embrace by lightning.]

Johann Franz von Palthen, twenty-three years earlier, had translated the same passage thus:

> In dem Augenblick ward aus seiner leeren Umarmung, (geheimnisvoller Himmel!) das schöne Mädgen zu Boden geschlagen, als geschwärzter Leichnam.[22]

[At that moment (mysterious heaven!) the beautiful maid was struck to the ground from his void embrace a blackened corpse.]

And Bodmer's translation presented Amelia's death as a complete act of cremation:

> Aus seinen Armen fiel, o des geheimen Schicksals!
> Das schöne Kind denselben Augenblick
> In einen Aschenhaufen. ("Celadon und Amalia," 56–58)

[From his arms fell, o secret fate! / The beautiful child that moment / Into a heap of ashes.]

Heinrich Harries rendered the same passage in the following way:

> Im Augenblick—geheimnisvolle Gottheit!
> entsinket seiner lustigen Umarmung
> das schöne Mädchen—eine schwarze Leiche—
> vom schnellen Blitz zu Boden hingestreckt! (*H: S*, 1444–47)[23]

[At that moment—mysterious deity! / Sinks from his lustful embrace / The beautiful maid struck by quick lightning to the ground—a black corpse.]

These four German versions of Thomson's lines differ in two major respects: they translate Thomson's "blacken'd corse," with the exception of Bodmer, by using "Leiche" or "Leichnam" (corpse), but differing in the adjective describing its color. Von Palthen is most faithful to Thomson's original, whereas Schubart reduces the intensity of the blackening. Harries's version of Amelia's corpse has changed color entirely, accentuating her transition from life to death. Brockes moves away from Thomson's participle construction. While the other translators do not mutilate the body's integrity, only Bodmer, whose translation is based on the 1730 text of the episode, completely changes Amelia's previously supposedly "perfect" body into a heap of ashes. Amelia's body has been marked, singled out, by God. It is no longer recognized as human and as the container of love. Instead, its alien status as a lifeless body differentiates it from its former mobile and emotionally driven individuality. Immovable and changed essentially, her petrified body is mirrored by Celadon's own.

The second respect in which the translations differ is the way in which the adjective defining the maid is rendered in German: with the exception of Schubart, the translators adopt literal translations of "beauteous." Instead, Schubart selects the phrase "schuldlose[s] Mädchen" (guiltless maid), a way of defining Amelia that recalls the opening passage of Thomson's original and casts her once more as innocent (as opposed to temptingly beautiful):

THEY lov'd. But such their guileless Passion was,
As in the Dawn of Time inform'd the Heart
Of Innocence, and undissembling Truth. (*S*, 1177–79)

Schubart had translated "guileless passion" as "schuldlose Liebe" (guiltless love). The contrastive conjunction "but" following Thomson's statement "They loved" indicates that the poet sought—as Schubart, too, would seek—to emphasize the lovers' blamelessness, a sense of innocence that is repeatedly compromised by the poet's description of the intensity of Celadon's and Amelia's love. Schubart's use of "schuldlose[s] Mädchen" in the concluding passage of the tale reiterates Amelia's innocence, while also implying guilt, an inference a reader can also make from Harries's translation of Amelia falling from Celadon's "void embrace." Harries is the exception among translators (who render the phrase literally) in that he translates "void embrace" as "lustige . . . Umarmung" (lustful embrace), a passionate, lust-driven embrace that, rhetorically at least, is far from the reading that Thomson appears to encourage. Johannes Tobler's otherwise unremarkable 1768 translation of *The Seasons* renders Thomson's "guileless Passion" as "betruglose Leidenschaft" (deceitless passion)[24] again, like Schubart and Harries, implying guilt through its very negation.

While Brockes obscures the meaning of Thomson's text,[25] Bodmer defines Celadon's and Amelia's love in terms of abstractions—"Es war nur Freundschaft, die von gleichen Wünschen, / Von süsser Hoffnung und von Sympathie / In holder Augen Licht belebet ward" ("Celadon und Amalia" [11–13]; It was but friendship animated by the same wishes, sweet hope, and sympathy reflected in the light of their lovely eyes). Harries, similarly, elevates their passion beyond erotic interest.[26] Schubart, by contrast, writes of "begeisternde Hoffnung, sympathische Gluth im begegnenden Blick" (elating hope, a sympathetic glow in their looks meeting one another),[27] echoing the passionate rhetoric of Wieland's *Erzaehlungen*. He thereby underscores the erotic charge he identifies in the lovers' looks and sighs. In this respect, the lovers' verbal exchanges are "sweet": they convey through this adjective of taste the desire with which the lovers live for each other alone. Schubart is the only German translator who consistently retains the erotic inscription of Thomson's original, even though he reduces some of the bodily erotic connotations in his revision of his 1788 "Proben einer neuen Uebersetzung, von Thomsons Jahreszeiten" (Specimens of a New Translation of Thomson's *Seasons*)[28] for the text he published in his edition one year later. His translation reveals the true import of Thomson's tragic-sentimental tale of a couple being everything to each other, idolizing one another at the cost of their devotional duties. Amelia's destruction and Celadon's petrifaction as lasting monument of his hubristic love are reminders to others of their tragic error and God's punishment of their transgression.

The presence in the German-speaking lands of Thomson's conception of the body was reflected not only in the translations of the interpolated episodes and *The Seasons* as a whole. It was also found—with the exception of those German poets loosely reworking and adapting material from the text for such works as Salomon Gessner's *Daphnis* (1754)[29]—in the actual rewriting of the Celadon and Amelia episode in the form of different versions of the story.

Unlike translators of Thomson's tale who, revising and revaluing the eroticism of the episode, faithfully rendered the story of the two lovers, a number of German authors rewrote significant aspects of the Celadon and Amelia tale. Ludwig Gotthard Kosegarten reworked the tale in the genre of the ballad. His "Romanze" "Allwill und Allwina," which appeared in his collection of *Gedichte* (Poems, 1788), reverses the roles of the lovers: Allwill is struck by lightning, whereas Allwina is left to mourn his death, even though this ending is foreclosed by the abrupt ending of the ballad.[30] There are numerous verbal echoes of Thomson's tale in Kosegarten's. It is the lovers' embraces, including their "Kuss und Kosen" (kiss and caress, 25),[31] however, that are ultimately responsible for their loitering and their being overtaken by the thunderstorm that will prove fatal to Allwin. Compared to Thomson, who denominates Celadon and Amelia merely as "lovers," Kosegarten legitimizes Allwin and Allwina's embraces by stating that they are spouses. Yet the role of the female is significantly reduced, as are references to her body and somatic-psychological responses to the storm. Even the petrifaction of the body of Allwin at the end of the poem is implicit, Kosegarten ensuring that the visual is suppressed in this catastrophe:

Hagel rasselt
Und Regen—Jäling stimmt
Im gellenden Getümmel
Ein Strahl daher—und ha!
Geheimnisvoller Himmel—
Entseelt lag Allwin da. (84–90)

[Hail and rain rattle—suddenly a flash appears in the shrill turmoil—and oh! mysterious heaven—Allwin lay soulless.]

Both the emphasis in the last two lines on religious intervention and Kosegarten's refusal to follow the Thomsonian model replace the act of memorialization by means of a statue in the Celadon and Amelia tale. Instead, Kosegarten describes Allwin's "soulless" person (as opposed to his body) functioning as a monument itself. None of the eroticism of the body found in the original is retained, however. When Kosegarten's "Allwill und Allwina" was reprinted in Wilhelm Julius Wiedemann's *Uebungen im Deklamieren für Knaben und Jünglinge* (Exercises in Declamation for Boys and Youths, 1800), Wiedemann not only identified the Thomsonian intertext but also reproduced the original. He also furnished his own translation of the text and clarified his position toward the notion of love depicted, for he emphasized the centrality of fidelity in his translation of Thomson's characterization of Celadon and Amelia's love, which the Scottish poet frames in terms of "innocence" and "undissembling truth" and *not* by referring to "fidelity." Wiedemann's statement that the lovers are possessed of "eine sich nie verstellende Treue" (a never dissembling fidelity) insists that their relationship is cemented by a bond akin to marriage.[32] This presents to his young readers a normative version of love based on lovers' declared faith in one another but also on the institution of marriage, which, in turn, resolves Celadon's and Amelia's unlicensed, non-married existence as lovers.

Another reworking of the tale by the twenty-eight-year-old Johann Heinrich Brumleu, entitled "Celadon und Amelia," initially concentrates on the natural spectacle of the thunderstorm, only in the end focusing on the effect the strike of lightning has had on Amelia's body.

Indem mit lauterem Gekrache fuhr
Ein Strahl daher. Die Höhen zitterten
Und Tiefen mächtiger. Den Waldungen
Von ihren Wipfeln bis zu'n Wurzeln hin
Erschauerte. Wie hallt 's von Fels zu Fels?—
Amelia lag da. Zu Bläße ward der Wange Purpur. Und das lichte blau [*sic*]
Der Augen wölkte sich:—So blinzt hervor
Aus Brunnens Tiefe trüber Wasser Schein;
So siehet durch ein flockigt Wölkgen hin
Der Aether.—Wie vom Wetterstrahl zugleich
Getroffen, taumelt' er, sank auf sie hin,
Warf seinen Arm um sie—
So lag er lang';
Wie über eine Trümmer Epheu her,
Die Ranken fest um sie verschlingend, liegt.[33]

[At the same time, a flash appeared with loud thunder. The heights trembled and the depths more powerfully. The woods, from their treetops to their roots, shuddered.

How it resounds from rock to rock!—Amelia lay there. The cheek's purple was transformed to pallor. And the light blue of her eyes was clouded.—Thus sparkles out of the well's depth the murky water's shine; thus appears the aether through a flaky cloud.—As if struck by the flash, he staggered, sank down upon her, threw his arms around her—thus he lay long, like ivy on a ruin, embracing it firmly.]

The female is no longer referred to as a corpse: the agency of speech and of movement to a place of safety is replaced by her stasis, her lying lifeless on the ground. Brumleu focuses on individual bodily features such as her cheek having lost its color and her dimming eyes no longer reflecting life; no reference is made to the blackening of the body or its physical destruction. These two physical features function as *pars pro toto* for the body as a whole. They also underscore the particularized feminine beauty of Amelia, something that is not present in Thomson's original. Brumleu's Celadon embraces Amelia at the end of the tale only, once he can hold her as a monument of his love. At that point, the physical contact between the two bodies can no longer be construed as transgressive but as a last effort on the part of Celadon to recreate the familiarity and closeness that characterized the lovers' relationship before they were overtaken by the storm. The poet's use of analogy to construct Celadon's grieving and embracing Amelia as natural is effected when the male lover collapses as if he had been struck by lightning. Likening his embrace to the covering of ruins by ivy reinforces his action as an act imitative of Amelia's death, rather than as an erotic search for physical proximity. The repetition of the verb "lag" (lay) furthermore serves to create the impression of Celadon re-enacting his lover's fatal death through his own collapse. Whereas the "lag" with reference to Amelia is used to denote permanent stasis and death, the "lag" referring to Celadon is relativized by "lang" (long). This restricting adverb limits the duration of his act of mourning and shows up a disjunction in the analogy between his embrace and the covering of ivy, as the vines of ivy over time in fact harden and petrify.

Even though Brumleu verbally echoes Thomson's tale closely, he delays the introduction of the discourse of the body until the very end of the poem. Whereas Thomson's Celadon at the end of the tale had transformed into a monument of grief "forever silent / And forever sad" (*S*, 1222), the difference in attitude—Celadon standing, whereas the dead Amelia is lying on the ground—emphasizes that the two spheres of life and death cannot be mediated. Brumleu's decision to approximate the two lovers by means of a final embrace, much like Thomson's original, results in a tableau. In Brumleu's case, however, this tableau conveys a stronger impression of Celadon's undying love for the deceased Amelia. By not relating the lover's gaze of Amelia's body, but by restricting observation to her face, the poet further reduces the erotic connotations of the dead body in favor of a celebration of its past beauties.

The different translations of the Celadon and Amelia tale, as well as the poems reworking the tale, demonstrate that Amelia's body was framed within a moral discourse that reduced both its physical eroticism and Celadon's desire to possess it. At the micro level of word choice, the translations reveal strategies to remove agency from Amelia's breasts, the heaving of which assert her fearful emotion as well as her biological distinction as a desirable woman. At the macro level, an attempt to regulate bodily desire in order to confirm moral orthodoxy can be discerned in all translations. Kosegarten's reversal of the roles of the lovers, Allwin being killed by lightning, represents the most radical intervention to control the female body by erasing it completely.

DAMON AND MUSIDORA: DENUDING, MALE DESIRE, AND THE GAZE

The body can only be acknowledged in its entirety at the end of Thomson's Celadon and Amelia tale, once its sexual potential has been neutralized. While it had been implied with reference to looks throughout the tale, the eroticized female body is on full show in the Damon and Musidora tale. Thomson offers a detailed description of Musidora's denuding in anticipation of her bathing, at the same time establishing a causal relationship between the slow undressing of one body and the arousal of another. In the Celadon and Amelia narrative, the bosom was used as a metaphor of the expressive force of bodily intuition, fear being expressed by its heaving. It is again invoked as containing Damon's beating heart. The poet refers to the bosom three times: initially to contain Musidora's love for Damon but her concealing it, then as a bodily space containing his arousal, and, finally, once the bosom is unwittingly unveiled to Damon's gaze, giving external, visible expression to the passion it previously contained. The bosom thus serves both as a metaphoric container of desire and a medium of it.

Schubart adopts the active verb structure of the original ("th' alternate breast, / With youth wild-throbbing, on thy lawless gaze, / In full luxuriance rose" (S, 1311–13). However, he does not exploit the ambiguity of the Thomsonian text where "to rise" is introduced as "rising" on Damon's "lawless gaze" and where it is associated with a rising movement of the breast as well, a reading that Harries reflects in his translation:

Nicht wilder pocht auf Ida's Fichtengipfel
des Hirten Herz, . . .
als, Damon, deins, da ihrer Lilienhüfte

und ihrem zarten Fuss, die umgekehrte Seide
sie leis' entstreifte, leiser aufgelöst,
der iungfräuliche Gürtel niedersank,
und schwelgerisch vor deinem irren Blick
ihr Busen durchs entfaltete Gewand
in wilder Jugendwallung stieg und sank— (*H*: *S*, 1551–57)

[Not more wildly does the shepherd's heart beat on Ida's piny summit . . . than yours, Damon, as the inverted silk is quietly stripped from her lily waist and her tender foot, even more quietly loosened, and the virgin zone lowered; as her bosom before your maddened gaze voluptuously rose and sank in a wild and youthful flush through the unfolded garment.]

Harries's translation adds a sound component to the derobing, which Thomson's text did not possess. The Thomsonian "lawless gaze" is transformed by Harries into one of madness. Damon is intoxicated by the erotic presence of Musidora, which makes him strain both his eyesight to capture her every move and his hearing so as to apprehend the sound that the shedding of clothes produces. Harries's introduction of sound conduces to building up gradation, "leis" (quietly), "leiser" (more quietly), culminating in the climactic deep focus on Musidora's bosom, which in Harries's translation is animated in ways that go beyond the textuality of the original.

Schubart's translation is more faithful than Harries's, specifically his rendering of Musidora's "soft touch" anticipating Damon's desire to bridge the distance between himself and his bathing lover. This distance heightens his arousal, while also facilitating the clandestine performance of Musidora's erotic identity:

> Ach da pocht' auf dem Fichtenhaupt Ida's dem Paris nicht wilder die Brust, . . . als Damon dir, da sie von den schneeigen Lenden, den zarten Fuessen die gekehrte Seide zog, da sie mit sanfter Berührung den jungfräulichen Gürtel löste, und durch das geteilte Gewand die wechselnde Brust,—wild aufpochend vor Jugend—vor deinem gesetzlosen Blik in voller Ueppigkeit stieg.[34]

[Ah, Paris's breast does not beat less wildly on the piny head of Ida than yours, Damon, as she pulled the inverted silk from her snowy waist and her tender feet and as she loosened with soft touch the virgin zone, her heaving breast—wildly beating because of her youth—rose in full luxuriance upon your lawless gaze through her divided garment.]

Schubart understands Musidora's role as orchestrating an erotic spectacle in order to arouse Damon's desire for her sexualized body. He introduces the idea, not found in *The Seasons*, of Musidora as magician, terming her

"Zauberin." Musidora's charm and her power over Damon are complicated, as—guided by "bashful coyness," which von Palthen renders as "schamhafte . . . Sittsamkeit" (shameful modesty)[35]—she transforms once more into a vulnerable female fearing the invasion of her privacy.

Both von Palthen and Schubart awkwardly render Musidora's consciousness that she may be observed, as well as the implicit recognition that she should not display her nude body even in the secluded pastoral setting of the tale. They are aware that Musidora's sense of shame may be read as a confirmation of her guilt by some and that this understanding of her as immodest and accepting of Damon's presence may induce readers to comprehend her as an immoral siren firing his desire. Thomson writes: "fair-expos'd she stood, shrunk from herself, / With Fancy blushing at the doubtful Breeze / Alarm'd, and starting like the fearful Fawn" (S, 1318–20). Von Palthen and Schubart are unable to grasp the meaning of "Fancy blushing at the doubtful Breeze," the former translating the lines as: "und sie schon entblößet da stand, für sich selbst zitternd, in schamrother Phantasie, durch ein zweideutiges Lüftgen in Unruhe versetzt, und gleich einem furchtvollem Rehkalbe zusammenfahrend" (and stood there already denuded, trembling, in shame-red fancy, and made uneasy by a suggestive breeze—like a fearful doe starting).[36] Schubart's translation, by contrast, reads: "die Zauberin da stand, lieblich entdeckt, vor sich selbst zusammenfahrend, über fremde Triebe errötend, aufgeschreckt vom zweifelnden Lüftchen, und gleich dem furchtsamen Rehe stuzzend" (there stood the magician, lovely and uncovered, startled by herself, blushing because of strange desires, frightened by the doubting breeze, and, like the fearful doe, hesitating).[37] Von Palthen's "schamrothe . . . Phantasie" (shame-red . . . fancy) changes the part of speech of Thomson's "blushing," using it as an adjective. By contrast, Schubart's choice of the phrase "über fremde Triebe errötend" (reddening because of strange desires) reveals Musidora's recognition that she, the bathing nude, could potentially function as the foil for sexual fantasies. Schubart's translation emphasizes the objectification of the nude but also the recognition on the part of Damon's lover that the spectacle she performs is a guilty pleasure that calls for her to adopt one more role: a transition from charmer to female likened by means of simile to a woodland animal known for its shyness. Musidora's "Fancy," then, is a reflective faculty that helps the reader to glimpse her multidimensional character, specifically that her motivations may be less straightforward than initially assumed. This ambiguity in the lover is also highlighted at the beginning of the tale when the speaker is unable to assign a definitive motivation for Musidora concealing her love from Damon: "falsely he [Damon] / Of MUSIDORA's Cruelty complain'd. / She felt the Flame; but deep within her Breast, / In bashful Coyness, or in maiden Pride, / The soft Return conceal'd"

(*S*, 1275–79). It is at this point that her bosom is the impenetrable container of her feelings. Schubart translates: "Sie fühlte seine [Damon's] Liebe; aber tief in ihrem Busen verbarg sie aus züchtiger Sprödigkeit, oder aus Mädchenstolz, die sanften Gegengefühle" (She felt his love, but deep in her bosom she concealed—out of chaste prudery or out of maidenly pride—her soft reciprocating feelings).[38] In following Thomson accurately, Schubart places emphasis on the female's pride, whereas Harries, as the only translator to do so, inverts Thomson's sequence, emphasizing Musidora's pride and only tentatively conceding the possibility of her modest coyness:

Sie fühlte seine Flamme; tief jedoch
verschloss ihr Busen noch—aus Mädchenstolz,
und aus verschämter Sprödigkeit vielleicht—
die holde Gegengluth.[39]

[She felt his flame; but her bosom deeply concealed—out of maidenly pride and out of bashful prudery perhaps—the lovely, reciprocating glow.]

Like Damon, Thomson's speaker can admire Musidora's beauty and be aroused by the erotic charge of her nudity. Again, like Damon, he can only view the surface of the body, unable to divine her motivation and thus depending on her agency to confirm her love. Only once love is acknowledged will the clandestine gaze be authorized and transformed into a private one that facilitates access to her body beyond the aural.

The Damon and Musidora tale was visualized three times for German book illustrations, first in Brockes's 1745 edition (which included a simplified version of the "Summer" plate William Kent had contributed to the 1730 quarto edition published in London) and then in von Palthen's 1758 Rostock edition, where it featured as part of a full-page multistory tableau. It was illustrated again, this time as a title-page vignette, for Tobler's translation of *Sommer* that Orell, Gessner, and Füssli published in Zurich in 1761. In addition, in 1777 Johann Friedrich Bause engraved a design of "Damon und Musidora" by Johann Sebastian Bach (the grandson of the composer), which was not meant for inclusion in editions of translations of Thomson's work but was instead retailed as a stand-alone print. Given that only one other of Thomson's interpolated stories—Celadon and Amelia—was illustrated in Germany and that the illustration was derived from a print that had first been published in England in 1766,[40] Damon and Musidora were given a central position in the visual paratexts of German translations of *The Seasons*.

The illustrations that were published between 1745 and 1761 depict Musidora disrobing and Damon, barely concealed by brushwork, excitedly looking on. Kent's tableau introduced Damon and Musidora as part of an allegorical landscape in which not only the two lovers are visible in the foreground, but the two females, Amoret and Saccharissa, whom Thomson would eliminate for the 1744 version of *The Seasons*, are also present (Figure 7.1). The physical distance between Damon and the standing Musidora is slight. In fact, in scaling down the original quarto print to be accommodated by the octavo format of Brockes's volume, the distance is further reduced. The barrier of the tree, which Damon embraces, serves as a physical placeholder for the bodies of the females he observes. It does not prevent his unlicensed looks, although the group of bathers appear to be unaware of his presence. While the illustration centrally highlights Damon's desire, he being literally at the center of the composition, the presence of three women, as opposed to Musidora on her own, makes the erotic scene less particular than when Damon and Musidora are the only human protagonists of the scene. Even though the simplified execution of the plate does not alter the design, Brockes—aware of the eroticism on display—likely caused a four-line caption to be added that did not accompany the original English plate. The author of the caption does not centralize the voyeuristic scene introduced to the reader but focuses instead on the health-giving benefits of bathing in summertime.[41] The caption thus depersonalizes a scene that is dominated by persons and personages both human and allegorical.

In contrast to the Hamburg version of Kent's design, the vignette for Tobler's translation does not depict anything but the lovers. The full-page plate that Gottlieb Leberecht Crusius contributed to von Palthen's edition is more ambitious, however (Figure 7.2a). Looking at the lower right-hand corner where Musidora is depicted, it is barely possible, without magnifying the image, to discern Damon, a figure that becomes visible on enlarging the detail from the image (Figure 7.2b). Crusius's mythopoeic tableau separates the group of people on the left from the Musidora–Damon group on the right by a pillar of smoke—a more effective barrier than the tree Kent had introduced. This division allows the reader to view what the group on the left is not allowed to see. The compressed scene depicting the two lovers reduces the distance between the female preparing to bathe and her lover, who appears to be facing her directly. But this direct gaze is mediated by the miniature format of this illustrative component, necessitating that the reader pay particular attention to identifying Damon's presence in this erotic scene. As an indication of her modesty, Musidora is not facing the reader; instead, even though she is casting her look down onto the leg she is tending to, she is directly confronting Damon. All that is discernible of Damon is his head, emerging from the cross-hatched background, his eyes almost on the same level as Musidora's. Immersed in the image by focusing on the detail, identifying Damon's line of vision, as well as the frontal-facing constellation of the lovers, the reader

Da die erhabne Sonn auf uns nun in geraden Stralen blitzt,
Die Erndte reifft, die Früchte Kocht, die Erde Fluht und Lufft erhitzt;
Wird man im Schatten Kühler Wälder vor ihrer schwühlen Glut geschütt,
Dabey auch oft die frische Fluht im Baden der Gesundheit nützt.

Figure 7.1. William Kent, "Sommer," *B. H. Brockes aus dem Englischen übersetzte Jahreszeiten des Herrn Thomson* (Hamburg: Herold, 1745).
Reproduced from a copy in the author's collection.

Figure 7.2a. G. L. Crusius, "Sommer," in *Jacob Thomsons Jahrszeiten aus dem Englischen nach der neuesten Ausgabe übersetzt von Johann Franz von Palthen*. **Mit Kupfern (Rostock: Koppe, 1757).**
Reproduced from a copy in the author's collection.

Figure 7.2b. Detail from Figure 7.2a.
Reproduced from a copy in the author's collection.

becomes complicit in the voyeuristic act of spying on the nude Musidora, replicating Damon's role in Thomson's tale. More subtle than most British illustrations visualizing the Damon and Musidora story, Crusius's engraving nevertheless captures the erotic charge of the scene, in the process implicating the reader in its sexual poetics.

Salomon Gessner's vignette for the 1761 edition of *Sommer* attempts to neutralize the sexual charge of the scene rendering the two lovers as cherub-putti (Figure 7.3). Watching the little Musidora from behind the foliage of some bushes, Damon shows unabashed, childlike interest in what Musidora is about. The main feature defining Musidora's body as that of a female is her hair, although the roulette work on her chest may indicate breast development. Unlike any other illustration of the tale, both lovers are naked, but their nudity is contextualized in terms of the conventions of the Rococo vignette, according to which nude putto figures frequently served as ornamental head- or tail-pieces. Gessner's title-page vignette, however, serves an interpretive function, visualizing a tale from the season. As in Crusius's illustration, the reader of Gessner's image has to willingly suspend disbelief and take for granted that Musidora is not aware of Damon's presence, even though Tobler's translation may cast some doubt on this. At the same time, an attentive reader recognizing the illustrative-interpretive function of the title-page illustration will need to reflect on how—through the lens of childhood—the erotic charge of Thomson's tale is sublimated; in this respect, the nude bodies of Damon and Musidora are only defensible because they have not reached sexual maturity as yet and are therefore removed from the desires of the adult lovers of Thomson's tale. Still, reading the vignette as paratextually meaningful endows the childlike body with erotic potential that its sexual immaturity should preclude.

Figure 7.3. Salomon Gessner, title vignette, in *Sommer* (Zurich: Gessner und Orell, 1761).
Reproduced from a copy in the author's collection.

For his 1777 print of "Damon und Musidora," Bach attempts to reinscribe the young Damon's presence at Musidora's bathing scene by significantly extending the physical distance between the lovers (Figure 7.4). Whereas Kent's Damon stared at Musidora, Bach's rendering of Damon depicts him looking down, not seeking eye contact with his lover. His downcast eyes are focused on the piece of paper he is about to place on the tree trunk rather than on Musidora's nude body. Kent's Damon was still partly concealed, and so was Crusius's. Bach's, however, is not shaded to indicate concealment. His posture indicates the modesty that is also reflected by Musidora's, the female seemingly unaware of her lover's presence. Compared with the two earlier illustrations, Bach's illustration situates the lovers in a sublime natural setting—for which reason the print was also classified as a "landscape"[42] and the role of Damon redefined as that of a poet (rather than a lover).[43] It is the sublimity of the scene, rather than a sense of intimacy between the lovers, that is being conveyed. In Anke Fröhlich's view, it is this sublime-idyllic mode of rendering Musidora as *venus pudica*, which distinguishes it from the complex ensemble and action-driven tableau of Kent.[44]

Illustration strategies range from the addition of a caption to the Kent plate and adopting the putto mode of presentation in the vignette for Tobler's translation to creating a physical barrier between Damon and Musidora and widening the compositional distance between the figures' bodies and a repositioning of their gazes. From these strategies, it seems reasonable to

190   *Chapter Seven*

Figure 7.4. Johann Sebastian Bach, "Damon und Musidora" (1777).
Reproduced from a copy in the author's collection.

assume that those responsible for the inclusion and production of illustrations in their editions were sensitive to mediating the desire on display in each of the images. They were conscious that the illustrations affect how the erotic bodies of Thomson's tales were understood in their translations. The illustrations thus shape interpretations of the morality, as well as of the attitudes toward the body and desire, that underscore the episodes. The consistent efforts to adopt a strategy to either move away paratextually from the erotic focus of the illustration (as in the case of the German adaptation of Kent's plate) or to desexualize the encounter between Damon and Musidora (as reflected in the vignette and Bach's print) point to the perceived desirability of muting or, at least, reducing the sense of sexual tension that readers may have gleaned from the text. The translations, like the illustrations, offer strategies to negotiate too explicit an understanding of the eroticism of Thomson's tales.

PALEMON AND LAVINIA: DESIRE, FANTASY, AND CLASS DIFFERENCE

The third interpolated episode, that of Palemon and Lavinia, introduces the love-at-first-sight encounter of two individuals from supposedly different classes—Palemon, the master and wealthy landowner, and the impoverished Lavinia, gleaning his fields. The underlying class and power politics complicate the male viewer's perception of Lavinia's bodily existence. Before Palemon encounters Lavinia for the first time, Thomson characterizes her as "unstain'd, and pure, / As is the Lily, or the Mountain Snow" (*A*, 193–94). The very combination of "unstain'd" and "pure"—supposedly pleonastic—poses a problem for a translator who is aware of the litotical residue of "stain" in "unstained." Friederike Magdalene Jerusalem, the translator of a separately issued version of the tale, "Die Ährenleserin. Eine Erzählung nach dem Englischen, aus Thomsons Jahreszeiten" (The Gleaner. A Tale after the English, from Thomson's *Seasons*),[45] chose not to render this characterization of Lavinia at all. Instead, she opts for a floral analogy to convey her moral and physical purity:

Hold, wie sich früh die junge Ros' erhebt,
Wenn Morgenthau auf ihren Blättern bebt,
Nein wie der Schnee auf unbesuchten Höhen,
Wie Lilienglanz, dem Wohlgerüch' entwehen,
So lieblich war Lawiniens Gestalt.

[Lovely, as when the young rose, morning dew quaking on its leaves, rises early, / No, like the snow on unfrequented heights, / Like lily brilliance, exudes perfumes, / So lovely was Lavinia's person.]

Deciding against a literal translation, Jerusalem contracts Thomson's meaning into an unambigious text that highlights the female's (moral and bodily) loveliness: she utilizes the meaning of the lily as a metaphor for Lavinia's purity to this end. Since the translation also appeared in *Pomona*, a journal specifically aimed at instructing "Teutschlands Töchter" (Germany's Daughters), Jerusalem redacted the sexual politics of the tale so as to confirm the high opinion of Thomson as moral author that the journal's editor, Sophie La Roche, advocated to her female readers.[46]

Whereas Lavinia's body is only implied in Thomson's comment on her innocence, once Palemon has witnessed her "charms," his attraction is immediate. In the confessional, private mode of a soliloquy he admits his attraction but also gives vent to his (erotic) interest in Lavinia. In the process of realizing his love for the gleaner, who is then identified as the daughter of his deceased benefactor, Acasto, he fantasizes her being touched by another man, specifically an unrefined, lower-class individual. It is clear that the landowner's regret at Lavinia's fate of being lost to the world in a sphere that cannot do justice to her worth is not selfless. Channeling his own desire for Lavinia through imagining "the rude Embrace / Of some indecent Clown"

(*A*, 241–42) not only increases his longing for Acasto's daughter but also the experience of the "Embrace." Palemon's attempt to sublimate his desire by reflecting on Lavinia's supposedly low station thus fails: rather, it impresses upon him the reality of his using the placeholder figure of the "Clown," a male figure acting out his own desire.

The female translator of "Die Ährenleserin," aware of the dubious morality of even fantasizing about an act of tactility between a man and Lavinia, passes over the physical encounter between the gleaner and "some indecent Clown." Instead, she opts for a paraphrase that eliminates the meaning of "indecent" and that focuses on a (married) union of the two individuals. By contrast, Johannes Tobler's translation had gone further than the original by rendering the fancied embrace as the "eckelhaften rohen Umarmen / Eines ungeschliffenen Bauern" (the disgusting embrace of an unrefined peasant). Unlike Tobler, Schubart does not judge this embrace as disgusting and repulsive; rather, he highlights the roughness and lack of polish on the part of the lower-class man, which puts into relief the contrast between Palemon and the "Clown." The difference between Lavinia and the "clown" impresses upon the reader that their union would not be a union of (social and moral) equals. At the same time, Schubart shifts from the Thomsonian embrace to the mere mention of "des Schäfers rauhem Arme" (the shepherd's rough arms), thus dissolving the friction that Palemon's imagining of an erotic meeting of bodies suggests. The mention of the arm is not over-determined in the way that an embrace is; it is less directly associated with the privilege of touch that Palemon assigns to it. Harries adopts a fundamentally different position in his translation in that he does not reference the bodily existence of the "Clown"; rather, he sees the advances of the "clown" as inevitable, holding that Lavinia will sacrifice herself by remaining in this sphere of life: "der rauhen Buhlschaft eines Hirtenburschen / sich opfern muss" (having to sacrifice herself for the rough paramour of a shepherd swain).

The very diverse ways in which German translators rendered Palemon's fantasy indicate that more than linguistic and semantic equivalence with the original was at stake. Translators were clearly aware of the erotic implications of the embrace and sought to negotiate this emphasis on the objectified body by means of paraphrases that muted or completely removed these associations. At the same time, they may have been aware of the conflict of reconciling Palemon's (jealous) fantasy with his being supposedly selfless in his preservation of innocence—especially when his desire for Lavinia is not understood in Platonic terms. All translators appear to have conceived of this part of Palemon's soliloquy as problematic and therefore redacted it in the interest of furnishing a morally unambiguous version of the landowner to German readers. It was the imagining of the (real) body's attractive force that posed a danger to a reading that should emphasize the moral perfection of Palemon. Equally, translators repeatedly omitted the Thomsonian combination of "love and chaste desire"—the two affective responses that Palemon experiences on perceiving Lavinia for the first time. Even as Thomson qualifies "desire" by defining it as chaste, the Platonic notion of love jars in conjunction with "desire," irrespective of whether the poet insists that Palemon's "desire" is "chaste." As a result, in Jerusalem's "Ährenleserin" Palemon is described as feeling "reinste Lieb'" (purest love), as opposed to any desire that would involve physicality and the erotic body. Tobler, by contrast, renders the original more faithfully but opts for the infelicitous plural form in "keuschen Begierden" (chaste desires).

CONCLUSION

It would be an overstatement to claim that the German translations rewrote the ideological mesh that makes up *The Seasons*. At the same time, these translations introduced the poem to German readers who would have approached *belles lettres* with certain (moral) expectations in mind. According to Ludwig Schubart, his translation aimed to recreate accurately "die verschlungene Subtilität" (the labyrinthine subtlety)[47] of Thomson's subjects, while also domesticating the work and adapting it to the mores and moral fabric of eighteenth-century German-speaking reading communities. In the preface to his translation, Schubart hailed Thomson's work as promoting morality. He did not engage explicitly with the interpolated tales, which seemed to counteract and question some of the prevailing moral dicta concerning the erotic and sexual identities of men and women. None of the translators who rendered these tales into German explicitly questioned their value; Georg Friedrich Herrmann, the editor of an annotated school edition of the text and teacher of English and French at the Wismar Lyceum, even termed them "meisterhaft" (236; masterful). Yet that translators did see the necessity to redact not only the wording used by Thomson but also the ideas that too directly engage with non-marital sexual desire has been demonstrated. The primary reason for these redactions is likely to have been the effort on the part of editors and publishers to consolidate the reputation of *The Seasons* as a primarily didactic poem infused with religious morality. To render the eroticism of the body characteristic of the interpolated episodes faithfully would have detracted from this primary aim of assigning a purpose to the work. The pedagogical uses of Thomson's text in both Britain and the German-speaking lands furthermore recommended that the erotic content of the tales be muted. Nevertheless, a shift from heavy redaction in the translations of Bodmer and

Brockes to the acknowledgment of Thomsonian (erotic) ambiguity in the translations of Schubart and Harries indicates that a change in the way the erotic body was viewed occurred in the half-century that separates Brockes from Harries. It was precisely in this period that Wieland's own conception of the erotic body received much attention from readers. By the mid-1790s, the preacher from Bruegge, Harries, no longer felt as apprehensive as Bodmer and Brockes had about the erotic underfelt and sexual politics of the interpolated episodes.

From the 1740s, the decade in which Bodmer and Brockes produced their translations, to the 1780s, when a 1781 English-language edition of *The Seasons* was published in Leipzig by Engelhard Benjamin Schwickert and an amatory epistle inspired by *The Seasons—Bey Übersendung einer Übersetzung aus Thomsons Jahrszeiten, im April 1783* (On Sending a Translation of Thomson's Seasons, April 1783)—was printed,[48] the English language had become considerably more common in Germany.[49] Whereas in the mid-century few readers would have been able to consume Thomson's work in the original English, this situation had changed by the 1790s, when Herrmann's edition catered to those learning the English language. The translations of the interpolated episodes considered in this chapter demonstrate that *The Seasons* represented a site of cultural negotiation on which debates regarding the ways in which the body and sexuality could be meaningfully engaged with by *belles lettres* were carried out. The translators' various choices to make sense of the body-focused narratives of Thomson are part of this debate, while at the same time representing them as works of morality. They reflect the mechanisms utilized to recruit *The Seasons* as a modern classic and as a model for nature descriptive and reflective poetry that would subsequently thrive in such Thomsonian works as Justus Friedrich Wilhelm Zachariae's *Die Tageszeiten* (1756).

NOTES

1. Work on this article was supported by the award of a Hiob Ludolf Senior Fellowship (funded by the Thyssen Stiftung) at the Forschungszentrum Gotha.

To date, only Knut Gjerset's very old doctoral dissertation has examined the different translations of *The Seasons* systematically, if not in the detail they require. See Knut Gjerset, *Der Einfluss von James Thomson's "Jahreszeiten" auf die deutsche Literatur des achtzehnten Jahrhunderts* (Heidelberg: E. Geisendörfer, 1898). A translation-historical study of *The Seasons* in Germany has not been attempted, although I have recently focused on the visual paratexts of the editions of these translations. See Sandro Jung, "Print Culture and Visual Interpretation in Eighteenth-Century German Editions of *The Seasons*," *Comparative Critical Studies* 9, no. 1 (2012): 37–59.

Older research publications have focused on the reception of Thomson's text by German-language poets. See C.H. Ibershoff, "A German Translation of Passages in Thomson's *Seasons*," *Modern Language Notes* 26, no. 4 (1911): 107–09.

2. Ludwig Schubart, ed., *Jakob Thomson's Jahreszeiten. Neuübersetzt. Mit fünf Kupfern nach Smith, Wilson und Jones, nach Genelly* (Berlin: Christian Friedrich Himburg, 1789), 140 note. All references to Schubart's translation will be by page number and given in the notes.

3. I have traced the fortunes of Thomson's interpolated tales via illustrative media in Sandro Jung, *James Thomson's "The Seasons," Print Culture, and Visual Interpretation, 1730–1842* (Bethlehem, PA: Lehigh University Press, 2015). The book argues for the significance of transnational perspectives on the ways in which these interpolated episodes were adapted by other nations. See also Louise L. Stevenson, "The Transatlantic Travels of James Thomson's *The Seasons* and Its Baggage of Material Culture, 1730–1870," *Proceedings of the American Antiquarian Society* 116, no. 1 (2006): 121–63. For the transnational mobility of illustrations visualizing the interpolated episodes, see Sandro Jung, "*Les Saisons* (*The Seasons*) de Thomson: mobilités textuelles et étude bibliographique des échanges iconographiques," *Revue des Sciences Humaines* (forthcoming, 2019).

4. James Thomson, *The Seasons: in Four Books* (London: printed for J. French, 1777), 205. On critical responses to Musidora as "nude" or "prude," see Ralph Cohen, *The Art of Discrimination: Thomson's "The Seasons" and the Language of Criticism* (London: Routledge & Kegan Paul, 1964), 291–95. Cohen notes that "Musidora represented the vulgarity of popular taste" (293).

5. Ritchie Robertson, "Wieland's Nude Bathers: Visual Pleasure and the Female Gaze," *German Life and Letters* 64, no. 1 (2011): 32. According to Robertson, the "motif of naked bathing expresses the Enlightenment's fascination with the concept of nature. Undressed, exposed, vulnerable, the bather . . . involuntarily offers himself or herself to the pleasurable gaze of others" (32). Thomson constructs Musidora's bathing as an inverted rise of Aphrodite from the sea foam.

6. *I. Thomsons Iahrszeiten, mit kritischen, ästhetischen und erklärenden Anmerkungen von I.P. und I. Horn*, two volumes (Halle: Verlag bei Ioh. Christian Hendel, 1800), volume 1, 164.

7. William Hamilton had produced the design for this plate for the 1802 edition of *The Seasons* published by Francis Isaac Du Roveray.

8. Elizabeth Boa, "Sex and Sensibility: Wieland's Portrayal of Relationships between the Sexes in the *Comische Erzählungen*, *Agathon*, and *Musarion*," *Lessing Yearbook* 12 (1980): 195.

9. Three eighteenth-century meanings of "Trieb" are at the center of the erotic contexts that Wieland generates in his poetry. D1: "innerer drang, lust, energie," D2a "die triebe sind die primitivsten natürlichsten Regungen," and D2b: "am meisten tritt der *trieb der liebe* hervor." See *Deutsches Wörterbuch von Jacob und Wilhelm Grimm* (www.dwb.uni-trier.de/de). Accessed on November 20, 2018.

10. Simon Richter, *Missing the Breast: Gender, Fantasy and the Body in the German Enlightenment* (Seattle, Washington: University of Washington Press, 2006), 104, 105, 106.

11. Christoph Martin Wieland, *Erzaehlungen* (Heilbronn: Franz Joseph Eckebrecht, 1752), 28. See Thomas Lautwein, *Erotik und Empfindsamkeit: C. M. Wielands "Comische Erzählungen" und die Gattungsgeschichte der europäischen Verserzählung im 17. und 18. Jahrhundert* (Frankfurt a.M.: Lang, 1996).

12. All quotations from *The Seasons* are from James Sambrook's variorum edition of the text, specifically to the final version of *The Seasons* published in Thomson's lifetime, unless otherwise stated: James Thomson, *The Seasons*, ed. with an introduction and commentary by James Sambrook (Oxford: Clarendon Press, 1981). Line numbers will be given parenthetically in the text. *S* refers to *Summer*, *A* to *Autumn*.

13. See Sandro Jung, "Image Making in Thomson's *The Seasons*," *SEL: Studies in English Literature* 53, no. 3 (2013): 583–99.

14. Thomson, *The Seasons*, ed. Sambrook, 114, 115.

15. Georg Friedrich Herrmann, who edited *The Seasons* for use in schools in Germany, glossed "heavy" (strangely) as "ahndend," whereas his translation of "to heave" is "sich heben; schwellen," the latter of which—"to swell"—Thomson frequently uses in scenes of growth. See *J. Thomsons Jahrszeiten: mit unterlegter Konstruction und grammatischen, historischen und andern Anmerkungen erleichtert für Lernende* (Weißenfels: Severin und Comp., 1798), 238.

16. In order to highlight the details of differences between translations of *The Seasons*, I have opted to translate the German as literally as possible, regardless of how awkward this may look in English.

17. Johann Jakob Bodmer, "Celadon und Amalia," in *Thirsis und Damons freundschaftliche Lieder*, ed. M. Samuel Gotthold Lange (Halle: Carl Hermann Hemmerde, 1749), 207. All line references are given parenthetically in the text.

18. *Herrn B. H. Brockes, Com. Palat. Caes. und Rahts-Herrn der Kayserl. freyen Reichs-Stadt Hamburg, aus dem Englischen übersetzte Jahres-Zeiten des Herrn Thomson. Zum Anhange des Jrdischen Vergnügens in Gott* (Hamburg: Herold, 1745), 239. All line numbers will be given parenthetically in the text, preceded by the abbreviation "*Br.*"

19. Bodmer reviewed Brockes's translation in 1745 and included his translation, "Celadon und Amalia," in this review. See *Freymüthige Nachrichten von Neuen Büchern, und andern zur Gelehrtheit gehörigen Sachen* 2 (1745): 108–9.

20. O. Christian Heinrich Schmid, *Anweisung der vornehmsten Bücher in allen Theilen der Dichtkunst* (Leipzig: in der Weygandschen Buchhandlung, 1781), 272.

21. *Jakob Thomson's Jahreszeiten. Neuübersetzt. Mit fünf Kupfern* (Berlin: Christian Friedrich Himburg, 1789), 143.

22. Johann Franz von Palthen, ed. and trans., *Jacob Thomsons Jahreszeiten* (Rostock: Johann Christian Koppe, 1758), 62. All references to the translation will be given by page number in the notes.

23. Heinrich Harries, ed. and trans., *Thomsons Jahreszeiten. In deutschen Jamben* (Altona: bey I. F. Hammerich, 1796). All line numbers will be given parenthetically in the text.

24. Johannes Tobler, trans., *Die Jahreszeiten* (Basel: bey Johannes Schweighauser, 1768), 155.

25. Brockes does not succeed in making sense of the Thomsonian original: "Die Freundschaft war es, die erhöhte, / Bey einem sanften Wechsel-Wunsch, der Hoffnung süssen Reiz; es glimmt' / Ein holdes sympatisch Feuer aus ihren Augen" (237; It was friendship, which heightened—through a tender mutual wish—the sweet charm of hope; a lovely sympathetic fire gleams from her eyes).

26. "Nur Freundschaft war's, erhöht durch Wechselwünsche" (*H*, 1398; it was friendship only, heightened by mutual wishes).

27. Schubart, trans. *Jakob Thomsons Jahreszeiten*, 147.

28. These "Proben" were published in *Neue Litteratur und Völkerkunde. Ein periodisches Werk* 2, no. 1 (1788): 50–53. While Schubart's early version of his translation differs in only a few instances (such as changed word order and epithets) from the later version, in two instances the translator in the 1789 text significantly departs from his earlier renderings of Thomson's tale. As part of his translation of Thomson's lines—"on Celadon her eye / Fell tearful, wetting her disordered cheek"—Schubart, in 1788, anthropomorphizes Amelia's tears: "Thränen zitterten die bleiche Wange hinab" (*Neue Litteratur*, 52; tears trembled down her pale cheek). This is later translated as "Thränen schauerten die bleiche Wange hinab" (tears showered down her pale cheek) as a means to underscore the animatedness of her body, the trembling of which is extended to the tears running down the female's cheeks. The trembling tears thus fulfil a metonymical function not only representing Amelia's fearful response to the storm, but the tears—which symbolically and mythologically are frequently linked to love—are endowed with special meaning as part of which Amelia's very love for Celadon is under threat by the elements. In addition, in his attempt to reassure his lover that she will be safe from the harmful influence of the weather, Celadon, in Schubart's 1789 translation, is made to say: "Sicher ist, wer in Deine Nähe flüchtet, und so die Vollkommenheit an den Busen drückt" (143; He is safe who seeks refuge near you and thus presses perfection against his bosom). The neutral statement at the start of the line emphasizing safety is, however, more rhapsodically rendered in the 1788 variant. In the earlier text, "O der Wonne, in deine Nähe zu flüchten, und so die Vollkommenheit an den Busen zu drücken" (52; O what joy, to seek refuge near you and thus to press perfection against his breast), Schubart synchronizes the state of delight experienced with the sense of perfection experienced by the person embracing Amelia. The interjection introducing "Wonne"—and its being linked with the physical contact with the "Busen"—emphasizes the eroticism, which is toned down by the later variant.

In addition to his rendering of the "Celadon and Amelia" story, Schubart also contributed an early version of his translation of the "Damon and Musidora" tale to *Neue Litteratur*, 45–50.

29. See Otto Ritter, "Gessner und Thomson," *Archiv für das Studium der neueren Sprachen und Literaturen* 111 (1908): 170.

30. For a similar inversion of the Thomsonian model, see Sandro Jung, "An American Parody of Thomson's Celadon and Amelia Tale," *American Notes & Queries* (forthcoming).

31. Ludwig Gotthard Kosegarten, *Gedichte*, two volumes (Leipzig: Ernst Martin Gräff, 1788), volume 1, 181. All line references are given parenthetically in the text.

32. Wilhelm Julius Wiedemann, ed., *Uebungen im Deklamieren für Knaben und Jünglinge; bestehend in einer Sammlung deutscher Gedichte, nebst einigen prosaischen Aufsätzen mit voraufgeschickten und begleiteten Hülfsregeln versehen* (Magdeburg: Johann Adam Creutz, 1800), 139.

33. Johann Heinrich Brumleu, *Einige Gedichte* (Helmstädt: Kühnlin, 1782), 49–51.

34. Schubart, trans. *Jakob Thomsons Jahreszeiten*, 148–49.

35. von Palthen, ed. and trans., *Jacob Thomsons Jahreszeiten*, 63.

36. von Palthen, ed. and trans., *Jacob Thomsons Jahreszeiten*, 64.

37. Schubart, trans. *Jakob Thomsons Jahreszeiten*, 149.

38. Schubart, trans. *Jakob Thomsons Jahreszeiten*, 147.

39. Harries, ed. and trans., *Thomsons Jahreszeiten. In deutschen Jamben*, 140.

40. See Jung, *Thomson's "The Seasons," Print Culture, and Visual Interpretation*, 115–17.

41. The caption reads: "Da die erhabne Sonn auf uns nun in geraden Stralen blitzt, / die Ernte reifft, die Früchte Kocht, die Erde Fluht und Luft erhitzt, / Wird man im Schatten Kühler Wälder vor ihrer schwühlen Glut geschützt, / Wobey auch oft die frische Fluht im Baden der Gesundheit nützt" (As the sublime sun flashes on us in straight beams, / ripens the crop, cooks the fruit, and heats the earth, the flood, and the air, / one is protected from its humid heat in the shade of cool woods / where oft the fresh flood of the bath serves health).

42. The print is listed as "Damon und Musidora, eine Landschaft" in "Verzeichnis aller Bauseschen Blätter von 1760–1785, von dem Künstler selbst in diese Ordnung gebracht," *Miscellaneen artistischen Inhalts* 27 (1786): 164.

43. In *Anhang zu dem fünf und zwanzigsten bis sechs und dreysigsten Band der allgemeinen deutschen Bibliothek*, it is observed that "In einem reizenden waldigen Thale siehet man hinter einen steilen Felswand, einer von da hinunter stürzenden klaren Bach, in demselben die badende Musidora, und zwischen den Bäumen, den dichtenden Damon" (801; In a charming woody vale, behind a steep rockface, a descending clear brook is visible, as are the bathing Musidora and, between the trees, the poet Damon).

44. Anke Fröhlich, *Zwischen Empfindsamkeit und Klassizismus: Der Zeichner und Landschaftsmaler Johann Sebastian Bach der Jüngere (1748–1778)* (Leipzig: Evangelische Verlagsgesellschaft, 2007), 248.

45. This translation was published with minor variations and under the different title of "Lavinia, eine Erndte Erzählung aus Thomson's Jahreszeiten" in Sophie La Roche's *Pomona für Teutschlands Töchter* 8 (August 1784): 730–47.

46. On La Roche and Thomson, see Ulrike Weckel, *Zwischen Häuslichkeit und Öffentlichkeit: Die ersten deutschen Frauenzeitschriften im späten 18. Jahrhundert und ihr Publikum* (Tübingen: Niemeyer, 1998), 410–13.

47. Schubart, trans. *Jakob Thomsons Jahreszeiten*, xxxv.

48. The preface to Schwickert's edition noted that the edition "being chiefly intended for the use of schools, correctness and cheapness have been more consulted

than that elegance and splendour, which too often exceeds the narrow circumstances of the diligent, but indigent youth." James Thomson, *The Seasons*, ed. Engelhard Benjamin Schwickert (Leipzig: Schwickert, 1781), i.

49. See Bernhard Fabian, *The English Book in Eighteenth-Century Germany* (London: The British Library, 1992).

Chapter Eight

Student Experiences
John Stuart Blackie and William Edmonstoune Aytoun in Germany (1829–1830 and 1833–1834)

Bernhard Maier

In their own days, John Stuart Blackie and William Edmonstoune Aytoun were probably among the most conspicuous public figures teaching in the University of Edinburgh, the former as Professor of Greek (from 1852), the latter as Professor of Rhetoric and Belles Lettres (from 1845). Blackie and Aytoun also share the distinction of having significantly contributed to introducing the Scottish public to the work of Johann Wolfgang von Goethe: the former published both a translation of *Faust* (in 1834) and an anthology of thematically organized extracts from Goethe's poetry and prose in English translation, entitled *The Wisdom of Goethe* (in 1883); and the latter produced, together with Theodore Martin, *Poems and Ballads of Goethe* (in 1859). Another feature that both men had in common is that they spent some time in Germany when they were just twenty years of age and that this time spent in Germany left a deep and lasting impression on them. By the end of Queen Victoria's reign, a substantial number of Scotsmen could claim to have spent a summer in one of the German universities at about that age. Yet what sets Blackie and Aytoun apart from the vast majority is that they were among the very first to have done so, having traveled to Germany many years before such a journey became fashionable.

As we shall see, going to Germany for the summer semester was becoming an increasingly commonplace experience in the second half of the nineteenth century. In around 1830 it certainly was not, however, and if we wish to understand the way in which Blackie and Aytoun responded to the German language and literature, we should not assume that we can infer this from the ways in which Scottish students responded to German culture in the 1870s and 1880s; by this time students could consult numerous personal travelogues and a substantial amount of secondary literature to prepare them for the experience. Indeed, Blackie and Aytoun had a very different experience from that of their successors. It was dissimilarities in family background, religion, and literary interests that drove their individual responses to their German experiences.

The lay of the land for Scottish students studying in Germany at the end of the nineteenth century could not have looked more unlike that of Blackie and Aytoun's time. In 1898 eight Scottish theologians published a humorous anthology entitled *The Clerical Life: A Series of Letters to Ministers*, in which they set before their readers a formidable spectrum of well-known theological types, including "a minister whose sermons last an hour," "a minister who regards himself as a prophet of criticism," "a minister who is asked to many tea-parties," and "a minister who has studied in Germany."[1] The latter is presented as someone who not only constantly refers to the authority of his continental teacher, "the learned Professor Hammelfleisch, of Bonn," but who has also published *Translations from Heine and Uhland* and has allegedly claimed of his six months in Germany: "To say that these six months gave a colour to my after life would ridiculously understate their influence. They have saturated my inmost consciousness. I might almost say, without exaggeration, that I think and dream in German."[2] Evidently, the Scottish student of divinity who returns from his sojourn on the Continent brim-full of German scholarship and poetry had become a familiar figure by the end of the nineteenth century. A real-life match of the literary stereotype might be found in Robert William Barbour, who on his return from a visit to the University of Tübingen started a list of the theological and non-theological books in his study with a "row of pure German theology," continuing his description with a formidable array of German works from the *Nibelungenlied* to more recent *belles lettres*, and featuring poets mentioned by name, including Heinrich Heine, Goethe, and Ludwig Uhland.[3] A lasting result of this particular craze for all things German can be found not only in substantial innovations in Scottish theology, but also in the much-quoted saying, "Theology is created in Germany, corrected in Scotland and corrupted in America." Although this saying has been attributed to an anonymous wag, one likely source for it was the Paisley-born Hugh Ross Mackintosh, who had been a student at Freiburg, Halle, and Marburg.[4]

Despite the familiarity that the type of the Scottish theologian steeped in German scholarship and literature had achieved by the end of the Victorian period, it was a comparatively recent development, which had come under way only gradually since the 1840s. As Alexander MacEwen recalled in his 1896 biography of John Cairns, who was among the first notable Scottish theologians of the Victorian period to have studied in Germany (in 1843–1844),

It would be difficult to exaggerate the isolation and insularity of British theology during the first half of this century. The dominant systems of doctrine were those which had been formulated prior to the great intellectual movement which revolutionised European thought before the eighteenth century closed, and such treatises on dogmatics and exegesis as were produced bore no relation to the currents of speculation and criticism then prevalent on the Continent. As a rule, German and French thinkers were either completely ignored or passed by with unintelligent denunciation.[5]

The fact that even leading Scottish theologians tended to be largely ignorant of German prior to the middle of the nineteenth century is confirmed by David Masson, who noted of Thomas Chalmers: "Of German writers or German speculation he knew nothing—with the single far-back exception of Leibnitz [sic], whom he had got at through the Latin or the French; and this defect of German (which, however, he shared with most of his countrymen of that day) was a great pity for him eventually, though it made things easier at the time."[6] Or, as William Garden Blaikie wryly put it in his biography of Chalmers: "He was just beginning to know something of German philosophy when he died."[7] Yet although John Cairns was remarkably early in comparison with the vast majority of Scottish students of divinity who chose to spend some time in a German university, John Stuart Blackie's visit to study in Germany predated that of Cairns by some fourteen years. Blackie was later to turn his back on theology and achieve considerable fame as Professor of Greek at the University of Edinburgh, where he assumed the dual role of propagator of German educational ideas and champion of Celtic Studies in Scotland.[8] However, before we take a closer look at Blackie's student experience in Germany, it is worth putting this experience in a wider chronological perspective.[9]

One of the most glowing appraisals of the positive effect that a semester in Germany could have on a Scottish student is provided by the Scottish Old Testament scholar George Adam Smith, who had been a divinity student in Tübingen in 1876 (at the same time as Robert William Barbour). Smith writes about this period in his life more than twenty years later in his biography of Henry Drummond, who had been a student in Tübingen some two years before Smith went there:

> The glory of the southern spring and summer; the first sight of vineyards and the first tramp through a real forest; the mediaeval castles and churches, Urach and Lichtenstein, Hohenzollern and Bebenhausen, the hospitality and "gemüthlichkeit" of the Swabians; the genuine piety, with other forms and larger liberties than Scottish religion has allowed itself; the social side of the students' life, their "kneipes," their music, and their duels; the first impression of the thoroughness of German scholarship, and of the depth of German thinking; the gradual mastery of the great language, and the entrance upon the vast new literature—with

all these it is not wonderful that so many of us at Tübingen should have wakened for the first time to what Nature is, and even found there, in a sense, the second birth of our intellect.[10]

Just how much of "the vast new literature" nineteenth-century Scottish students could actually absorb during their stay is of course difficult to ascertain. Of John Watson, better known by his pen name Ian Maclaren, who was one of the editors of *The Clerical Life* and had gone to Tübingen in 1874, it was later said, somewhat apologetically, that "one may be pardoned for suggesting that the insight he gained into German life in the 'kneipes' [sic] at the Schottei, or Mullerei, in the Whitsuntide excursion into the Black Forest, and in summer evening strolls to Waldhörnle, Bebenhausen, or the Wurmlinger Kapelle may have been the most valuable advantage he reaped from the semester at Tübingen."[11] Of Henry Drummond, a post-Victorian critic even claimed that he had in fact "carefully avoided lectures" at Tübingen, inferring this "from the fact that neither of the two fellow-students (destined to be lifelong intimates) who accompanied him was ever able to say what courses he attended or what were his studies."[12] Be that as it may, in the very same summer of 1876, which George Adam Smith spent in Tübingen, William Robertson Smith (yet another Free Church theologian) and two of his younger sisters also traveled through Germany, accompanied by Smith's artist friend George Reid.[13] Again we get a glowing description, in an unpublished travel diary, of the pleasure they had: "The best thing that one can do in Köln is to cross the bridge of boats and sit under the horse chestnut trees by the river-side in the garden of the hotel Bellevue in Deutz. The view is finest by moonlight aided by Grünehauser. We had it this time in the afternoon through a silvery haze as we drank our coffee after dinner. Voilà."[14] Significantly, when Smith's younger sister Alice wrote an account of her upbringing and early life for the benefit of her grandchildren more than fifty years later, she also gave a vivid and touching description of that afternoon on the banks of the Rhine in Cologne and of the overwhelming impression it had made upon her as a young girl.[15]

Relating these documents from the 1870s to the much earlier experiences of Blackie and Aytoun, two points may be made. The first concerns the number of the students involved. Although there is no complete survey of how many Scottish students spent time at a German university in the century between the end of the Napoleonic Wars and the outbreak of the First World War, the matriculation records in the Tübingen University Archive give some sense of the numbers involved. From these it appears that Scottish students were first attracted to Tübingen in the 1850s and that they were particularly numerous in the 1870s. After the end of the Victorian period, however, they were few and far between. Although we do not have comparable figures for other German universities that were popular with Scottish students, the evidence that we do have suggests that what we find at Tübingen faithfully reflects the general picture. Therefore, Blackie traveling to Germany in 1829 and Aytoun following suit in 1833 may well be regarded as a harbinger of what became fashionable and to some extent commonplace only several decades later. Until the 1830s, German universities and German student life were a rather niche topic, as may be gleaned from such ephemeral productions as "The University of Bonn" and "Recollections of a Göttingen Student," two articles published anonymously in the *Monthly Magazine, or, British Register*, and the *New Monthly Magazine and Literary Journal*, respectively.[16] From the early Victorian period, by contrast, prospective students who were interested in going to a German university could fall back on several manuals that had been written expressly for the purpose of supplying vital information and advice. Notable both for its early date and its wide influence is *The Student-Life of Germany*, which William Howitt published in 1841, following the prolonged residence of the author and his family at Heidelberg, which is in turn described in detail by Howitt's wife Mary in her posthumously published autobiography.[17] As Howitt focused his attention almost exclusively on the social aspects of German student life, dwelling lovingly on the picturesque rituals, quaint songs, and raucous festivities of German students, his work could be supplemented by *German University Education*. This concise and much more prosaic account was published four years later by the English historian, classicist, and barrister Walter Copland Perry, who endeavored to cover in eight chapters both the past and the present of the German university system and rounded off his account with an appendix containing the syllabus of lectures in the University of Berlin for the year 1844.[18] Presumably, both the expectations and the experiences of Scottish students who had prepared themselves for their German sojourn with the help of such manuals would tend to be rather more uniform than they had been in previous decades.

Another point that deserves to be stressed in this context is that many Scottish students who spent only a few months in Germany can hardly be assumed to have acquired a comprehensive knowledge of German, especially when they had not previously been exposed to the language. As James Stalker was ready to admit in his "Memorial Chronology" of Robert William Barbour, the latter's short stay in Tübingen "opened to him the treasures of German theological literature, though his stay was too short to give him a real mastery of the language."[19] That said, there were considerable differences depending on individual circumstances, interests, and talents. Thus Allan Menzies, who studied at Erlangen in 1867, was exceptional in that he had already lived in Germany for three years before he went there as a student, having acquired and practiced the language together with his siblings in a German secondary school at Stuttgart. Here, "they learnt their Greek and Latin through German, and worked well under the careful German system; they acquired a thorough knowledge of German and of the local dialect, Schwäbisch, which they never forgot and always delighted to speak in later years."[20] Similarly, John Cairns' biographer confidently claimed of his subject, "German he picked up as a plaything"[21]; he quotes a letter in which the young student had told a friend: "In one week I have contrived to get through the grammar, and I am beginning to translate. It is far easier than French. Don't be afraid of it. Its difficulty is immensely exaggerated by young ladies, both male and female, whose minds have not been strengthened by the classics. A month of continuous learning will make me translate anything."[22]

BLACKIE, THEOLOGY, AND GERMAN CELTICISM

Being decades ahead of the trend, Blackie's experiences of Germany were to be markedly different to those of his successors. In stark contrast to many later Scottish students, for example, Blackie was most probably rather exceptional in his mastery of the German language. When fifteen-year-old Kuno Meyer, later famous as a Celtic scholar, met the illustrious professor in Edinburgh in the summer of 1874, he subsequently told his parents in a letter with unconcealed excitement and admiration: "He speaks German just like you and me."[23] Blackie's sojourn in Germany certainly had a great impact on his later scholarly and literary career. This is clear if we take as a starting point one of his less well-known books, *Lay Sermons*, which Blackie published in 1881, one year before his retirement.[24] Blackie dedicated this volume of popular lectures to his Edinburgh friend, Sir Arthur Mitchell, Fellow of the Royal Society of Antiquaries of Scotland and Commissioner of Lunacy for Scotland, praising him in his dedication as "an efficient public servant, a sound archaeologist, and a man wise in the best wisdom of life."[25] Blackie gave one copy of the book to another trusted friend, the Edinburgh Free Church minister, Walter Chalmers Smith, writing on the fly-leaf: "To Walter Smith with warm prayers for his growth in the knowledge of the indivisible Trinity of the three holy Ps Piety, Poetry and Philosophy from John Stuart Blackie."[26] Today best known as the author of the hymn "Immortal, invisible, God only wise," Walter Chalmers Smith enjoyed considerable popularity in his day not only as a preacher, but also as a poet, publishing some of his works under the German pen name of Hermann Kunst.[27] Moreover, he was commissioned in 1894 to edit a posthumous selection of the poems of yet another friend of Blackie's, the Skye-born lawyer and man of letters, Alexander Nicholson, a journalist and supporter of William Robertson Smith.[28]

Significantly, Blackie, Walter Chalmers Smith, Sir Arthur Mitchell, Alexander Nicolson, and William Robertson Smith were all closely associated with what one might call the urban, middle-class, theologically progressive, and liberal wing within the Free Church of Scotland (as distinct from the much more conservative Free Church to be found in the Highlands and Islands of Scotland).[29] This urban segment of the Free Church upheld fairly close ties with Germany, from which it had drawn and indeed continued to draw a good deal of its theological and philosophical inspiration. Blackie's dedicatory admonition to Walter Chalmers Smith may therefore safely be taken to reflect his view that German poetry and philosophy were necessary correctives of traditional Scottish piety. This emerges most clearly from the sheer number of times he refers to German poetry and philosophy in his *Lay Sermons*. Blackie significantly steers clear of the "monistic cosmogony of Haekel [sic], which is only Darwinianism followed out in its consistent absurdity."[30] His heroes, instead, were Goethe and Friedrich Schiller, the only German poets whom he not only referred to in passing, but repeatedly quotes verbatim either in an English translation or in the original German.[31] Not surprisingly, German Biblical scholarship is also referred to with approval: he cites the likes of lexicographer, Wilhelm Gesenius, Christian Karl Josias von Bunsen, and August Dillmann.

While we can glean the later results of Blackie's reading of German literature and philosophy from his *Lay Sermons*, for the details of Blackie's involvement with Germany as a student, however, we largely have to rely on aspects of his biography.[32] Born in Glasgow in 1809, Blackie was first educated at Merson's Academy, Aberdeen, and afterwards at Marischal College. After a brief interlude at an Aberdeen lawyer's office, he enrolled at the University of Edinburgh, where he studied for another four years, the last two of which as a candidate for the ministry in the Church of Scotland. In the spring of 1829, a friend of his father's advised that he should complete his education in Germany, and thus Blackie traveled to the small university town of Göttingen. There Blackie attended various courses and lectures, most notably those of the historian Arnold Heeren, who specialized in the political systems of modern Europe, the anthropologist Johann Friedrich Blumenbach, who was the author of a widely used *Manual of Comparative Anatomy*, and the classical philologist Karl Otfried Müller, who was a leading representative of the so-called *Sachphilologen*, who advocated the integration of Archaeology, Numismatics, and Epigraphy into the philological study of Classical Literature.

In the autumn of 1829, Blackie left Göttingen for Berlin. There, he told his aunt in a letter, he visited the theater as regularly as the church, in order to perfect his German: "I go conscientiously whenever a fine piece of Goethe,

Schiller, Kotzebue, or any other bright constellation of literary stars which has of late shone over Germany, is brought on stage."[33] One of the major attractions in this respect would no doubt have been the Berlin Schauspielhaus, which had opened in 1821. As regards the professors whose lectures and courses Blackie attended, there were, most notably, the classical philologist August Boeckh, the historians, Friedrich von Raumer and Leopold von Ranke, and the Protestant theologians, August Neander and Friedrich Schleiermacher. Both in Göttingen and in Berlin, Blackie was clearly at pains to constantly improve his German. Soon after his arrival, he received a letter from his father demanding that he should on no account take up lodgings with the two Scottish friends who had accompanied him on his journey, as this would stand in the way of his rapid acquisition of German. Thus Blackie and his two Scottish fellow-students "spoke German to each other, imposing a fine of two Pfennige for every relapse into English."[34] In Berlin, Blackie tried to secure lodgings in the household of a professor, but was told by von Raumer that this was not common practice. Thus Blackie finally took lodgings in the house of a retired army officer and his wife, enlisting the help of German fellow students to improve his command of German. In the words of his biographer, Stoddart:

> He made the acquaintance of a young theologian, a proficient in Greek, whom he engaged to read Homer with him four times a-week. They translated into German, so that from their work he reaped a double benefit. He soon made friends amongst the students, and with one of them he concluded terms of mutual edification. He undertook to teach his friend English in return for five hours' weekly help with the German classics. The contract repaid both, and on John's side led to a careful study of Goethe's "Faust," while we find him brushing up his own language for the benefit of his friend.[35]

From Berlin, Blackie moved on to Rome in the autumn of 1830, where he came under the influence of the Prussian diplomat and private scholar, who made such a powerful impression on him that he is said to have stated several decades later: "My father's teaching, the nature God gave me, and Bunsen's influence have been the great shaping forces of my life."[36] The reason for this verdict appears to have been the fact that it was in Rome and chiefly due to Bunsen's guidance that Blackie finally decided to give up the study of theology and try to make a career in classical philology. As is well known, Bunsen had formerly been an assistant to the historian Barthold Georg Niebuhr and later became Prussian ambassador in England. In this capacity, Bunsen was pivotal in mediating between German and English scholars, and introducing German Protestant theology to the British public, one of his best-known protégés being Friedrich Max Müller at Oxford.[37]

In considering the influence that Blackie's time in Germany had on his later career, perhaps the first thing to note is that, despite his having attended the courses of August Boeckh and Karl Otfried Müller, this influence was not very prominent in the field of Classical Philology. Although Blackie produced a translation of Aeschylus in 1852 and four volumes entitled *Homer and the Iliad* in 1866, these books were not written in close contact with German classicists, and Blackie's insistence that Ancient Greek should be pronounced like Modern Greek was held to be rather idiosyncratic. Likewise, the fact that Blackie had studied with eminent German historians like Heeren, Ranke, and Raumer did not prompt him to become a historian himself. He did, however, write two articles on the German Liberation War for *Tait's Edinburgh Magazine*, which he later incorporated into his book *War Songs of the Germans*, published at the time of the Franco-Prussian War in 1870.[38] Much more important was his early and lasting immersion in the works of Goethe, *The Wisdom of Goethe* being published a year after his retirement.[39] As stated in the dedication, Blackie held his Goethe anthology to be a "manual of wise words, for guidance in fruitful action and sound thinking,"[40] the topics covered ranging from "life, character, and morals," "religion," "politics" via "literature," "philosophy" and "nature," to "art," "women," and "education and culture." Having noted that the wisdom of Goethe "is generally acknowledged, even by those who entertain the most unfavourable views of his character," he claimed that he "had reason to thank God that at an early period of my life I became acquainted with the writings of this great man."[41] Significantly, *The Wisdom of Goethe* was dedicated to the Reverend Walter Chalmers Smith. Although Blackie had given up academic theology on his return from Germany, he continued to be fascinated by the practical consequences of the Christian faith for society, and his favorite motto, which ultimately came to be engraved on his monument in St. Giles' Cathedral, was *Aletheuein en Agape*, "Speak the truth in love," taken from St. Paul's Letter to the Ephesians (4:15).

Trying to understand the influence of Blackie's early stay in Germany on his later career, mention must also be made of his interest in all things Celtic, including the *Poems of Ossian*, first published between 1759 and 1765 by James Macpherson. A particularly interesting piece of evidence in this context is Blackie's book *Altavona*, first published in 1882.[42] As Blackie points out in his preface, the book's subtitle, *Fact and Fiction from my Life in the Highlands*, was inspired by that of Goethe's autobiography *Aus meinem Leben* (From my Life), subtitled *Dichtung und Wahrheit* (Poetry and Truth). A more obvious model for Blackie's book, however, is *Noctes ambrosianae*, the celebrated series of imaginary colloquies first published from 1822 to 1835 in *Blackwood's Magazine* by Blackie's former Edinburgh professor,

John Wilson alias Christopher North. Like *Noctes ambrosianae*, *Altavona* consists mainly of a series of rambling dialogues between the members of a heterogeneous party traveling through the Western Highlands. This party includes Roderick MacDonald, a Highlander educated at Oxford and Göttingen, representing what Blackie calls the "Gaelic Presbyterian type," Roderick's sister Flora MacDonald, representing the "old Catholic and high-Highland type," Roderick's college chum from Oxford, the Reverend Christopher Church, representing the "English Episcopo-Oxonian type," and, finally, Roderick's German friend and fellow student of Göttingen days, Dr. Hermann Bücherblume, representing the "European or cosmopolitan type." Historically, the book is remarkable not least because of its commitment to the cause of the Highland crofters, and in the first edition of the book, Blackie made some highly critical remarks on the role of the notorious factor Patrick Sellar during the Sutherland Clearances. These remarks provoked the anger of Sellar's eldest son, who demanded that these references be purged from the second edition. Threatened with legal proceedings, Blackie felt compelled to comply with this request, so in the second edition he inserted a footnote stating that his account was "in no wise intended as an inculpation of any person in particular."[43]

Closely related to Blackie's championing the case of the crofters was his interest in the *Poems of Ossian*, the authenticity of which was still hotly debated in his time. Here Blackie steadfastly or stubbornly adhered to the view that the Gaelic version that had finally been published after much discussion in 1807 was the original of Macpherson's version, although it was of course exactly the other way round, Macpherson's English text having been translated into a kind of modern Scottish Gaelic. Again, we can see the influence of Blackie's stay in Germany in this debate, for in *Altavona* Blackie has Dr. Hermann Bücherblume extol the achievements of German Celticists. In principle, this was a fair assessment, as the upsurge of Celtic Studies in the second half of the nineteenth century was largely due to the publication of the seminal *Grammatica Celtica* by Johann Kaspar Zeuss in 1853. However, in discussing the *Poems of Ossian*, Flora tells Bücherblume that she has just been "dipping into a metrical German version of *Fingal* by a Dr. Ebrard, which reads much more naturally and pleasantly than the somewhat stilted and attitudinising prose Ossian of MacPherson."[44] Evidently Blackie regarded the theological writer August Ebrard as a highly respectable authority on the Ossianic question: in 1875 he had commissioned and revised an English translation of the latter's essay "Ueber Alter und Echtheit von Ossian's Gedichten" (On the Age and Authenticity of Ossian's Poems).[45] In fact, however, professional Celtic scholars of the period were well aware that Ebrard was a mere amateur in the field of Celtic, and Blackie appears to have taken the superiority of German scholarship for granted, without making himself familiar with all the details. Among those who frowned at what they perceived to be Blackie's rather misguided championing of the Gaelic version of *The Poems of Ossian* was the celebrated folklorist John Francis Campbell of Islay, who had spent considerable energy, time, and scholarship on repudiating the claim that the Gaelic texts published in 1807 were part and parcel of a living oral tradition. That said, the establishment of the Edinburgh "Chair of Celtic Languages, Literature, History and Antiquities," filled in 1882 by the Gaelic native speaker Donald MacKinnon, was largely due to Blackie's tireless efforts. The use of "Celtic" instead of "Gaelic" to this day reflects Blackie's esteem for German Comparative Philology. As early as 1876 Blackie had scathingly condemned the view of those who "would still persistently believe that Celtic means Gaelic, and nothing more, which was just as logical as to say that a dog meant a Skye terrier." Needless to say, the use of the umbrella term "Celtic" as advocated by Blackie was also bound up with romantic notions about *Volksgeist* (spirit of a people), reflecting the idea—which may ultimately be traced back to Herder—that a comparison of individual Celtic traditions would yield insights into what was quintessentially Celtic across space and time. This approach is also evident in the collection of Gaelic proverbs compiled by Blackie's close friend, Alexander Nicolson, who sometimes comments on a Gaelic proverb by noting that it exemplifies a typically "Celtic" feeling or sentiment or is just "very Celtic."[46] In Blackie's days, this line of reasoning was closely associated with the writings of Ernest Renan and Matthew Arnold, who extrapolated the characteristics of a Celtic "race" from their own highly subjective interpretations of a very small selection of medieval texts. The bracketing together of "Languages, Literature, History and Antiquities" most probably reflects the comprehensive concept of philology that Blackie's teachers, Karl Otfried Müller at Göttingen and August Boeckh at Berlin, had advocated in the field of Greek, arguing that the interpretation of Greek and Latin literature should be informed by all sorts of specialized archaeological and historical studies.[47]

Blackie's efforts on behalf of the campaign for a Celtic Chair at the University of Edinburgh were also part of a much larger struggle to emulate in Scotland the model of German or rather Prussian universities, a struggle in which Blackie was joined by James Lorimer, James Donaldson, and Sir Richard Burdon Haldane.[48] Blackie articulated his educational aims when he stressed the need for a Celtic Chair before the General Council of the University of Edinburgh in 1877:

> All persons of education and intelligence in this country are now convinced that we have been for some generations back allowing our higher education to drift along with a current of the most vulgar utilitarianism, which, if consistently

carried out, would drag down our institutions of highest culture to the level of mere polytechnic schools, or dispensaries and retail shops of the results of high learning and scientific research, acquired everywhere except in Scotland. Enough of evil has been done already to our Universities by the prevalence of this degraded ideal; and it will not be the least triumph of the Celtic Chair that, while on the one hand it asserts the importance of the national and historical element in University study, it at the same time stands up as a grand practical protest against the debasing notion that University teaching is only valuable in proportion as it helps people make money by the subservience of intellectual culture to professional advancement; and that the worth of an Academical Chair in the social organism is to be estimated mainly, like the prosperity of a bazaar, by the number of customers whom it invites, and the number of shillings which it turns over.[49]

This aspect of Blackie's work was already highlighted by a contemporary educationalist, who remarked soon after Blackie's death "that Professor Blackie was 'made in Germany,' and it is equally certain that he was well and truly made, for he lost all his narrowness and gained a conception of the whole duty of a teacher which egged him on persistently in after years to use both pen and voice in his attempts to make university teaching in Britain more of a reality than it, at that time, was."[50] As Stuart Wallace points out in his recent biography of Blackie, the Edinburgh professor of Greek supplied many Edinburgh students with introductions to German scholars. Aside from his enthusiasm for Goethe and, to a lesser extent, Schiller, Blackie does not seem to have made much use of his knowledge of German poetry and drama in enticing students to German culture. Thus his encouragement of students "to go and sample the rich research culture of German universities . . . was perhaps his most valuable contribution as an Edinburgh professor."[51]

AYTOUN'S POETIC PROGRESS

As a translator of Goethe's *Faust*, Blackie had a remarkable counterpart in William Edmonstoune Aytoun, who was Blackie's junior by four years and visited Germany at exactly the same age four years later. Comparing and contrasting the two, we find that there are both conspicuous similarities and differences. Both came from a rather similar social background, belonging to the affluent urban middle class: Blackie hailed from Glasgow and was the son of a banker, whereas Aytoun was born in Edinburgh's New Town, the son of Roger Aytoun, Writer to the Signet, a member of a body of solicitors conducting cases in the Scottish Court of Session. That said, Aytoun's family could point to a much longer history than Blackie's, and they adhered to the Scottish Episcopal Church rather than the Church of Scotland. This accounts not only for Aytoun's Jacobite sympathies, as seen in his *Lays of the Scottish Cavaliers* (1848), but also for his impatience with the demands of the Evangelicals within the Church of Scotland and, after 1843, those of the Free Church of Scotland. Significantly, Aytoun is said to have been the author of an anonymous pamphlet entitled *Our Zion, or Presbyterian Popery*, championing patronage and state control of the Church, which was published at the height of the Ten Years' Conflict in 1840. Significantly, too, there is a letter to his parents from Germany, in which Aytoun tells them that he found the German way of celebrating Sunday rather agreeable.[52] This position formed a marked contrast to that of most Scottish students with a Presbyterian background, whose reaction to Continental Sundays tended to range from uneasiness to horror and disgust.

Like Blackie, Aytoun went to Germany at the age of twenty to supplement his education by learning German and studying some of its literature. However, while Göttingen appears to have been a natural choice in the case of Blackie as a result of its long-standing association with the house of Hanover and thus with Britain, it is by no means obvious why Aytoun should have gone to Aschaffenburg in Bavaria. Göttingen, in those days, could boast a university of international renown, but the University of Aschaffenburg had, in fact, just been downgraded to a *Lyzeum*, a kind of high school focusing on philosophy and theology. According to Theodore Martin's *Memoir of William Aytoun*, the choice of place had been Aytoun's and was subsequently approved by his father, but unfortunately he does not give us the reasons behind it.[53] In any case, Aytoun appears to have been fortunate in securing as his private tutor Joseph Merkel, professor of Philology and Philosophy, librarian, and a close friend of the Brentano family.[54] Like Blackie, Aytoun is said to have relished the German theater. But his social life was very different from that of Blackie (and in fact from that of most other Scottish students in Germany), inasmuch as he appears to have held completely aloof from such student life as there was in Aschaffenburg, making some rather scathing remarks on it in his letters.[55] Blackie, by contrast, was enthusiastic about German student life in later years and even tried to introduce some of its features into Scotland.[56] Probably as a result of his comparative isolation, Aytoun does not seem to have formed any lasting friendships with Germans of his age during his stay in Germany, although he did remain in contact with Joseph Merkel. On the publication of his poem *Bothwell* in 1856, Merkel sent Aytoun a letter in which he called him "my unforgotten friend" and "my dear intellectual foster-son." Aytoun visited his old teacher once more and, as it turned out, for the last time, in the summer of 1862.[57]

Trying to ascertain the influence of Aytoun's early stay in Germany on his later literary and academic career is, on the whole, rather difficult. Aytoun's published writings include a vast number of short pieces both in prose and in verse, which did not find their way into monographs and moreover were frequently unsigned, so that his authorship is not always beyond doubt. Another drawback results from the fact that the main source for his highly successful career as professor of English consists of unpublished lectures, with the most extensive and detailed treatment of this unpublished material dating back to the 1960s.[58] As in the case of Blackie, Martin claimed in his *Memoir* that Aytoun's stay was a turning point in his life.[59] This is certainly true to the extent that for both men their stay in Germany ultimately served as a starting point for their later literary and academic careers. However, there may well be a substantial difference, for while Blackie's outlook on life appears to have changed considerably in Germany, Aytoun's did not, or at least not to the same extent. For him, the German influence was not so much related to general views on philosophy, history, theology, and education, but much more closely bound up with the perception and interpretation of literature.

The difference between the two men is neatly illustrated by the kind of German poetry that appealed to them and the ways in which they responded to it. As is well known, both Blackie and Aytoun boldly attempted to translate Goethe's *Faust* at a surprisingly early age. But while Blackie was enthusiastic enough to publish his translation in 1834, Aytoun ultimately refrained from doing so. Aytoun eventually made his name as a translator of Ludwig Uhland, whose poetry does not seem to have appealed to Blackie, and was cherished by Aytoun on account of its resemblance to the work of Walter Scott. Moreover, Blackie's enthusiasm for Goethe clearly extended far beyond Goethe's literary achievement, making him compile his practical manual *The Wisdom of Goethe*, whereas Aytoun's admiration of Uhland was confined to the latter's ballads and certainly stopped short at endorsing Uhland's liberal political ideas.

The different ways in which both men responded to German poetry was further related to a remarkable difference in character. "Though ready to make fun at the expense of others," Stuart Wallace notes, "Blackie always took himself seriously—perhaps the reason why, as a close friend noted, he could not laugh. 'His nearest approach was an explosive splutter and hiss that was anything but pleasant.'"[60] Aytoun, by contrast, appears to have been far less serious about his own doings (and literary production) and was certainly more inclined than Blackie to see things in a humorous light, as may be gleaned from his *Book of Ballads*, first published under the pseudonymous editorship of Bon Gaultier in 1845. Three years before the publication of this book, which was to make him famous, he and his friend, Sir Theodore Martin, had published in *Tait's Edinburgh Magazine* an anonymous article entitled "Lays of Loyalty."[61] In this article, the anonymous authors boldly claim that Uhland had happened to be present during Queen Victoria's visit to Edinburgh in the autumn of 1842. Sitting at the breakfast table in his hotel near Waterloo Place (we are told), the German poet suddenly realized that a magnificent parade was passing by outside. He rushed out into the street, saw the Queen, and composed a spirited ballad in his native German:

Sass Ich da in dem Hotelle,
Frey am Sinn, am Herzen frey,
Suppte Klatzsch vom kauldsten Parritsch,
Saurstes Butter-Milch vorbei.

Sang der Kettel an dem Feuer,
An dem Tafel Kaffee stand,
Waren Butter da und Eier,
Pfenning-Rollen, Baps genannt.

Rolle-Sleis hatt' ich gebüttert,
Kupf von Kaffee ausgepört,
Eier hatt' ich auch erschüttert,
Als die Freud' mir war zerstört.

Horch! Vom fernen Kastel-Hügel,
Donnern die Kanonen laut!
Ach Gott! Haben sie die Kügel,
Graut mir's nun am ganzen Haut.

Nein! Sie haben keine Kügel,
Frichtet sollen sie nicht sein.
Horch! Wie von dem Kalton Hügel
Die erfreute Volken schrei'n!

Kommt die Königinn! Und plötzlich,
Butter-Brod stoss' Ich herab,
Umkehr' die Kaffee so ergötzlich,
Sturz' hinaus am meinem Stab.

Lawt und lawter auf der Strasse
Schallt des freuliches Geschrei,
Dumpf erbrausend durch die Gasse,
Kommt der prachtvoll Zug herbei.

Folgen sie viel stolze Ritter,
Glänzt ein Engelbild darin—
Ach! Mein Herz fühlt ein Getwütter,
Himmel! 'S ist die Königinn!

Und Fürst Albrecht ihr zur Seite,
Ihr Gemahl so himmel-süss,
Der um Liebe kam von Weite,
Seine saure Kraüte liess.

Damenschrei von den Balkonen
Grüsst das Konigliches Paar:
Schottland's grüne Cupidonen
Schützen sie auf immerdar.

For the benefit of illustrating the abundant Scotticisms in this poem, it might be rendered into English as follows:

As I was sitting in my hotel
Carefree and in cheerful mood,
Had a bowl-full of cauld parritch
And sour buttermilk forbye,

Kettle singing on the fire,
On the table, pots with caps,
Eggs and butter were abundant,
Also penny-rolls, called baps.

Just as I had cut some butter,
And some coffee I had poured,
Ate some eggs that I had shattered,
All my joy was brought to naught.

Hark! From where the castle rises
Cannons boom with mighty roar!
Jesus! If the guns are loaded,
I'll take fright as ne'er before.

No! The cannons are unloaded,
Are as harmless as a toy,
Hark! From yonder Calton Hill
Cheerful people shout with joy.

Here she comes! The Queen they greet,
And I drop the buttered rolls,
Throw the coffee to the gutter
And rush out into the street.

Ever louder on the pavement
Sound the shouts of accolade,

As with rising noise approaches
The magnificent parade.

Stately knights in shining armor
Highlight a seraphic sheen—
Ach! My heart in rapture quivers!
Heaven! 'T is herself, the Queen!

And Prince Albert sits beside her,
Consort of angelic mind,
From afar he came to woo her,
Left his sauer Kraut behind.

Ladies hail the Royal Couple
From the balconies with "hurray!"
Royal Archers, like green cupids,
Pledge to guard their love for ay.

Metrically, the ballad closely reflects Uhland's celebrated poem "Die Kapelle" (based on the Wurmlingen chapel near Tübingen), the two opening lines "Sass Ich da in dem Hotelle, / Frey am Sinn, am Herzen frey" bearing some resemblance to Uhland's "Droben stehet die Kapelle, / Schauet still ins Tal hinab." In terms of spelling, grammar, and vocabulary, however, the ballad represents a curious hotchpotch of misspellings ("lawt" for "laut" and "Kraüte" for "Kräute"), incorrect adjectival endings ("saurstes" for "sauerste"), incorrect use of the definite article according to both gender and case ("an dem Tafel" for "an der Tafel"), mistaken plural formations ("Kügel" for "Kugeln"), and English and Scottish words spelled as if they were German (*Parritsch* for *parritch*, *Kettel* for *kettle*). Suffice to say, with this level of German and the mistakes in it, the ballad could not have been by a native German, let alone by Uhland. Moreover, the very use of Scotticisms (and the extent to which the poem works once translated back into English) makes it plain that Aytoun was its author.

Taken together, all of the misspellings, mistakes, and Scotticisms in "Der Morgenzug" make for good comical effect. But this poem also highlights the central difference between Aytoun and Blackie. Even though they were temporally so close, Blackie's and Aytoun's experiences of student life in Germany between 1829 and 1834 could not have had more markedly different results. While the lessons learned by Blackie were to color his career as a theologian and an academic, Aytoun's German experiences led him down the route of poetic composition. And while Aytoun had no problem in using the model of Uhland as a mere vehicle for his own type of humor, it is difficult to envisage such levity from Blackie, in whose imagination German poetry appears to have been bound up indissolubly with a high moral purpose. Even in 1870, as the Franco-Prussian War was about to usher in a new era in European politics and many in Britain were already voicing their misgivings, Blackie confidently published a selection of patriotic German songs by Ernst Moritz Arndt, Theodor Körner, Nikolaus Becker, and Matthias Claudius both in the original and in English translations, as he wished "to produce in the British mind a lasting respect for that people to whose intellectual labors Europe has been under such great obligations, and whom we now at length, in insular Britain, see so much cause to admire, as our emulators and rivals in the world of policy and of action."[62]

NOTES

1. John Watson, Marcus Dods, T.C. Edwards, James Denney, T.H. Darlow, T.G. Selby, W. Robertson Nicoll, J.T. Stoddart, *The Clerical Life: A Series of Letters to Ministers* (New York: Dodd, Mead and Company, 1898), 167–75.

2. Watson et al, *The Clerical Life*, 168.

3. Robert William Barbour, *Letters, Poems, and Pensées* (Glasgow: Maclehose, 1893), 162–63.

4. See Randle Manwaring, *From Controversy to Co-existence. Evangelicals in the Church of England 1914–1980* (Cambridge: Cambridge University Press, 1985), 75; and Alasdair Heron, "James Torrance: An Appreciation," in *Christ In Our Place: The Humanity of God in Christ for the Reconciliation of the World. Essays presented to Professor James Torrance*, ed. Trevor A. Hart and Daniel P. Thimell (Alison Park, PA: Pickwick, 1989).

5. Alexander R. MacEwen, *Life and Letters of John Cairns, D.D., LL.D.* (London: Hodder and Stoughton, 195), 148.

6. David Masson, *Memories of Two Cities: Edinburgh and Aberdeen* (Edinburgh and London: Oliphant, Anderson & Ferrier, 1911), 74.

7. William Garden Blaikie, *Thomas Chalmers* (Edinburgh and London: Oliphant, Anderson & Ferrier, 1896), 95.

8. See Anna M. Stoddart, *John Stuart Blackie: A Biography*, two volumes (Edinburgh: Blackwood, 1895). For a comprehensive modern biography, see Stuart Wallace, *John Stuart Blackie: Scottish Scholar and Patriot* (Edinburgh: Edinburgh University Press, 2006).

9. For a wide-ranging study of Scottish-German academic links in the period before the First World War, see Stuart Wallace, "Scottish University Men and German Universities before 1914," in *Aneignung und Abwehr: Interkultureller Transfer zwischen Deutschland und Großbritannien im 19. Jahrhundert*, ed. Rudolf Muhs, Johannes Paulmann and Willibald Steinmetz (Bodenheim: Philo, 1998), 227–61. For Scottish students of divinity who traveled to Germany in that period, see Todd Statham, "'Landlouping students of Divinity': Scottish Presbyterians in German Theology Faculties, c. 1840 to 1914," *Zeitschrift für Kirchengeschichte* 121 (2010): 42–67.

10. George Adam Smith, *The Life of Henry Drummond* (New York: Doubleday & McClure Company, 1898), 51.

11. William Robertson Nicoll, *"Ian MacLaren": The Life of the Rev. John Watson, D.D.* (London: Hodder and Stoughton, 1908), 64.

12. Donald Carswell, *Brother Scots* (New York: Harcourt, Brace and Company, n.d.), 7.

13. See the classic biography of W.R. Smith by John Sutherland Black and George W. Chrystal, *The Life of William Robertson Smith* (London: Adam and Charles Black, 1912), and the more recent study by Bernhard Maier, *William Robertson Smith: His Life, his Work and his Times* (Tübingen: Mohr Siebeck, 2009).

14. See Bernhard Maier, "Ritus und Mythos bei William Robertson Smith. Theologische Voraussetzungen einer religionswissenschaftlichen Theorie," in *Liturgie und Ritual in der Alten Kirche*, ed. W. Kinzig, U. Volp und J. Schmidt (Leuven: Peeters, 2011), 224.

15. See Maier, *William Robertson Smith*, 98–99.

16. See "The University of Bonn," *Monthly Magazine, or, British Register* 5 (1828): 391–98, and "Recollections of a Göttingen Student," *New Monthly Magazine and Literary Journal* 26 (1829), 515–23, 28; (1830), 12–20, 145–54, 245–54, 340–48, 423–35.

17. See William Howitt, *The Student-Life of Germany: containing nearly forty of the most famous student songs, with the original music, adapted to the piano-forte, by the Herr Winkelmeyer. From the unpublished ms. of Dr. Cornelius, illustrated with engravings by Sargent, Woods, and other eminent artists* (London: Longman, Brown, Green, and Longmans, 1841), and cf. Mary Howitt, *Mary Howitt: An autobiography*, ed. Margaret Howitt, two volumes (London: Isbister, 1889).

18. See Walter Copland Perry, *German University Education, or, the Professors and Students of Germany* (London: Longman, 1845).

19. See Barbour, *Letters, Poems, and Pensées*, xvi.

20. See Allan Menzies, *A Study of Calvin and Other Papers, with a Memoir by His Daughter* (London: Macmillan and Co., 1918), 7.

21. MacEwen, *Life and Letters of John Cairns*, 113.

22. MacEwen, *Life and Letters of John Cairns*, 126.

23. See Bernhard Maier, *Ein Junge aus Hamburg im viktorianischen Schottland: Kuno Meyers Briefe an die Familie, 1874–1876* (Würzburg: Ergon, 2016), 125. Meyer himself had come to Edinburgh with hardly any English at all, and although he was famous for his command of the language in later years, one can see from his numerous early letters that it took him about a year to become fluent in it.

24. John Stuart Blackie, *Lay Sermons* (London: Macmillan and Co., 1881).

25. Blackie, *Lay Sermons*, v.

26. Copy now in the author's possession.

27. See Hermann Kunst, ed., *Olrig Grange* (Glasgow: Maclehose & Sons, 1872). The American edition (Boston: James R. Osgood & Company, 1872) gives the editor's name as "Künst."

28. See Bernhard Maier, "A Kaleidoscope of Victorian Scotland: The Life of Alexander Nicolson (1827–1893)," *Scottish Gaelic Studies* 26 (2010): 35–65.

29. See, for example, Callum G. Brown, "Religion, Class and Church Growth," in *People and Society in Scotland II 1830–1914*, ed. W. Hamish Fraser and R.J. Morris (Edinburgh: John Donald, 1990), 310–35.

30. Blackie, *Lay Sermons*, 49.

31. See, for example, Blackie, *Lay Sermons*, 34, 62–63, 74, 123, 148, 300.

32. For what follows, see Stoddart, *Blackie*, I, 1–129; and Wallace, *Blackie*, 11–75.

33. Blackie, cited in Wallace, *Blackie*, 53.

34. Stoddart, *Blackie*, I, 53.

35. Stoddart, *Blackie*, I, 76–77.

36. See I.F.M., "John Stuart Blackie: Professor and Poet," *The Leisure Hour* (May 1895): 434.

37. On Bunsen, see Frank Foerster, *Christian Carl Josias Bunsen: Diplomat, Mäzen und Vordenker in Wissenschaft, Kirche und Politik* (Bad Arolsen: Waldeckischer Geschichtsverein, 2001).

38. John Stuart Blackie, *War Songs of the Germans, with Historical Illustrations of the Liberation War and the Rhine Boundary Question* (Edinburgh: Edmonston and Douglas, 1870).

39. See John Stuart Blackie, *Faust: A Tragedy. By J. W. Goethe, Translated into English verse, with notes, and preliminary remarks* (Edinburgh: Blackwood, 1834), and John Stuart Blackie, *The Wisdom of Goethe* (Edinburgh: Blackwood, 1883).

40. Blackie, *Wisdom of Goethe*, v.

41. Blackie, *Wisdom of Goethe*, x–xi.

42. John Stuart Blackie, *Altavona: Fact and Fiction from my Life in the Highlands* (Edinburgh: David Douglas, 1882).

43. See Wallace, *Blackie*, 286–87.

44. Blackie, *Altavona*, 31.

45. See August Ebrard, "On the Authenticity of the Poems of Ossian," *An Gaidheal* 4 (1875): 279–88, 313–18. The original German version of this article had been published as an appendix to Ebrard's translation of *Fingal*, published under the title *Ossian's Finnghal: Episches Gedicht, aus dem Gälischen metrisch und mit Beibehaltung des Reims übersetzt* (Leipzig: Brockhaus, 1868). For a modern assessment of August Ebrard as a Celticist, see David Stifter, "Christian Wilhelm Ahlwardt, Stephan Ladislaus Endlicher und Johann Heinrich August Ebrard im Kontext der Keltologie des 19. Jhs.," in *Johann Kaspar Zeuss im kultur- und sprachwissenschaftlichen Kontext (19. bis 21. Jahrhundert)*, ed. Hans Hablitzel and David Stifter (Wien: Praesens, 2007), 209–53, especially 231–43.

46. See Alexander Nicolson, *A Collection of Gaelic Proverbs and Familiar Phrases* (Edinburgh: MacLachlan and Stewart, 1881), 17, 153, 211, 216, 218, 221, 238, 243, 276.

47. Recent studies of this topic include Annette M. Baertschi and Colin G. King, eds., *Die modernen Väter der Antike: die Entwicklung der Altertumswissenschaften an Akademie und Universität im Berlin des 19. Jahrhunderts* (Berlin: de Gruyter, 2009); William M. Calder and Renate Schlesier, eds., *Zwischen Rationalismus und Romantik: Karl Otfried Müller und die antike Kultur* (Hildesheim: Weidmann, 1998); Christiane Hackel, ed., *August Boeckh: Philologie, Hermeneutik und Wissen-*

schaftspolitik (Berlin: BWV, 2013); and Christian Pietsch, "August Boeckh und die methodische Grundlegung der Philologie als Leitwissenschaft des 19. Jahrhunderts," in *Philologie als Literatur- und Rechtswissenschaft*, ed. Claudia Lieb (Heidelberg: Winter, 2013), 53–71.

48. See Wallace, *Blackie*, 222–38.
49. John Stuart Blackie, "The Celtic Chair," *An Gaidheal* 6 (1877): 154.
50. Thomas Cartwright, "Modern Educational Reformers: XXV.—John Stuart Blackie," *The Practical Teacher* (November 1896): 252–53.
51. See Wallace, *Blackie*, 206–07, 216n94.
52. See Theodore Martin, *Memoir of William Edmonstoune Aytoun* (Edinburgh: William Blackwood and Sons, 1867), 46.
53. See Martin, *Aytoun*, 35–36.
54. See Brigitte Schad, *Die Aschaffenburger Brentanos: Beiträge zur Geschichte der Familie aus unbekanntem Nachlass-Material* (Aschaffenburg: Geschichts- und Kunstverein, 1984), especially 89–90.
55. See Martin, *Aytoun*, 44–45.
56. See especially John Stuart Blackie, *Musa Burschicosa: A Book of Songs for Students and University Men* (Edinburgh: Edmonston and Douglas, 1869).
57. See Martin, *Aytoun*, 192–93.
58. See Erik Frykman, *W.E. Aytoun, Pioneer Professor of English at Edinburgh: A Study of his Literary Opinions and his Contribution to the Development of English as an Academic Discipline* (Stockholm: Almqvist & Wiksell, 1963); Mark A. Weinstein, *William Edmonstoune Aytoun and the Spasmodic Controversy* (New Haven: Yale University Press, 1968).
59. Martin, *Aytoun*, 48.
60. Wallace, *Blackie*, 220, quoting the Rev. Alexander Stewart.
61. Anon., "Lays of Loyalty," *Tait's Edinburgh Magazine* 9 (1842): 721–24.
62. Blackie, *War Songs*, 135.

Select Bibliography

The books, essays, and articles listed in this bibliography constitute a selection of the works cited in the contributions to the present volume. To this end, rather than being an exhaustive account of literature on the topic of Anglo-German literary and philosophical exchange in the period, this bibliography is intended as a reference to the research literature cited in this volume that the reader may wish to revisit.

Anderson, Benedict. *Imagined Communities: Reflections on the Origin and Spread of Nationalism*, revised edition. London and New York: Verso, 2016.

Angerson, Catherine. "'A friend to rational piety': The Early Reception of Herder by Protestant Dissenters in Britain." *German Life and Letters* 69, no. 1 (2016): 1–21.

Apter, Emily, *Against World Literature: On the Politics of Untranslatability*. London and New York: Verso, 2013.

Bachleitner, Norbert. "English Plays on the Austrian Lists of Banned Books between 1750 and 1848." In *Anglo-German Theatrical Exchange: "A sea-change into something rich and strange?"* edited by Rudolf Weiss, Ludwig Schnauder, and Dieter Fuchs, 19–41. Leiden and Boston, MA: Brill, 2015.

Barnaby, Paul, and Tom Hubbard. "The International Reception and Literary Impact of Scottish Literature of the Period 1707–1918." In *The Edinburgh History of Scottish Literature, Volume Two: Enlightenment, Britain and Empire (1707–1918)*, edited by Ian Brown and Susan Manning, 33–44. Edinburgh: Edinburgh University Press, 2007.

Barnett, Pamela. *Theodore Haak, F.R.S.: (1605–1690). The First German Translator of "Paradise Lost."* 's-Gravenhage: Mouton, 1962.

Bassnett, Susan, and André Lefevere. *Constructing Cultures: Essays on Literary Translation*. Clevedon: Multilingual Matters, 1998.

Boerner, Peter. "National Images and Their Place in Literary Research: Germany as Seen by Eighteenth-Century French and English Reading Audiences." *Monatshefte* 67, no. 4 (1975): 358–70.

Brewer, Wilman. *Shakespeare's Influence on Sir Walter Scott*. Boston, MA: Cornhill, 1925.
Bridgwater, Patrick. *The German Gothic Novel in Anglo-German Perspective*. Atlanta, GA, and Amsterdam: Rodopi, 2013.
Brown, Hilary. *Benedikte Naubert (1756–1819) and her Relations to English Culture*. Leeds: Maney, 2005.
Carlson, Julie. *In the Theatre of Romanticism. Coleridge, Nationalism, Women*. Cambridge: Cambridge University Press, 1994.
——. "Unsettled Territory: The Drama of English and German Romanticisms." *Modern Philology* 88, no. 1 (1990): 43–56.
Casanova, Pascale. *The World Republic of Letters*. Translated by M.B. DeBevoise. Cambridge, MA, and London: University of Harvard Press, 2004.
Charles, Robert Alan. "French Intermediaries in the transmission of German literature and culture to England, 1750–1815." PhD dissertation, Pennsylvania State College, 1952.
——. "French Mediation and Intermediaries, 1750–1815." In *Anglo-German and American-German Crosscurrents*, edited by Philip Allison Shelley, Arthur O. Lewis Jr, and William W. Betts Jr, 1–38. Chapel Hill, NC: University of North Carolina Press, 1957.
Cox, Jeffrey. "Ideology and Genre in the British Antirevolutionary Drama of the 1790s." *ELH* 58, no. 3 (1991): 579–610.
——. *In the Shadows of Romance*. Athens, OH: Ohio University Press, 1987.
Eldridge, Sarah Vandegrift. "Expanding the Eighteenth-Century Novel between England and Germany: Sentiment, Experience, and the Self." In *Repopulating the Eighteenth Century: Second-Tier Writing in the German Enlightenment*, ed. Michael Wood and Johannes Birgfeld, 90–106. Rochester, NY: Camden House, 2018.
Engel, Manfred, and Jürgen Lehmann. "The Aesthetics of German Idealism and Its Reception in European Romanticism," in *Nonfictional Romantic Prose: Expanding Borders*, edited by Steven P. Sandrup, Virgil Nemoianu, and Gerald Gillespie, 69–95. Amsterdam and Philadelphia, PA: John Benjamins, 2004.
Erken, Günter. "Deutschland." In *Shakespeare-Handbuch: Die Zeit—Der Mensch—Das Werk—Die Nachwelt*, edited by Ina Schabert. Fourth edition, 635–60. Stuttgart: Kröner, 2000.
Even-Zohar, Itamar. "The Position of Translated Literature within the Literary Polystystem." *Poetics Today* 11, no. 1 (1990): 45–51.
——. "Translation Theory Today. A Call for Transfer Theory." *Poetics Today* 2, no. 4 (1981): 1–7.
Ewen, Frederic. "John Gibson Lockhart, Propagandist of German Literature." *Modern Language Notes* 49, no. 4 (1934): 260–65.
Fabian, Bernhard. *The English Book in Eighteenth-Century Germany*. London: The British Library, 1992.
Farese, Carlotta. "The Strange Case of Herr von K: Further Reflections on the Reception of Kotzebue's Theatre in Britain." In *The Romantic Stage. A Many-Sided Mirror*, edited by Lilla Maria Crisafulli and Fabio Liberto, 71–84. Amsterdam: Rodopi, 2014.

Fritz, Bärbel. "Kotzebue in Wien: Eine Erfolgsgeschichte mit Hindernissen." In *Theaterinstitution und Kulturtransfer II: Fremdkulturelles Repertoire am Gothaer Hoftheater und an anderen Bühnen*, edited by Anke Detken, Brigitte Schultze, Horst Turk, and Thorsten Unger, 135–53. Tübingen: Narr, 1998.

Gamer, Michael. "Authors in Effect: Lewis, Scott, and the Gothic Drama." *ELH* 66, no. 4 (1990): 831–61.

———. *Romanticism and the Gothic*. Cambridge: Cambridge University Press, 2000.

Gaskill, Howard, ed. *The Reception of Ossian in Europe*. London: Continuum, 2004.

Geng, Zhao, Robert S. Laramee, Tom Cheeseman, Alison Ehrmann, and David M. Berry. "Visualizing Translation Variation: Shakespeare's Othello." In *Advances in Visual Computing*, edited by George Bebis et al, Part I, 653–63. Berlin and Heidelberg: Springer, 2011.

Gjerset, Knut. *Der Einfluss von James Thomson's "Jahreszeiten" auf die deutsche Literatur des achtzehnten Jahrhunderts*. Heidelberg: E. Geisendörfer, 1898.

Greg, Walter Wilson. "English Translations of 'Lenore': A Contribution to the History of the Literary Relations of the Romantic Revival." *The Modern Quarterly of Language and Literature* 2, no. 5 (1899): 13–26.

Grieder, Theodor. "The German Drama in England, 1790-1800." *Restoration and 18th Century Theatre Research* 3, no. 2 (1964): 39–50.

Gundolf, Friedrich. *Shakespeare und der deutsche Geist*. Berlin: Bondi, 1911.

Guthke, Karl S. "Deutsche Literatur aus zweiter Hand. Englische Lehr- und Lesebücher in der Goethezeit." *Jahrbuch des freien deutschen Hochstifts* (2011): 163–237.

———. *Englische Vorromantik und deutscher Sturm und Drang*. Göttingen: Vandenhoeck & Ruprecht, 1958.

———. "Themen der deutschen Shakespeare-Deutung von der Aufklärung bis zur Romantik." In *Wege zur Literatur: Studien zur deutschen Dichtungs- und Geistesgeschichte*, edited by Karl S. Guthke, 109–32. Bern: Francke, 1967.

Halbjan, Jernej, and Fabienne Imlinger, eds. *Globalizing Literary Genres: Literature, History, Modernity*. London and New York: Routledge, 2016.

Hale, John K. "The Significance of the Early Translations of Milton's *Paradise Lost*." *Philological Quarterly* 63 (1984): 31–53.

Hall, Dan. *French and German Gothic Fiction in the Late Eighteenth Century*. Bern: Lang, 2005.

Houswitschka, Christoph. "The Political Reception of German Drama in Britain in the Period of the French Revolution." In *Anglo-German Theatrical Exchange: "A sea-change into something rich and strange?"* edited by Rudolf Weiss, Ludwig Schnauder, and Dieter Fuchs, 171–91. Leiden and Boston, MA: Brill, 2015.

Isbell, John Claiborne. *The Birth of European Romanticism: Truth and Propaganda in Staël's "De l'Allemange," 1810–1815*. Cambridge: Cambridge University Press, 1994.

Johns, Alessa. *Blue-Stocking Feminism and British-German Cultural Transfer, 1750–1837*. Ann Arbor, MI: University of Michigan Press, 2014.

Johnson, Christopher. "Scott and the German Historical Drama." *Archiv für das Stuidium der neueren Sprachen und Literaturen* 233, no. 1 (1996): 2–36.

Jung, Sandro. *James Thomson's "The Seasons," Print Culture, and Visual Interpretation, 1730–1842*. Bethlehem, PA: Lehigh University Press, 2015.

———. "Print Culture and Visual Interpretation in Eighteenth-Century German Editions of *The Seasons*." *Comparative Critical Studies* 9, no. 1 (2012): 37–59.

Kinzel, Till. "Gotthold Ephraim Lessing und Johann Joachim Eschenburg als Leser und Vermittler Samuel Richardsons. Wege der deutschen Anglophilie im achtzehnten Jahrhundert." In *Britisch-deutscher Literaturtransfer 1756–1832*, edited by Lore Knapp and Eike Kronshage, 39–52. Berlin and Boston, MA: de Gruyter, 2016.

Klieneberger, H.R. *The Novel in England and Germany: A Comparative Study*. London: Wolff, 1981.

Knapp, Lore, and Eike Kronshage, eds. *Britisch-deutscher Literaturtransfer 1756–1832*. Berlin and Boston, MA: de Gruyter, 2016.

Kob, Sabine. *Wielands Shakespeare-Übersetzung: Ihre Entstehung und ihre Rezeption im Sturm und Drang*. Frankfurt am Main: Lang, 2000.

Kreuder, Hans-Dieter. *Milton in Deutschland. Seine Rezeption im latein- und deutschsprachigen Schrifttum zwischen 1651 und 1752*. Berlin: de Gruyter, 1971.

Kristmannsson, Gauti. *Literary Diplomacy*, two volumes. Frankfurt a.M.: Lang, 2005.

Lamport, Francis. "'Shakespeare has quite spoilt you': The Drama of the Sturm und Drang." In *Literature of the Sturm und Drang*, edited by David Hill, 117–39. Rochester, NY: Camden House, 2003.

Lawson-Peebles, Robert. "Translation in Uncertain Times: The Case of Bürger's 'Lenore.'" In *Revolutions and Watersheds: Transatlantic Dialogues, 1775–1815*, edited by W.M. Verhoeven and Beth Dolan Kautz, 7–25. Rodopi: Amsterdam, 1999.

Liebert, Kira. "Die kreative Aneignung Shakespeares im Werk von Karl Philipp Moritz." In *Britisch-deutscher Literaturtransfer 1756–1832*, edited by Lore Knapp and Eike Kronshage, 171–91. Berlin and Boston, MA: de Gruyter, 2016.

Lindsay, David W. "Kotzebue in Scotland, 1792–1813." *Publications of the English Goethe Society* 33, no. 1 (1963): 56–74.

Magon, Leopold. "Die drei ersten deutschen Versuche einer Übersetzung von Miltons Paradise Lost. Zur Geschichte der deutsch-englischen Literaturbeziehungen im siebzehnten Jahrhundert." In *Gedenkschrift für Ferdinand Josef Schneider*, edited by Karl Bischoff, 39–82. Weimar: Böhlau, 1956.

Maier, Bernhard. "A Kaleidoscope of Victorian Scotland: The Life of Alexander Nicolson (1827–1893)." *Scottish Gaelic Studies* 26 (2010): 35–65.

Mander, John. *Our German Cousins. Anglo-German Relations in the 19th and 20th Centuries*. London: John Murray, 1974.

Maurer, Michael. *Aufklärung und Anglophilie in Deutschland*. Göttingen: Vandenhoeck & Ruprecht, 1987.

McLelland, Nicola. "German as a Foreign Language in Britain: The History of German as a 'Useful' Language since 1600." *ANGERMION* 8 (2015): 1–33.

———. *German Through English Eyes: A History of Language Teaching and Learning in Britain 1500–2000*. Wiesbaden: Harrassowitz, 2015.

Mennie, Duncan. "Walter Scott's Unpublished Translations of German Plays." *Modern Language Review* 33, no. 2 (1938): 234–39.

Moretti, Franco. *Atlas of the European Novel 1800–1900*. London and New York: Verso, 1998.
——. *Graphs Maps Trees: Abstract Models for Literary History*. London and New York: Verso, 2007.
——. *Distant Reading*. London and New York: Verso, 2013.
Morgan, Bayard Quincey, and A.R. Hohlfeld, eds. *German Literature in British Magazines: 1750–1860*. Madison, WI: University of Wisconsin Press, 1949.
Mortensen, Peter. *British Romanticism and Continental Influences: Writing in an Age of Europhobia*. Basingstoke: Palgrave Macmillan, 2004.
Murnane, Barry. "Radical Translations: Dubious Anglo-German Cultural Transfer in the 1790s." In *(Re)-Writing the Radical: Enlightenment, Revolution and Cultural Transfer in 1790s Germany, Britain and France*, edited by Maike Oergel, 44–60. Berlin and Boston, MA: de Gruyter, 2012.
Needler, G.H. *Goethe and Scott*. Toronto: Oxford University Press, 1950.
Ochojski, Paul M. "Sir Walter Scott's Continuous Interest in Germany." *Studies in Scottish Literature* 3, no. 3 (1966): 164–73.
Oergel, Maike, ed. *(Re)-Writing the Radical: Enlightenment, Revolution and Cultural Transfer in 1790s Germany, Britain and France*. Berlin and Boston, MA: de Gruyter, 2012.
Oz-Salzberger, Fania. *Translating the Enlightenment: Scottish Civic Discourse in Eighteenth-Century Germany*. Oxford: Clarendon Press, 1995.
Paulin, Roger. *The Critical Reception of Shakespeare in Germany 1682–1914: Native Literature and Foreign Genius*. Hildesheim: Olms, 2003.
——. *The Life of August Wilhelm Schlegel: Cosmopolitan of Art and Poetry*. Cambridge: Open Book Publishers, 2016.
——, ed. *Shakespeare im 18. Jahrhundert*. Göttingen: Wallstein, 2007.
Perry, Walter Copland. *German University Education, or, the Professors and Students of Germany*. London: Longman, 1845.
Price, Lawrence Marsden. *Die Aufnahme englischer Literatur in Deutschland, 1500–1960*. Bern and Munich: Francke, 1961.
——. *English>German Literary Influences. Bibliography and Survey. Part I. Bibliography*. Berkeley, CA: University of California Press, 1919.
——. *English Literature in Germany*. Berkeley, CA: University of California Press, 1953.
——. *The Reception of English Literature in Germany*. Berkeley, CA: University of California Press, 1932.
Price, Mary Bell, and Lawrence Marsden Price. *The Publication of English Literature in Germany in the Eighteenth Century*. Berkeley, CA: University of California Press, 1934.
Redekop, Benjamin W. *Enlightenment and Community: Lessing, Abbt, Herder, and the Quest for a German Public*. Montreal and Kingston: McGill-Queen's University Press, 2000.
Reitemeier, Frauke. *Deutsch-englische Literaturbeziehungen: Der historische Roman Sir Walter Scotts und seine deutschen Vorläufer*. Paderborn: Schöningh, 2001.

Richter, Sandra. *Eine Weltgeschichte der deutschsprachigen Literatur*. Munich: Bertelsmann, 2017.

Robertson, Ritchie, and Michael White, eds. *Fontane and Cultural Mediation: Translation and Reception in Nineteenth-Century German Literature*. Cambridge/Leeds: Modern Humanities Research Association/Maney, 2015.

Saggini, Francesca. *The Gothic Novel and the Stage*. London: Pickering & Chatto, 2015.

Schmidt, Wolf Gerhard. *"Homer des Nordens" und "Mutter der Romantik": James Macpherson's "Ossian" und seine Rezeption in der deutschsprachigen Literatur*, four volumes. Berlin and New York: de Gruyter, 2003–2004.

Sellier, Walter. *Kotzebue in England: Ein Beitrag zur Geschichte der englischen Bühne und der Beziehungen der deutschen Litteratur zur englischen*. Leipzig: Schmidt, 1901.

Steimer, Carolin. *"Der Mensch! die Welt! Alles." Die Bedeutung Shakespeares für die Dramaturgie und das Drama des Sturm und Drang*. Frankfurt am Main: Lang, 2012.

Stevenson, Louise L. "The Transatlantic Travels of James Thomson's *The Seasons* and Its Baggage of Material Culture, 1730–1870." *Proceedings of the American Antiquarian Society* 116, no. 1 (2006): 121–63.

Stockhorst, Stefanie, ed. *Cultural Transfer through Translation: The Circulation of Enlightenment Thought in Europe by Means of Translation*. Amsterdam and New York: Rodopi, 2010.

Stockley, Violet. *German Literature as Known in England, 1750–1830*. London: Routledge, 1929.

Stokoe, F.W. *German Influence in the English Romantic Period 1788-1818, with Special Reference to Scott, Coleridge, Shelley and Byron*. Cambridge: Cambridge University Press, 1926.

Strout, Alan Lang. "Writers on German Literature in *Blackwood's Magazine* (With a footnote on Thomas Carlyle)." *The Library* 9 (1954): 35–44.

Summers, Montague. *The Gothic Quest*. London: Fortune, 1838.

Tautz, Birgit. *Translating the World: Toward a New History of German Literature Around 1800*. University Park, PA: Pennsylvania State University Press, 2017.

Thompson, Lionel Field. *Kotzebue, a Survey of his Progress in France and England*. Paris: Champion, 1928.

Venuti, Lawrence. "Local Contingencies: Translation and National Identities." In *Nation, Language, and the Ethics of Translation*, edited by Sandra Bermann and Michael Wood, 177–202. Princeton and Oxford: Princeton University Press, 2005.

———. *Translation Changes Everything: Theory and Practice*. London and New York: Routledge, 2013.

———. *The Translator's Invisibility: A History of Translation*, second edition. London and New York: Routledge, 2008.

Wallace, Stuart. "Scottish University Men and German Universities before 1914." In *Aneignung und Abwehr. Interkultureller Transfer zwischen Deutschland und Großbritannien im 19. Jahrhundert*, edited by Rudolf Muhs, Johannes Paulmann, and Willibald Steinmetz, 227–61. Bodenheim: Philo, 1998.

Waterhouse, G. "Schiller's *Räuber* in England Before 1800." *Modern Language Review* 30, no. 3 (1935): 355–57.

Waszek, Norbert W. "The Scottish Enlightenment in Germany, and its Translator, Christian Garve (1742–98)." In *Scotland in Europe*, edited by. Tom Hubbard and R.D.S. Jack, 55–71. Amsterdam and New York: Rodopi, 2006.

White, Michael. "Herder and Fontane as Translators of Percy's *Reliques of Ancient English Poetry*: The Ballad 'Edward, Edward.'" In *Fontane and Cultural Mediation: Translation and Reception in Nineteenth-Century German Literature*, edited by Ritchie Robertson and Michael White, 107–19. Cambridge/Leeds: Modern Humanities Research Association/Maney, 2015.

Wiggin, Bethany. *Novel Translations: The European Novel and the German Book, 1680–1700*. Ithaca, NY: Cornell University Press, 2011.

Willenberg, Jennifer. *Distribution und Übersetzung englischen Schrifttums im Deutschland des 18. Jahrhunderts*. Munich: Saur, 2008.

Willoughby, L.A. "English Translations and Adaptations of Schiller's *Robbers*." *Modern Language Review* 16, no. 3/4 (1921): 297–315.

Wolffheim, Hans. *Die Entdeckung Shakespeares: Deutsche Zeugnisse des 18. Jahrhunderts*. Hamburg: Hoffmann & Campe, 1959.

Wood, Harriet Harvey. *Lockhart of the "Quarterly": "Prince of Biographers."* Edinburgh: Sciennes Press, 2018.

Wood, Michael. "'An old friend in a foreign land': Walter Scott, *Götz von Berlichingen*, and Drama Between Cultures." *Oxford German Studies* 47, no. 1 (2018): 5–16.

———. "Notes on a Scandal: Robison, Scott, and the Reception of Kotzebue in Scotland." *Notes and Queries* 65, no. 3 (2018): 314–16.

———. "On Form and Feeling: German Drama and the Young Walter Scott." *German Life and Letters* 71, no. 4 (2018): 395–414.

Index

Page references for figures are italicized

Aböllino, der große Bandit (Zschokke), 30, 36–41
Act of Union (1707), 52
Addison, Joseph (1672–1719), 11, 148, 149, 150; *Cato*, 11
Adelphoe (Terence), 108
Aeschylus, 209
"Die Ährenleserin" (Jerusalem), 191–92, 193
Alighieri, Dante (1265–1321), 163
"Allwill und Allwina" (Kosegarten), 178–79
Almanach Dramatischer Spiele zur geselligen Unterhaltung auf dem Lande (Kotzebue), 107, 111–12
Altavona (Blackie), 209–10
The Analytical Review, 48
Ancrum Moor (battle of, 1545), 62, 64
Anderson, Benedict, 4, 10
Anne of Geierstein (Scott), 81
The Anti-Jacobin Review, 23, 24, 33
Apter, Emily, 71
Aristotle, 121; dramatic unities, 28, 29, 70, 71, 73–75, 77–78, 80–81, 82, 88, 117, 119, 120–21, 122–23, 126. *See also* Neoclassicism; rule-based poetics

Arndt, Ernst Moritz (1769–1860), 218
Arnold, Matthew (1822–1888), 211
Aurelio and Miranda (Boaden), 28
Aurora, 163
Austen, Jane (1775–1817), 23
Aytoun, William Edmondstoune (1813–1865), 16–17, 201–2, 204–5, 212–18

Babo, Joseph Marius von (1756–1822), 80; *Otto von Wittelsbach*, 79, 80, 82
Bach, Johann Sebastien (1748–1778), 184, *189*, 190
Baillie, Joanna (1762–1851), 87–88, 94n47; *Plays on the Passions*, 87–88
ballad, 13, 47–68
"Balsora" (Wieland), 172
Barbauld, Anna Laetitia (1743–1825), 57
Barbour, Robert William (1854–1891), 202, 203, 205, 206–7
Barnett, Pamela, 147
Barruel, Augustin (Abbé) (1741–1820), 32
Basedow, Johann Bernhard (1724–1790), 104
Bäuerle, Adolf (1786–1859), 96

Bause, Johann Friedrich (1738–1814), 184
Becker, Nikolaus (1809–1845), 218
Bentley, Richard (1662–1742), 150
Berge, Ernst Gottlieb von (1649–after 1710), 147
Berlin Schauspielhaus, 208
Bertram (Maturin), 23, 70
Biographia Literaria (Coleridge), 73
Blackie, John Stuart (1809–1895), 16–17, 201–2, 203, 204–5, 206–12, 213, 214–15, 217–18; *Altavona*, 209–10; *Lay Sermons*, 206–7; *The Wisdom of Goethe*, 201, 209, 214
Blackwood's Magazine, 12, 209–10
Blaikie, William Garden, 203
Blanckenburg, Christian Friedrich von (1744–1796), 34
"The Bleeding Nun" (Lewis), 24, 24–29, 41
Blumenbach, Johann Friedrich (1752–1840), 207
Boaden, James (1762–1839), 28, 29, 40; *Aurelio and Miranda*, 28; *The Secret Tribunal*, 29, 31–33, 36
Bock, Jean-Nicolas-Étienne (Baron de) (1747–1809), 31, 33
Bode, Johann Joachim Christoph (1731–1793), 104
Bodmer, Johann Jakob (1698–1783), 1, 2, 15, 16, 147, 148–53, 154, 155, 160, 175, 176–77, 181, 193–94; *Critische Abhandlung von dem Wunderbaren in der Poesie*, 149
Boeckh, August (1785–1867), 208, 209, 211
Boïeldieu, Adrien (1775–1834), 98
Bonaparte, Napoleon (1769–1821), 5
Bonneville, Nicolas de (1760–1828): *Nouveau Théatre [sic] Allemand*, 74
book illustration, 16, 170, 184–90
The Borderers (Wordsworth), 29
Bouilly, Jean-Nicolas (1763–1842), 97
bourgeois tragedy. *See* domestic tragedy

"The Braes of Yarrow" (Hamilton), 60–61
Brandes, Johann Christian (1735–1799): *Der Gasthof; oder, trau, schau, wem!*, 72
The Bravo of Venice (Lewis), 38–39
Breitinger, Johann Jakob (1701–1776), 15, 148, 150
The British Critic, 24
Brockes, Barthold Heinrich (1680–1747), 16, 175, 177, 181, 184, 185, 186, 193–94
Bruder Moritz (Kotzebue), 81
Brumleu, Johann Heinrich (1754–1822), 179–81
Bunsen, Christian Karl Josias von (1791–1860), 207
Bunyan, John (1628–1688): *The Pilgrim's Progress*, 11
Bürde, Samuel Gottlieb (1753–1831), 162
Bürger, Gottfried August (1747–1794), 13, 47–68; "Lenore," 13, 47–66; "Der Wilde Jäger," 51, 58, 62
bürgerliches Trauerspiel. See domestic tragedy
Burke, Edmund (1729–1797), 32
Burns, Robert (1759–1796): "Tam o' Shanter," 61–62
Byron, George Gordon (Lord) (1788–1824): *Manfred*, 70; reception of in German-speaking world, 8

Cairns, John (1818–1892), 202–3, 206
Calepio, Pietro (1693–1762), 148
Campbell, John Francis (of Islay) (1822–1886), 211
Campbell, Thomas (1777–1844), 47
Carlyle, Thomas (1795–1881), 12, 16
Casanova, Pascale, 9, 10
The Castle Spectre (Lewis), 27, 28, 29
Cato (Addison), 11
"Celadon and Amelia," 170, 171, 173–81

Celticism, in German-speaking world, 16, 210–12
Chalmers, Thomas (1780–1847), 203
chapbooks, 25, 27, 39
Chateaubriand, François-René de (1768–1848), 164
Cheeseman, Tom, 117
"The Child of Elle," 50–51
Clarissa (Richardson), 6
Claudine von Villa Bella (Goethe), 62
Claudius, Matthias (1740–1815), 218
Clerk, John (of Eldin) (1728–1812), 72
Coleridge, Samuel Taylor (1772–1834), 12, 16, 17, 23, 29, 70, 73, 161–62; *Biographia Literaria*, 73
Collyer, Mary (1716–1763), 11
Colman, George (the Elder) (1732–1794), 14, 98, 107–8; *The Jealous Wife*, 98, 107–112
Comische Erzählungen (Wieland), 172–73
Congress of Vienna, 5, 14, 98–99, 104, 106, 110–12
Congreve, William (1670–1729), 24
Corneille, Pierre (1606–1684), 132
Covent Garden theater, 28, 39, 100
Cowper, William (1731–1800), 47
Cramer, Carl Gottlob (1758–1817), 82
Critische Abhandlung von dem Wunderbaren in der Poesie (Bodmer), 149
The Crusades, 49, 59–60
Crusius, Gottlieb Lebrecht (1730–1804), 185–87, *188*–189
Cumberland, Richard (1732–1811), 14, 98–106, 118; *The West Indian*, 98–106, 108, 111–12; *The Wheel of Fortune*, 99–100

Damon (Lessing), 125
"Damon and Musidora," 169–70, 171, 175, 181–90
Damrosch, David, 9, 10
Daphnis (Gessner), 178

De Quincey, Thomas (1785–1859), 12, 25
De Wilde, Samuel (1751–1832), 29
dialogue novel, 34–38, 87
Defoe, Daniel (1660–1731), 3, 7
Diderot, Denis (1713–1784), 76, 77; *Entretiens sur "Le Fils Naturel,"* 77
Dillmann, August (1823–1894), 207
Doctor Faust, 121
domestic tragedy, 70, 76–77, 88
domestication, 50–51, 53–54, 57, 59–62, 63–64, 65–66, 74, 77–78, 82, 87, 103–4, 110, 149, 150, 156, 158, 159–60 170–71, 175, 179, 192–94
Donaldson, James (1831–1915), 211
Douglas (Home), 69
dramatic realism, 41, 75, 76–77, 83–87, 88, 102–3, 134–35
Drummond, Henry (1851–1897), 203–4
Drury Lane theater, 39, 99, 107–8
Dryden, John (1631–1700), 157
The Dunciad (Pope), 2
Dunlap, William (1766–1839), 39
Dusch, Johann Jakob (1725–1787), 158
Duval, Alexandre (1767–1842), 97
Duval, Georges (1777–1853), 98

Ebert, Johann Arnold (1723–1795), 1, 2
Ebrard, August (1818–88), 210–11
The Edinburgh Literature Society, 57
The Edinburgh Review, 12
Der Educations-Rath (Kotzebue), 97
"Edward, Edward," 53, 55–57
Die eifersüchtige Frau (Kotzebue), 98, 107–12
Elliston, Robert William (1774–1831), 39
Emilia Galotti (Lessing), 74–75, 76–77, 80, 86
Empfindsamkeit (Sentimentalism), 157–64. *See also* Sentimentalism
Engel, Johann Jakob (1741–1802), 34, 101
English Goethe Society, 11

Enlightenment, 6, 33, 104; early, 118, 125, 127, 128, 129, 134, 135; radical 32; Scottish 13–14, 71–73, 75, 77–78, 79, 87–89
Entretiens sur "Le Fils Naturel" (Diderot), 77
eroticism, 169–70, 171, 172–73, 174, 175, 177–78, 179, 181–83, 184, 185–88, 190, 192, 193–94
Erzaehlungen (Wieland), 172
"The Eve of St. John" (Scott), 48–49, 62–66
Even-Zohar, Itamar, 4

Faculty of Advocates (Edinburgh), 79, 81
"Fair Helen of Kirconnell," 59
Farley, Charles (1771–1859), 28
Faust (Goethe), 17, 162–63, 201, 208, 212, 214
Ferguson, Adam (1723–1816), 72, 75
Fielding, Henry (1707–1754), 3, 7; *Tom Jones*, 108
"The Fire-King" (Scott), 62
folk culture, 51–53, 155–56, 211
The Foreign Quarterly Review, 11
formal innovation, 13, 14–15, 29, 30, 33–36, 41–42, 71, 73–79, 80–81, 82, 88, 89, 123, 130, 136
Forsyth, Neil, 153
The Fortunes of Nigel (Scott), 88
Foucault, Michel, 18n3
France: as mediator between Britain and German-speaking world, 30–31, 39, 72, 74–75, 91n19; 148, 152, 203; cultural influence of, 1, 2–3, 11, 34, 51, 69, 79, 120, 149; revolution in. *See* French Revolution
Frederick II of Prussia (Frederick the Great) (1712–1786), 54, 59
Frederick I (Holy Roman Emperor) (1122–1190), 59, 60
French Revolution, 30, 32, 40, 41
Friedel, Adrien Chrétien (1753–1786): *Nouveau Théatre* [sic] *Allemand*, 74

"The Friar of Orders Gray," 50–51
Fröhlich, Anke, 189
Fust von Stromberg (Maier), 79, 80, 82

Garrick, David (1717–1779), 69, 99, 108
Garside, Peter, 71
Gärtner, Karl Christian (1712–1791), 1, 2
Gaskill, Howard, 21n27
Der Gasthof; oder, trau, schau, wem! (Brandes), 72
Der Geisterseher (Schiller), 25
Gellert, Christian Fürchtegott (1715–1769), 1, 2, 3, 33, 152; *Das Leben der schwedischen Gräfin von G****, 3, 7
Genie. See genius
genius 1, 2
The German Hotel (Holcroft), 72
Gerstenberg, Heinrich Wilhelm von (1737–1823), 119, 120, 121, 126
Geschichte des Agathon (Wieland), 7
Die Geschwister (Goethe), 99
Gesenius, Wilhelm (1786–1842), 207
Gessner, Salomon (1730–1788), 178, 188–89; *Daphnis*, 178; reception of in Britain, 11; *Der Tod Abels*, 11
Gillies, Robert Pearse (or Pierce) (1789–1858), 11, 12
Giseke, Nikolaus Dietrich (1724–1765), 1, 2
Gleich, Alois (1772–1841), 96
Gleim, Johann Wilhelm Ludwig (1719–1803), 1–2
"Glenfinlas, or, Lord Ronald's Coronach" (Scott), 62
Goethe, Johann Wolfgang von (1749–1832), 11, 15, 30, 66, 75, 79, 80, 99, 119, 120, 122–23, 126, 162–63; *Claudine von Villa Bella*, 62; *Faust*, 17, 162–63, 201, 208, 212, 214; *Die Geschwister*, 99; *Götz von Berlichingen*, 75, 81, 82, 94n47, 128; *Iphigenie auf Tauris*, 49, 132;

Die Leiden des jungen Werthers, 7; "Mahomets Gesang," 162; reception of in Britain, 8, 23, 201, 207–8, 209, 212, 214; *Wilhelm Meisters Lehrjahre*, 34
Golo und Genovefa (F. Müller), 130
gothic, 13, 56, 70; gothic novel, 12–13; German gothic novel, 12–13, 30–31, 33–36, 81–82; German gothic novel in Britain, 12–13, 23–46, 60; gothic drama in Britain, 12–13, 23–46
Göttinger Hainbund, 53
Göttinger Musenalmanach, 48
Gottsched, Johann Christoph (1700–1766), 3, 11, 14, 15, 74, 110, 120–21, 122, 127, 128, 147, 149, 150, 151–52, 154, 155, 162; *Sterbender Cato*, 11, 74; *Versuch einer critischen Dichtkunst vor die Deutschen*, 110, 120–21
Gottsched, Luise (1713–1762), 152
Götz von Berlichingen (Goethe), 75, 81, 82, 94n47, 128
Graf Benjowsky (Kotzebue), 97
Grand Tour, 16
Greg, Walter Wilson, 56, 59
Grosse, Carl Friedrich August (1768–1847), 30
growth of readerships, 4
growth of spectatorships, 95–97, 130
Gundolf, Friedrich, 122

Haak, Theodore (1605–1690), 146–47
habeas corpus, 40
Haldane, Richard Burdon (1856–1928), 211
Hale, John K., 148
Haller, Albrecht von (1708–1777), 150
Hamburgische Dramaturgie (Lessing), 75–76
Hamilton, William (of Bangour) (1704–1754): "The Braes of Yarrow," 60–61
Hamlet (Shakespeare), 124, 161

Harries, Heinrich (1762–1802), 175, 176–77, 181–82, 184, 194
Hart, Gail K., 38
Hayley, William (1745–1820), 47
Hazlitt, William (1778–1830), 29, 40, 41
Heath, Stephen, 10, 71
Heeren, Arnold (1760–1842), 207, 209
Hegel, Georg Wilhelm Friedrich (1770–1831), 207
Die heilige Vehme (Wächter), 81–87
Das heimliche Gericht (Huber), 31, 33
Heine, Heinrich (1797–1856), 202
Herder, Johann Gottfried (1744–1803) 19n11, 51–53, 55, 58–59, 123, 145, 155–57, 211; *Volkslieder*, 51, 58–59
Herrmann, Georg Friedrich, 193, 194, 196n15
Herrmann, Leonhard, 100
Herrmann von Unna (Naubert), 24, 30–33, 34–36, 40
Historic Survey of German Poetry (Taylor), 51, 52
historical drama, 31, 33
Hoffmannswaldau, Christian Hoffmann von (1616–1679), 151
Hog, William (fl. 1682–1702), 146–47
Holcroft, Thomas (1745–1809): *The German Hotel*, 72
Home, Henry (Lord Kames) (1696–1782), 72
Home, John (1722–1808): *Douglas*, 69
Homer, 149, 154, 155, 208, 209
L'homme à trois visages (Pixérécourt), 30, 39
The House of Aspen (Scott), 29, 70, 71, 79, 81–87, 94n47
Howitt, William (1795–1879), 205
Huber, Joseph Karl (1726–1760), 1, 2
Huber, Ludwig Ferdinand (1764–1804): *Das heimliche Gericht*, 31, 33
Huber, Martin, 34, 38
Hume, David (1711–1776), 72, 78; *A Treatise of Human Nature*, 78

Die Hussiten vor Naumburg (Kotzebue), 30
Hutcheson, Francis (1694–1746), 75, 78

Ida, oder das Vehmgericht (Komarek), 31
Idealism (German), 70
ideological coding, 9, 52
ideological suspicion, 5, 12, 23, 24, 30, 32–33, 40
Iffland, August Wilhelm (1759–1814), 80, 95–96, 119; *Die Jäger*, 134; *Die Mündel*, 79, 80, 82, 86; reception of in Britain, 24, 30, 79
Inchbald, Elizabeth (1753–1821): *Lovers' Vows*, 98
intermedial transfer, 1–3, 12, 16, 23–46, 71, 79, 88–89, 170–71, 184–90
interpersonal exchange, 146, 157–58, 210–18
Iphigenie auf Tauris (Goethe), 49, 132

Jacobinism, 12, 23, 30, 41
Die Jäger (Iffland), 134
The Jealous Wife (Colman), 98, 107–12
Jerusalem, Friederike Magdalene (?1750–1836): "Die Ährenleserin," 191–92, 193
Johanna von Montfaucon (Kotzebue), 100
Johns, Alessa, 6, 18n11

Kalchberg, Johann von (pseud. Johann Nepomuk Komarek) (1765–1827), 31
Keenan, Joseph J., 101
Kemble, John Philip (1757–1823), 28
Kent, William (1685–1748), 184–86, 189, 190
Das Kind der Liebe (Kotzebue), 98
Die Kindermörderin (Wagner), 126
Klinger, Friedrich Maximilian (1752–1831), 119
Klischnig, Karl Friedrich (1766–before 1825), 158

Klopstock, Friedrich Gottlieb (1724–1803), 1, 2, 8, 146, 151, 152–53, 156–57; *Der Messias*, 152
Knapp, Lore, 7, 11
Komarek, Johann Nepomuk: *Ida, oder das Vehmgericht*, 31. See also Kalchberg
Körner, Theodor (1791–1813), 218
Kosegarten, Ludwig Gotthard (1758–1818), 178–79, 181; "Allwill und Allwina," 178–79
Koselleck, Reinhart, 3–4
Kotzebue, August von (1761–1819), 80, 95–116, 119, 308; *Almanach Dramatischer Spiele zur geselligen Unterhaltung auf dem Lande*, 107, 111–12; *Bruder Moritz*, 81; *Der Educations-Rath*, 97; *Die eifersüchtige Frau*, 98, 107–112; and French theater, 97–98; in Germany, 95, 105–6, 111–12; *Graf Benjowsky*, 97; *Die Hussiten vor Naumburg*, 30; *Johanna von Montfaucon*, 100; *Das Kind der Liebe*, 98; *Menschenhaß und Reue*, 72, 98, 99; reception of in Britain, 7–8, 14, 23, 30, 69–70, 72, 81, 98, 99–100; *Die Spanier in Peru*, 8, 23, 98; *Die Spardose*, 97; as translator and adapter of English plays, 14, 98–112; *Der Westindier*, 98, 102–6, 111–12; *Der Vater von ungefähr*, 97; *Der Verschwiegene wider Willen*, 98; *Das zugemauerte Fenster*, 97
Kronshage, Eike, 7, 11
Kummer, Paul Gotthelf (1750–1835), 107, 109–110
Kunst, Hermann. *See* Smith, Walter Chalmers
Kurz, Joseph Felix von (1717–1784), 95

La Roche, Sophie von (1730–1807), 33, 173, 191
Lafontaine, August (1758–1831), 33

Index

Lamartelière, Jean-Henri-Ferdinand (1761–1830), 39
language-learning, 5, 24, 49, 59, 194, 203–4, 205–6, 207–8, 213
Laokoon (Lessing), 154–55
latin, as mediating language between Britain and German-speaking world, 148, 203
Lawson-Peebles, Robert, 54
The Lay of the Last Minstrel (Scott), 60
Lay Sermons (Blackie), 206–7
Das Leben der schwedischen Gräfin von G*** (Gellert), 3, 7
Lee, Sophia (1750–1824): *The Recess*, 31
Leibniz, Gottfried Wilhelm (1646–1716), 203
Die Leiden des jungen Werthers (Goethe), 7
Leisewitz, Johann Anton (1752–1806), 119
Lesage, Alain-René (1668–1747), 97
Lesser, Auguste Creuzé de (1771–1839), 97
Lessing, Gotthold Ephraim (1729–1781), 1, 2, 3, 11, 14, 15, 74–77, 80, 86, 88, 89, 119, 120, 121–22, 134, 154–55; *Damon*, 125; *Emilia Galotti*, 74–75, 76–77, 80, 86; *Hamburgische Dramaturgie*, 75–76; *Laokoon*, 154–55; *Nathan der Weise*, 49, 80
"Lenore" (Bürger), 13, 47–66
Lenz, Jakob Michael Reinhold (1751–1792), 119, 123
Lewis, Matthew Gregory (1775–1818), 24, 25, 28, 38–40, 59; "The Bleeding Nun," 24, 25–29, 41; *The Bravo of Venice*, 38–39; *The Castle Spectre*, 27, 28, 29; *The Monk*, 24, 25, 28; *Rugantino*, 39–40; *Tales of Wonder*, 59, 62
Lillo, George (1691–1739): *The London Merchant*, 77
Literarisches Wochenblatt, 107

literary prints, 171, 184
Locke, John (1632–1704), 157
Lockhart, John Gibson (1794–1854), 12, 80
Lohenstein, Daniel Casper von (1635–1683), 151
The London Merchant (London), 77
Lorimer, James (1818–1890), 211
Lovers' Vows (Inchbald), 98, 115n35

Mackenzie, Henry (1745–1831), 13–14, 71–79, 80, 81, 87, 89; *The Man of Feeling*, 72
Macpherson, James (1736–1796), 8, 52, 209, 210. *See also* Ossian
"Mahomets Gesang" (Goethe), 162
Maier, Jacob (1739–1784), 80; *Fust von Stromberg*, 79, 80, 82
Mallet, David (ca. 1705–1765): "William and Margaret," 59
The Man of Feeling (Mackenzie), 72
Mander, John, 8
Manfred (Byron), 70
Mannheim National Theater, 107
Martin, Theodore (1816–1909), 201, 213, 214
Martus, Steffen, 6
marvelous. *See* supernatural
Masson, David, 203
Maturin, Charles (1782–1824): *Bertram*, 23, 70
medievalism, 70, 92n33
Meisl, Karl (1775–1853), 96
melodrama, 12, 41, 88, 131; in America, 39; in Britain, 24, 29, 33, 70, 71; in France, 30
Menander, 120
Menschenhaß und Reue (Kotzebue), 72, 98, 99
Menzies, Allan (1845–1916), 205
Merkel, Joseph (1788–1866), 213
Mesmer, Franz Friedrich Anton (1734–1815), 110
Der Messias (Klopstock), 152
Meyer, Kuno (1858–1919), 206

A Midsummer Night's Dream (Shakespeare), 128
migration of people, 6, 11, 16–17, 146, 157–58, 201–18
Milton, John (1608–1674), 3; *Paradise Lost*, 2, 15, 145, 147–67; *Paradise Regained*, 163; reception of in German-speaking world, 1, 2, 8, 15, 145–67
Minstrelsy of the Scottish Border (Scott), 59
mixing genre, 71–72, 75–77, 77–78, 82, 89
Molière (1622–1673), 97
The Monk (Lewis), 24, 25, 28
The Monthly Magazine, 49, 50, 51, 56, 205
The Monthly Review, 24
morality, 12, 14, 16, 23, 24, 61, 73, 75–76, 77–79, 80–81, 87, 101, 105–6, 109–10, 111–12, 122, 158, 169–70, 171–73, 175, 179, 181, 183, 190, 191–94
Moretti, Franco, 9, 118
Moritz, Karl Philipp (1756–1793), 15, 157–60
Mudford, William (1782–1848), 100
Müller, Friedrich (1749–1825): *Golo und Genovefa*, 130
Müller, Friedrich Max, (1823–1900), 208
Müller, Karl Otfried (1797–1840), 207, 209, 211
Die Mündel (Iffland), 79, 80, 82, 86
Muratori, Lodovico Antonio (1672–1750), 148
Musäus, Johann Karl August (1735–1787), 25–27, 28
muse, 1, 2, 11, 29, 155, 156–57
The Mysterious Mother (Walpole), 69

Über *naïve und sentimentalische Dichtung* (Schiller), 161
Nathan der Weise (Lessing), 49, 80
National Theater movement, 95

Naubert, Benedikte (1752–1819), 12, 30–31, 40, 82; *Herrmann von Unna*, 24, 30–33, 34–36, 40
Neander, August (1789–1850), 208
Neoclassicism, 29, 51, 69, 70, 71, 73–74, 77–78, 80–81, 89, 120–21, 128, 131, 133, 136, 148, 156, 162
Nestroy, Johann Nepomuk (1801–1862), 96
New Monthly Magazine, 205
Das Nibelungenlied, 202
Nicolson, Alexander (1827–1893), 206–7, 211
Niebuhr, Barthold Georg (1776–1831), 208
Noctes ambrosianae, 209–10
normative poetics, 69, 73–75, 76, 77–81, 88–89, 120–21, 122–23, 126, 127, 128, 130, 131, 132, 134, 136, 149, 156
North, Christopher. *See* Wilson, John
novel: dialogical, 34–38, 87; position in Anglo-German exchange, 5, 6–7, 8–9, 10; rise of in German-speaking world, 3, 7, 12, 33; rise of in Europe, 4, 6; role of in nation-building, 4, 6; theory of, 33–35
Nouveau Théatre [sic] *Allemand* (Friedel and de Bonneville), 74

Opitz, Martin (1597–1639), 150
orality, 10, 47, 53, 54
origins of language, 15, 154–55, 159–60
Ossian, 8, 51–53, 145, 155, 209, 210–12
Otto von Wittelsbach (Steinsberg, after Babo), 79, 80, 82

Pain, Joseph-Marie (1773–1830), 97
"Palemon and Lavinia," 170, 171, 175, 190–93
Palthen, Johann Franz von (1724–1804), 176, 181, 183, 184, 185, *187*, *188*
Paradise Lost (Milton), 2, 15, 145, 147–67
Paradise Regained (Milton), 163

patronage, 73, 77, 120, 147
Paulin, Roger, 16
Percy, Thomas (1729–1811), 13, 50; reception of in German-speaking world, 51–53; *Reliques of Ancient English Poetry*, 13, 50, 60
Perry, Walter Copland (1814–1911), 205
Pestalozzi, Johann Heinrich (1746–1827), 104
Picard, Louis-Benoît (1769–1828), 97
The Pilgrim's Progress (Bunyan), 11
Piozzi, Hester Lynch (also Thrale) (1740–1821), 28–29
The Pirate (Scott), 65
Pittock, Murray, 52
Pixérécourt, René Charles Guilbert de (1773–1844), 30; *L'homme à trois visages*, 30, 39
Pizarro (Sheridan), 8, 23, 30, 98
play of chivalry, 60, 87
Plays on the Passions (Baillie), 87–88
political suspicion, 5, 12, 23, 24, 30, 32–33, 40
Pomona für Teutschlands Töchter, 173
Pope, Alexander (1688–1744), 2, 3, 158, 170; *The Dunciad*, 2
Price, Lawrence Marsden, 7, 17n1, 145–46
Prins, Yopie, 10
Prinz Zerbino (Tieck), 126
Prior, Matthew (1664–1721), 155
puritanism, 147–48
Pye, Henry James (1744–1813), 48, 57, 59
Pyra, Jacob Immanuel (1715–1744): *Thirsis und Damons freundschaftliche Lieder*, 175

Radcliffe, Anne (1764–1823): *The Romance of the Forest*, 31
Ramler, Karl Wilhelm (1725–1798), 1, 2
Ramsay, Allan (the Elder) (1686–1758): *The Tea-Table Miscellany*, 59

Ranke, Leopold von (1795–1886), 208, 209
Die Räuber (Schiller), 8, 40, 73, 78, 82, 86, 134, 160–61, 162, 163
Raumer, Friedrich von (1781–1873), 208, 209
The Recess (Lee), 31
Reich, Philipp Erasmus (1717–1787), 11
Reid, George (1841–1913), 204
Reliques of Ancient English Poetry (Percy), 13, 50, 60
Renan, Ernest (1823–1892), 211
Richardson, Jonathan (1667–1745), 154
Richardson, Samuel (1689–1761), 3, 7, 11, 72, 145; *Clarissa*, 6
Richter, Simon, 172
Rinaldo Rinaldini (Vulpius), 24
Ritson, Joseph (1752–1803): *Scottish Songs*, 59
Ritterdrama. See play of chivalry
Ritterstück. See play of chivalry
Robertson, William (1721–1793), 72
Robinson, Henry Crabb (1775–1867), 12, 16
Robison, John (1739–1805), 32–33, 41
Rogers, Samuel (1763–1855), 47
The Romance of the Forest (Radcliffe), 31
Romanticism, 12, 110; English, 12, 161–62, 164; French, 164; German, 8, 34, 70, 163
Romeo and Juliet (Shakespeare), 128, 143n29
Rowe, Nicholas (1674–1718), 1, 2, 3
Royal Society, 147
Royal Society of Antiquaries of Scotland, 206
Royal Society of Edinburgh, 72
Rugantino (Lewis), 39–40

Sage, Victor, 39
Sagen der Vorzeit (Wächter), 81
Sand, Karl Ludwig (1795–1820), 14, 106

Index

Sattelzeit (Saddle Period), 6, 11, 12, 17, 117; definition of, 3–4, 18n3

Schiller, Friedrich (1759–1805), 15, 30, 39, 78, 79, 80, 86, 119, 160; *Der Geisterseher*, 25; *Die Räuber*, 8, 40, 73, 78, 82, 86, 134, 160–61, 162, 163; reception of in Britain, 24, 70, 73, 79–80, 86–87, 207–8, 212; *Über naïve und sentimentalische Dichtung*, 161; *Die Verschwörung des Fiesco zu Genua*, 79–80, 86; *Wallenstein* trilogy, 73; *Wallensteins Lager*, 135; *Wilhelm Tell*, 131

Schlegel, August Wilhelm (1767–1845), 16, 17, 163

Schlegel, Friedrich (1772–1829), 34, 118, 129, 141n7

Schlegel, Johann Elias (1719–1949), 1, 2, 3, 15, 120, 121, 142n15; *Vergleichung Shakespears und Andreas Gryphs*, 121

Schleiermacher, Friedrich (1768–1834), 208

Schmid, Christian Heinrich (1746–1800), 175

Schröder, Friedrich Ludwig (1744–1816), 114n23

Schubart, Ludwig (1765–1811), 169, 171, 175, 177–78, 181, 182–84, 192, 193, 194

Schwickert, Engelhard Benjamin (1741–1825), 194

Scots Musical Museum, 59

Scott, Harriet Hepburne (1772–1853), 57

Scott, Walter (1771–1832), 11, 13–14, 29, 47–49, 51, 57–68, 69–72, 78–89, 214; *Anne of Geierstein*, 81; "The Eve of St. John," 48–49, 62–66; "The Fire-King,", 62; *The Fortunes of Nigel*, 88; "Glenfinlas, or, Lord Ronald's Coronach," 62; *The House of Aspen*, 29, 70, 71, 79, 81–87, 94n47; *The Lay of the Last Minstrel*, 60; *Minstrelsy of the Scottish Border*, 59; *The Pirate*, 65; *Tales of My Landlord*, 88–89; *The Voyage of the Pharos*, 65; "William and Helen," 58–62, 65

Scottish Songs (Ritson), 59

The Seasons (Thomson), 2, 15–16, 169–99

secret societies, 23, 32–33, 39–40, 41. *See also* secret tribunal

secret tribunal, 31, 32–33, 35, 40–41, 81–83

The Secret Tribunal (Boaden), 29, 31–33, 36

Seneca, 120

Sentimentalism, 35, 31, 41, 52, 54, 56, 70, 73–74, 80–81, 83–84, 89, 99, 101, 157, 164. *See also Empfindsamkeit*

sexuality, 169–70, 171, 174, 181, 183, 188, 191, 193–94

Shakespeare, William (?1564–1616), 24, 69, 88, 94n47 157, 158; and German drama, 8, 11, 14–15, 82, 117–43; *Hamlet*, 124, 161; *A Midsummer Night's Dream*, 128; reception of in German-speaking world, 7–8, 17, 145–46, 155–56; *Romeo and Juliet*, 128, 143n29

Shelley, Percy Bysshe (1792–1822), 17

Sherbo, Arthur, 99

Sheridan, Richard Brinsley (1751–1816), 8; *Pizarro*, 8, 23, 30, 98; *The Stranger*, 72, 98

Siddons, Sarah (1755–1831), 28

"Sir Patrick Spence," 58–59

Smith, Adam (1723–1790), 72

Smith, George Adam (1856–1942), 203–4

Smith, Walter Chalmers (pseud. Hermann Kunst) (1824–1908), 206–7, 209

Smith, William Robertson (1846–1894), 204, 206–7

Die Spanier in Peru (Kotzebue), 8, 23, 98

Die Spardose (Kotzebue), 97
spectacle in the theater, 28–29, 37, 38, 41
Spencer, William Robert (1769–1834), 48, 57, 59
Spivak, Gayatri Chakravorty, 5
The Spectator, 108, 148, 152
Southey, Robert (1774–1843), 47, 73, 162
Stanley, John Thomas (1766–1850), 48
Stäel, Germaine de (1766–1817), 12, 16, 164
Stein, Charlotte von (1742–1827), 99
Steinsberg, Karl Franz Guolfinger von (1757–1806), 80; *Otto von Wittelsbach* 79, 80, 82
Sterbender Cato (Gottsched), 11, 74
Sterne, Laurence (1713–1768), 7, 73; *Tristram Shandy*, 105
Stewart, Dugald (1753–1828), 57, 78
Stockley, Violet, 11
The Stranger (Sheridan), 72, 98
Sturm und Drang (Storm and Stress), 8, 15, 73, 82, 117, 119–20, 121, 122–23, 125–27, 128, 129, 130, 131, 132–33, 134, 135, 136–40, 146, 151, 162–63
Summer (Thomson), 169, 174
supernatural, 15, 25–28, 41, 60, 61, 148–51
"Sweet William's Ghost," 13, 53–56, 57, 59, 60, 63, 64, 65–66
Szondi, Peter, 77

Tait's Edinburgh Magazine, 209, 215
Tales of My Landlord (Scott), 88–89
Tales of Wonder (Lewis), 59, 62
"Tam o' Shanter" (Burns), 61–62
Tautz, Birgit, 9
Taylor, William (of Norwich) (1765–1836), 13, 48, 49–52, 56–57, 59, 60, 62; *Historic Survey of German Poetry*, 51, 52
The Tea-Table Miscellany (Ramsay), 59
Terence: *Adelphoe*, 108

Thalia, 31
Thirsis und Damons freundschaftliche Lieder (Pyra), 175
Thompson, Lionel F., 99
Thomson, James (1700–1748), 2, 3, 8, 15–16, 145, 169–99; *The Seasons*, 2, 15–16, 169–99; *Summer*, 169, 174
Tieck, Ludwig (1773–1853), 118, 129, 141n7, 163; *Prinz Zerbino*, 126
Tobler, Johannes (1732–1808), 177, 184, 188, 192, 193
Der Tod Abels (Gessner), 11
Tom Jones (Fielding), 108
tragic-sentimental tales, 169, 173–194
A Treatise of Human Nature (Hume), 78
Tristram Shandy (Sterne), 105
Turnerbewegung, 111, 115n42

Uhland, Ludwig (1787–1862), 202, 214–16
Universities: Aberdeen (Marischal College), 207; Aschaffenburg, 213; Berlin, 205, 207–8, 211; Edinburgh, 78, 201, 203, 206, 207, 211–12; Erlangen, 205; Freiburg, 202; Göttingen, 207, 210, 213; Halle, 202; Heidelberg, 205; London, 11; Marburg, 202; Oxford, 209, 210; Tübingen, 202, 203–5;
Uz, Johann Peter (1720–1796), 1, 2

Der Vater von ungefähr (Kotzebue), 97
Vehmgericht. *See* secret tribunal
Venuti, Lawrence, 4
Vergleichung Shakespears und Andreas Gryphs (J.E. Schlegel), 121
Der Verschwiegene wider Willen (Kotzebue), 98
Die Verschwörung des Fiesco zu Genua (Schiller), 79–80, 86
Versuch einer critischen Dichtkunst vor die Deutschen (Gottsched), 110, 120–21
Victoria (Queen of United Kingdom) (1819–1901), 201, 215

Vieillard, Pierre-Ange (1778–1862), 97
Vienna Congress. *See* Congress of Vienna
Vienna *Spektakelfreiheit*, 95
Virgil, 149
Volkslieder (Herder), 51, 58–59
Voltaire (1694–1778), 148
The Voyage of the Pharos (Scott), 65
Vulpius, Christian August (1762–1827), 12, 82; *Rinaldo Rinaldini*, 24

Wächter, Leonhard (pseud. Veit Weber) (1762–1837), 81, 85; *Die heilige Vehme*, 81–87; *Sagen der Vorzeit*, 81
Wagner, Heinrich Leopold (1747–1779), 119; *Die Kindermörderin*, 126
Wallace, Stuart, 212, 214
Walpole, Horace (1717–1797): *The Mysterious Mother*, 69
Wallenstein trilogy (Schiller), 73
Wallensteins Lager (Schiller), 135
war: Napoleonic Wars, 5, 106, 204; Seven Years War, 11, 54; Thirty Years War, 25
Watson, John (1850–1907), 204
Weber, Veit. *See* Wächter, Leonhard
Wegleiter, Christoph (1659–1706), 147–48, 157
Weimar Classicism, 9, 73, 119, 125, 126–27, 128, 129, 131–32, 133, 134, 135
Weimar Liebhabertheater, 99
Weishaupt, Adam (1748–1830), 32
The West Indian (Cumberland), 98–106, 108, 111–12
Der Westindier (Kotzebue), 98, 102–6, 111–12
The Wheel of Fortune (Cumberland), 99–100
Wiedemann, Wihelm Julius, 179

Wieland, Christoph Martin (1733–1813), 1, 2, 33, 34, 122, 135, 141n7, 143n29, 170, 171, 172–73, 194; "Balsora," 172; *Comische Erzählungen*, 172–73; *Erzaehlungen*, 172; *Geschichte des Agathon*, 7; "Zemin und Gulhindy," 172
"Der Wilde Jäger" (Bürger), 51, 58, 62
Wilhelm Meisters Lehrjahre (Goethe), 34
Wilhelm Tell (Schiller), 131
"William and Helen" (Scott), 58–62, 65
"William and Margaret" (Mallet), 59
Williams, Stanley T., 99
Wilson, John (pseud. Christopher North) (1785–1854), 209–10
Winckelmann, Johann Joachim (1717–1768), 155
The Wisdom of Goethe (Blackie), 201, 209, 214
Wordsworth, William (1770–1850), 29, 42, 47; *The Borderers*, 29
World Literature, 9, 71
Wright, George, 169

Young, Edward (1683–1765), 145, 155

Zachariae, Justus Friedrich Wilhelm (1726–1777), 1–3, 11, 16, 153–54, 155, 194
Zeitung für die elegante Welt, 110–11
Zellweger, Laurenz (1692–1764), 148
"Zemin und Gulhindy" (Wieland), 172
Zeuss, Johann Kaspar (1806–1856), 210
Zschokke, Heinrich (1771–1848), 12, 30, 36–41; *Aballino, der große Bandit*, 30, 36–41
Das zugemauerte Fenster (Kotzebue), 97

About the Authors

Johannes Birgfeld teaches Modern German Literature at the University of the Saarland. He studied in Hamburg, London, and Bamberg before completing his PhD in Saarbrücken in 2009. His thesis was published in 2012 as the two-volume study *Krieg und Aufklärung*, dealing with German-speaking literature's reaction to experiences of war between 1700 and 1800. Before his present position at the University of the Saarland (since 2003), he taught German literature after 1500 at the Universities of Bamberg and Oxford. His main areas of research are German literature of the eighteenth, twentieth, and twenty-first centuries; war and literature in the eighteenth century; and the history of theater and drama in German from 1500 to the present. He has published on a wide spectrum of writers and issues.

John Guthrie is Emeritus Fellow of Murray Edwards College founded as New Hall, Cambridge. He studied for his BA Hons. at the University of Western Australia and completed a PhD thesis on the plays of J.M.R. Lenz and Georg Büchner in Cambridge. He has held teaching posts at the University of Leicester, the University of Leeds, and the University of Cambridge, where he was Director of Studies in Modern Languages at Murray Edwards College until his retirement. Publications on German and comparative literature include *Schiller the Dramatist: A Study of Gesture in the Plays* (2009); *Alexander Pope: Epilog zu den Satiren: Dialog I; in der ungedruckten Übertragung von Lenz* (2014); *Friedrich Schiller: The Conspiracy of Fiesco at Genoa* (2015); and *Friedrich Schiller: Don Carlos Infante of Spain. A Dramatic Poem* (2018).

Sandro Jung is Distinguished Professor of English at the Shanghai University of Finance and Economics and Past President of the East-Central American Society for Eighteenth-Century Studies. He is the author of *David Mallet, Anglo-Scot: Poetry, Politics, and Patronage in the Age of Union* (2008), *The Fragmentary Poetic: Eighteenth-Century Uses of an Experimental Mode* (2009), *James Thomson's "The Seasons," Print Culture, and Visual Interpretation, 1730–1842* (2015), and *The Publishing and Marketing of Illustrated Literature in Scotland, 1760–1825* (2017). He co-edited the 2015 MHRA *Yearbook of English Studies* (on "The History of the Book"), edited the 2013 *Essays & Studies* volume (on "British Literature and Print Culture"), and is currently working on a new book, *Illustration and Literature*.

Bernhard Maier studied Comparative Religion, Comparative Philology, and Celtic in Freiburg, Aberystwyth, and Bonn, where he did his PhD and second doctorate (Habilitation) in 1989 and 1998, respectively. From 2004 until 2006 he was Reader and Professor in Celtic at the University of Aberdeen; since 2006 he has been Professor of Religious Studies and the European History of Religions at Tübingen University. His main research interest is in the religious history of the Celtic-speaking peoples from antiquity to the present and in the history of Religious Studies as an academic discipline, especially in the nineteenth century.

Barry Murnane is Associate Professor of German at the University of Oxford. His main areas of research are the literature and culture of the "threshold period" between 1780 and 1830, modernism, and contemporary drama. He has published widely on the gothic, Anglo-German relations, and medical humanities, including a monograph on Franz Kafka (2008), two volumes on the German *Schauerroman* in 2011 and 2012 (co-edited with Andrew Cusack), and on Hanns-Heinz Ewers in 2014 (co-edited with Rainer Godel). He is currently working on a volume exploring the relationship between literature and pharmacy in the "long" eighteenth century and on a volume about the origins of literary criticism in Germany around 1700 for Wallstein (due out in early 2019).

Nils Reiter studied computational linguistics and computer science at Saarland University. He did his PhD in a collaborative project between classical indology and computational linguistics at Heidelberg University (on ritual dynamics). He now works at Stuttgart University as a scientific coordinator and investigator in the Centre for Reflected Text Analytics. Since Summer 2017, he is also the principal investigator of the mixed-methods project QuaDramA on the quantitative analysis of dramatic texts. With colleagues, he initialized a shared task with the goal of creating annotation guidelines for narrative levels. His research interests mostly relate to operationalization questions, particularly with respect to literary research questions and concepts.

Marcus Willand studied Linguistics, Literature, Psychology, and Sociology in Darmstadt, Berlin, and Turku (Finland) between 2002 and 2008. His dissertation was on "Lesermodelle und Lesertheorien" (Theories and models of the reader) (Narratologia 41, Berlin 2014); Willand is a former member of the PhD-Net: "Das Wissen der Literatur" (the knowledge of literature) (J. Vogl) and former scholarship holder of the Studienstiftung des deutschen Volkes. He was a visiting research scholar at Princeton University, in 2009. Willand is a research assistant to Professor Andrea Albrecht, first assisting her in Stuttgart, and now in Heidelberg (SoSe2018). He is editor of *Scientia Poetica*, and principal investigator of the Volkswagen Foundation–funded mixed-methods project "QuaDramA" (Quantitative Drama Analytics). Publications and research are mainly in the fields of hermeneutics, literary theory, and digital humanities.

Lucy Wood gained her PhD from the University of Edinburgh in 2016 with a thesis entitled "Fragments of the Past: Walter Scott, Material Antiquarianism, and Writing as Preservation" (as Lucy Linforth). Her thesis was awarded the Saltire Society's Ross Roy Medal in 2017, and in early 2018, she held the British Association for Romantic Studies/Wordsworth Trust Early Career Fellowship researching William Wordsworth's collections at Dove Cottage in Grasmere. Her research interests predominantly lie in writers from the eighteenth and nineteenth centuries and matters of collecting, both literally and figuratively, and in ways of making research into these objects and works accessible to the public. She currently works for the Abbotsford Trust and for the Royal Collections Trust.

Michael Wood is British Academy Postdoctoral Fellow in the School of Literatures, Languages and Cultures at the University of Edinburgh. Prior to this, he was the Susan Manning Postdoctoral Fellow at the Institute for Advanced Studies in the Humanities at Edinburgh. His current project focuses on Walter Scott's reception of German drama, and he is more widely interested in matters of intercultural exchange, World Literature, and the roles of drama and performance in these. He has published on topics ranging from eighteenth-century drama to contemporary performance and post-dramatic theory, and has recently co-edited a collection of essays with Johannes Birgfeld on *Second-Tier Writing in the German Enlightenment* (2018). He is the author of *Heiner Müller's Democratic Theater: The Politics of Making the Audience Work* (2017).

www.ingramcontent.com/pod-product-compliance
Lightning Source LLC
Chambersburg PA
CBHW062135300426
44115CB00012BA/1928